A Passion for Survival

DUNDEE UNITED FC,
A COMPREHENSIVE HISTORY 1909–1945

Steve Gracie

Arabest Publishing Dundee

© Steven F Gracie 2008

Published by Arabest Publishing

ISBN 978 0 9558341 0 3

British Library Cataloguing in Publications Data

A catalogue record for this book is available from the British Library

All photographs © D C Thomson & Co Ltd and Dundee United FC

Set in Minion Pro 11pt

Cover designed by Clare Brayshaw

Prepared by:
York Publishing Services Ltd
64 Hallfield Road
Layerthorpe
York YO31 7ZQ
Tel: 01904 431213
Website: www.yps-publishing.co.uk

Foreword by Denys Carnegie, Former Director, Dundee United FC

It was a great honour to be asked by Steve Gracie to write this foreword. The Carnegie family have been supporters and Directors of Dundee United Football Club over five generations and I am very proud to have been part of that history.

Steve has researched and written a history of the Club from 1909-1945 which will be unsurpassed in its detail. It could have just been a series of names and dates but his racy style has made it a fascinating read of the trials, tribulations and high points of the Club. The story tells how the various Directors, over those years, kept the Club alive in extremely difficult circumstances, often using their own money. The contribution of each Manager and player is also a vital part of the Club's past and as a boy watching the team since the early 1930s, I well remember some of the characters brought to life again in this book. The years of the Second World War witnessed some of the most difficult years for the Club, with an astonishing turnover in players, but Dundee United survived against considerable adversity.

This book is a fitting memorial to those United men who had the Black and White blood flowing through their veins.

Denys Carnegie

August 2007

Authors Notes and Acknowledgements

It was while I was working for Dundee United as a contributor to T&B Magazine that I first started researching the history of Dundee United. As a reference source, *Rags To Riches* by Mike Watson was a good starting point but did not tell the whole story and it was necessary to undertake much more extensive investigation using several sources but mainly the local newspapers. The advent of the internet also opened up countless stores of information. I spent time examining player records at the SFA in Glasgow, and visited the National Library of Scotland, Scotland's National Archives and obtained information from Companies House.

This project began in the latter part of 2002, primarily to satisfy my own desire to find out everything I could about Dundee United FC, the team I have supported since I was a boy. However, it grew to become an all-consuming passion and as time went on, I decided to put together a detailed history of the Club. This book covers the period from the formation of Dundee Hibernian in 1909, to the end of season 1944-45 and I plan to add two further volumes to complete the story. The second book will begin at the post WW2 years, giving an account of the Club's progress to the end of season 1978-79. To coincide with the centenary year of Dundee United FC, the third book will chronicle the most recent years. My intention is to tell the full Dundee United story.

In today's newspapers, we are spoiled for information on the Club with virtually daily bulletins and match reports at every level from the first team through to Reserves and Youths. This was not the case in the infancy of the Club. The formation of Dundee Hibernian in 1909 received much attention but once the season was under way only brief reviews and reports were published. Team line-ups in the early years were difficult to ascertain. It must also be borne in mind that the early records of Dundee Hibernian/Dundee United contain frequent gaps for various reasons. Limitations of space in local newspapers (which contain the only truly reliable reports) meant that precedence was given to Scottish League clubs. The Northern League and others such as the Central League and the Scottish Alliance were often given scant regard. And, as if anyone needs reminding, there were two World Wars during which football was, quite rightly, a minor issue and was therefore given less coverage at the time. When compiling match details, player information and statistics, all possible care has been taken to ensure accuracy.

I would like to acknowledge the assistance of D C Thomson & Co Ltd., without whom it would have been impossible to complete this project. Special thanks are owed to Anne Swadel and her team for all their help throughout the last few years. D C Thomson & Co Ltd also provided the vast majority of photographs used in this book. Wherever possible, photographs of players, managers and directors have been included and whilst I accept that most of the images are not of a high quality, I felt that readers would be interested to see what the personalities looked like.

I am grateful to staff at the Local Studies Department of Dundee City Libraries for providing access to their bound newspaper volumes and microfilmed archives, and to Richard McBrearty, Curator at The Scottish Football Museum at Hampden, for allowing me access to player registration records. *The Dundee United Who's Who* by Pat Kelly was utilised to confirm some player information. I also gained access to records at Dundee United FC and I was especially honoured to receive on loan through Peter Cabrelli, several very early original minute books and cashbooks. I would also thank Mike Watson who supplied me with statistics for most of the period 1909-1939. Statistics were obtained from several sources and used as a basis but were all checked to at least one separate source. Any errors are therefore mine alone.

My close friends Scott Carnegie, Denys Carnegie, Finlay Noble, David Cargill, Bill Campbell and Keith Haggart helped out enormously as test subjects for the book in its early forms. Their comments and encouragement were extremely helpful and shaped the final version that went to print.

Thanks also to Shug Falconer who first planted the idea for this book, although he probably will not remember. I would also thank Kirsten McCarle who (almost) volunteered for the job of editing the early versions of the book and Alison Farrell, who undertook the final proof reading. Duncan Beal and his staff at York Publishing Services Ltd were extremely patient and understanding and kept me on track in the final stages.

However, the most grateful thanks of all go to my long-suffering wife, Carol-Anne who had to tolerate my eternal ramblings about the history of Dundee Hibernian/Dundee United. Good job she too is an Arab!

To her I dedicate this History of Dundee United F C 1909-1945.

Season By Season 1909–1945

THE DUNDEE HIBERNIAN ERA

Thirty Years in the Making

Dundee United Football Club is an institution. Like all football clubs, no matter how grand or how small, the Club is the passion of the supporters and the Club belongs to them. Chairmen, Directors, Managers and players will come and go but the supporters are eternal. The history of Dundee United FC (formed initially as Dundee Hibernian Football and Athletic Club) is long and proud. There have been many high points in the years since the Club was founded, and many lows but that is the nature of the game. Football fans the world over have one thing in common. They may owe their allegiance to a myriad of clubs but they all feel the same emotions and each knows the passion of the other.

In Scotland, football had emerged as the popular sport of the working man in the latter quarter of the 1800s and clubs sprang up all over the country. Several leagues existed by the turn of that century but the county association competitions, such as the Forfarshire Cup, were more popular in the early days and the Scottish Cup was the biggest prize prior to the advent of the national leagues.

Football in Dundee travelled many paths in the last quarter of the 1800s and many teams came and went until just two senior sides remained in the city by 1914. St Clements were probably the first team in the area, starting life in the mid 1870s at which time there is also a record of a Dundee FC. However, the latter appears to have had a short existence and St Clements were gone within ten years. In the mid 1880s, there were around twenty senior teams in Forfarshire with several located in Dundee. These included the 3rd F.R.V. (Forfar Volunteer Rifles) Dundee Highlanders, Balgay, Perseverance and West End. The latter three of this group were in the Scottish Cup at various times over 1883-86 but they all appear to have folded by the end of that decade.

Formed in 1885, Wanderers (who took over Clepington Park in 1890) were another successful local side, playing in the Scottish Cup until 1890. They then amalgamated with Johnstone to form Johnstone Wanderers for a short time. A further amalgamation in 1894, with Strathmore, created Dundee Wanderers who then had one season in the Scottish League Division 2 and another three seasons in the Scottish Cup. Strathmore had been a successful outfit in their own right since 1876 and regulars in the Scottish Cup over 1880-89.

There were also teams on the outskirts of the city, with Broughty making their mark. They played in the Scottish Cup between 1885 and 1891 before they too became defunct. Lochee FC are also recorded as a senior side and played in the Scottish Cup from 1887 to 1890. They were replaced in 1892 by Lochee United who took part in the Northern League but eventually joined the junior set up. The two teams who amalgamated in 1893 to create Dundee FC were East End (who played on Clepington Park until 1890) and Our Boys. Both played regularly in the Scottish Cup.

The dawn of Dundee Hibernian, later to become Dundee United, began long before the Club was formed in 1909. The foundations were laid with the arrival of migrant Irish workers during the 1800s as they came to Dundee looking for work in the jute industry. There was a desire amongst this immigrant population for a football team to follow but attempts over thirty years to satisfy that need invariably failed, until the formation of Dundee Hibernian in 1909.

A team bearing the name Dundee Hibernian took part in the first round of the Scottish Cup in season 1882-83, losing 2-1 to Our Boys. They lost out again a year later to Perseverance (Arbroath) apparently on a walk over after a 0-0 draw. This Hibernian appears to have folded quite quickly and the local side favoured by the Dundee Irish was Dundee Harp, formed in 1879.

Dundee Harp were relatively successful and won the Forfarshire Cup three times in succession from 1885. They also took part in the Scottish Cup over ten seasons and made their first appearance in October 1881 losing 5-3 to Our Boys. In the following season, Harp knocked out Perseverance (Arbroath) 7-2 and Aberdeen 3-1 in a replay after a 2-2 draw but lost 5-0 to Dunblane in the third round. Season 1883-84 saw Harp progress to the fourth round with a 9-0 win over Angus (a Forfar club), a walk over past Vale of Atholl and a 2-1 victory over Arbroath following a 1-1 draw. They were eventually knocked out 6-0 by Vale of Leven in the fourth round as one of the last eighteen clubs in the competition.

A year later, the Harp faced a first round exit, beaten 3-2 at Arbroath but created a piece of history in the tournament a year later on the way to another fourth round appearance. They recorded a 35-0 win over Aberdeen Rovers and that would have been a record but for a 36-0 win by Arbroath over Bon Accord on the same day! Harp went on to beat Our Boys 4-1 and Vale of Teith 8-1 before losing 6-0 at Vale of Leven again. In 1886-87, Harp won 4-3 against Kirriemuir based Lindertis and after twice drawing 3-3 with Strathmore (Arbroath) both teams qualified for the next round where they met again. Harp won 8-1 and then received a bye into a best ever last sixteen meeting with Dumbarton. The sides drew 2-2 in Dundee but Dumbarton won the replay with a walk over. Harp faced a 2-1 first round exit in the next Scottish Cup against Lindertis but had another relatively good run in 1888-89. Starting with a 4-3 win over Strathmore (Dundee) they then beat Broughty 4-2 before losing out to Our Boys by the odd goal in three.

The Harp's Scottish Cup run lasted just two rounds in the next two seasons. In 1889-90, they won 5-3 at Arbroath but were knocked out when they were beaten 5-3 by Our Boys. A year later advancement to the second round came after a walk over against Lochee but then Arbroath knocked Harp out with a 5-1 win. From that point on, Dundee Harp faced a gradual decline before they were expelled from the SFA in 1894 for failure to pay match guarantees to visiting teams. A completely new outfit calling itself Dundee Hibernian was set up, lasting around two years before Dundee Harp was resurrected for another season. However, in 1897, they were again in financial distress and disbanded. Later, a junior side bearing the name of Dundee Harp emerged. By 1898, the only sides playing in senior leagues were Dundee Wanderers and Lochee United in the Northern League and Dundee FC in the Scottish League.

Prior to the creation of the new Dundee Hibernian, it had therefore been almost twelve years since the Dundee Irish had a senior team to follow. Formation of the Club was achieved through the efforts of a group of local businessmen with Irish origins, who began the process in March 1909. The driving force behind the move was a local bicycle trader, Pat Reilly. Discussions were held with officials of the Northern League and the Forfarshire Association at Dens Park on 20th March 1909, in connection with the proposed new club. Reilly had already stated his intention on behalf of the fledgling Dundee Hibs, to apply for membership of the Northern League, which was then in dire need of teams to compete. It had been reduced to only six clubs (Brechin City, Forfar Athletic, Montrose, Dundee Wanderers and the reserve sides of both Aberdeen and Dundee) following the departure of St Johnstone and Arbroath to the new Central League. In the *People's Journal* that weekend a local reporter warned against the "enormity of the task" but wished the founding members well in their efforts.

Matters moved on quietly but deliberately over the next two weeks and by 10th April 1909, Reilly announced the choice of venue was to be Clepington Park. This came as a surprise for three reasons. Firstly, the supporter base was located mostly in the west of the city, with the Lochee area housing the majority of Hibs' potential following. Secondly, Dundee FC were located only yards away at Dens Park and it was reasoned that the close proximity had hindered the progress of Dundee Wanderers to a very large extent. Thirdly, and probably most significantly, Dundee

Pat Reilly

Wanderers were already playing on Clepington Park! The landlords however, accepted the offer from the newly formed Club to lease the ground and Dundee Wanderers were notified of eviction. At the time, it was feared that Dundee Wanderers would fold completely but they survived, at least until 1913.

'Citizen' in the *Dundee Advertiser* of 12th April 1909, reported that some surprise had been created with the announcement that the steering committee were entering into the lease of Clepington Park. "I am sorry." he said, "I cannot congratulate the promoters on their choice. It is no doubt convenient to get a ready made ground, but in setting up in business next door to the Dens Park club, a blunder is being made. For not only will the new team have to compete with the Scottish League games, but also with those of the new Second Eleven League, which promises to be of considerable importance. It would have been better if the Hibs had gone to another quarter of the city, where they might have gathered together a following of their own."

By that he probably meant that Hibs should have remained in their own back yard, Lochee. When quizzed on this fact a few days later, Reilly revealed that situating at a ground in the west of the city had been the first consideration but negotiations for a suitable site had broken down at an advanced stage. He did not however, disclose the location that had been under discussion. He declined also to make any further comment on the Clepington Park situation until the end of the month by which time presumably the deal would be signed and sealed.

Reilly was determined that the Club would become established at the highest possible level, and at a meeting of the Forfarshire Football Association on 15th May 1909, he put forward Dundee Hibs' application for membership. The Forfarshire Association declined to make a decision on admission. This rejection followed hard on the heels of a refusal by the SFA to grant membership and conspiracy theories abounded with letters to the editors of the local papers. In fact all that had happened was that both the SFA and the Forfarshire Association had deferred their decision, as Dundee Hibernian were not formally in existence and did not have a registered ground. Clepington Park was still the home of Dundee Wanderers until their lease expired on 28th May 1909.

There was considerable bad feeling between Dundee Wanderers and the group forming Dundee Hibernian. A very public argument ensued between the two camps but in the end there was little Wanderers could do. Before leaving Clepington Park however, they instructed removal of everything possible including the stand, changing rooms, boundary fence and even the goal posts! These were all advertised for sale in the *Dundee Courier*. The Dundee Hibs group were rebuffed when they offered to buy these items from the company carrying out the demolition work. Hibs therefore had to start from scratch when they eventually took over. Within a short space of time, Hibs were able to reconstruct the ground and it was renamed Tannadice Park. At the time, it was stated that the cost of all the work had totalled around £3,000, but it is worth pointing out that, when the Limited Company was created four months later, the pre-formation costs were just £930. If the founding members of the Club did spend £3,000, they certainly did not recover the money when the Company was set up.

There has previously been some debate as to the actual date of the formation of Dundee Hibernian Football Club but it can be confirmed that the Club was officially formed on 24th May 1909 at a meeting in the Crown Hotel, Dundee. It is a pity there is little evidence of this meeting other than a report in the *Evening Telegraph and Post* the following day. The office bearers were elected from the group of local businessmen who had started the ball rolling two months earlier. It was also agreed to contact every senior club in Scotland, seeking support for Dundee Hibs' entry to the Second Division and Reilly had letters ready for mailing the very next day.

The elected officials at that historic meeting were Honorary President, Councillor P McCabe and Honorary Vice President J Hennessy. In the executive roles were Thomas Hannick (President), Samuel Johnstone (Vice President), Thomas Timmons (Treasurer) and Patrick Reilly (Secretary and Team Manager). Also elected were Committee Members Patrick Doyle, James Glover, Thomas Heraughty, John Kennedy, Thomas Malone and John Naulty.

Little could that committee know how the history of the Club would unfold as the years progressed. There is no doubt they were ambitious,

DUNDEE HIBS F.C.

APPOINT CLUB OFFICE-BEARERS.

FRASER'S BENEFIT ARRANGED.

Jamie Turnbull and Manchester.

FORFARSHIRE C.C.'s MATCH OFF.

The general meeting of the Dundee Hibs Football Club was held in the Crown Hotel last night, when the undernoted office-bearers were appointed for the forthcoming season:— Hon. president, Councillor P. M'Cabe, J.P.; hon. vice-president, Mr J. Hennessy; president, Mr T. Hannick; vice-president, Mr S. Johnstone; secretary and manager, Mr P. Reilly, 55 Perth Road, Dundee; treasurer, Mr T. Timmons, 7 Eden Street, Dundee. committee—Messrs J. Glover, J. Naulty, P. Doyle, J. Kennedy, T. Heraughty, and T. Malone. Rules have been drawn up along with a circular which is to be sent to every secretary in the First and the Second Divisions of the Scottish League to support the application for the Second Division. Secretary Reilly has some good First League players on his list who have offered their services to the new organisation. If the Hibs obtain admission to the Second Division they intend to have a team second to none in the Second Division of the League. The headquarters of the club is Tannadice Park, late Clepington, to which the club enter into occupancy on Friday.

Article from Evening Telegraph 25th May 1909

but could they possibly conceive that from such humble beginnings the Club would bring every major piece of Scottish silverware back to Tannadice? In their wildest dreams could they have foreseen a Club that would reach the final of one European trophy event and the semi final of the premier European competition? Probably not. But the founders in general are owed a great debt of gratitude, especially Pat Reilly who worked tirelessly in Hibs' cause.

Four days after the first general meeting of the Club, the SFA admitted the Dundee Hibernian claim for membership. Shortly afterwards, a meeting of the Forfarshire Association was planned to formalise Hibs' application there.

The 1909 attempt to gain entry to the Scottish League failed with the votes going in favour of more established clubs. Bottom clubs Arthurlie and Cowdenbeath were re-elected with 21 and 17 votes respectively. The four clubs unsuccessful in their attempts to gain entry were Johnstone (11 votes), Renton (8 votes) Wishaw Thistle (5 votes) and Dundee Hibernian (3 votes). In truth, Reilly and his fellow committee members probably did not expect to be successful in this first attempt but the groundwork done would result in acceptance into the Scottish League within twelve months.

In the meantime, for their inaugural season in senior football, Hibs were accepted into the Northern League on 12th June 1909. It had not been clear cut, with the vote in favour split at 4-2. Dundee Wanderers would most likely have voted against Hibs, for obvious reasons and they found like minded support from one other member club. The four clubs voting in favour almost certainly included Aberdeen and Dundee, who would have been aware that the inclusion of Dundee Hibs was a positive step for the struggling Northern League.

Although initially formed as an unincorporated body, the founding committee were anxious that a Limited Company was created as soon as possible and the minutes of a meeting on 8th July 1909 confirm that this change was set in motion. Tom Hannick became the first Chairman of the new company. Reilly and Kennedy along with Patrick Rock were the other Directors when Dundee Hibernian Football and Athletic Club Ltd was formed on 9th September 1909 with capital of £1,000. The major shareholders were Pat Reilly with 445 and Patrick Rock who took 430. There were just a handful of other shareholders but no single person held a majority.

1909-10

The First Eleven

With the infrastructure and all the formal documentation in place, Pat Reilly in his role as Manager began to put together a team. Even before the SFA and Forfarshire Association had accepted Dundee Hibs into the fold, Reilly had been lining up players. It would have been folly to wait and in any event, membership of the Northern League was virtually assured despite the differences with Dundee Wanderers. On 28th May 1909, Tom Boland from St Joseph's was the first Dundee Hibs player signed and he was soon joined by Forfar Athletic inside forward Jamie Docherty and experienced full back Jack Hannan who had been with Celtic, Everton, and St Johnstone. Another Forfar Athletic inside forward, Tom McDermott signed along with centre half James Ramsay from Brechin City. Half back James Strachan joined from Dundee Violet, followed by full back Christopher Gallacher from Dundee Wanderers and the left wing pairing of Tim Dailly from Dundee 'A' and Henry Brown from Kirkcaldy United. The trainer was Joe 'Dod' McNally who had been with Dundee Wanderers and Forfar Athletic as a player.

To complete the team, goalkeeper John Brady from Lochgelly United and outside right Tom Flood from Dundee 'A' were recruited in the first week of July. These players were then the first starting eleven and lined up to meet the Hibs of Edinburgh in a friendly on 18th August 1909:-

Brady, Hannan and Gallacher; Strachan, Ramsay and Boland; Flood, McDermott, Docherty, Dailly and Brown.

The decision to face the Edinburgh Hibs was a wise one, as the newly formed Club would not wish to run the risk of a potential heavy defeat from the other obvious choices, Glasgow Celtic and near neighbours Dundee. The first match at Tannadice Park took place in front of a crowd of 7,000 who witnessed an entertaining game. A ceremonial kick off was performed by Lord Provost Urquhart who received an engraved silver cigarette case as a memento. A further presentation was made to John O'Hara of the Edinburgh Hibs as the scorer of the first goal. He was given a bicycle donated by Pat Reilly for this achievement, after he opened the scoring in the first half. Jamie Docherty netted the equaliser in the second half for a 1-1 draw, and for scoring that first goal for Dundee Hibs, he was presented with a commemorative gold medal.

For much of season 1909-10, Brady would wear the keeper's jersey with Tom Timmons, registered as an amateur, his able deputy. At full back, Hibs were able to choose from Hannan, Gallacher, Strachan and Boland. The latter would become a stalwart of the side for years to come. Also available were Ramsay and former Clyde man James Loney, who signed on a loan deal just before the Qualifying Cup exit at the beginning of September. Others defenders signed included James Mudie who would feature regularly but ex-Dundee Wanderers player James Snee could count his appearances on one hand. In the forward line the regulars were Docherty, Brown, Dailly, and Peter Yule (ex-West End) with Flood used more often than not. Over the season, other players signed were E F Gibb (an amateur), James Burns, Archie Downie, James Carroll and Simon Fraser, who all played a few games for Hibs without becoming first choices. The Manager also signed Charlie Donnachie, a very experienced player who had been with both Rangers and Chelsea. He had just returned from America and signed late in the season at the same time as former Glossop forward Thomas 'Rocky' Cairns, but neither made the expected impact. Another who failed to make an impression was Irish international James Sheridan signed from Alloa Athletic.

It was ironic that the first league visitors to Tannadice were Dundee Wanderers. The still homeless club exacted a measure of revenge, beating the new tenants 2-1 in the opening fixture of the Northern League on 21st August 1909. Hannan missed a penalty that would have earned a share of the points and overall, Hibs were unlucky to lose. The next match was a charity event at Arbroath in aid of the Artisan Golf Clubhouse at Elliot. Hibs won the match 2-0, their first recorded win, with goals from Strachan and Burns. Montrose were the next visitors to Tannadice and a crowd of around 6,000 watched a good 1-0 win for Hibs in the Northern League but the score line did not reflect the dominance of the 'Irishmen' throughout.

The Forfarshire section of the Qualifying Cup had drawn Hibs away to Brechin City on 4th September and a large travelling support went to Glebe Park on a special train organised by the Club. The fans returned disappointed after the home side won 2-1 with two first half goals to Hibs' solitary counter after half time by Loney, making his debut. The guest reporter for the *Dundee Courier* was former Brechin City player James Fowler and he felt that Hibs deserved at least a replay.

Hibs returned to Northern League business and won comfortably at home, 2-1 over Forfar Athletic and 3-0 over Brechin City, with Burns hitting two goals in each match. There was also a friendly against Dumbarton Harp at Tannadice and although it was a good work out for both sides, there were no goals. Unfortunately for Flood, a dislocated elbow during that match ruled him out for almost three months. There were 7,500 spectators present at a friendly against First Division Morton two days later, but a 4-1 defeat only proved that Hibs were well short of Scottish League standard.

A Northern League record crowd of 10,000 turned up for the match against Dundee 'A' on 9th October and the stronger fitter Dark Blues eventually overcame Hibs 3-0. A visit to Montrose was next in the league and Hibs, inspired by McDermott, won 4-1. A 1-1 draw with Dundee Wanderers at home and a 3-1 defeat at Brechin City ended any slim chance of winning the league title. Although the next match was a mere friendly against junior opposition Arbroath Strollers, it is significant in that Peter Yule recorded the first hat-trick for a Hibs player in the 6-2 win on 6th November.

After an entertaining 3-3 draw with Aberdeen 'A' and a 1-1 result at Forfar Athletic towards the end of 1909, the league campaign was all but over. The last Northern League match against Dundee 'A', two months later, resulted in a 4-2 home defeat and an inauspicious debut for Sheridan. The league programme was never completed, with the away match against Aberdeen 'A' not played as a date could not be arranged and Hibs finished in third place. Although significant because it was the first league in which the Club campaigned, the Northern League from that point onwards became little more than a testing ground to keep reserve players fit and try out potential new players.

As a result of failing to reach the Scottish Cup proper, Dundee Hibs took part in the aptly named Consolation Cup, instigated by the SFA in 1908. On 8th January 1910 the opposition was Brechin City, and just as in the Qualifying Cup, Hibs lost. Strachan got the only goal of the first half from the penalty spot but after the interval Brechin City asserted enough pressure to overcome a rather weak Hibs. The defence made basic errors, allowing a couple of soft goals in the 4-1 reversal. Prior to this meeting, Hibs had played three matches in four days between 1st and 4th January including friendlies against Second Division Cowdenbeath and Raith Rovers. Such a hectic schedule must surely have hindered any chance of progress in the cup.

One of the biggest crowds of the season packed into Tannadice for the Forfarshire Cup tie against Dundee 'A' on 19th February and they saw Hibs just eased out 2-1 but the team did enough to warrant a second bite at the tie. Dundee went in front but Mudie equalised before half time. The visitors then grabbed the winner but Hibs missed chances to level before the end.

Success however, was achieved in one of the cups, albeit this particular competition, the Carrie Cup was restricted to local senior clubs. As members of the Forfarshire Football Association, Dundee Hibs entered the Carrie Cup (also known as the Forfarshire League), a subsidiary competition for Northern League clubs who were also Forfarshire members. The teams competing were Dundee Hibs, Forfar Athletic, Brechin City, Montrose and Dundee Wanderers. Arbroath were also included, even although they had deserted to the Central League. This was the only time that Hibs played for the trophy, and they topped the table in the competition with six wins, two draws and just one defeat. However, it should be noted that Brechin City, Hibs' nearest challengers for the trophy, still had fixtures to honour in the competition including their home tie against Hibs. The Angus side ran out of available dates to play the ties and Dundee Hibs were awarded the trophy. At home to Forfar Athletic in the last Carrie Cup match of the season, Brown scored the only goal from a cross by Timmons, the Hibs goalkeeper having "abandoned the sticks" for a centre forward role that day.

Off the field, significant events that would have a direct bearing on the future of Dundee Hibs were taking place. On 2nd March at an Extraordinary General Meeting, the proposed merger of Ayr and Ayr Parkhouse fell through when the share holders voted 120 for and 120 against the motion, and the chairman refused to exercise his casting vote. Instead, he deferred the final decision on the merger to the AGM scheduled for late April. Events were being closely monitored by Dundee Hibs and they were no doubt relieved when the merger was finally approved. The two clubs in Ayr emerged as Ayr United.

In early May, Reilly again wrote to the Scottish League clubs, soliciting support for entry and extolling the facilities at Tannadice, which by then boasted hot and cold running water in the fully fitted dressing rooms. The Club was debt free having paid in full the cost of renovation works at Tannadice. The new stand could accommodate 1,200 spectators and the ground could hold 15,000 to 20,000. If enlarged he said it might be able to take as many as 40,000, although this claim may have been somewhat exaggerated. In his letter twelve months earlier he had quoted the number of people of Irish extraction, living in the area at 30,000, but by May 1910 this estimate had risen to an astonishing 50,000! Another exaggeration? It didn't matter, as the other league clubs eventually voted in favour of the inclusion of Dundee Hibernian in the Second Division for season 1910-11.

Match reports of Hibs' first season, and indeed for many in the early years of the Club, are not as comprehensive as they are today, and it must be remembered that the Tannadice outfit were then a club in its infancy. Records of line ups and goal scorers are difficult to obtain, but it is known that a number of the outfield players found the net during the season. Yule was top scorer with just seven to his name and Docherty and Brown are each recorded as scoring six times. News reports of Dundee Hibs throughout season 1909-10 frequently referred to the team as 'The Irishmen'. From the beginning though, the Club was definitely non sectarian, and included players who were non Irish and non Catholic. Later, another nickname, 'The Greens' would also emerge.

In an inconsistent season, the highlight was undoubtedly the Carrie Cup success and generally the Directors must have been satisfied with Hibs' debut in senior football. Late in the season, friendly matches were arranged against St Mirren 'A' and a Clyde XI. Hibs lost 5-1 when they went to Paisley, although the Tannadice side did not play all that badly. Cup finalists Clyde sent a strong team for the match at Tannadice and there was little to choose between the sides in a 3-3 draw. However, with the prospect of Second Division football ahead, this again demonstrated that the squad would need to be strengthened. Almost 30 players had faced the challenges of the inaugural season, but it was not surprising that most were released and only Boland, Carroll, Docherty, Timmons and Yule would see service with Hibs in the next campaign. Loney returned to Clyde after his loan period, but he would soon be back.

1910-11

The First Scottish League Season

During the close season the Manager had several irons in the fire. He had lodged applications with the Central League and with the Scottish League but the former was merely a precaution in case he was unsuccessful with the latter. The merger of Ayr Parkhouse and Ayr FC to form Ayr United left a vacancy in the Second Division as expected and Dundee Hibernian were admitted at the Scottish League meeting on 7th June 1910, just over a year from the date the Club were formed. The votes cast at the meeting to fill the two places available were Cowdenbeath 26, Dundee Hibs 20 and St Johnstone 10. Reilly's lobbying of the Scottish League clubs a year earlier did much to assist Hibs' cause. Four days later the Northern League re-admitted the Tannadice side for season 1910-11.

The Manager knew that to compete in the Scottish League he would need to improve his squad. The vast majority of players that had seen the Club through the 1909-10 season had already left and all through the summer Reilly set about building a new team. Loney returned on loan from Clyde again on 16th May but it took a few weeks before he was joined by others. On 21st June, goalkeeper James Tullis was signed from Carnoustie Panmure followed a few days later by centre forward William Swan from Arbroath and full back William Welsh from Hearts. Yule re-signed, and outside right Tom Collins joined from Airdrieonians in the first week of July. Boland re-signed on 16th July, just after Reilly had added another half back, John Robertson, then with Arthurlie. Centre half George Fyfe, a former Watford and Hibernian player signed on the same day.

James O'Gara, who had been with Middlesbrough and Airdrieonians, was added to the squad and Carroll was re-signed although he never featured during the season except in friendlies, and was released a year later. Reilly tried and failed to sign Tom Dorward of Dundee who went to Arbroath instead. Hibs were also particularly unfortunate to lose out on the signature of former Celtic and Brighton defender Bob Craig.

The *Dundee Courier* reported favourably on Hibs' prospects for their first season in the Scottish League as signings continued with Docherty putting pen to paper for another season. With the first game of the new season just a week away, John Collins, an outside left with the Edinburgh Hibs, was Reilly's next acquisition. The season opened with friendly matches against a Dundee Junior Select and St Johnstone. The first match brought a 2-0 win and the second a defeat by the same score line and some trialists were put through their paces but only John Darroch (ex-Dundee) was added to the growing list of playing staff. Tommy Miller, an ex-international who had been with Falkirk and Chelsea, was then signed on loan in time for the first league game on 20th August.

Dundee Hibs played their first Scottish League match at Tannadice against Leith Athletic but lost by the odd goal in five. The Irishmen should have taken more from the game but the Edinburgh side were well organised, whilst Hibs played like a team that did not know each other very well, which was of course true! The first league side, with five players making debuts in the green of Hibs lined up:-

Tullis, Welsh and Miller; Loney, Robertson and Boland; T Collins, O'Gara, Fyfe, Yule and J Collins.

During August there was only one league match played, although two were in the fixture list. The match at East Stirlingshire on 27th August was a scheduled league game but the referee failed to turn up! After an unsuccessful search to locate a suitable replacement, the clubs agreed to play the match as a friendly and Hibs lost 2-0. Three days earlier, Hibs lost by the same score at Arbroath in a benefit match for George Guild, a popular Red Lichties stalwart. In return, Arbroath played Hibs at the end of October in a benefit game for the "Hibs Brake Fund", in effect the Supporters' Club. That one ended in a 1-1 draw.

Further signings were made in early September. William Graham, a former Dundee Wanderers player was brought in along with the respected Airdrieonians goalkeeper Bill Monteith, formerly with Beith and Kilmarnock. Reilly had tried to sign the keeper a few months earlier and now finally got his man. Both the new players went straight into the side for the Qualifying Cup tie against Arbroath on 3rd September and despite a Swan goal for a half time lead, Hibs lost the tie 2-1 as Arbroath controlled the second half. At the end of September, forward Alexander Marshall arrived from Motherwell just as James Mudie left to join Cardiff City. The squad was by now so large that Hibs gave serious consideration to putting forward a team for the Second Eleven League. That ambitious idea was not followed through, but in November, the Club was inviting teams to play Hibs' second eleven at Tannadice, whilst the first team were away from home.

Despite a 4-3 defeat at St Bernard's in the second match of the campaign, the league season progressed well for Hibs initially. A 4-1 home win over Abercorn was regarded as a particularly good result and that was followed by a goalless draw at Albion Rovers. Cowdenbeath were beaten 2-0 at Tannadice on 1st October and then a 1-1 draw was achieved at home to Vale of Leven. During this period, Charlie Dunnian arrived on trial from Carlin Shamrock but he did not sign until 24th February 1911 after a spell with Hibernian in Edinburgh. Tom Waterston signed from Hearts and made an immediate impact, scoring in each of his first three appearances which saw successive wins over Port Glasgow Athletic, 2-1 Arthurlie, 2-0 and Abercorn, 2-1. That left Hibs in third place at the half way stage, albeit teams below them had games in hand.

Hibs then went on a nine-game run but this time it was without winning. Between mid November and early January, only two points were collected from 1-1 draws against Ayr United and Leith Athletic in early December. The other seven games resulted in defeats with only three goals scored and nineteen conceded. During that period, new signing John Dwyer and John J Smith were tried out unsuccessfully but James Izatt was brought into the side on 17th December from the ranks of the Edinburgh juniors to shore up Hibs' leaky defence. Although the improvement was not immediate, he emerged as the signing of the season as his arrival coincided with gradually improving form. John Dunn, James Govan and Charles Young also arrived in late December but took little part as the remainder of the season unfolded. Similarly, Percy Bryson, from junior side Dundee Harp, hardly featured in the league, although he made a significant contribution in the Consolation Cup run.

The prospect of facing the re-election lottery to retain Scottish League status must have been very real with just four games left and the visit of league leaders Albion Rovers on 7th January 1911 was anticipated with some trepidation. However, Hibs played well and won 1-0 with a good first half display and a goal from O'Gara, but it took some solid defending to preserve the lead.

At this point the Consolation Cup intervened. Hibs began a good run in the tournament with a replay win over Montrose. The first match, postponed due to snow a week before, ended in a 2-2 draw. With Montrose leading 2-1, the officials called time (the officials being the Montrose captain, Montrose linesman and Montrose secretary!) but the referee played on and Hibs levelled right at the end. Protests were a common feature in football during that era and Montrose challenged the result as the referee had allowed more than the allotted ninety minutes. The SFA however, rejected the protest on the basis that the referee had merely permitted injury time. The match was replayed at Tannadice where Hibs were by far the stronger side and deservedly won 6-1. Montrose finished with ten men after Whyte was ordered off.

The next round brought Dunfermline Athletic to Tannadice and it finished 3-2 to Hibs in a game they really should not have won, as the Fife side had played the better football. In the next round Hibs had to travel to Cowdenbeath. With the score at 0-0, the first meeting was abandoned due to torrential rain twenty minutes into a second half with Hibs controlling the game and looking likely to win. In the rescheduled match a week later, a spirited performance by Hibs was not enough to stop Cowdenbeath running out 3-1 winners.

Cup football continued with a Forfarshire Cup tie against Montrose who were again humiliated by Hibs. The Tannadice men practically scored at will in a 4-0 win and actually netted a fifth. The ball definitely crossed the line and bounced back out but the referee never saw it happen! In the final against Arbroath two weeks later, Hibs struggled, but won by a single goal in the second half when O'Gara's shot was parried by the keeper and Dunnian netted the rebound. The Forfarshire Cup went to Tannadice for the first time and the gate money was a record for a Forfarshire Cup final with total receipts of £126.

In between these two ties, Dunnian scored a hat-trick as Hibs played their best league game of the season to win 4-1 over Port Glasgow Athletic. A goalless draw against East Stirlingshire brought the last point of the season on 1st April and with it, Scottish League safety. Two weeks later newly signed Dan Gibson from Dundee North End made his debut as Dumbarton won the Second Division championship with a 3-1 win over Hibs.

Having won the Forfarshire Cup, Hibs were then paired with King's Park in the Dewar Shield, a trophy donated by the Dewar's Whisky family of Perth. The shield was contested by the winners of the county cups of Forfarshire, Aberdeenshire, Perthshire and Stirlingshire. After having a penalty claim denied, when Dunnian was bowled over in the box, Hibs eventually lost by a single goal.

The season ended with Dundee Hibs surviving in the Scottish League but only on goal average. The team scored 29 league goals and Swan was the top scorer with just six of those in his eight appearances. Still, the Board must have been pleased with the final outcome. In only their second season in existence Dundee Hibs had consolidated a Scottish League place and secured a trophy, adding the Forfarshire Cup to the Carrie Cup won last term. Financially, Dundee Hibernian Football and Athletic Club Ltd was not performing as well as could be expected and Directors Reilly and Rock between them had been forced to inject more cash in the form of loans totalling around £200.

On the same day that the last ball was kicked, 29th April 1911, players were on the move. Fyfe went back to Edinburgh to rejoin Hibernian, Miller returned to Falkirk and Loney to Clyde. Welsh also left, but would return to Tannadice within a couple of years. With such a big squad of players it was perhaps inevitable that there would be a number released. Fringe men Darroch, Marshall, Waterston, P Docherty, J Timmons, J J Smith, Dunn and Young, were allowed to go, leaving eighteen others to face the challenge of the next season. However, even some of those would fail to feature again, including Gibb, Dunnian, Yule, Dwyer, Graham, Tom Timmons, Carroll and both Collins. Perhaps the biggest surprise was the loss of Monteith who moved to Albion Rovers because he was unwilling to continue the regular commute to Dundee by train.

1911-12

Surviving a Second Scottish League Season

As soon as the first season of Scottish League football at Tannadice had ended, Reilly began signing players for the next campaign. In May 1911 he secured the services of Welsh outside left Idwal Evans. A month later, outside right George (Jock) Low from Forfar Athletic and Henry Taylor, a right half and captain of East Fife, were also enlisted. Around the same time Tullis, Gibson and Govan, all re-signed for the next campaign, whilst Carroll, Collins, Dunnian, Robertson, Swan and Yule were transfer listed.

On the national scene, the Second Division clubs of the Scottish League were, not for the first time, seeking a system of automatic promotion to the First Division. The motion was soundly defeated at the League AGM on 6th June 1911. For the next month or two, news of the Irishmen was hard to find. Then on the 5th August the signing of right back John Sharp from Third Lanark and former Dundee and Clyde outside right Alex Mitchell were announced. By then, Boland had re-signed for his third season with the Club.

On Monday 7th August the *Dundee Courier* previewed Hibs forthcoming season saying, "Hibs' prospects for next season are bright. They enter on their second term in the Scottish Second League. Hibs did well during the first three months of last season but owing to injuries which laid aside three or four of the team they were unable to maintain their form.......... Hibs now have almost got their team into order. One or two places however, are to be filled up with experienced men. Loney, Robertson, Fyfe, Welsh, Monteith, O'Gara, Collins and Graham have all gone to other quarters. Manager Reilly informs me they are to have all their players training at Tannadice Park next season. The drawback last year was that the members of the team came in from various places for the matches. The Irishmen mean to make a bold challenge for the championship." Unfortunately that last statement would come back to haunt Pat Reilly!

A new trainer, Mr Callary, formerly of Leith Athletic, replaced Joe McNally.

Izatt and Bryson re-signed by mid August along with the versatile former Celtic back Bob Craig. Reilly had chased Craig's signature a year earlier but had lost out to Darlington. The following day he signed another ex-Celt, John Young, and the team was ready to face the challenge of the new season which began with a 2-1 friendly win over junior side Dundee Celtic.

The opening league fixture away to East Stirlingshire on 17th August ended in a 3-1 defeat, with only a late Gibson consolation goal to offset the three scored against. Worse still for Hibs was the injury to John Sharp which ensured that the player would never again don a Hibs shirt after just one game! O'Gara returned to Tannadice in time for the home match against Leith Athletic, one of the strongest league sides. The Greens were on the defensive against a lively Leith and worked hard for a 1-0 win. By the end of the August, the hunt for players to strengthen the side yielded forwards James Robertson and John Brown from Partick Thistle.

For the third year in succession Hibs fell at the first hurdle in the Qualifying Cup. A win had been expected against Forfar Athletic but despite having more of the play and chances galore, Hibs lost 2-1 at home. The Manager moved to strengthen the side and Loney was again brought back on loan from Clyde in mid September. He made his return on the same day that goalkeeper Jim Crumley made his debut against Albion Rovers in a 1-0 defeat. Hibs went another seven league games without a win, managing only a point each in draws with Arthurlie, St Bernard's and Abercorn. Whilst there were some narrow defeats, the same could not be said of the visits to Ayr United where Hibs lost six goals without reply and to St Bernard's where the home side won 7-1. Crumley, who had been heavily criticised in both these defeats, surprisingly kept his place in goal for all but one game after he signed. Hibs signed two more centre forwards in October; William Finlay from St Andrews University and David Scrimgeour but neither had the desired impact and a run of poor results went on. New signing from Lochee Harp, William Galloway headed the only goal of the game against St Johnstone on 11th November in a match which saw Hibs off the bottom of the table, but only just.

New centre half, John Burns, was signed in November and inside forward Willie Linn joined Hibs from Dundee North End to begin a long association with the Club. At the same time O'Gara left for Portsmouth. James Robertson was transferred to Ayr United and George Fyfe arrived from Dumbarton in early December. These moves were quickly followed by the return of Hannan who had been with Brechin City for a short spell.

In late November 1911 the *Dundee Courier* announced that Mr David Wallace, who had already put up several trophies for local swimming and cycling competitions, had donated a trophy called the Loftus Cup. At inception it was contested between Dundee Hibs, Dunfermline Athletic and St Johnstone, on a two leg basis. Hibs' first match in the tournament was against St Johnstone on

23rd December at the Recreation Ground, Perth. The home side won 4-0 easily in a bad tempered match that saw Izatt of Hibs and Colombo of Saints ordered off late in the game.

Performances in the second half of the season were not much better than in the first. Seven league games yielded just two points from draws with Arthurlie and Ayr United, leaving Hibs in dire straits on the eve of the visit of East Stirlingshire on 6th January 1912. Inside forward William Donaldson joined Hibs in time to make his debut in this match with Hibs desperately needing a win. They got it, scraping home 1-0, with a goal from Gibson. League business then went on hold for the early rounds of the Consolation Cup. Forfar Athletic were the opposition in the first round and Donaldson played his second and last game for Hibs in a dull 0-0 draw at Station Park. For the replay at Tannadice, Izatt was suspended after his sending off at Perth and Hannan was cup tied with Brechin City, so Hibs signed Andrew Richardson from Blairgowrie Our Boys to cover. There was no mistake this time, as Hibs won comfortably 4-1. This set up a derby with Dundee Wanderers at Tannadice and with Hibs in top form, they romped to a 5-1 win, although the visitors were handicapped by an injury to a player in the second half.

It was back to league matters on 10th February with a 3-1 away defeat at Abercorn that made league survival precarious again. But Hibs had the advantage of home games against Dumbarton and Cowdenbeath to end the season. Both were strong sides but both matches had to be won to avoid the prospect of seeking re-election.

Dumbarton came calling first, having scored six against Ayr United the week before. To add further interest, they had to win to prevent Ayr United taking the championship flag. There was therefore, quite a build up to the match. Surprisingly, Hibs took the lead through Gibson early in the game and Linn scored a second before Dumbarton pulled one back from the spot. Hibs took a three-goal advantage in the second half with goals from Gibson and Richardson. Right at the end, the visitors pulled another one back, but the day belonged to Hibs with a 4-2 win after one of their best displays of the season. The result handed Ayr United the title and with only East Stirlingshire of the other re-election contenders gaining a point, Hibs were that bit closer to safety.

Due to the intervention of yet more cup commitments, there was a wait of almost two months before Hibs knew their fate for certain. First up in the cups was the Consolation Cup match against St Bernard's. With memories of their 7-1 thrashing there only three months before, Hibs were too cautious and in an evenly matched contest they lost 1-0 to exit the competition. Next came a Forfarshire Cup tie against Dundee Wanderers who had signed former Hibs man Peter Yule only days before. It was a poor game overall, with Hibs just marginally the better side winning 2-0 to set up a semi final with Dundee. Before that, Hibs' next match was in the Loftus Cup at Dunfermline Athletic and the Greens won 1-0.

Dundee had difficulty agreeing a date for the Forfarshire Cup semi final at Dens Park and several attempts to fix up the tie failed. Frustrated by this, Hibs intimated their intention to claim the tie if Dundee kept refusing to play on the dates suggested. At the eleventh hour a date was agreed and Dundee fielded their reserve side as they were entitled to do. It became an ill-tempered encounter in which Hibs carved out a 2-2 draw against a well organised Dundee. The Dens Park side then lodged a protest claiming Andrew Richardson of Hibs was ineligible as he had played in a Perthshire tie. Hibs offered no defence and the protest was upheld and a replay ordered. Reilly was severely censured, but the unfortunate Richardson received a very harsh penalty. He was suspended for six months! Hibs then decided to withdraw from the tournament citing a conflict between national and county rules as both demanded priority, thus creating fixture difficulties.

Perhaps the decision to scratch from the competition was fuelled by the earlier problems trying to arrange the tie or maybe it was indeed because of the conflict between national and county rules. But there may also be some significance in the fact that Hibs were about to go into the last league game of the season at home to Cowdenbeath, knowing that almost all the other sides in Division Two had completed their programmes. At least a point was still required to ensure the Irishmen did not finish in second bottom place and as a consequence, seek re-election. As it turned out, Hibs had a four goal half time lead through Gibson, Scrimgeour, and two from Linn. The Fife side scored twice in the second half before Gibson scored again to wrap up the points in a merited 5-2 win, which ensured Scottish League football at Tannadice for another year.

Two more Loftus Cup matches were played to end the season. The return match against St Johnstone was won 2-0 with goals from Galloway and Gibson and that set up a cup decider against Dunfermline Athletic. The Fife side needed only to draw to lift the trophy and brought a train load of around 700 supporters to back them in their bid. Labelled the game of the season by the *Dundee Courier* of 22nd April, "the play was keen, fast, exciting and devoid of the finer points but none the less it whet the jaded football appetite of the public." Hibs played well in defence but could not prevent the visitors from taking the cup with a 2-1 win.

Hibs continued to compete in the Northern League but due to fixture congestion they were again unable to complete their programme. By the end of the season however, Hibs decided that the Northern League commitment was too onerous and on 16th April, gave notice of their intention to withdraw. Shortly after that it was reported that the Northern League was in serious danger of collapsing altogether but it struggled on for two more years and Hibs remained involved.

On 5th May, Reilly revealed that, yet again, the lower league clubs were proposing a system of automatic promotion to the First Division. On the same day, Hibs withdrew from the Forfarshire Association on the grounds that the demands for preference by the county association and the Scottish League created a conflict. There was also a county rule precluding any match by an associated club within a five mile radius of a Forfarshire tie. This affected Hibs more than any other side because, as well as Dundee's home matches at Dens Park, the Forfarshire Cup final was normally played there. A very public series of accusations and counter accusations followed. Hibs stood by their decision with Chairman Peter Ross giving a full and final explanation of Hibs' actions on 15th May.

At the end of the season, Reilly admitted he was unhappy with the way the team had performed overall. His side had managed only 21 league goals with Gibson the top scorer on six. The Manager let the supporters know that there would be several changes in the playing staff for the next season. Many players were freed, including Fyfe, Burns, Brown, Docherty, Taylor, Dwyer, Evans, Findlay and Galloway. Only a dozen or so of the squad for 1911-12 would see service with Hibs again.

Reilly wanted 'heftier lads' more suited to the Second Division and wasted little time in getting started. Right half Sam Whyte signed from Forfar Athletic on 13th May, forward John Ross from Arbroath ten days later and, in early June new keeper James Elrick from Brechin City replaced Jim Crumley who left Scotland to live in Canada. Hibs however, retained Crumley's registration as a player and the keeper would return to Tannadice years later. Low re-signed almost as soon as the season ended and was soon joined by Scrimgeour, Govan and Gibson.

1912-13

Another Season of Struggle

There was no real surprise expressed around Tannadice when yet again, at their AGM on 4th June 1912, the Scottish League rejected automatic promotion from the Second Division. The excuse was that First Division bottom club, St Mirren would become the relegated club, but because the Paisley side had already committed to a First Division wage structure, it would be unfair to change the rules. Perhaps as a compromise the Second Division was extended to 14 teams, with the inclusion of Dunfermline Athletic and Johnstone.

The *Dundee Courier* correspondent did not seem to be aware of the Scottish League decision. He displayed a hint of optimism when reporting on Hibs' prospects on 27th July writing, "…..the Hibs intend to be more than an 'also ran' should promotion honours be served out."

With just two weeks left before he had to name his side for the first league match of the season, the Manager had still not signed enough players. George Forbes from Dundee joined Hibs at the end of June followed by the return of Mudie but supporters were told they "should just wait for news of new captures". Despite the lack of signings, season tickets went on sale at five shillings (25p) and there was a lot of interest.

Izatt and Boland re-signed at the end of July, along with new outside right Harry Black and left back Alex McDonald, both from Arbroath. This double signing was quickly followed by the news that Linn had re-signed. Right back John McGinness was signed just before the friendly against St Johnstone on 15th August that ended in a 3-3 draw. Hibs were then ready for the season with a team made up mostly of local men, which made it easier to get together for training.

In the first league match against East Stirlingshire at Tannadice, Hibs lost by the odd goal in five to a bigger, stronger side. The squad however, was not complete. Inside right David 'Chappie' Gowans, formerly with Dundee, was added before

7th October 1912 – Forbes of Dundee Hibs challenges Husson of Dundee 'A'

the visit to Leith Athletic where Hibs lost 2-0. By the third league game of the season, in which Hibs beat Arthurlie 3-1, Gowans was Hibs' captain. Indifferent league form continued through September with a 2-1 defeat from Vale of Leven and 4-1 reversal at Arthurlie but in October, Hibs recorded a good 1-0 win over a strong Dundee 'A' side in a friendly.

After receiving a bye in the first round of the Qualifying Cup, Hibs went on a good run in the competition, knocking out Montrose 3-0 with the aid of a Linn double, Forfar Athletic 3-1 with a Scrimgeour hat-trick and Broxburn United 1-0 with Linn getting the only goal. The next round brought a trip to Inverness Caledonian and Hibs looked to have won the tie with a Govan goal two minutes from the end.

However, the Highland League side were not to be denied and equalised straight from the restart. Hibs were expected to win the replay at Tannadice but were eliminated, losing 2-0 despite bombarding the Caley goal for much of the game. Scoring chances were passed up whilst the visitors snapped two opportunist goals to win. Unfortunately the cup run came at the expense of league results with defeats at St Johnstone, 2-0 and Albion Rovers, 5-1. To make matters worse it had been costly, with Hibs barely breaking even financially, although they had gained entry to the Scottish Cup for reaching the fourth round of the 'QC'.

Loney re-signed in late October but did not feature again until December and Hibs had also signed international goalkeeper Donald Cameron from Sheffield United in time to travel to Inverness Caledonian for the Qualifying Cup tie. Outside right, Michael Lamb arrived from St Bernard's just before the replay on 9th November. League form in November and December was indifferent with full points taken just once in a 2-1 win against Leith Athletic. The other matches resulted in draws against Ayr United, 0-0 St Johnstone, 1-1 and Cowdenbeath, 0-0 with away defeats at Dumbarton, 2-0 and at St Bernard's, 3-0. Also, a poor showing against Arbroath Amateurs resulted in a 4-1 defeat in a friendly.

It was around this time that Reilly intimated an interest in signing Herbert Dainty, then with Bradford City. Despite being willing to pay what would have been a Second Division record fee of £250, it would take almost two more years to eventually acquire the player. Dainty would have been a welcome addition to the team and would almost surely have improved attendances, which were very much in decline. By the end of November, Hibs' gate money was as little as £5-£10 each game and not nearly enough to pay wages, the upkeep of Tannadice, plus payments to the visiting sides. The call went out for the support to back the team in the numbers that had been anticipated. So dire was the financial shortfall that the Directors were considering the issue of shares to the general public if income did not improve. Publicly, the Board appeared optimistic but in fact, Hibs were facing the possibility of going out of business.

To strengthen the squad, Tom Gallacher was signed from Dundee in early December and Docherty returned after a spell at Partick Thistle. Hibs also recruited a new trainer, Michael Fox (formerly with Dundee Harp, the junior side). By the mid-way point in the league Hibs were bottom and still trying to find the right blend. Ned MacDonald was then brought in from Glossop and Craig went to Southend United on loan, whilst former player Welsh returned to Tannadice.

The Club went into the second half of the campaign desperate to avoid re-election. A much improved Hibs took 15 points from thirteen games, losing just twice more in the league. A 3-3 draw at home to Dumbarton on 1st January 1913 was followed by a 1-1 result against St Bernard's, also at Tannadice. Hibs then lost 4-1 at Johnstone but won 1-0 at home against Ayr United who went on to win the Second Division. The next match brought the highlight of the league campaign, a 7-1 thrashing of Johnstone with Scrimgeour scoring a hat-trick. A 2-2 draw at Vale of Leven then set up Hibs for their first Scottish Cup tie, at Hampden, against Queen's Park,

Handicapped by the loss of the injured Whyte, attempts were made to obtain players on loan from Third Lanark, Raith Rovers and Dunfermline Athletic but without success. Other clubs were not keen to have players cup tied for future rounds. When the big cup day came, a special train was organised to carry the team and 1,000 Hibs supporters to Glasgow. With a total of around 11,000 watching, Hibs struggled for much of the first half and conceded three goals. The home side went four up before Hibs rallied and pressed forward. Boland and Scrimgeour pulled it back to 4-2 to give the home support a worrying last few minutes but Hibs still went out. The gate receipts of £280 gave the Club something to offset the financial losses made in the Qualifying Cup run.

The next six league matches brought an unbeaten run starting with a 1-1 draw at Cowdenbeath on 15th February. A 3-0 win at home to Abercorn followed and then Hibs drew 0-0 at Dunfermline Athletic and 1-1 at East Stirlingshire before recording an excellent 2-1 win at home to Albion Rovers. A league point was taken from a 1-1 draw with Dunfermline Athletic and Hibs finished tenth in the league after losing the final match 2-0 at Abercorn on 29th March. It was just a slight improvement on the previous season but the Club were at least well clear of the bottom two. Linn had proved his worth in twenty six appearances and he was top scorer with twelve league goals. There had also been a good Qualifying Cup run and a first entry to the Scottish Cup.

By the end of March, Young had returned to Celtic and Low had gone to Clyde.

It was also announced that Chappie Gowans was going to Canada and a friendly match was organised on 7th April with Dundee 'A' as the opposition. Dundee won it 2-0 and Gowans was presented with a purse of sovereigns by Mr William Wallace (Dundee FC) at half time. Scrimgeour also left, joining Portsmouth on 21st April and he was soon followed south by Gibson. There was also a series of Loftus Cup matches at the end the season and Hibs were undefeated drawing 3-3 at St Johnstone and winning 2-1 at home to Dunfermline Athletic. The third Loftus Cup match ended 1-1 at Dunfermline Athletic but the cup was withheld as Hibs final match against St Johnstone could not be arranged.

The rift that had occurred between Hibs and the Forfarshire Association was healed when the county association accepted that Hibs had been unfairly treated the previous season. The rules which had caused the problem were deleted. Hibs then re-applied and were unanimously re-elected to the Forfarshire Association. A major surprise came from the Board in early May. Bearing in mind all the reports of financial problems at the turn of the year, a profit of £200 was announced and a dividend of 10-15% was proposed. Despite this announcement, the financial position at the Club was still problematic and by this time there were Director's loans totalling £760 due by the Club. Still in need of cash therefore, Hibs advertised the issue of 1,000 shares of £1 each. The actual take up of the offer was not made public but the Directors later reported it had been a success. However, it transpired that only 153 shares had actually been taken up with 100 of these by John Bogue, later to become a Director.

A bigger surprise followed on 9th May when Reilly revealed that Hibs were applying for one of the two new First Division places! The Scottish League had previously announced a restructure, with the First Division increasing from eighteen teams to twenty, while the Second Division was to reduce from fourteen teams to only twelve. The rules of the Scottish League then permitted a maximum of thirty two member clubs. Realistically, Hibs' chances of gaining entry to the top flight were negligible with only Aberdeen openly supporting the application.

The Manager was still not satisfied with the team's performances and the squad was consequently trimmed. Substantially over staffed, several players were released by the Club, including Ross, Richardson, Docherty, Mudie, Black, Elrick and George Parker, who managed only two games at centre in January. More surprisingly, Izatt also ended his Tannadice career. Still at the Club but on the transfer list were, Tullis, Carroll, John Collins and Dunnian and they were now joined by Bryson, Crumley (although he was still in Canada!), Gallacher, Hannan, Lamb, Loney, Mitchell, Alex McDonald, McGinness and Yule. In late May, with Forbes and Boland back for another season, the Manager began the hunt for experienced players with the potential to compete in First Division football. With this in mind, he signed the former Dundee, Hearts and Bradford City centre half Bill Henderson from Grimsby Town on 14th June.

1913-14

Finding a Blend

Not surprisingly, Hibs were left disappointed when their application to join the elite of the First Division received a mere handful of votes. Ayr United were voted in with little difficulty and they were joined in the top flight by Dumbarton on the casting vote of the Chairman. Cowdenbeath were the side that lost out on the casting vote, followed by Dunfermline Athletic with Hibs a long way behind in the ballot.

There was however, still plenty of transfer activity. In early June, Hibs began gearing up for another season in the Second Division. Donald Cameron left to join Cowdenbeath and Hibs signed outside right Pat Currie, formerly of East Fife, a week later. At the end of the same month, half back Alex McDonald re-signed and outside left Fred Stoessel from Dundee was added to the squad.

There was considerable optimism around Tannadice by the end of July with a big demand for season tickets. Much of the pre-season enthusiasm was attributable to the signing of David 'Collie' Martin, formerly of Dundee and Brechin City. Over the next two seasons he racked up almost 50 goals for Hibs and was the Second Division's top scorer two years running. The former Hearts goalkeeper Charlie McPhilips was signed around the same time, along with local junior player William Brown. Hannan came off the transfer list and re-signed on 13th August in time for the start of the season. By then, Linn, Govan, Ned MacDonald, Welsh and Whyte were already in pre-season training.

The opening league match of the season on 16th August ended in a goalless draw at Perth against St Johnstone. In the next two matches Hibs took three points with a well deserved 1-0 win against Arthurlie in which Collie Martin scored his first goal for the Club, followed by a 1-1 draw at Leith Athletic. The good start to the league campaign encouraged more season tickets sales and a second printing was required on 26th August. The Qualifying Cup paired Hibs with Brechin City in the first round on 13th September. Hibs strolled through the match and should have won by more than the two goals they scored.

It was back to league business with a 2-0 defeat in Paisley from Abercorn, followed by a 2-0 win over Vale of Leven courtesy of another Martin double, before the next round of the Qualifying Cup brought Dunfermline Athletic to Tannadice. A crowd of 7,000 witnessed an outstanding team performance by the Irishmen who won 3-0, with one from Stoessel and two from Martin. That win was followed by the 5-0 thrashing of Johnstone and yet again Martin got two of the goals. Arbroath keeper George Sutherland signed in October along with Frank Leckie and St Joseph's player Andrew Crawford.

Hibs played only four more league matches until the end of 1913 but won only once, 3-1 at home to East Stirlingshire on 8th November. The three defeats suffered were all away from home and all by a single goal. At Albion Rovers the home side won 2-1, at Dunfermline Athletic it was 1-0 and Arthurlie won 3-2. Most of the attention at the end of that year was on the Qualifying Cup, but with replays required in the third round, semi final and final it was a strength sapping tournament for the Tannadice side.

A third round away tie on 18th October at East Stirlingshire that ended in a hard fought 1-1 draw earned a replay a week later. In the replay, Martin and Linn scored in a dazzling display against their more fancied opponents and the 2-1 win brought a quarter final home tie against Forfar Athletic on 1st November. Tannadice had been extended in anticipation of a bumper crowd and the ground was packed as Hibs emerged 1-0 winners with a good team display and a second half strike by Whyte.

In the semi-final against Inverness Caledonian at Tannadice on 29th November, Hibs were expected to win comfortably, but played what was probably their worst game of the season and were lucky to get a second chance against their Highland League opponents after a 1-1 draw. In Inverness a week later, Hibs played to form and two goals from Stoessel were enough to set up a final against Albion Rovers. It took three matches, all played in Edinburgh, before a cup winner would emerge and for each game Hibs fielded the same line up:-

Action from the Qualifying Cup Final

McPhilips, Hannan and Forbes; Whyte, Henderson and Boland; Brown, E McDonald, Martin, Linn and Stoessel.

With Albion in front in an evenly balanced first game on 13th December, Brown fired in a great shot to earn a re-match. A week later, the first replay produced a dour struggle with both teams opting for caution, which hindered any chance of a good match. Albion scored first again but Linn equalised within a minute. In the second replay on 27th December, Albion adapted better to the poor conditions under foot. Although Hibs were unlucky on more than one occasion in front of goal, they were comprehensively beaten 3-0.

Due to the cup commitment, league form seemed to have suffered and by the half way point only ten points had been accumulated. Fixture congestion was a problem as evidenced by the need to play three matches in three days over the period 1st to 3rd January 1914. Losing 3-1 to St Bernard's in the third of these matches, the team showed they were tired from the effects of playing a Loftus Cup tie the day before. The tie had been held over from the previous year's competition and Hibs beat St Johnstone 3-1 to win the trophy with the help of a Martin hat-trick. Hibs had been involved in a Northern League match before that.

The second half of the season saw a revitalised Hibs mount a genuine challenge for the championship. A 1-1 draw at Leith Athletic was followed by a 3-1 win at East Stirlingshire and a 2-1 win at home to Abercorn. Inexplicably, the Tannadice side travelled to Johnstone, who were languishing near the bottom of the league, and lost by a single goal. A Scottish Cup tie with Airdrieonians was played the following week and in an audacious move, Hibs had offered the First Division side £200 plus half of the gate money to switch the tie to Tannadice. Airdrieonians rejected the request of course, but the move showed the level of the Board's ambition. No other Second Division club had the wherewithal to make such a unique offer, especially to a First Division side. Hibs' chances of creating an upset were gauged as slim because, a week prior to the cup tie, whilst Hibs were losing to lowly Johnstone, Airdrieonians were beating Morton 7-1. Hibs did however, surprise their First Division opponents at Broomfield and held out until half time but conceded a goal within a minute of the restart. After that Hibs were overwhelmed and lost 5-0.

The league challenge was still real and William Duncan was added to the playing staff in February. Hibs were back on track the following week with a 2-2 draw at home to fellow challengers, Albion Rovers. Dunfermline Athletic were then beaten 2-1 at Tannadice and Hibs continued their good league form into the Forfarshire Cup trouncing Brechin City 7-1, with a hat-trick from Martin in a very one-sided affair. League leaders Cowdenbeath were the next visitors to Tannadice and Hibs won comfortably 3-0. However, it was a completely different story in the return match a week later in Fife as Hibs were soundly beaten 7-0. Cowdenbeath could not then be caught and they went on to take the Second Division title. This result must have had a demoralising effect as Hibs went into the Forfarshire Cup final a week later against Arbroath. Hibs led by a Stoessel goal before Guild equalised. The match set a record of £140 for gate receipts at a Forfarshire Cup tie beating the record set by the same two sides in 1910. In the replay a week later, won 2-1 by Arbroath, both sides improved and entertained the crowd with a match full of incident and goal mouth action.

More signings came at the end of the season with four local juniors, William Spence, Joe Hughes, Willie Cavanagh and Alex Grieve all taking part in the final matches of the season. Hibs beat Vale of Leven 2-1, St Bernard's 2-1 and St Johnstone 3-2 to secure a best ever fourth spot in the Second Division. The name of Herbert Dainty was again being linked with Hibs but these rumours were firmly quashed on 4th April following the news that Dainty had signed as player/manager at Ayr United. Hibs then signed outside right Gordon Bannerman from St Johnstone on 14th April but he left within weeks. It was the only season at Tannadice for goalkeepers Sutherland and McPhilips who were both released. Also ending their Hibs careers after 1913-14 were Duncan and Hannan. Boland, Brown and Welsh remained initially but joined the armed forces as soon as WW1 began.

Having participated in two cup finals and finishing only five points off the top of the league, Reilly and the Directors must have been satisfied with Hibs' season. However they must also have considered what might have been if the Qualifying Cup run had not been so protracted. Financially the cups had brought in much needed income, but Reilly expressed his concern saying "it was an absolute scandal" that the second Division was left with only twelve teams and no automatic promotion. The clubs had nothing to aim for in the league and had to rely heavily on cup revenue to supplement league income. He also criticised the Second Eleven set up which charged only 4d (about 2p), while Second Division sides were obliged to charge 6d (2½ p). This would of course have affected Hibs more than most other sides with Dens Park only yards away. But the financial situation was at least improving and the Directors loans were now just £500. It will come as no surprise to learn that the matter of automatic promotion was on the Scottish League agenda again.

1914-18

The First World War Years

During the build up to the new season, there was a belief in the Hibs camp that further success was achievable. Many of the squad were expected to sign up again and Hibs fans were delighted with the news that Martin had decided to remain at Tannadice despite several offers from English clubs. Also the subject of much interest from south of the border, Forbes re-signed in mid May and Linn signed up for his fourth season at around the same time. Ned MacDonald, Cavanagh, Govan, Grieve, Spence, Hughes, Stoessel and the dependable Boland all re-signed, whilst Low returned after a year with Clyde and Alex Chaplin was added to the squad in late May.

As the summer months went by, football news in the local press lost significance, with much more space given over to unrest within Europe. The continent was in political turmoil and on the brink of war. But football life went on as Dundee Hibs advertised season tickets for sale at five shillings (25p). Despite the declaration of war on 4th August 1914, the Qualifying Cup draw was made as normal a week later with 94 teams in the first round scheduled for 27th September. Hibs were drawn at home to Forfar Athletic.

The immediate effect of the war on football was the reduction in playing staff. Many players, including Boland, Stoessel, Whyte and others from Hibs, joined the armed services in the early months of the conflict. Linn is reported as 'taking the colours' but not until April 1915. Throughout the war years, registered players on active service would turn out for Hibs if they could, when home on leave. Hibs' Directors, like those of most clubs, decided to continue to pay the wages of these players, although later they were reduced to half the usual rate.

As the season kicked off, there was heated public debate around whether or not football should be cancelled altogether. In Scotland, the national leagues, the Qualifying Cup and other minor cup competitions went ahead. St Johnstone petitioned the SFA to stop all football, and at a meeting of the SFA on 8th September, Mr Munro of Inverness also proposed abandoning football completely. It was agreed that a deputation should go to London to discus the matter. After that meeting it emerged that the War Office was in favour of the game continuing, but the four International Associations agreed to cease all matches if so ordered. It was generally felt that allowing football to carry on did not hinder recruitment and was good for morale at home. However, the major cups of each association were postponed and international matches were suspended.

There were hardly any new signings at Tannadice as the season progressed, with just James Cheyne arriving in late August and then a local junior, John Knowles signed on 9th September. The absence of several senior players meant that the Greens had to field a relatively inexperienced side, relying heavily on Forbes, Linn and Martin to help the younger players through, but in the early stages of the campaign they struggled. After losing the opening match 3-1 at Dunfermline Athletic, Hibs took a point from a 3-3 draw with Arthurlie but then lost against St Johnstone, Cowdenbeath, Clydebank and Leith Athletic, before beating Lochgelly United 4-3 on 3rd October for the first win of the season. Hibs had also faced an early exit from the Qualifying Cup on 8th September when Forfar Athletic ran up a 4-0 win with ease. There was not even a Consolation Cup to look forward to as the war resulted in the cancellation of that tournament.

After leaving Hibs at the end of season 1909-10, Flood returned on 7th October and was in the side at Tannadice three days later when a single Martin goal against St Bernard's gave Hibs the points. They could not however, maintain any consistency and lost to Abercorn, East Stirlingshire, Albion Rovers and Dunfermline Athletic. The inexperience of the players was frequently exposed as the side remained in the lower reaches of the league for much of the season.

Facing undefeated Clydebank away on 14th November appeared to be a tough task but it proved instead to be the turning point of the season as Hibs won 3-2 with goals from Cavanagh, Martin and Linn. After that result, points were gradually accumulated as Hibs clawed their way from the bottom to finish eleventh. There were commendable draws with Cowdenbeath and Vale of Leven and an excellent 6-1 home win over Albion Rovers on 19th December with Martin scoring five times. He also netted twice in a 3-0 win over Johnstone on 1st January 1915 and scored another two in the 3-1 victory over St Johnstone the following day. He continued his good form with yet another brace as Hibs beat Abercorn 2-1. All of these results were achieved on home turf, but on away trips it was the complete opposite as Hibs collected just three away points all season.

In the second half of the season, Hibs experienced a keeper crisis. Henry Steel took the jersey for the last two league matches in January as the Club beat Abercorn 2-1 but then lost 5-1 at St Bernard's. William Connolly was the next keeper signed and he played in goal for three matches. His debut was at Dunfermline Athletic where the home side hammered Hibs 6-0 on 30th January in the Loftus Cup. He then played in the last two league games as Hibs lost 4-3 at East Stirlingshire but recorded a fine 4-1 win over Vale of Leven at Tannadice in the final league fixture of the season on 13th February. The fourth goalkeeper of the season was Charlie Bruce of Brechin Hearts who joined Hibs on 19th February.

The remaining ten weeks of the football season were taken up with Northern League matches and other minor cup tournaments. A sizeable crowd witnessed a good performance by Hibs to produce a 3-1 win at Tannadice against a strong Dundee 'A' in the semi final of the Forfarshire Cup on 6th March. The visitors took the lead early in the game but Cheyne equalised before half time. Hibs were the better side after the interval and Martin netted twice to set up a repeat of the previous year's final against Arbroath. Hibs were not so well organised a few days later and lost 4-0 when they met Dundee at Dens Park in a friendly. In the first half hour of the Forfarshire Cup final on 27th March, Arbroath looked the more likely side, but Cheyne scored two quick goals for Hibs who then controlled the game until the end to win the cup for the second time.

As a result of winning the Forfarshire Cup, Hibs entered the Dewar Shield and beat St Johnstone 2-0 at Tannadice with goals from Low and Govan to set up a final against Aberdeen 'A'. Before that, St Johnstone were the opposition again, in Perth, where the home side won a Loftus Cup tie 3-2. In the Dewar Shield final, Hibs were the better side on the day, but the trophy went north to Aberdeen as a result of a goalkeeping blunder by Bruce in extra time. The unfortunate keeper took his eye off the ball and allowed a harmless shot to slip through his hands and drop over the line.

One very important change took place at Tannadice in late April 1915 as the season drew to a close. Pat Reilly gave up the post of Manager but remained as Club secretary. The new Player/Manager had been in Hibs' sights for two years and they finally got their man, obtaining the signature of Herbert Dainty from Ayr United. The fee of £100 was a record, although considerably short of the £250 Ayr United might have expected under normal circumstances. The former Dundee and Bradford City player held a Scottish Cup medal from Dundee's 1910 win over Clyde. He had business interests in Dundee and had been trying to return to the city for some time.

As season 1915-16 began, the *Dundee Courier* reported under the headline, "Full Team Serving with The Colours – Dundee Hibs Record", on 5th July 1915 that "Edward MacDonald, left half of the Dundee Hibs, has joined the Cameron Highlanders. This brings the total of Tannadice players serving with the colours up to eleven, i.e. Sutherland, Welsh, Boland Crawford, MacDonald, Stoessel, Flood, Linn, Cheyne, Cavanagh and Brown. The number of Dundee Hibs who have joined the colours compares favourably with the roll of honour of any Northern club." Many players from other teams had joined up, most notably a full eleven from Hearts, all on the same day.

First Division football was set to continue, but most of the Second Division sides had found that financial problems made it difficult to fulfil a league programme under war conditions. As a result, on 14th July 1915, all fourteen of the Second Division clubs decided to abandon the national league in favour of an East and West split. Hibs of course took part in the Eastern League into which a number of Central League sides were invited to bring the total to twelve teams. The twelve comprised seven from the Second Division and five from the Central League which was suspended. All guarantee payments to visiting clubs were cancelled. Another effect of the new set up was that Hibs were able to field players who were not actually signed to the Club as the Eastern League was not run under the auspices of the Scottish League. So, although Hibs had two dozen players registered with the Scottish League throughout the remaining war years, many others turned out for the Greens and were only required to sign if taking part in cup ties. Similarly Hibs players could play for other teams.

International meetings and national cup competitions were again suspended, so there was no Qualifying Cup, Consolation Cup or indeed Scottish Cup. Instead the clubs made do with their local county cups, and an Eastern Cup and Western Cup were introduced. Prices were reduced from 6d to 4d and players' wages went down to £1. St Johnstone went as far as discontinuing all football but gave over their Recreation Park ground to the military for matches. Dunfermline Athletic on the other hand actually had East End Park requisitioned, and for a short period had nowhere to play home matches!

By the time training started on 10th August, Hibs had acquired ex-Dundee Wanderers man David Ferguson from Forfar Athletic to add to Bruce, Forbes, Hughes, Dainty, Spence, Govan, Low, Cheyne, and Martin. Dainty then added Bert Neal who had been with Northampton Town, Dundee and St Johnstone, along with James Ritchie from Arbroath and David Gillies from Hearts. As the season unfolded there would be frequent personnel changes due largely to the uncertainty of the times. The goalkeeping position for example would see six custodians, Charlie Bruce, Jim Crumley, Robert Blackwood (on loan from Johnstone), McKerracher, O'Rourke and Gordon Kerr. Several guest players, juniors and trialists also turned out in Hibs colours.

The addition of former Dundee, Arsenal, Rangers and Fulham full back Jamie Sharp from Chelsea on 11th September caused considerable excitement around Tannadice and Val Lawrence, formerly with Newcastle United and Manchester City, and James McGuire from St Johnstone, also signed in September. Five years after Reilly tried to sign him from Dundee, Tom Dorward arrived from Arbroath in early October along with George Nicolson just after Ritchie had 'left the city', an expression which presumably meant he had joined his regiment elsewhere. John Brown and Frank Leckie were also back at Tannadice and the following month, a local junior, Tom Murray was signed. There was also heightened excitement at the prospect of former Hearts and Spurs star Tom Collins turning out as a guest, but it never happened as clearance could not be obtained. Late in the season, junior international John Aitken, Partick Thistle's George McGregor and James Herron from Arbroath joined Hibs but each made just a few appearances.

Hibs failed to impress over the season, with only six wins and one draw from twenty one games played in the Eastern League and the fixture list was not completed. Hibs lost the first two matches, 2-1 at East Stirlingshire and 5-4 to Lochgelly United but then notched a 4-3 victory at East Fife with the help of a Martin hat-trick. After losing 3-0 to Bathgate, a point was taken in a 3-3 draw at Kirkcaldy United. Hibs then lost 2-1 to Leith Athletic but gained a well deserved two points when they beat a strong Dunfermline Athletic on 2nd October by the same score line. After a 4-0 friendly defeat by Dundee at Dens Park, the next six matches ended in defeat, and Hibs plunged down the table. It was not until 20th November that they won again, beating East Stirlingshire 2-1. Defeat to Cowdenbeath followed before another good victory was achieved in a 5-2 win over St Bernard's. But another 4-0 friendly defeat was suffered, from the 2/7th Argyll & Sutherland Highlanders XI.

The remainder of the season was a mixture of league and cup matches. In the last six league encounters, spread over four months, a 1-0 win against Kirkcaldy United and 3-0 victories at home to Broxburn United and at Lochgelly United were enough to lift Hibs into ninth place but that was far below what was expected. The single pleasing aspect of the league campaign was the continued scoring form of Martin who netted eleven of Hibs' goals to become top scorer at Tannadice for the third season. In the cup competitions there were mixed fortunes even allowing for the circumstances, and the Board would have been unhappy with the overall showing. The Eastern Cup brought a 0-0 draw at Broxburn United and Hibs won the replay 3-0 but lost in the next round, 3-0 at home to Leith Athletic. Hibs also lost a Loftus Cup tie 3-2 at Dunfermline Athletic on New Year's Day 1916.

The Forfarshire Cup deserves a mention, despite a losing final. The semi-final against Arbroath took three games before it was settled at the third time of asking on 11th March, by a single McGuire counter. In the final, Hibs played Montrose, but it was Montrose in name only. The Angus side were in fact represented by the entire team of the 2/7th Argyll & Sutherland Highlanders complete with players from both English and Scottish First Divisions. The army side had gone the whole season undefeated and won the Forfarshire Cup final 2-0 with little difficulty. The winning ball was sent to the regiment on active service as a memento and no doubt a great boost to morale.

At the beginning of season 1916-17, Hibs still had the same two dozen registered players, several of whom were still in the armed forces. Another season in the Eastern League was in prospect, but Leith Athletic and Kirkcaldy United dropped out leaving only ten teams and they agreed that the league programme would wind up at the end of December. All national cups were again off the fixture card and the Forfarshire Association, with only Dundee and Hibs left playing, decided to abandon the cup competition.

Before the season got under way Neal had joined the forces. Herron left to make the short journey up Tannadice Street to join Dundee, after playing only three matches for Hibs at the end of April 1916. Many of the players who had turned out for Hibs in 1915-16 would not be seen again at Tannadice. It was expected that Hibs would begin the new term with a few new players, along with several players from the previous season's team and that is just how it turned out. Dainty, Spence, Forbes and McGuire would play a large part in the campaign alongside 'Ref' Ferrier, Vic Outerson and Archie Taylor. The latter would end the season as top scorer with twelve goals to his credit. Others such as John Robertson and John Ross who had both been at Tannadice before, played their part too.

Dainty was successful in signing North End goalkeeper Kennedy, who missed only one match during the season. Hibs had also secured the services of Charlie Dinnie from Huddersfield Town and Michael Lamb from Dundee. Bob Husson, also from Dundee, was drafted into the side by late August and became a stalwart in a season which saw uncertainties in team selection as never before. Jack Brown, a soldier with Middlesbrough connections, joined Hibs in September and a month later former Dundee forward McCabe was in the green of Hibs also. Junior international Charlie McKenzie played once for Hibs and would turn out once more a season later. It was felt that the Greens were strong enough to mount a serious league challenge and early results seemed to bear this out.

In the opening match against Lochgelly United, who had retained only one player in their side from the previous season, the Irishmen were a goal in front at half time and went on to hit four more for a final score of 5-1. Defeats away to East Stirlingshire and at home to Bathgate followed, but a good 4-2 win was achieved with the help of a Taylor hat-trick at Lochgelly United on 9th September to begin a sequence of five wins in a row. A 3-0 home victory over Dunfermline Athletic was followed by a 2-1 win at Broxburn United, a 2-0 win at home to East Stirlingshire and another Taylor hat-trick resulted in a 3-2 win at Bathgate to keep Hibs in the leading group. The side were in such good form that it is hard to believe the rest of the league campaign provided just another two points from a 0-0 draw with Broxburn United and a 1-1 result at St Bernard's. Significantly, Lamb left to join the army at the end of October, and what had been a relatively settled line up was thereafter frequently chopped and changed because of injuries and players' unavailability.

In one particularly bad defeat, Hibs lost five without reply at East Fife. Hibs keeper Kennedy was unavailable for that game and his place was taken by Baird, an off duty soldier, who despite letting in five goals, did in fact keep the score down with some fine saves. Again the league programme was incomplete and several clubs did not honour all their fixtures. This included Hibs who failed to play Armadale, both at home and away. Two Loftus Cup matches were played and brought a 1-1 draw at home to East Fife on 28th October and a 5-2 home defeat by East Stirlingshire on New Year's Day 1917. In April, Hibs ended the season with two friendlies. They played Dainty's XI but the score is not recorded and against a Royal Garrison Artillery side the Greens won 4-2.

In the only match Hibs played in the Eastern Cup, the 7-0 defeat at the hands of Dunfermline Athletic on 7th March may look bad but there were circumstances to mitigate the disastrous score line. There is no doubt that the Fife side were a better team and fully deserved to win the match on the day. But it is only fair to mention that Hibs were grossly under strength with five regular players unavailable for selection. To make matters worse they actually fielded only ten players at kick off. They were handicapped this way until twenty minutes into the first half when an eleventh man came on. He was a local lad, probably stepping in after he had gone home to get his boots! In a season that saw Hibs take part in just 21 games, there is no way success or failure can be measured but the Club was doing its best to aid the war effort and maintain morale.

At a meeting on 6th June 1917, the SFA made a few crucial decisions. They decided that there would again be no internationals, Scottish Cup, Qualifying Cup or Consolation Cup. Also, Dundee were to be suspended from the Scottish League along with Aberdeen and Raith Rovers because of travel restrictions. This left the Scottish League made up largely of west coast teams plus Hibernian, Hearts and Falkirk.

Raith Rovers and Dundee were therefore invited to join the Eastern League. At the same time, East Stirlingshire, Lochgelly United, St Bernard's, Bathgate and Broxburn United all dropped out, leaving only seven teams in the competition. In order to maintain interest in football it was agreed the clubs would play each other home and away twice. From the previous campaign only Dundee Hibs, Armadale, East Fife, Dunfermline Athletic and Cowdenbeath remained.

Herbert Dainty was by then heavily involved in raising funds for the war effort with Dainty's XI and he was elevated to the Board at Dundee Hibs. To replace him, Pat Reilly returned as Manager and Charlie Craig, who had been with Dundee Wanderers and Violet, was the new trainer. The team assembled for the new season consisted of Grieve, Husson, Ferrier, Dainty, Spence, John Ross, McCabe, McGuire, Taylor and Outerson, but before the campaign was under way Husson returned to Dens Park. Former Dundee player, Jimmy Bellamy joined Hibs in August along with Charles Rennie and in September, two more Dundee players, forward Tom McCulloch and half back David 'Napper' Thomson were added to the squad.

Keeper Dave Balfour, who was also ex-Dundee, signed in late October and Reilly then brought in another former Dundee player, Sam Gilligan along with former Hibs player Henry Brown from St Johnstone and local junior Johnny Fitzpatrick. Fitzpatrick was one of a family of five brothers all with a strong football pedigree. Of the Fitzpatrick brothers, Owen was with Montrose, Tom was captain of Cowdenbeath, Charlie was a well known junior in Dundee and Joe was a junior international.

During 1917-18, many trialists, juniors, guests and players on temporary transfers would don the green of Hibs including Ernest Levett from the Newcastle area, youngster Matthew Wilson and former Everton player William Stalker. One very notable absentee was Collie Martin who was killed in action in 1917. George Low had also been a casualty of war and would never play again following a severe leg wound.

To open the season on 18th August, Hibs faced Dundee in the first ever league derby. The result was a heavy defeat for the Tannadice side which lined up with:-

Grieve, Rennie and Taylor; Ferrier, Dainty and Spence; Ross, Bellamy, Boland, McCabe and Outerson.

Hibs had Boland home on leave and in an unaccustomed centre forward role and were up against a strong Dundee side but gave a good account of themselves for thirty minutes before Dundee went ahead. Outerson equalised shortly after that and at half time the sides were level. The Dark Blues were the better side in the second half, but Hibs were not as poor as the 5-1 defeat suggests. Hibs lost 2-1 to East Fife the next week. By 1st September, Napper Thomson was in the side, but even his presence in the half back line could not prevent Hibs' third defeat in a row, 3-1 at Dunfermline Athletic.

Around this time there were rumblings of discord in the dressing room, with several players not satisfied with the wages they were receiving. It took a while to resolve this problem but it was settled in time for the Loftus Cup ties. Some of the players may have made some extra money in a more novel way. Boxer Charlie Williams was using Tannadice from time to time for training, and players were often found with him as his sparring partners!

In the league campaign, a 3-1 win against Armadale was followed by a 2-0 defeat by Dundee, both at Tannadice. There was a 1-0 win at East Fife on 22nd September but thereafter, results in October and November were generally poor with just draws at home to Raith Rovers and Cowdenbeath to cheer the Hibs fans.

A notable encounter with Dundee took place in the Loftus Cup on 10th November 1917. It ended 1-1 but surely no derby in Dundee or anywhere else for that matter, has ever included such a unique line up. Hibs fielded eight former Dundee players! Balfour, Thomson, Taylor, Bellamy, Dainty, McCabe, McCulloch and Gilligan were the eight, plus Fitzpatrick, McGuire and Brown. The replay was won 2-1 at Tannadice two weeks later by Dundee.

The remainder of the season produced very little for the Hibs fans to enthuse over with sometimes wildly varying results. Take for example a bizarre series of consecutive home results in December, starting with an emphatic 4-1 win against Dunfermline Athletic followed by a 6-1 defeat by Cowdenbeath and then a 5-1 win over East Fife.

Amongst only three wins in the second half of the season, there was a derby victory to celebrate. On 26th January 1918, Hibs met Dundee at Dens Park to record a landmark first derby win at first team level for the Tannadice side. Hibs were two up within the first ten minutes before Dundee were reduced to ten men. Dundee's centre half John Stirling went off with an injury just before half time and did not return to the play until midway through the second half. The Dark Blues then pulled one back but Hibs held out for the 2-1 win. For the record, the scorers were Burge and Thomson and the line up was:-

Balfour, Stalker and Taylor; Ferrier, Thomson and Fitzpatrick; Bellamy, McCulloch, Burge, McGuire and McCabe.

The other victories came in a 2-0 win over Armadale and a surprise 3-0 result at Dunfermline Athletic, as the league season stuttered to its conclusion. Hibs ended the campaign fifth in the seven team league but yet again some teams failed to complete their full quota of fixtures.

Two more derby matches were played at the end of the season. Hibs met Dundee in the Penman Cup final and the Dens Park side were fortunate to win the trophy. The Eastern Cup final was originally scheduled for 2nd March, but following severe snow storms, both Dens Park and Tannadice suffered damage to the stands and the pitches were covered in snow, half a metre deep in places. So the eighth and last derby of 1917-18 was held over until the end of the season. When the match was eventually played, Hibs were in front through Wilson in a rousing game. Dundee pulled level only for Hibs to take the lead again when Fraser netted. Dundee had a late goal chalked off but netted in the last minute to deny Hibs the cup. The replay could not be arranged and was held over until the following season, but it does not appear to have taken place. In any event the close season would herald the end of league and cup football for Dundee Hibs. Matches in 1918-19 would consist only of friendly and charity meetings.

1918-23

The Wilderness Years

By the beginning of season 1918-19, football in Scotland generally had gravitated to local competitions. There was still a First Division made up of the bigger west coast sides together with Falkirk, Hearts and Hibs of Edinburgh, whilst the remaining west coast teams made up a Western League of eight teams but the Eastern League was abandoned. Dundee Hibs still had Boland, Bruce, Cavanagh, Chaplin, Cheyne, Crawford, Crumley, Currie, Dainty, Ferguson, Flood, Forbes, Grieve, Henderson, Hughes, Leckie, Linn, Low, MacDonald, Spence, Stoessel and Whyte as registered players and the list held by the Scottish League had remained unaltered since season 1916-17, except for the name of Collie Martin. Every player was technically available for selection but many were on active service and could not turn out for the Club.

Of the registered players, only Crumley took part in the first game of 1918-19, a friendly against the Highland Light Infantry on 21st September that ended in a 2-2 draw. In the next match, a 6-2 win over a Labour Garrison XI, Forbes was the only registered player in the eleven. Many of the others that turned out in those first two matches had played for Hibs in past campaigns during the war years and 'Napper' Thomson, Archie Taylor, Jimmy Bellamy, 'Ref' Ferrier, James McGuire and Tom McCulloch featured regularly in the line ups of late 1918. There was nothing at stake in these matches but they were usually highly entertaining and served up some good football with plenty of goals. A McGuire hat-trick was the highlight of the 6-2 win over the Labour Centre Garrison XI. Matthew Wilson scored five in a 7-2 win over an RAF side on 7th October. Tom Murray scored four in a 6-2 win over an Army Select and Wilson was again in top form netting four in a 5-3 win against the Royal Garrison Artillery, who until then had been undefeated. Shortly after that match the war ended, and matches against forces XIs and selects came to an end over the next three months as the forces personnel in the area dispersed. Over the remainder of November and December, only four matches were played and then, after drawing 2-2 with a Canadian XI on 1st January 1919, Hibs were without another game for a full month until a meeting with Dainty's XI on 1st February. Although leading 3-0 at one stage, Hibs eventually went down 6-4 to a very strong representative side.

Three friendlies took place against strong select sides in February 1919 as it was important to get match practice against quality teams. It was expected that the Scottish League would re-establish a Second Division for the following season and therefore, by March 1919, Hibs were arranging matches against the local senior teams and junior sides. Hibs' line ups for these matches were varied, with a mixture of signed players, trialists, guests and juniors but after almost a year without real competitive action the lack of adequate training was very evident. Hibs suffered some heavy defeats in the spring of 1919, even with the return of players such as Fitzpatrick, Stoessel, Linn, McCabe and Hughes. Success was generally achieved only against the juniors.

Results did little to enhance the reputation of Dundee Hibs, who again planned an audacious bid for a place in the First Division of the Scottish League. A decision to increase the number of teams to twenty two had been reached but the Scottish League voted not to reinstate the Second Division, leaving a large number of clubs without a competition. Hibs stepped up their efforts to join the top flight and Club Treasurer, David Simpson lobbied for support along with Herbert Dainty, who was by then the Hibs Chairman. They travelled to Glasgow carrying a letter which guaranteed that the Club could raise an additional £1,000 of capital without relying on public subscription. Indeed, more new shares had been taken up by Joseph Bell and John Findlay and later in the year Thomas Leddie, Patrick Cameron and David Wallace also became shareholders. None however, purchased great quantities and, since the initial £1,000 was received to set the company up, only a further 500 shares had been issued. One positive aspect of the Club's finances however, was that the Directors' loans had been repaid and there was just a small overdraft at the bank.

In their favour for inclusion in the First Division, Hibs had a groundswell of potential support. They could also boast a high standard of facilities at Tannadice and well proven transport links. Against, the Club had to compete with the longer established clubs for a place in the league and in the end the bid failed. Aberdeen, Dundee and Raith Rovers were welcomed back into the First Division to retake their places and that left one vacancy. Along with Cowdenbeath, Albion Rovers polled ten votes for the last available place in the First Division. As in 1913-14 the casting vote of the Chairman was required and with it, Albion Rovers were elected. The other three applicants, Dunfermline Athletic, Vale of Leven and Dundee Hibs were not in the running.

Left with no option, Hibs joined the resurrected Eastern League on 14th May 1919 and on 11th June withdrew from membership of the Scottish League. The Directors felt that it was unfair for Hibs to be bound by Scottish League rules whilst unable to take part in a national league. The Manager was then free to approach unsigned players with Scottish League clubs and offer them terms without having to pay a transfer fee. Of the players signed to Hibs at the time only Crumley and Hughes would remain for season 1919-20. John Mulholland and George Wilkie, both of whom had turned out for Hibs in the previous season, also signed up for the Eastern League campaign. They were soon joined by David Millar, Tom Murray, Dan Gibson, Alex McDonald, John Smith and William Stalker who had all played in Hibs' colours before.

In early July, there were rumours that Dundee players 'Napper' Thomson, Bert McIntosh and Davie Brown might sign for Hibs as they were dissatisfied at Dens Park. It never happened, but Brown did play for Hibs during 1920-21. Two former Dundee players, David Cargill and Jimmy Bradley did sign for Hibs before the season started. Both were in the side that began the Eastern League campaign of 1919-20 with a comfortable 2-0 win over Montrose. The second and decisive goal was a hotly contested penalty scored by Bradley. Two more former Dundee players, John Stirling and James Herron (who had been with Hibs late in 1915-16), were signed in time to face Arbroath in the first home match of the season. They helped Hibs to another 2-0 win and for the second game in succession, a disputed Bradley penalty sealed the points. The good start to the season continued with a 3-1 victory over Forfar Athletic in the Qualifying Cup with Bradley netting his third penalty in as many games, this time to open the scoring. Then, St Johnstone were overcome at Tannadice by the same score line to maintain top spot in the Eastern League, a position Hibs would retain for the entire season. A fifth former Dark Blue, Frank Murray, was signed just after that match. He became possibly the most significant signing of the campaign, and played a vital role in the successful team that went on to win the Eastern League.

Murray made his debut in the Qualifying Cup second round defeat at Cowdenbeath and Hibs were really no match for the Central Park club who won 3-1. Next, Hibs drew 1-1 with Dundee 'A' to continue an undefeated run in the league. An unexpectedly large crowd of over 10,000 witnessed this match. After impatience near kick off led to a gate being forced open, 2,000 of those gained free entry. Of the six wins that followed, none produced much out of the ordinary but Hibs, with Frank Murray in top form, showed the consistency that was required to win the championship. Cargill scored twice at Forfar Athletic as Hibs won 2-1 and Frank Murray got his first goal for the Club in a 2-0 win over Cowdenbeath. He scored the only goal against Raith Rovers 'A' on 18th October and another 1-0 win was recorded at Arbroath where a rare Mulholland goal gave Hibs a fortunate two points. Forfar Athletic then fell to Hibs, 2-0 at Tannadice. Hibs were lucky again in the 3-2 win over Raith Rovers 'A', but a dramatic defeat at home to Montrose on 15th November brought the first reversal in the campaign. Although Montrose had mastered the bone hard frosty pitch, with five minutes left it looked likely that Hibs, 2-1 down, might salvage a point. What happened next demonstrates how football fortune can easily turn in an instant. Patterson of Montrose was through on goal and in a race for the ball, Hibs keeper Crumley appeared to be the favourite. However, a collision between Crumley and Stirling allowed the ball to trickle over the line to put Montrose further ahead. The two Hibs players were carried off and did not return. With only nine men on the pitch it was no surprise when Montrose notched a fourth right at the end.

Hibs recovered well from that defeat to win 5-2 at Brechin City on 29th November, with Gibson notching a hat-trick. Lochgelly United were then beaten 4-0 at Tannadice and this time Frank Murray was the hat-trick hero. In the 1-1 draw at St Johnstone that followed, emotions were running high between the two old rivals. With Hibs a goal in front, St Johnstone levelled with the last kick of the ball to spark a pitch invasion by the Perth side's ecstatic fans. Joe Wilson signed from Blackburn Rovers and made his debut in the match. A 2-0 defeat at Dundee 'A' followed, but the title challenge was back on track when Hibs won 3-1 at Lochgelly United, very much against the run of play, in the last league game of December 1919. The result was all the more commendable as Hibs had lost the calming influence of keeper Crumley. He had moved south to join Swansea Town, tempted by an offer of a weekly wage of £6. Local junior George Aimer made his debut in the match at Lochgelly along with new keeper William Miller from Stobswell. Only two matches remained in the Eastern League and Hibs required just one point to secure the title. Then the weather intervened to postpone the final outcome.

The new goalkeeper was not seriously tested in three matches in the Northern League, and he could not be held at fault as Hibs lost 3-1 to a strong St Johnstone side in the Loftus Cup on the last day of January. The penultimate Eastern League match of the season was scheduled for the following Saturday and the Directors offered a substantial bonus to the players to win the title on the day. But it was a nervy Hibs that lost 3-0 at Cowdenbeath on 7th February. The remainder of that month was spent on cup duty, with a 2-2 draw in the Eastern Cup against St Johnstone sandwiched between two Forfarshire Cup ties against Forfar Athletic. The Angus side were eventually eliminated 2-0 at Tannadice after a 2-2 draw at Station Park.

The final Eastern League match was therefore played on 13th March. Hibs still needed a point to be absolutely sure of the title as the nearest challengers, Dundee 'A', were three points behind with two games in hand. As it turned out, Hibs had an easy 4-1 win against Brechin City, with all Hibs' goals coming in the first half. But it was academic, as Dundee 'A' lost rather tamely to Lochgelly United. Hibs were the league champions and the big crowd at Tannadice celebrated.

The season continued with local cup competitions and it took two matches to dispose of Montrose in the Forfarshire Cup semi final. The Angus side came from behind twice to draw 2-2 and earn a replay at Tannadice where they snatched an early lead. Hibs then took control gradually, and emerged 2-1 winners. Former Blackburn Rovers half back James Webster made his debut in the replay. The Eastern Cup replay with St Johnstone was another 2-2 draw and then Hibs lost 2-0 in a friendly against a Forfarshire Junior Select, with Andy Henderson in goal for Hibs. Miller was back in goal as Cowdenbeath ended Hibs' involvement in the Penman Cup with a rather easy 4-1 win. Yet another 2-2 draw came against Raith Rovers 'A' in the Loftus Cup with former Dundee keeper Bob Crumley making his only Hibs appearance. In their sixth match of the month, Hibs finally settled the Penman Cup tie with a 3-1 win over St Johnstone. By then, goalkeeper Henderson had signed from Falkirk and he would be in the side throughout most of the following season. Full back, James Morrison from St Patrick's also played a couple of times in April 1920 and he too made his major contribution the next term. A match against a Dundee Junior Select on 19th April had to be abandoned.

The Forfarshire Cup final was the last event of 1919-20. With Hibs leading 1-0 from a Bradley free kick against Dundee 'A', a protest against "David Gibb of Montrose" was handed by Dundee captain Fleming to the referee, with the match still in progress! Listed in the team sheet as Anderson, the centre was indeed David Gibb of Montrose. It appears he had been playing for Hibs since early April under an alias, a fairly common practice at the time. Immediately after the match, a meeting of the Forfarshire Association upheld the protest and ordered a replay. Hibs accepted the situation and the lack of any sanctions against Club or player tends to suggest that a genuine error had been made. Furthermore, Gibb was not cup tied as he had not played for Montrose in the earlier rounds and he did in fact turn out at inside right for Hibs in the replay a week later! The result was the same with Gibson scoring the only goal to win the cup. The season ended with a 4-1 win against St Johnstone in a testimonial for their trainer, John McVean.

Several prominent players in the Eastern League campaign would not be seen playing for Hibs again, with, most notably, top scorer Frank Murray, Cargill, and Bradley moving on. In a season with thirty matches played, nine Hibs players made more than twenty appearances and it was this consistency of selection that made everyone at Tannadice delighted with the most successful season so far in the history of the Club. The measure of the Club's confidence in the future could be seen in June, as work was under way to refurbish the pavilion and dressing room areas. The improvement programme had been announced as far back as February and when the work was completed in August, the Tannadice facilities were second to none outwith the First Division. Also in June, Hibs announced a profit of £347 with the Club debt free. Much of the upgrading of Tannadice was carried out in anticipation of a return to the Second Division and to this end, Hibs re-applied for membership of the Scottish League. However, at the Scottish League AGM in early June things did not go according to the script.

As the agenda progressed, Hibs were indeed re-admitted, but the motion to reinstate the Second Division was defeated. This effectively abolished the Second Division which until then had merely been suspended. In the view of the excluded clubs, the First Division sides were not prepared to jeopardize their elite position and the lower league sides were extremely dissatisfied with the outcome. As a result, they resigned en masse and at the end of June formed a new Central League in direct competition with the Scottish League. However, it is interesting to note that the reserve sides of both Hearts and Falkirk were permitted to join the new set up. Once again Hibs were in a position to offer contracts to First Division players without having to pay transfer fees to their clubs and made an outrageous, albeit unsuccessful attempt to sign Patsy Gallacher of Celtic.

Henderson, Aimer, Gibb, Morrison and Webster re-signed at the end of the previous season and they were soon joined by William Miller, Mulholland, Stalker, Hughes, Stirling, Herron, Wilson and Wilkie. By mid July, John McMahon from Hamilton Academical, former Dundee man George Lamb and Willie Kay from Plymouth Argyle had been acquired. Just a week before the season kicked off, Adam Brown from Forthill Athletic joined Hibs and the side were set for the challenge of the Central League.

The season opened with a Loftus Cup tie and a 10,000 crowd at Dunfermline Athletic witnessed their star man Andy Wilson scoring the only goal of the game. Davie Brown came to Hibs, on loan from Dundee, in time for the first Central League match against Armadale. It ended in a 3-2 defeat despite Hibs facing nine men for the last third of the match, after two Armadale players went off injured. Hibs then put together a run of three home wins in the league; 2-0 against St Johnstone, 1-0 over Falkirk 'A' and 2-1 against Lochgelly United. On each occasion Hibs were well worth the two points, although the results were close. Brown ended his short spell at Tannadice at the end of August and returned to Dundee.

The Qualifying Cup came next with an away tie at long time rivals Arbroath, and an even contest ended 1-1. With a hectic fixture list in prospect, Hibs had to play a rescheduled league match at St Johnstone four days later and lost narrowly 2-1, even with Linn back in the side. The next two Saturdays were taken up with cup replays against Arbroath. After another 1-1 draw, the third match, at Station Park Forfar, ended in a 3-0 defeat for Hibs to exit the 'QC'. It was the last time Hibs would ever take part in that competition.

John Waugh was signed from Dunfermline Athletic, but the new man had little effect and Hibs lost the next two league matches by the same 4-1 score line, away to Bathgate and then at home to Bo'ness. A much changed side lined up to face St Johnstone on 4th October in the Penman Cup and Hibs won 1-0. Full back Wilkie played in goal for that match with both regular keepers unavailable. Inside forward, Joe Allison of Banknock Juniors joined the squad in late October, just before Willie Kay left on a free transfer.

The Manager made frequent changes to the line up over the next few games but could never seem to find the right combination and varying results were achieved over the remaining months of 1920. After losing 2-1 at home to St Bernard's, Hibs drew 0-0 at East Stirlingshire and, with man of the match Waugh starring against his old club, a 2-1 win was achieved in a hard fought match against Dunfermline Athletic. Poor finishing contributed to a 0-0 draw at King's Park but at home to Alloa Athletic the 3-0 win was deserved, although the visitors played with just ten men in the second half. Perhaps the best indicator of the way Hibs were playing can be seen in the 6-3 defeat at Lochgelly United on 13th November. Hibs netted twice in the first half of that match through Waugh and Gibb to lead 2-0. Lochgelly then scored three for a half time lead. After the interval Lochgelly scored again before Gibb pulled one back but the home side scored two in the last few minutes to win.

In late November, ex-Osborne and Brechin City centre forward Frank Gray was signed and around the same time Waugh was transferred to Gillingham. Hibs lost 3-2 at home to King's Park on 20th November and followed that with goalless draws at Falkirk 'A' and East Fife, but the Greens were full value in the 3-2 win over Hearts 'A'. At Cowdenbeath on Christmas Day 1920, Hibs were just not good enough and lost 2-0 with Scotland's top scorer Paterson netting twice to bring his season to date goals tally to 44.

More changes were made to the line up, particularly in attack, as Hibs played four games in a very hectic first five days of January 1921. With keeper Andy Henderson suspended after a sending off against East Fife, the goalkeeping duty was shared between St Joseph's Joe Kinsella and two trialists. On Saturday 1st January, Hibs played out a scrappy 1-1 draw with Broxburn United in the league and on Monday, lost 2-0 at Dunfermline Athletic in the Loftus Cup. Bathgate were at Tannadice on league business the following day and Hibs won 2-1 with a trialist, Macfarlane scoring both goals. Wednesday brought a friendly at Montrose, with a win by the odd goal in three for the home side. Tom Dick signed from Bonnybridge Thistle after satisfactory trials and was one of a tired looking Hibs side that lost too easily in the league 2-0 at Stenhousemuir on 8th January, Hibs fifth game in eight days.

A week later, Qualifying Cup winners East Fife were the visitors at Tannadice and a solid Hibs performance produced a well deserved 4-0 win. A 1-1 draw with St Bernard's followed but unfortunately the apparent upturn in form proved to be a false dawn as the Greens then went on a run of seven league defeats, beginning with home and away reversals to lowly Clackmannan. Interspersed with this run of matches, Hibs met Arbroath in a Forfarshire Cup tie. On 2nd February at Tannadice it ended 0-0 and the replay at Arbroath, three weeks later, was a 2-2 draw. At neutral Dens Park a third match ended level at 1-1 after extra time. All three matches had produced entertaining football, but the fourth attempt to settle the tie produced a dull match played at Arbroath in atrocious conditions and after extra time it was 0-0 as the match ended in near darkness. Finally at Dens Park, Hibs were eliminated in the fifth match on 16th March, as Arbroath won 2-0, taking the advantage after scoring in the first minute.

Meanwhile the Greens had tumbled down the league and even a hard fought 1-0 win over Armadale on 19th March gave little consolation. In the Loftus Cup, Hibs were beaten 3-1 at Raith Rovers 'A' and 1-0 at St Johnstone but managed a 2-1 win when the Perth side made the return trip to Tannadice. In the league, Hibs could only draw 1-1 with Stenhousemuir and lost 2-0 to Alloa Athletic. After a 2-2 draw with a Forfarshire Junior Select in a friendly and a 1-0 defeat by Dundee in a charity match, the last league match brought a win against East Stirlingshire, with trialists George Adams from Montrose and Norman Thain from Forthill Athletic in the side along with James Ritchie from the ranks of Aberdeen reserves. Goals from Wilkie, Aimer and Gray gave Hibs a good 3-0 win in front of less than 1,000 fans but it was far too little far too late. To end the season, a 2-0 win over Lochgelly United set up a Penman Cup final against Alloa Athletic but the Greens lost rather tamely 2-0 at East End Park on 5th May.

The thorny subject of a Second Division, and along with it automatic promotion and relegation, was of course back on the national agenda. In December 1920, both the Central League clubs and the Scottish League were discussing the situation. But this time at least, the prospect of a decision in favour, including automatic promotion, looked better than it ever had. The Scottish League openly invited clubs to apply for membership and at the AGM in June the motion was finally approved after years of wrangling. The Central League negotiated entry for all sixteen of their clubs, who were joined by Arbroath, Forfar Athletic, Johnstone and Vale of Leven. At the end of season 1921-22, one club would be promoted and three would be relegated from Division One. The two bottom clubs in Division Two would then drop out completely from the Scottish League. With a poor season just completed, Hibs would have to rebuild to have any hope of competing as it appeared that the current squad was not up to the task.

Probably Hibs best player, Aimer left Tannadice at the end of the season to make the short trip up the road to join Dundee. From a total of thirty players and numerous trialists used in 1920-21, just ten remained. They were regulars Henderson, Mulholland, Wilkie and Linn plus Ned MacDonald and Kinsella. Also re-signed were Ritchie, Adams, Thain and Lowingham Braidford, who had all joined Hibs late in the campaign.

Before the end of May 1921, Reilly added Willie Hogg from Montrose, Tom Bannister from Dundee and Dan Gibson again signed for Hibs. In July, the signature of Edinburgh Hibs' Horace Williams was obtained. He was quickly joined by Dan McInnes. formerly of St Johnstone and Raith Rovers. In early August, Dundee Hibernian were "on the brink of the greatest season in their history" according to one prominent Hibs official. Every effort was being made to get ready for the challenge of the new campaign, including the laying of a new pitch.

Dundee Hibernian 15th August 1921
Standing: Bannister, McInnes, Henderson, Adams, Mulholland, Wilkie
Seated: Boland (Trainer), Hogg, Linn, Williams, Braidford, Ritchie, Small (Referee)

The new season opened with a 1-1 draw in a friendly against St Johnstone and as they lined up for the team photograph, most of the Hibs players were in fairly confident mood for the season ahead. In the opening four matches the side was unbeaten, with 2-2 draws at Bo'ness and then at home to Johnstone followed by home wins against East Stirlingshire, 2-0 and St Johnstone, 3-1. The addition of former Dundee player George Stuart from Leeds United and Barney Smith from the Hibs of Edinburgh, looked to have added strength to the squad. Unfortunately Smith did not last long and a month later he was released. This left an opening for St Joseph's defender David McKimmie, signed earlier as a reserve. Defeats at Armadale, 3-1 and Bathgate, 4-2 did not ring immediate alarm bells, with Hibs 7-1 thrashing of Clackmannan following soon afterwards. Then, after a 4-1 reversal at Dunfermline Athletic, Hibs beat Forfar Athletic 1-0 with new signing James Headrick, from Stirling Emmet, in the defence. Surprisingly, Headrick had been on trial with Clackmannan, and had played against Hibs during the 7-1 win! Over the next five games, the Tannadice side slipped slowly down the table gaining only one point in a 0-0 draw at East Fife. Concerns were expressed in some sections of the local press that Hibs were placing too much reliance on players from the junior ranks, when more experienced players were available.

Some confidence was restored with the help of a Williams hat-trick in a 4-0 win over Lochgelly United and a 2-0 victory at King's Park, but Alloa Athletic came to Tannadice on 10th December and won easily 4-0. New signing Tom Houston from Roselea made his debut in that match and like the rest of the team was shell shocked by the result. From that point on, the season went downhill all the way, with few highlights on the road to the exit door of the Scottish League. In the next twelve matches, only four points were gathered in draws with Stenhousemuir, Lochgelly United, Vale of Leven and Forfar Athletic, and that sent Hibs into free fall. They also lost 3-1 against Dundee in a friendly on 11th January 1922 and went out of the Scottish Cup, beaten 2-0 at home by Broxburn United. New signing Peter Kelly, in the forward line from December, made little impact. Both William McDonagh from Croy Celtic and John Rae from Arbroath, signed for Hibs in late January whilst Dan Gibson was given a free transfer at his own request. Edinburgh pair, David Duncan from Hearts and Hibs' Patrick Maxwell came into the side in late February. But the Dundee Hibs fans were dealt a blow with the news that top scorer Horace Williams was being sold to Gillingham. Even then, at the end of the season he was Hibs' top scorer with thirteen goals in his twenty four appearances in the league.

In Early March, Hibs signed Alex McCulloch and several trialists came and went during the spring. Hibs recorded their first win in three months with a 2-0 victory over St Bernard's at Tannadice but that was followed by 3-0 defeats at both Stenhousemuir and Alloa Athletic and although a 1-0 win was achieved against Broxburn United, the chance of survival began slipping away after a 3-2 reversal at East Stirlingshire. The fans still clung to a last hope and after losing 3-0 to Raith Rovers in a Penman Cup tie, Hibs snatched a 1-0 victory at home to Dunfermline Athletic but it was not enough. Hibs lost by the same score at home to East Fife and then drew 1-1 at Clackmannan which made the 4-1 win over Armadale in the last game of the season irrelevant. The Club were three points adrift in second bottom place and out of the Scottish League. The Manager's efforts to rescue the season had include the signing of former Blackburn Rovers and Wigan Borough player Joseph Bibby and even Fred Stoessel stepped into the breach but it was all to no avail.

In the midst of the battle for survival, Willie Linn, Hibs' long serving forward, was granted a testimonial with Dundee as the opposition. This was the first and only time a Dundee Hibs player was granted such an honour, so it was perhaps disappointing that only 2,000 spectators were in attendance to witness the 1-1 draw on 12th April 1922.

When it was all over there was still a slim chance that Hibs would survive the cut, with Airdrieonians in particular, keen to retain both Hibs and bottom club Clackmannan. Many of the other Second Division clubs were also in favour of amending the rules to retain Hibs, in view of the quite substantial cheques received as their share of gate receipts. Alloa Athletic for example, received £120 after their visit. The motion was tabled at a meeting of the Scottish League on 18th May 1922 but the rules remained unaltered and Hibs were left searching for a competition for season 1922-23. As a consolation, Hibs were granted exemption from the Qualifying Cup and entered directly into the Scottish Cup draw.

WHAT HIBS ARE TO DO

Alliance Door Shut

By UNOMI.

"We may be out of the Scottish League, but we are by no means out of Scottish football," declared a Dundee Hibs' official, referring to the exclusion of the Club from the Scottish League.

"Of course," he continued, "we are disappointed, but we are not to sit down quietly under the blow, and allow things to drift. We are to keep the flag flying at Tannadice, so that when the times comes we shall be ready to take our place in the big competition.

"The set-back we have experienced will naturally affect the carrying out of the plans we had in view in connection with our ground, and these will be modified, or perhaps postponed, but the Club is to go on."

Admission was sought to the Scottish Alliance League at the annual meeting of that body in Glasgow last night, but, as it was decided to restrict the membership to 14, and as there were Clubs to that number already admitted, no new applications were entertained. Brechin, Montrose, Clackmannan, and Queen of the South shared a similar fate.

Will Fight for Qualifying.

Probably as a sort of consolation gift, the Hibs were voluntarily granted exemption from the Qualifying Cup-ties. This means, of course, that the Club is ensured of at least one game for the Scottish Cup. But this is not what the management want at all. They realise that they must have games if the Club is to be carried on, and exemptions are not in the programme. Consequently the Hibs will take their chances in the Qualifying Cup competition, and make a bold, determined effort not only to reach the fourth round, which means admission to the Scottish ties, but to lift the Cup.

Up to the present not a single player has been engaged for Tannadice Park, but, as already stated, that does not mean that the Club is to become defunct. The energies of the officials are to be directed towards arranging a programme of friendly games. An effort may even be made to resuscitate the Northern League, a step that would have the support of Montrose and Brechin. Fraserburgh and Peterhead would doubtless entertain the idea, and some of the Perthshire Clubs might be induced to enter.

No matter what is done, the Hibs will have a hard struggle, but the officials appreciate the seriousness of the position, and their commendable enthusiasm will doubtless meet with its due reward. I sincerely hope so.

People's Journal
20th May 1922

The Club had no alternative but to look elsewhere and the best option was the Scottish Alliance, in effect the reserve league for the First Division sides. A place in this competition would at least allow Hibs to compete against strong opposition and keep them in touch with the Scottish League. An application to the national league would be possible again in the next season.

However, the Scottish Alliance had decided to restrict membership to fourteen teams. Hibs were too late in applying and were denied entry, as were Brechin City, Montrose, Clackmannan (who had also been awaiting the outcome of the motion to change the rules) and Queen of the South. Consequently, there was a suggestion that the Northern League could be resurrected. Brechin City and Montrose showed interest, as did Highland League clubs Fraserburgh and Peterhead together with some of the Perthshire sides, but it never happened.

Instead, Hibs and a number of other sides revived the Eastern League. By 3rd June 1922 the Eastern League had ten teams; Hibs, the reserve sides of Aberdeen, Dundee, Raith Rovers, Hearts and Falkirk together with Montrose, Brechin City, Leith Athletic and Clackmannan. With a league to compete in but no players signed, Hibs then began team building. The first to sign were Henderson, Morrison and Bannister, the only players to remain after the disastrous 1921-22 season. The majority of the others had moved on to other clubs to secure a job in the season ahead.

The general uncertainty also led to the resignation of more than half of the Board, with Thomas Leddie, Peter Ross and Patrick Cameron all standing down. It was rumoured that Hibs might in fact disband. But at the AGM on 30th June it was revealed that the Club had a healthy bank balance and was determined to keep going, aiming for a return to the Scottish League. New Directors William Hogg, James Dickson and William Burke were appointed and each purchased 50 shares. They joined Herbert Dainty, Pat Reilly and Treasurer David Simpson. A few days later Dundee Hibs were advised that a vacancy had arisen in the Scottish Alliance, following the withdrawal of the Celtic reserve side. Hibs and Montrose both applied for the place, but with the influential backing of Celtic, and some of the other First Division sides, Hibs were the successful applicants and were offered the place on 12th July.

Now in two leagues, the Manager began a frantic search for more players, as the first match was only five weeks away. By the end of July, Hibs had signed Dundee reserve keeper Bowman and former Hamilton Academical left back James Scullion, although he would not feature until October. Half backs Russell Sutherland (ex-Dundee and Barrow) and William Stewart (Arbroath) were joined by Aberdeen forward Peter Fisher who had played with Hibs in season 1919-20. A week before the season began, former Hull City player, George Stoddart signed and just days before the first game, he was joined by John Young (Morton), James Terris (Millwall), James Balloch (ex-Clackmannan and Hearts), W Thomson (described only as an army footballer) and Willie Wilson (Raith Rovers).

In August 1922 both Hibs and neighbours Dundee applied for permission to use the city coat of arms on their team jerseys but at a meeting of magistrates on 30th August both teams were unanimously refused the consent. Lord Provost Spence commented that the clubs "be recommended to get badges of their own." In the team photograph a year later however, Hibs players sported a badge with the letters D and H intertwined between the representations of the griffins that form part of the official City of Dundee Coat of Arms.

The Scottish Alliance season opened poorly for Hibs and some inconsistent play brought just two points in the first five matches. Hibs' first match ended in a 2-2 draw at Partick Thistle 'A' but they then lost home and away to St Mirren 'A' and at home to Hearts 'A' before drawing 2-2 at Aberdeen 'A'. The Greens also lost a Penman Cup tie 2-1 to Raith Rovers 'A'. Robert McDonald joined the squad in late August and George (Dod) Hutcheson, a Fife junior, arrived in early September, with Joseph Murray signed at the end of the same month. A 2-1 defeat at Queen's Park Strollers was followed by 1-1 home draws against Rangers 'A' and Aberdeen 'A' and on both occasions, Hibs were the better side. The first victory of the season came on 14th October, when a single Scullion goal proved to be the winner against Raith Rovers 'A'. After a 1-0 defeat at Ayr United 'A' and a 1-1 draw at home to Airdrieonians 'A', it was becoming clear that most of the First Division reserve sides were more than a match for Hibs. However, a good second half performance resulted in a 4-0 win against Albion Rovers 'A' on 11th November and a fortunate 1-0 victory over Kilmarnock 'A' two weeks later brought some cause for celebration at last for Hibs' followers.

A 0-0 draw at Raith Rovers 'A' at the beginning of December prompted action. Now with the addition of William Hutchison as a Director following his purchase of 50 shares in September, the Board announced the appointment of the experienced Peter O'Rourke as Manager on 6th December and Pat Reilly took charge of the team for the last time three days later in a 2-1 defeat at Kilmarnock 'A'. O'Rourke had a good reputation, having played with Celtic 20 years earlier. He had then been transferred to Burnley and then to Bradford City where he had been player/manager. His last position, before coming to Hibs, was manager at Pontypridd.

Peter O'Rourke

The new Manager brought in his two sons Michael and Peter and persuaded former Queen's Park, Clyde and Third Lanark player, Willie McAndrew to join Hibs. A new outside right, John Chester, was also signed but there was no improvement in performance all through December and the New Year period, with a 6-1 drubbing by Dundee 'A' at Dens Park, home and away 1-0 defeats by St Johnstone in the Wallace Cup and a 3-0 defeat by Dundee 'A' at Tannadice.

Andy Henderson left Hibs at the end of December and the replacement keeper was Joe Baillie, signed from Edinburgh Hibs. Several attempts were made to find a new centre forward before Carlisle's John Clark arrived on loan for a month in January. He made his debut in a comfortable 3-1 win over Beith in the Scottish Cup on 13th January 1923. That win brought the reward of a home tie against Nithsdale Wanderers and qualification for the next round was confidently expected. Harry Smillie was signed from St Johnstone in time to make his debut against Nithsdale Wanderers but he and indeed everyone of the Hibs persuasion was stunned when the Sanquhar side grabbed the only goal of the game to win the tie. On the day, in near gale force wind, neither side was able to master the conditions. Poor finishing was also a major factor in Hibs' downfall, but the defence made a crucial mistake with fifteen minutes left, allowing McConnell room to scramble the ball home. Hibs ended the month with a friendly at St Johnstone that ended goalless as both sides tried out new players.

Half back Walter Mackintosh was signed and February saw some improvement from the team, with only one defeat that month. A 1-1 draw at home to Partick Thistle 'A' was followed by a close game at Albion Rovers 'A' that ended 1-0 to the home side. But in the Forfarshire Cup on 14th February, Arbroath were easily beaten 3-1 and at the match there were a number of scouts. St Johnstone were keeping close tabs on Wilson, whilst Wigan were showing interest in Bannister and Hearts watched Michael O'Rourke. The next matches brought home wins of 1-0 against Ayr United 'A' and 3-1 against Third Lanark 'A' but in March, Hibs' weaknesses were again exposed. The pressure proved too much for the new Manager and after just four months in the job he resigned following a 5-0 beating from Hearts 'A' on 3rd March. His resignation came as a major surprise because, despite that big loss, it was felt that he was making progress.

Willie McAndrew took over as Player/Manager until the end of the season. His first match in charge resulted in a 2-2 draw with Third Lanark 'A' on 24th March but he then lost 3-2 to Rangers 'A'. He too came under pressure following a 1-1 draw against Forfar Athletic in the Forfarshire Cup, and a 7-0 thrashing by Airdrieonians 'A' in the league. Wilson had left to join St Johnstone in January and the outside left position was not properly filled until March with the arrival of new signing Adam Lindsay. Centre forward Fred Howard was signed in April from Clyde. The situation on the pitch worsened as the final weeks of 1922-23 rolled by. Hibs drew the Forfarshire Cup replay 0-0 with Forfar Athletic and then lost the second replay 1-0 at Dens Park.

Willie McAndrew

Everyone connected with Dundee Hibs was no doubt glad to see the end of season 1922-23 approach. In the *People's Journal* of 17th March 1923 'Unomi', the sports columnist had reported, "With only the County Cup to interest the Club this season, no special effort is being made meantime to strengthen the playing power in the team, but the officials are keeping their eyes open in order to secure nothing but the best in players for the new season. How successful they will be remains to be seen but I am assured money will not stand in the way of the talent wanted. Of course, Hibs are not making such plans with the intention of taking part in the Scottish Alliance! It is confidently expected that the Club will be members of the Second Division."

Queen's Park Strollers won 3-1 at Tannadice in the last Scottish Alliance match of the season on 28th April and Hibs' final placing of third bottom in the Scottish Alliance only served to underline the inadequacies of the team. Involvement in the Eastern League had been restricted to just five matches over the season and Hibs failed to play the rest of the scheduled fixtures. The last match of the season ended 0-0 as a Hibs XI met Aberdeen in a charity match, in aid of Lord Roberts Memorial Workshop, on 12th May 1923, and the Hibs Select included Jimmy Brownlie in goal. He was by then a signed player and shortly afterwards was confirmed as the new Manager for the first of his three stints in charge.

News emerged that a Scottish Third Division was to be created and Hibs, along with Brechin City, Montrose, Leith Athletic, Queen of the South, Nithsdale Wanderers, Peebles Rovers, Arthurlie, Royal Albert, Helensburgh, Dykehead and Galston, were invited to join. Hibs declined the offer as the Directors took a calculated gamble on achieving admission to the Second Division. They wasted little time in soliciting the support of the Scottish League clubs for the bid to return. William Hutchison and James Dickson were the main ambassadors for the Club, drawing on their considerable business experience to put forward a persuasive argument for Hibs.

One prominent Hibs official said, "We are all out to gain admittance to the Second Division, and I can assure you we will do our utmost to secure that end. It is most important that we get back again. Our present season in the Scottish Alliance League has been an utter failure and we dare not look forward to another year of the same. In short, Dundee Hibs will be forced to go to the wall if the application for the Second Division is turned down. With our return to the League, the future success of my Club is assured. Again, we are prepared to lay out a goodly sum to secure a strong team – one capable of securing promotion to the First Division."

The vote at the Scottish League AGM did not go as readily in favour of Hibs as had been expected and a large number of the clubs who earlier indicated their support were not as good as their word. Along with Hibs and Queen of the South, Arbroath and East Stirlingshire (the two clubs relegated from the First Division) were seeking re-election. The first round of voting saw Arbroath comfortably through with 26 votes polled. East Stirlingshire gained 19 and Hibs 17 with Queen of the South a long way behind. Only Hibs and East Stirlingshire contested the second round and Hibs won through with 23 votes to 15. Mr Hutchison stressed the effort that had gone into securing the return saying, "…none but those who are intimately connected with the Club will ever know the work we have accomplished." He thanked those clubs who had supported Hibs' bid and also 'Unomi' of the People's Journal, who always had "a word of cheer and encouragement" during a difficult season.

'Unomi' (who was in fact sports writer Bob Millar) has, it appears, one major claim to fame in the history of Dundee Hibs. It was he who apparently first publicly suggested that the support, and thus the fortunes of the Club would improve with a change of name. On 20th January 1923 he suggested "Were 'Dundee Rovers' or 'Dundee City' substituted for Dundee Hibs the barrier that keeps many from giving personal practical support to the Club would be broken down, attendances would increase to a healthy level, with a consequent growth in revenue and a strengthening of the financial foundations." The inference was quite clear – the 'Hibernian' connection was politically incorrect at a time of trouble in Ireland. The Directors readily acknowledged that a change of name was a sound idea and 'Unomi' even went so far as to say "….you may take it as official that, with the curtain ringing down on this season, the name of Dundee Hibs will pass into oblivion."

The Directors were however, reluctant to make any changes too quickly. The application to the Scottish League, if made in the name of Dundee City as was suggested, might have hindered the prospect of a return to the Scottish League, because it would in effect have been a new club. It was therefore decided to defer the change of name until Scottish League status was assured as this was the primary aim. Whether or not 'Unomi' was in fact the instigator of the change may be contested. What is important is that the change did take place a few months later, and within two years the Club were playing First Division football for the first time. Jimmy Brownlie used his influence and personal connections within Scottish football to ensure that Dundee United would become an established league club after Dundee Hibernian had spent so many years in the wilderness.

DUNDEE HIBS TO CHANGE NAME

The "People's Journal" Tip Adopted

By UNOMI.

IN last week's "People's Journal" I dealt with the position of Dundee Hibs and what a change of name would mean to the Club, financially and otherwise. To say the least of it, the article created a sensation in local football circles. It is generally admitted that the proposed change of name would certainly mean a turn in their fortunes.

When I visited Tannadice Park on the occasion of Nithsdale Wanderers' Scottish Cup-tie visit I heard the proposal discussed on all hands, while at the close of the game I had the opportunity of discussing the matter with several of the Hibs' Directors in the Boardroom. All are agreed that the "People's Journal" suggestion is a thoroughly sound one, and you may take it as official that, with the curtain ringing down on this season, the name of Dundee Hibs will pass into oblivion. What the procedure will be is not exactly known, but the rules of the Scottish League will have to be carefully noted.

The Tannadice Parkers are to apply to the Scottish League for readmission to the Second Division. Should they do so under the suggested new name of "Dundee City" they will be treated as an entirely new Club, and they may lose a place to some other Club, who, while not such an old combination as the Hibs, would claim priority on the grounds that the Hibs, having adopted a new name, must be treated as a new Club.

With such a position, it may be taken for granted that the officials will apply to the Scottish League in the name of Dundee Hibs, and should they be successful in securing a place in the Second Division, a further application will be made to have the name of the Club changed to that of "Dundee City."

In a talk I had with a prominent official of the Hibs it was admitted that the present name of the Club only stands for misfortune and bad luck both in a financial and playing sense, and that a change would do the Club all the good in the world.

Now's the time for reconstruction, ye Tannadice officials. Get to work immediately. My advice to my Hibernian friends is to secure young talent, coach them properly, and be ready to take their place in the Second Division under the name of "Dundee City." I make the suggestions in all good faith, and, should it be followed, I am sure the Tannadice Parkers will enter into an era of prosperity never before enjoyed by the Club.

People's Journal
27th January 1923

1923-24 – Part 1

The End of an Era

The new Manager immediately began assembling his team and although he considered bringing in another keeper, he made that position his own. Hibs were keen to retain Millwall player Terris but, faced with a fee of £250, they decided to let him go. All of the other players had already moved on and most had found new clubs.

When the new season began every one of the starting eleven would therefore be making their Hibs debut. One of the first signatures obtained by Brownlie was his former team mate at Third Lanark, Jock Kay a full back who had also played at Armadale. Outside left George Hannah, who had been with Hamilton Academical and Broxburn United, signed the same week. These two were soon joined by Jim Porter (Hearts), Bobby McEwen (Dumbarton) and Sandy Gilmour (Raith Rovers). By early August, the Manager had also acquired former Celtic centre forward Joe O'Kane, centre half Dave Richards (Port Vale) and former Hamilton Academical and Luton Town forward Tom Cottingham.

Meanwhile, at Dundee Hibs AGM, held in the Mathers Hotel in mid July 1923, the same Directors were re-elected with the exception of William Burke who stepped down and was replaced by Alexander Lamb. He and David Godfrey were two new shareholders who took 100 shares each bringing the total capital of the Company to 1,966 shares. An Extraordinary General Meeting was called on 20th August by the Board and afterwards they confirmed the intention to press on with plans to change the team name. The new name of Dundee City had been intimated to, and accepted by, the Board of Trade after they initially rejected the first choice of Dundee Athletic Association. The Club colours of green and white were also changed; black and white was chosen instead. It was expected that the SFA would quickly ratify Dundee City as the new name. But then it became apparent that the change would not be plain sailing as an objection was planned by Dundee.

Standing: Mr Hutchison, Mr Simpson, Richards, Brownlie, O'Kane, Mr Lamb, Robertson
(Trainer), Mr Hogg
Sitting: Gilmour, Kay, Porter, Hannah, Mr Dickson,
Kneeling: McEwan, Knox, Cottingham, Stirling
This is the last known photograph of Dundee Hibernian and shows the players sporting a club badge.

In early August 1923, Celtic's Eddie Gilfeather arrived on loan and next to join the Tannadice ranks was Dundee reserve half back, Ed Stirling followed by Bobby Knox from Third Lanark. This ensured that Hibs had a solid base of players to begin the season. Sporting their new white shirts and black shorts, the opening match was a friendly against St Johnstone which Hibs lost 2-0. Despite the defeat the team played well, although the forwards showed their lack of understanding and missed several good chances.

The league season opened with the change of name still awaiting formal approval by the SFA. Hibs were showing some early promise in the league and the point taken against Cowdenbeath in the goalless first match was well deserved. A single Cottingham goal gave Hibs two points at Alloa Athletic but it was a costly win, with Brownlie receiving a serious leg injury. He aggravated the problem at Albion Rovers and although Hibs won 2-0, the Player/Manager had to rule himself out of the match at Stenhousemuir. Without a reserve keeper, a trialist was fielded but he was not to blame for the 3-0 loss. Hibs just failed to perform well enough on the day.

James Mackie, signed from Bo'ness on 8th September, made his debut the following week and scored in the 2-0 Wallace Cup win over St Johnstone. Just after the 1-1 home draw with Johnstone three days after, former Clydebank defender John Swan was signed and made his debut against Arbroath. With Brownlie missing again, Hibs lost 2-1. But by then, the Tannadice spotlight moved off the field and onto the matter of the Club's new name.

Hibs' first attempt to change the name to Dundee City FC was beaten by an objection from Dundee on the basis that the new name would cause confusion between the two. The matter was referred to a council meeting of the SFA on 19th September and when it came time to the vote, Dundee's objection was upheld, but only on the casting vote of the Chairman, Tom White (Celtic). However, three council members did not vote, including Mr McLoughlin (Alloa Athletic) who had seconded the motion for the change of name. He had already left to catch a train along with Mr Adamson (Raith Rovers) who was also in favour. Perhaps if they had realised how tight the vote might be they would not have left. As it was, the vote was split evenly until the casting vote was used in favour of Dundee's objection. It also came to light that, if promoted, Hibs might meet with opposition to their current name, as the Hibs of Edinburgh would almost certainly oppose the use of 'Hibernian' by any other team in the First Division. The day after the meeting Hibs appealed to the SFA who then contacted both Dundee clubs suggesting they get together to find a solution. But neither side would alter their stance. Dundee were adamant that Dundee City was not to be the name, whilst Hibs were just as determined to become Dundee City.

As the two Dundee clubs pondered their next move, the team carried on the business of gathering league points. They beat Vale of Leven 3-1, with some good forward play and a fine display in goal by Brownlie. On the first Saturday of October, Hibs met Dundee at Tannadice in a Forfarshire Cup tie. They beat their more fancied First Division opponents by a single Mackie goal after half an hour. No doubt there was some discussion about the change of name in the Boardroom after the game but still no solution emerged and it took almost another three weeks to resolve the problem. The next league match was at Dunfermline Athletic and resulted in a 1-0 defeat but only by a second half penalty. At home to East Fife a week later, a goalless encounter might have had a more positive outcome for Hibs had Swan netted from the spot instead of firing straight at the keeper.

The appeal regarding the change of name by Hibs was discussed at another SFA meeting in their Carlton Palace offices on 17th October and was initially turned down, but their letter was left 'on the table'. Mr McIntosh of Dundee left the meeting to go into an ante room with Messrs Hutchison, Dickson and Brownlie for more discussions. Eventually McIntosh agreed to support Hibs if they dropped 'Dundee City' in favour of another name. The new team name was hastily agreed, although it may be that both sides had previously arrived at this compromise. Tom White was advised that Dundee would not object to the name Dundee United. The new name was verbally agreed, to be ratified at the next full SFA meeting. Official records however, confirm that Dundee Hibernian

Football and Athletic Club Ltd changed its name to Dundee City Athletic Club Ltd on 31st October 1923 and the Club continued to trade with that name until June 1925, although playing under the name Dundee United!

The new name of Dundee United could have been used on 20th October but instead, the last game played by Dundee Hibernian took place that day against King's Park, and Hibs won. It was 2-2 at half time with Mackie getting both goals for the Greens in a frantic ten minute spell which also saw former Hibs player Scullion get two for his new side King's Park. After the break, Gilmour scored what proved to be the winner and the last goal scored by Dundee Hibs. When the team next took to the field it would be as Dundee United. Along with the name of Dundee Hibernian, the nicknames of the Greens and the Irishmen also went into the void, to be replaced by the 'Black and Whites', until decades later.

DUNDEE UNITED

1923-24 – Part 2

A New Outlook

Some newspapers still listed Dundee Hibernian playing away at Dumbarton on 27th October but it was in fact the first match for Dundee United. They played poorly and the loss of three goals without reply gave the Club an inauspicious start. Following the match against Dumbarton it became known that Hannah was unwell and would be out of the team for some time (indeed he would never play again) and United were in dire need of a replacement outside left. The matter came up during a conversation between United and Dundee officials and, unprompted, Dundee offered former Arniston Rangers player Jimmy Walker on loan until the end of the season. Walker was at first reluctant but after discussion he agreed to move. Bobby Bauld from Raith Rovers also signed in time for United's first home game on 3rd November 1923 in which the "Tannadice Parkers" recorded a 3-2 win over St Bernard's. It was a hard won two points with the visitors taking a two goal lead before Walker and Bauld levelled the match and finally Mackie netted the winner.

A good run of results followed, with a 0-0 draw at Forfar Athletic and a narrow 1-0 win at Tannadice against Lochgelly United. O'Kane scored the only goal of that game, running half the length of the pitch and then chipping the ball over the advancing keeper. Just prior to beating Broxburn United 2-1, it was announced that Cottingham and McEwan had been freed, as neither had achieved the standard that Brownlie was looking for. Archie Taylor, who had played with Dundee Hibs and Dundee, where he had also been assistant trainer, joined United as the new trainer on the same day that United picked up another valuable away point at Armadale in a 1-1 draw.

The next three games produced only one point from a goalless draw at home to Bo'ness and exposed United's lack of a centre forward capable of taking the chances that were certainly being created. The Manager decided to release Mackie near the end of December and he signed for King's Park. He was replaced by Tommy Simpson from Osborne, who would prove to be one of the best signings of the 1920s.

In a dramatic match at Cowdenbeath on 31st December, United were twice two goals behind but on both occasions they drew level and it ended 4-4. Then on 2nd January 1924, United's unbeaten home record went to a solitary goal by Wood of Alloa Athletic. Another 0-0 draw was registered against Lochgelly United, followed by a stunning 4-0 win over Armadale, at the time considered something of the league's shock troops. After Armadale dominated the opening half hour, United stepped up a gear and rattled in four goals without reply. The Manager was still searching for a centre forward to solve the goal scoring problem and it seemed that he had found what he was looking for when trialist Jimmy Russell from Rosslyn Juniors scored twice in that match. The player then signed and although he turned in some good performances, he never hit the goal trail as expected. In fact the top scorer in the league turned out to be O'Kane who played in all three central attacking positions over the season.

The match at East Fife on 19th January was nothing to enthuse over as United were stretched defensively and were fortunate to return from Methil with a point from yet another 0-0 result. Perhaps the players' thoughts were elsewhere, as the following week, United were due to play at Easter Road in the Scottish Cup in a match that would test the Club's ambitions for a top flight place. As an added incentive, the players on cup duty were being offered a substantial bonus to either draw or win. The team travelled to the capital on the day before the match in relaxed mood. The Manager even took the players to the theatre on Friday night! The next day, 16,000 spectators, including a sizeable United support, were packed into Easter Road. They saw United put up a good fight, but lose to a single goal from Ritchie with half an hour played. Very much on the defensive in the first half, United tried hard to knock Hibs out of their stride but were unable to make any real impression on the Edinburgh side's defence. It was then back to league business with goal scoring still a major problem for the Manager to solve. The final league table shows that United drew fifteen matches over the campaign; more than any other side in the league and testament to the lack of a good finisher.

All the league matches in February were at home but goals were difficult to come by. The standard of play was at best average and just four points were gained, with a 1-1 draw against St Johnstone, a goalless game with King's Park and a 2-0 win over Arbroath. In March, all five league matches were away from home and United could only muster a point at each of Vale of Leven, St Bernard's and Bo'ness. The slow but sure accumulation of points over the season had long since secured Scottish League safety and the Directors were now looking to the future. They were determined that the Club would prosper and with their sights firmly set on a place in the First Division, plans for further improvements to Tannadice were announced in February 1924. Most importantly the pitch, which had a noticeable slope, was to be levelled out and re-turfed and new drainage was planned, with installation in time for the 1925-26 kick off.

By this time, Brownlie had decided to stop playing to concentrate on managing, although he retained his player registration. The highly regarded Frank Bridgeford, from Forfar Celtic, was signed as a replacement after trials in March. Brownlie, with sixteen international caps to his name, was a man who certainly knew a good goalkeeper when he saw one. The following season would prove what a good judge he was.

In an end of season flurry of matches, United notched a 2-1 win over Albion Rovers in the league and then played Arbroath in a Forfarshire Cup tie at Gayfield, losing by the odd goal in three. But the match is significant in that United played in this cup competition under two different names. In the earlier round, against Dundee, the Tannadice players turned out as Dundee Hibernian.

In other competitions, United lost heavily to Dundee in an Eastern League match. They were also involved in the second leg of the Wallace Cup against St Johnstone, who had been the promoted side a year earlier. In an ill tempered 3-3 draw, both sides were fortunate to end the match with eleven players. United had played the first leg as Dundee Hibs and perhaps this was another unique situation; a team playing two legs of a cup tie under different names. Interspersed with these three encounters, United ended the league campaign with four home matches. Starting with a good 2-0 win over Bathgate, they then lost 1-0 in a poor display against Stenhousemuir. Against Dunfermline Athletic, United were behind after the Pars scored twice from the spot but a late rally earned a 2-2 draw. Finally a drab Angus derby against Forfar Athletic was won 2-0, with goals from Gilfeather and O'Kane.

After all the drama of the first few months of season 1923-24 the campaign ended without much fanfare. But viewed against the history of a struggling Dundee Hibernian over the previous fourteen years, finishing in ninth place must have been regarded as quite a triumph. With 39 points gathered from thirty eight games, a goal average of exactly zero and 41 goals scored, Brownlie took careful stock of his playing staff. He decided to free Knox, Hannah, Stirling and Swan and of course Walker went back to Dundee. Gilfeather returned to Celtic but the Manager expressed an interest in retaining his services and the player was keen to stay. Initially Celtic refused permission but eventually relented and he came back on 24th June. At the same time James 'Snyder' Smith was signed from Clyde. The work to get these two players was carried out by Brownlie whilst he was back at his home in the west of Scotland and in regular contact with many clubs there.

Two more important decisions were made in late June. The first was made by Brownlie, who decided that he would live in Dundee. With his commitment secured, the Board then agreed to his request that United become a full time club to ensure that they had the best chance of making a bid for promotion. This was undoubtedly a bold financial gamble by the Board as at the time the Club were borrowing almost £2,000 from the bank and another £1,746 from the Directors. None of the other Second Division sides were full time and even in the First Division, several clubs were still part time. It would require a team performing at their best to keep the crowds coming in to help fund the increased wages bill. The Manager already had the basis of a good side with the retained players Bridgeford, Kay, Porter, Richards, Gilmour, O'Kane, Simpson, Russell and Bauld and there would soon be a few new faces added to the squad.

1924-25

Promotion !

Before a serious promotion challenge could be mounted, Brownlie had to complete the team building exercise. First he took former Kilmarnock right half James Harvey from St Johnstone to Tannadice. Another Perth based player, Johnny McRoberts, was already transfer listed, but the fee of £100 was more than United were prepared to pay. The Perth side were reminded that Willie Wilson was released by United and allowed to move to them a year earlier. This seems to have had the effect of softening St Johnstone's hard line on the price, and McRoberts then joined United to complete the pre-season player search.

In the opening league match at Bo'ness, 'Snyder' Smith was United's man of the match, scoring twice in a 2-2 draw. Bo'ness were the better side on the day and had plenty of chances, whilst Smith made the best of the only two real opportunities that fell United's way. A week later, newly relegated Clyde were the visitors and Smith won the match for United scoring the only goal of the game against his old club. Momentum was maintained with a 2-0 Forfarshire Cup win against Montrose with Russell at centre scoring both goals. Smith was back in the line up for the next league match, a 3-3 draw at Dumbarton but that was the last appearance of the strangely nicknamed 'Snyder' Smith. Russell returned for the 3-1 win over Johnstone. The centre forward position would again cause Brownlie much anxiety over the season, with no less than eight different players taking the role. In the end he never really solved the problem and the top scorer for the season was actually inside right Willie Oswald! A former Gillingham and St Johnstone player, Oswald had played for United as a trialist two years earlier and scored twice in a 4-1 win against Armadale. He returned in August 1924, initially for a one month trial but impressed enough to stay for the remainder of the season.

There may have been a problem at centre, but the team generally was playing well and an unbeaten league run continued with a 1-1 draw at King's Park where centre forward Andy Cant from Dunfermline Athletic made his debut. He was one of a number of players freed by the Fife side after a poor start to the season and he arrived with a good reputation, but during his stay at United, he showed only glimpses of his true form. United also signed defender John (Jacky) Osborne from Lochee Central after a successful trial in a 1-0 win over East Fife. Cant netted a brace of goals in a 2-2 draw with Bathgate but he was not among the scorers as United won the next three league matches against St Bernard's 3-0, Arbroath 1-0 and Arthurlie 4-1 but lost a friendly with Dundee, 2-0 in the midst of the winning league sequence. Top of the league after ten games, United had ridden their luck most of the way and a wake up call was delivered when Alloa Athletic came to Tannadice and won 2-1 on 25th October. After that match Cant was dropped and replaced by O'Kane, but he was only in the side for two weeks before being replaced by Willie Mackie, signed from Albion Rovers in the last week of October. With so many players available to fill one position it was perhaps inevitable that one would go and Russell left United to join Third Lanark on loan.

Throughout November, United continued to pick up points, taking seven from a possible eight with a 3-2 win at East Stirlingshire, a 2-1 home win over Forfar Athletic, a goalless draw at Dunfermline Athletic and a resounding 5-2 success against Armadale at Tannadice. The Black and Whites then lost only their second league game of the campaign when they went down by a single goal at Albion Rovers. What followed was described as 'an off day' as United suffered a 5-0 drubbing from fellow promotion hopefuls Clydebank. Brownlie however, quickly lifted the team and in the next four matches they again took seven points with a 1-0 win at Broxburn United, a 3-0 home win against Stenhousemuir, a closely fought 2-1 win over Bathgate at Tannadice and a 0-0 draw at Forfar Athletic on 1st January 1925. That run saw United achieve top spot again by the turn of the year.

Since the arrival of Osborne, Porter had been unable to get back into the side and on 20th December he accepted a move to join Bathgate. At the same time, Partick Thistle centre forward Hugh Collins was attracting United's interest but an attempt to bring him to Tannadice fell through. The former Hamilton Academical man did however join the squad in March but only until the end of the season.

Although United lost 3-0 at Clyde on 3rd January, Brownlie again rallied his team to take five points from the next three matches, with a 1-0 win against Clydebank, a goalless draw at home to Bo'ness and a 2-1 win at Arthurlie. Kay and McRoberts were both struggling with injury, so the results were all the more welcome. Signed from Lochgelly United, Robert Rintoul scored the winner on his debut in the match against Arthurlie. He was brought in to replace Gilmour who was injured and out of action for several weeks.

The next match was against Aberdeen University in the Scottish Cup and

United fans were confident of progressing to the next round. However, it almost did not go to plan. The non league side made life difficult for United and at half time the match was goalless. Brownlie no doubt had a few choice words for the players in the dressing room and in the second half United were a team transformed, virtually scoring at will to win 5-1. The highlight of the match was a hat-trick from O'Kane.

After a creditable 0-0 draw with Dumbarton in the league the following week, United geared up to face Partick Thistle in the Scottish Cup at Firhill. In front of a crowd of 20,000, this was very much a reversal of the game against Aberdeen University, with United as the underdogs. They held their own before the interval but after losing three goals in fifteen minutes in the second half, United were all but out. They did not give in though, and Oswald gave the travelling fans a glimmer of hope when he pulled one back, but the Jags then scored two more and it ended 5-1 to the home side. United returned home, knocked out of the competition but with great credit for a battling performance. In any event it may have been a blessing in disguise as all efforts were then focused on the league challenge.

Then, as now, there was frequent speculation and rumours to give the fans plenty to talk about. Take for example the case of Robert Rintoul who had played in three league matches and twice in the Scottish Cup. Rumours were circulating in Dundee that he had been ineligible and the Scottish League was planning to deduct six points from United. This caused genuine concern amongst United supporters but the rumour was a complete fabrication and the player was properly registered after his move from Lochgelly United. How the rumour started is not known but it was quickly quashed to allay the fans' fears.

In February, wins against Albion Rovers 3-2, East Fife 1-0, St Bernard's 2-1 and King's Park 2-0 put United in a strong promotion winning position. With the arrival of Hugh Collins, it was hoped the side would secure the points from the remaining matches to take United into the top flight. But it seemed to have the opposite effect and from four matches in March, United took only one point in a 1-1 draw with Arbroath. Particularly worrying was the 2-0 win for fellow promotion hopefuls Alloa Athletic but fortunately none of the other front runners took full advantage. At Johnstone, United won 2-0 playing Jim Cameron as a trialist and he scored one of the goals. Brownlie would keep an eye on this young outside left over the next three years and he would become a United player in December 1928. Cameron was in the side again as United faced East Stirlingshire at Tannadice needing just one point to make promotion a certainty. The Black and Whites won both points and First Division football was guaranteed. Mackie scored in just eight minutes for a one goal half time advantage and Richards made it 2-0 with a swerving 35 yard shot to seal the win. Although the visitors scored a late consolation, United celebrated with the Manager carried shoulder high off the pitch. A week later, a 2-2 draw with Broxburn United secured the championship. In between these two results United lost 1-0 to Dundee 'A' in a friendly.

After losing 2-0 to Arbroath in a Forfarshire Cup semi final, the last league match of the season was a 3-0 defeat at Stenhousemuir. The pressure was off and United relaxed just a little too much and the home side had United reeling with three quick first half goals. Perhaps the players were thinking about the challenges ahead in Division One. Certainly the Manager and the Directors were. They had already announced details of a new financial structure and had also confirmed that work would commence on the ground improvements. In celebration of the championship win, the players, Manager Jimmy Brownlie and Trainer Archie Taylor were gifted gold watches donated by Mr Henderson (probably of the well known Henderson the Jeweller in Dundee). The presentation was made at a dinner held in Morgan Academy after the end of season friendly with St Johnstone, in aid of Morgan Academy Sports Park Pavilion Fund. Archie Taylor was credited with much of the championship success as his advice in football matters and his positive attitude gave the Manager incalculable assistance during the campaign.

Even before the season ended, United announced that the purchase of Tannadice would take place. The cost was later confirmed at £2,830 and included land along Sandeman Street, to allow additional standing areas. A new stand was to be built, the pitch levelled, new drainage installed and new turf laid. It would be an expensive exercise and to pay for it, shares and debentures were offered by public subscription through a new Limited Company.

Work began almost as soon as the season was over. Very quickly rumours were circulating that the Scottish League were not satisfied with the condition of Tannadice and the Club were not being granted promotion. Instead, relegated Ayr United would be staying up. The rumour started after United were advised of a planned visit by an inspection committee from the Scottish League. The visit to Tannadice was standard procedure and the inspectors were also planning to check up on the grounds at Queen of the South and Nithsdale Wanderers. The inspection committee comprising; R C Liddell (Falkirk) Scottish League President, W Duffy (Motherwell) Vice President and committee members Colquhoun (Clydebank), Maley (Celtic), Roxburgh (Alloa Athletic) and McAndrew, duly arrived at Tannadice on 11th May. They viewed the plans and work in progress and initially expressed some doubt that United would be ready for the new season. However, after receiving assurances from the main contractor John Carnegie (John Carnegie & Son Ltd) that the work would be completed on time, the committee indicated that they were satisfied. That effectively ended the speculation around the promotion issue.

On the playing side, Brownlie was working behind the scenes to bring in new faces after retaining only Kay, Osborne, Simpson and Bauld for the First Division challenge. Most of the others had been freed except for Collins and Gilfeather who each returned to their own clubs after their loan deals expired.

SFA Inspection Visit to Tannadice 11th May 1925
Mr Hogg, Mr Roxburgh, Mr Hutchison, Mr Dickson, Mr Colquhoun, Mr Maley

With the plans for First Division football well under way, the next step was to find the cash to pay for the ground improvements, the proposed new stand and new players. Dundee United Football Company Limited was formed for this purpose and registered at Companies House on 3rd June 1925. One week later the prospectus dated 6th June was published in the *Dundee Courier*. On offer was total capital of £27,500 in the form of 15,000 shares of £1 each and £12,500 in debenture stock at 5% interest per annum, secured over the ground and repayable on 1st January 1935. The prospectus also confirmed the contract price for the purchase of Tannadice. The planned new stand would accommodate 3,000 supporters and with the standing accommodation extended the total capacity at Tannadice would rise to 35,000.

Initially the take up of the offer was good and two weeks later in the *Dundee Courier*, Brownlie was saying that demand had been high. "Shares are still available to intending investors although the market is likely to be closed after this week." he said "The sum subscribed up to the present reaches a respectable sum." Only days later however, in the *Evening Telegraph* it was a different story. The paper reported an appeal by Dundee United management regarding shares. "So far the response has been to put it frankly, very discouraging and the lack of subscribed capital is tying the hands of the management with regard to fixing up players they want... unless the sporting public of Dundee come away with the necessary cash, there will be little chance of a team worthy of the town being placed on the field." Unfortunately the appeal fell on deaf ears at a time when money was already tight. The launch of Dundee United on the big stage had arrived at an inopportune moment, with hard times just around the corner, and the effects of financial restraint already evident.

1925-26

Playing with the Big Boys

Aided by good weather, the improvements to Tannadice were on schedule and, although the work was likely to be completed on time, paying for it was a different matter. The share and debenture issue was grossly under subscribed with just 655 shares purchased initially. In addition, 1,966 shares were to be issued to Dundee City Athletic Club Ltd but those would not raise any cash being replacements for Dundee Hibs shares. Of the debenture stock, only around £2,800 was taken up to begin with. United therefore did not have enough money to pay the contractor. Instead, it was agreed that the company would be paid the balance over time from gate receipts. Later in the year it would appear that some £8,000 of debenture stock was issued to various creditors and some more shares were sold to bring the total to 1,140 but in essence the launch of Dundee United Football Company Ltd was a major disappointment to the Directors. The cash raised came nowhere near what was needed to underpin the Club. The biggest disappointment was the cancellation of plans to build a new stand. That would have to wait for almost 40 years!

Getting a team together was still the priority and with much less money available than was expected, the Manager was forced to lower his sights. He was still able to attract some experienced men to United. By mid May only Malcolm 'Micky' Campbell from Falkirk had been acquired but attempts to bring in Chelsea keeper Colin Hampton had fallen through. There was some good news on 23rd May when team captain McRoberts re-signed after a change of heart by Brownlie. On the same day two more signings took place. Firstly, Directors Sandy Lamb and William Hutchison along with Brownlie went to Perth to sign Jimmy Howieson from St Johnstone. From there they set off to Dunfermline where they added the signature of goalkeeper Bill Paterson. He was to prove one of the best buys of the season and played a crucial role on the field and in the dressing room all through the forthcoming First Division campaign. The big keeper was one of football's characters; he was the joker in the pack and did a lot to keep morale high in the dressing room.

Pre-season 1925–26
Standing: Campbell, D. Walker, Paterson, Bauld, McDonald, McRoberts.
Kneeling: Howieson, Osborne, Kay, T Simpson, Oswald.

Three of the squad from 1924-25 were still available and the Manager was considering re-signing them all but before he could, Richards accepted a move to Luton Town and Gilmour went to St Bernard's. That left only Oswald, who re-signed in early June.

Across the road at Dens Park, ex-Linfield and Blackburn Rovers outside left Jock McDonald had been unable to agree terms with the Dark Blues and when he was approached by Brownlie in early July he readily signed for United. Two weeks later half back Dave Walker was acquired from St Johnstone and to complete the pre-season signings, in August, Jimmy Walker was transferred from Third Lanark along with Hugh McBride from Hamilton Academical. It is a measure of the enthusiasm for United in the First Division that around 6,500 spectators turned up for the trial match which was held at Rockwell Park as the work at Tannadice was still not quite complete.

Sixteen years after the formation of the Club, it was finally time to put a team onto the big stage. The first game in the top flight was played at Starks Park, Kirkcaldy. The honour of playing for First Division Dundee United for the first time went to:-

Paterson, Kay and McBride; Campbell, D Walker and J Walker; T Simpson, Bauld, J Simpson, Howieson and McDonald.

The latest addition to the side was Jimmy Simpson, who had been signed only two days before from Newburgh West End. Not quite seventeen years old, he made his debut along with seven others. This may account for the lack of understanding between the players in the 4-2 defeat. Raith Rovers were a goal up in only three minutes, ahead by three at half time and 4-0 in front just after the interval. United rallied and Howieson scored twice to put a fairer reflection on the score line. The next league match was against Cowdenbeath and was also away from home. United, through Howieson, took an early lead but by half time the Central Park side were in front. In the second half, United collapsed to a 5-1 defeat. A midweek derby at Dens Park in the Penman Cup produced another poor showing as Dundee thrashed United 5-0. Even this early in the season it was beginning to look as if United might become the whipping boys of the league.

It was hoped that the next game would be something of a festival day for United as they played on the newly upgraded Tannadice pitch for the first time. Mrs Dickson (wife of Director James Dickson) hoisted the Second Division championship flag over Tannadice in the presence of several dignitaries including Mr Liddell, the Scottish League President. He complimented United on the improvements to Tannadice and wished the Club well for the season. Unfortunately his club, Falkirk were in no mood to be generous. United took the lead through Bauld and were good for at least a draw but lost 2-1 in the end. United were out of luck again a week later when Motherwell were the visitors. Leading by an Oswald goal, the Black and Whites lost McBride to injury. Whilst United were reduced to ten men the visitors levelled the match at 1-1 to steal a point. Outside right William MacDonald had signed from junior side Law Scotia and made his debut in that match but would feature only twice more in the season. Former Queen of the South player Joe Shandley was another new acquisition but he featured only three times.

The third home match in a row saw United lose 2-1 to Queen's Park and the lack of success had Brownlie back in the transfer market. Just before the trip to Perth on 12th September to face St Johnstone in the next match, the former Portsmouth and Southend United centre Peter McMillan was signed. He made his debut and scored the only goal of the game to give United their first league win of the season. United surprised the entire football community a week later at Tannadice when they won against eventual champions Celtic. The 1-0 win was built on a sound defensive display, with Paterson in goal playing at his best. After absorbing massive Celtic pressure, Howieson grabbed a late goal for a deserved two points. After that however, United suffered five defeats in a row. The same eleven that humbled Celtic could not reproduce the same form and lost rather meekly 2-0 to St Mirren. Arbroath then won a midweek Forfarshire tie by a single goal. But the 6-1 hammering from Clydebank after that was self inflicted as United brought in McRoberts at centre half and William MacDonald at centre forward. It was the last game for both and McRoberts would shortly leave to join East Stirlingshire. Brownlie was still trying to improve the squad and for the second time, came close to signing Patsy Gallacher but the well known Celtic forward eventually signed for Falkirk instead, as he wanted to remain closer to his business interests in the west.

Before the next match, against Hamilton Academical, twenty one year old forward Willie Welsh arrived on loan from Hearts where he had been for three years. He netted five goals in his first three games, with one on his debut. United were 2-0 up in that match but collapsed to a 5-2 defeat. Welsh scored in the next game against Queen's Park but United were already 2-0 behind at the time. New signing Andrew Findlay from Third Lanark also made his debut in that match. Welsh then scored a hat-trick on his third appearance to cancel out an early Kilmarnock strike and record only the third win of the campaign. Perhaps the arrival of Welsh and Finlay was seen as the answer to the problems up front. This may have prompted Brownlie to let Howieson go to St Mirren after only ten appearances for United. The move certainly came as a surprise and was completed very hastily, with Hull City also knocking at the door and forcing the Paisley side to a decision. Initially, Tom Barclay of the Buddies was to be exchanged in part payment but in the end the transfer went through for a straight cash payment, reported to be £1,000. It should not be forgotten that United were short of cash after the failure of the share and debenture issue and £1,000 would have been a welcome boost.

Over the next dozen or so games, United began to pick up points. Draws with Morton, Dundee and Hibs were well deserved and a good 2-0 win against Aberdeen was credited to some excellent forward play with well taken goals from Tommy Simpson and Campbell. The match against Partick Thistle was won by a single goal against the odds, with Finlay taken off injured in the first half. United were forced to play on the defensive and won with a penalty scored by Dave Walker. Unfortunately the momentum could not be maintained and United lost 3-1 at Hamilton Academical.

Near the end of the year, full back Tommy Gilroy was signed from Fauldhouse Juniors and went straight into the team to face Rangers on 19th December. United performed extremely well to beat the Ibrox side 2-1 and claim an unlikely Old Firm double. In the first half, Rangers were awarded a dubious penalty from which they took the lead but the Black and Whites showed great determination to level the match after the interval through Campbell, and Tommy Simpson netted the winner. That win was followed by narrow but deserved victories over Airdrieonians, 1-0 on Boxing Day 1925 and Kilmarnock, 3-2 on 1st January 1926 to leave United with twenty points after the festive programme finished and a good chance of First Division survival. However, United then lost 1-0 at home to Dundee and collected just one more league point in January with a 1-1 draw at Falkirk before losing at home again, 2-1 to Cowdenbeath.

Although league survival was the priority, the intervention of the Scottish Cup brought some much needed revenue to the Club. It took three games to settle the tie against Hearts but at the end of it all United received £1,100 as their share of the gate money. Two additions to the playing staff were hurriedly brought in before the first game against Hearts. With Dave Walker suspended, United acquired replacement centre half Dave Nicoll from Forfar Athletic. Arbroath's Bob MacFarlane was signed to cover for Willie Welsh who had contracted diphtheria and was unavailable. Osborne was seen as surplus to requirements and he left to join Forfar Athletic.

*Jimmy Brownlie in action at Tynecastle on
1st February 1926*

The first meeting with Hearts was at Tannadice and a crowd of 18,522 witnessed an enthralling match, played in torrential rain that created something of a mud bath. Bauld crashed a shot in to give United the lead but Hearts levelled to set up the first replay at Tynecastle. In front of 25,000 spectators, the replay produced another great game with the United defence taking all the plaudits. Hearts went ahead just after half time but Campbell equalised with only eight minutes remaining. Hearts pounded the United defence, but even after extra time the tie was not settled and another replay was required. For reasons of financial benefit, United agreed to play at Tynecastle again but this time United were overwhelmed by the home side. On 1st February, in front of another 20,000 crowd, Hearts won the second replay 6-0 with relative ease.

United had been forced to field Brownlie in goal following an injury to Paterson in the 3-1 league defeat at Morton two days earlier. Brownlie was not match fit and at 40 years of age, his reactions were not up to those of Paterson. The emergency keeper did however make some good saves but he also let in goals that Paterson would most likely have stopped. That said, the outfield players were not at their best and too much rested on the last line of defence.

The cup marathon definitely had the effect of draining the players. But that alone cannot account for poor league form during February. United suffered further defeats to Motherwell, St Mirren, Hearts and Partick Thistle to slip down the league and were soon in the relegation zone. There was also a 2-1 defeat in a friendly against Dundee. It is no coincidence perhaps that Welsh was missing from the side at the time. Even on his return he did not look fully fit and took a couple of weeks to get back to his best. The pressure was on as the last few games loomed and Mitchell McGregor signed from Stobswell but he was one for the future and made only one appearance. United also tried, unsuccessfully, to bring George (Geordie) Henderson to Tannadice from Rangers.

The final weeks of season 1925-26 were nail-biting for United fans. Safety was only finally secured in the penultimate match, a 0-0 draw with St Johnstone, in front of the largest home attendance of the season, 23,517. Prior to that United had lost to Airdrieonians, Aberdeen and Rangers but enough points were gathered in creditable home wins of 3-1 over Raith Rovers, 5-0 over Clydebank and 5-3 away to Hibernian. The latter was United's best performance of the season, coming from 3-1 down to win. By the time St Johnstone came to Tannadice a week later, United needed just that one point for safety. The last league game of the season pitted United against champions Celtic and the 6-2 score line in favour of the Glasgow side only served to emphasise the gap between the two. St Johnstone gained a measure of revenge against United in a 5-2 Wallace Cup first leg win in Perth.

Despite the narrow escape from relegation, the season was considered a success. The income the Club had received resulted in a profit of £1,842, for the year to 30th April 1926, although the figure was not announced until the AGM in August. At the end of April eight players were freed but of those, only Oswald, McBride and Finlay had made any significant contribution. Top scorer with eleven goals was Campbell and he re-signed along with Paterson, Gilroy, Bauld, Tommy Simpson and Jock McDonald. Jock Kay and Dave Walker initially held out for better terms but they also signed up again. Before the next campaign began, Jimmy Walker moved to take up the post of head teacher in Bishopbriggs and he gave up the game. He was not out of football entirely; and was at least once a guest reporter for the *Sunday Post*.

1926-27

A Losing Battle in the Basement

There was not much happening at Tannadice over the summer of 1926. The squad of players had been increased to only eleven following the re-signing of Jimmy Simpson and McGregor. A recent new addition was Johnny Hart, signed from St Johnstone on 4th June and it would be almost a month before the next player, Willie Welsh was added. Hearts had released him shortly after his loan deal at Tannadice ended. Welsh proved to be another inspired Brownlie signing, ending the season as top scorer with a total of fourteen league and cup goals. With kick off just days away United had a dozen players; not enough for the challenge ahead. They were also soon to lose trainer Archie Taylor who left to join Huddersfield Town in late September and he was replaced by former Dundee goalkeeper, Bob Crumley, trainer with Lochee United.

The opening three league matches all ended in defeat to Rangers, Hibs and Dundee, with United failing to find the net and conceding nine goals. Of these, five were scored by Dundee at Dens Park in the first derby of the season. Former Aberdeen half back John Moore was signed on 24th August but it was very much a panic buy. He made only one appearance, in the next match, a 2-1 defeat at home to Kilmarnock. Moore was joined by two other players making their debuts. Andrew Miller signed from Wishaw Juniors and Irish international and former Glenavon forward Eddie Carroll was acquired on loan from Aberdeen. Alex Henderson from local junior side North End was also signed but it would be two months before he turned out.

A 4-1 reversal at Cowdenbeath was the fifth defeat in a row, leaving United at the bottom of the table. The first win of the season came against Clyde, 3-1 on 18th September but the poor run continued, and in the next game, Falkirk beat United 5-3, albeit with more than their fair share of good fortune. United tried to shore up the defence with the signing of utility half back man, ex-Newry player/manager Frank Carroll (brother of Eddie) but he lasted only three games.

He helped the side take a point in a 2-2 draw with Queen's Park and another point in a 1-1 draw at Hamilton Academical but he played his last game a week later in a 2-0 defeat at Dunfermline Athletic. By now United were consigned to the basement and once again it was fairly obvious that the season would be a relegation battle. United tried to sign centre half Tommy Williamson from Third Lanark but after a fee of £1,000 was mentioned, Brownlie withdrew the offer. October concluded with a 4-2 defeat at home to Airdrieonians and a 0-0 draw with Morton, also at home. On 6th November, St Johnstone took an easy two points from United in a 4-1 win but an unexpected point was earned in a 2-2 draw with Aberdeen. Form deteriorated again as Motherwell won 1-0 at Tannadice and a visit to Celtic Park in the last match in that month exposed United's weak defence as Celtic won 7-2.

It came as quite a surprise when, a week later, United beat Hearts 5-3! After missing a penalty and then letting Hearts take the lead, United levelled through former Hearts man Welsh. Eddie Carroll bagged a hat-trick and McGregor got the other to make it 5-1, but slackness near the end allowed Hearts to score twice. United were still bottom with only eight points from seventeen games but then went on to collect another seven points from the next five games. The match on 11th December at Partick Thistle was a real coupon buster and yielded an unlikely point in a 2-2 draw! Over the festive programme United lost just once, to Morton 3-1 whilst the other matches brought commendable wins against St Mirren 2-1, Rangers 2-0 and Dundee 1-0. It did not last though, and league form dipped with a 3-0 defeat at Kilmarnock and then Cowdenbeath won 2-0 at Tannadice.

The Scottish Cup had drawn United against Arbroath Athletic and the non leaguers, with choice of venue, elected to play at Tannadice. The match was switched to a Wednesday to avoid a clash with Dundee, who were also at home. The 7-0 score line truly reflects United's dominance, with Johnny Hart scoring a hat-trick. It was a shame that only 2,000 turned up for the match. United then suffered a one goal league defeat at Clyde, but the worst news from that encounter was that Bill Paterson had injured a knee and would be sidelined for several weeks. The Manager had to move quickly to sign the replacement, James Dempster from St Johnstone. He made his debut in the next round of the cup as United comfortably disposed of Vale of Leven at Tannadice, winning 4-1 with Carroll netting twice.

On returning to league business again, Falkirk gave United a lesson in chance taking, when they won 2-0 at Tannadice and then Queen's Park continued an impressive run of form beating United 5-3 in Glasgow. This took the amateurs' tally of goals to fifteen in three league matches.

The Scottish Cup beckoned again and United faced Montrose, then in the Scottish Alliance League. The Angus side gave United a torrid time in a 2-2 draw at Tannadice, scoring first and last to earn a deserved replay. Montrose sold the

A crowd of just 1,000 watched United play Falkirk on 9th February 1927

ground rights to United and the replay was also at Tannadice. Again United had to battle all the way, with Montrose in front until nine minutes from the end when McGregor levelled the tie. In extra time he scored again, and Walker netted from the spot for a 3-1 win to set up a fourth round tie at Partick Thistle.

Meanwhile, United were making no headway in the league and remained rooted to the foot of the table. A 4-4 draw at home to Dunfermline Athletic on 26th February was the single point added since beating Dundee almost two months earlier. By now, United's problems were compounded by injury to key players. With no depth in the squad the Club were fortunate to obtain James Meagher from Dundee on loan until the end of the season and he made his debut in the 2-1 home defeat by Hamilton Academical. The next match was the Scottish Cup tie at Partick Thistle. Again short of players, for one game only, the Dens Park side allowed centre forward Andy Ramage to play for United alongside the other loaned player Meagher. Neither had much impact in the match as the Glasgow side won rather easily 5-0. United did however benefit from their share of the gate money produced by the 25,000 crowd.

The run of bad results continued with a 7-2 drubbing from Airdrieonians with five of those scored by McPhail. United's latest signing, Tom Fleming from Dundee, made his debut that day in defence. Narrow defeats at the hands of Hibs, 3-2 and St Johnstone, 2-1 followed before a single point was collected at Aberdeen in a 2-2 draw. Motherwell then drove the nail in further when they scored six against United, without reply. When the surprise score line of 3-3 with Celtic was recorded on 9th April, it merely emphasised the Club's inconsistency. United were actually 3-1 up but tired and allowed Celtic to equalise.

Two days later, with a few changes to the line up, United faced Dundee in a Forfarshire Cup tie. Andy Ramage who, only a month before was wearing the black and white of United, led the Dundee attack and scored four times as Dundee cruised to a 7-0 lead. Only then did United come into the match with Meagher and Carroll grabbing a couple of consolation goals.

There was just no accounting for the team's form. Already relegated and with the pressure off, United played Hearts at Tynecastle. In a match that was a personal triumph for Welsh, the former Hearts man scored both United goals in a 2-1 win. The same player also scored as United surprised everyone again by beating Partick Thistle 2-1 a week later. That afternoon the Tannadice stand was peppered with representatives of other clubs, including Middlesbrough, St Johnstone, Hearts and Raith Rovers, all there to run the rule over a number of United players. It was by then an open secret that United would listen to offers for any player. True to form, or rather true to the lack of it, United lost the last game of the season by the odd goal in seven against St Mirren at Love Street.

Surplus to requirements, Moore had been transferred to Arthurlie in early March. At the end of the season Meagher returned to Dundee and Eddie Carroll, who had scored thirteen of United's goals, went back to Aberdeen where he was immediately handed a free transfer. Frank Carroll was freed along with Dempster, but every other player was placed on the retained list. The Board were aware of the interest being shown in several players and by retaining them all, transfer fees would be payable. The Directors were acutely aware that a season or more in the Second Division would be costly and steps had to be taken to bring in cash.

It did not take long for the exodus to begin. Three days after the last game of the season, Hearts made an offer, reported at £1,000, for Miller and United accepted. On 12th May the highly rated Jimmy Simpson, still only eighteen years of age, was signed by Rangers who put in a bid reported as £2,500 and again United accepted. The transfer was processed very quickly to make sure that Simpson was signed by Rangers in time to be included in the Scotland party that was leaving to tour Canada. A week after that Gilroy, who had been attracting interest from Celtic, was snapped up by Falkirk for a fee later reported to be £550. On the same day it was announced that Bob Crumley had given up his job as trainer at Tannadice. Towards the end of May, Welsh was next through the exit door. He moved to Charlton Athletic for an estimated £1,000.

1927-28

The Arrival of the Hurricane

It was rumoured that Kay and Bauld were planning to go to America after being approached by an agent with an offer and with a reduced retained list, Brownlie had fixed up just two players by the end of June. Dave Walker was re-signed and half back John Bain had been recruited on 1st June from Dunfermline Athletic. Over a month passed before there was any more activity but on 5th July the Manager made a trip across to Fife and signed Duncan Hutchison, who had been released by Dunfermline Athletic. It proved to be one of the most inspired of Brownlie's signings. The man who became known as "Hurricane Hutch" was soon a great fans' favourite and enjoyed two spells at the Club. Indeed, in his first season he became top scorer with thirty one goals in his thirty nine appearances. Around the same time Hutchison arrived, Tommy Simpson went to Brighton & Hove Albion and Henderson re-signed.

By the end of July, Hart, McGregor, Campbell and Paterson had all re-signed for the 1927-28 Second Division campaign. New to Tannadice was trainer Jack Qusklay, a former professional boxer who had also played football and rugby locally. One player who would not be reappearing was Bauld. There had been a lot of interest in the player from south of the border, with Middlesbrough, Stoke City and Spurs all watching him at the end of the previous season. But the popular inside forward, renowned for his thunderous shooting, went to Bradford City for a fee of approximately £350. United had to be satisfied with that. If he had taken his other option and gone to America, the Club would have received nothing.

Jock Kay was still thinking over his potential move to America, but after several talks with Brownlie he re-signed for United at the start of August. Three further additions to the squad were made after the trial match at Tannadice on 9th August. Jock McDonald was re-signed and he was joined by Archie Ralston from Law Scotia and Jacky Kay from Motherwell Juniors. John Dorward then signed from local junior side Logie. With his team rebuilt, Brownlie was ready to face the rigours of the new season.

The first match of the campaign was against Bathgate at Tannadice and United won comfortably 4-2. At Clydeholm Park a week later, United were robbed of a point as Clydebank won 2-1 with a very late goal. United struggled through the next three matches and had the defence to thank for a point in each against Queen of the South, Forfar Athletic and King's Park, and away to Arthurlie, the Black and Whites were fortunate to win 3-1. New signing Jacky Kay was proving a hit in the forward line and his fifth goal of the campaign earned United two points against Albion Rovers in a 3-2 win on 24th September. A share of the spoils in a 1-1 draw with Morton kept United in the leading pack in the league but in the Forfarshire Cup, United lost by the odd goal in seven to Dundee at Dens Park. United should have had this tie wrapped up, leading 3-1 at half time, but the Dark Blues rallied in the second half to level and then snatched a winner four minutes from the end. The match also aggravated Paterson's injury and for the second season in succession United had to find a goalkeeping replacement quickly. Fortunately, Brownlie had already seen St Andrews United keeper, Alex Johnstone in action in the trial match in August and he was signed in time to face St Bernard's in the next league match on 8th October. The new keeper played his part in a 5-3 win in which two of United's goals came from Dave Walker penalties. He might have had a rare hat-trick of spot kicks if he had not missed from a third penalty awarded!

United moved into second place in the league with seven points from the next four games, a 0-0 draw at Alloa Athletic and victories over Leith Athletic 2-0, Stenhousemuir 5-3 and East Stirlingshire 3-1. Bill Taylor joined United from Longriggend Rob Roy and made his debut as a trialist in the last of these three wins. In early December, Harry Michie was drafted into the side. He was considered one of the most promising players in the junior ranks and had signed provisionally from Alva Albion Rangers on 1st November. A dip in form however, brought just one win, 3-1 at Dumbarton, in the next six encounters and United slipped out of promotion contention. On Christmas Eve 1927, United returned from Bathgate with a hard earned two points from a 2-1 win and the fans were then treated to a winning sequence all through the festive season. A disjointed Forfar Athletic were easily overcome 4-0 on Hogmanay, and that was followed by a 2-1 home win against Alloa Athletic and a 1-0 away victory at King's Park. Newly signed from Falkirk, George Mason made his debut in the latter match but made only one other appearance in the black and white of United before he was released.

In late December, the Club's AGM took place. Not surprisingly, a deficit was announced, but no account had yet been taken of the summer transfer fees received. John Carnegie Snr was formally appointed to the Board after being co-opted in August. Unfortunately Mr Carnegie was a Director for only two months and sadly died on 4th February 1928 after a short illness.

John Carnegie Snr

With United riding high in the Second Division several players were attracting attention from elsewhere. Burnley had scouts at the 2-2 draw at Dumfries with Queen of the South. The players under scrutiny were Jacky Kay and Duncan Hutchison, and although he had been with United mere weeks, Bill Taylor was also being watched.

With all the attention focused on these players it therefore came as quite a surprise when Arsenal came in with an offer for goalkeeper Paterson. Their manager, Herbert Chapman, arrived in Dundee on the evening of the Dundee United annual dance on 11th January and insisted on discussing the possible transfer of Paterson then and there! Terms were provisionally agreed and a week later, the deal was done. Full details are not known but the player was entitled to a payment of £390 from the fee, which must therefore have been quite substantial. Paterson's send off from United was a highly memorable 9-2 win over Arthurlie with Hutchison netting his first hat-trick for United. In truth, had United taken all the chances on offer, they might have scored another nine.

The loss of Paterson was not too keenly felt as United went into the Scottish Cup tie against East Fife at Methil. Reserve keeper Johnstone took over in goal in a 1-1 draw that earned a replay for United. At Tannadice it was a different story. Superior fitness ensured that United won through 2-1 with a late Hutchison strike. The next round of the cup drew United at home to Dundee. But before that, the league challenge took a knock with a 3-2 defeat away to St Bernard's.

United were well prepared for the Scottish Cup tie against Dundee and were the better side on the day, with Dundee a little fortunate to get a second chance. In a thrilling match, Kay and Hutchison scored for United but Dundee led 3-2 at half time. Hutchison equalised after the break and United passed up several chances to go in front, although in the closing stages Dundee nearly stole it. Newly signed from Burnbank Athletic, keeper John 'Jock' McHugh made his debut in the replay but the match came nowhere near the heights of the entertaining first encounter. On a windy day, a plucky fight by United was not enough and Dundee won by a single goal.

It was back to league business and United suffered a cup hangover from their midweek tie and lost rather tamely 2-0 to Albion Rovers but the promotion challenge was back on track with a 3-2 win over Morton at Tannadice a week later. The next three matches yielded four points from a 2-2 draw with Stenhousemuir, a 3-1 win over Leith Athletic and another 2-2 result with Clydebank but United struggled in each game. The 3-1 defeat at East Stirlingshire that followed might have hurt United more, but other results on the day went in favour of the

Tannadice side and kept them in second place. Brownlie was not happy with a forward line that lacked punch and he dipped into the transfer market again to bring Tom Parker on loan from Celtic. The versatile inside forward had only recently joined the Glasgow club from Bathgate for a fee of £400 following an impressive game for the West Lothian side against Celtic in the Scottish Cup. He made his United debut against fellow promotion hopefuls Third Lanark, and a Hutchison hat-trick was the highlight of the 4-3 win. After that however, United more or less hit the self destruct button by losing 3-2 to East Fife and 3-0 at Dumbarton. A narrow win by a single goal against Arbroath left United with a slim chance but a 7-1 thrashing at Ayr United ended promotion hopes. The season was over, concluding with a featureless 1-1 draw at home to Armadale. In the final table United finished sixth but just two points behind second placed Third Lanark. The fans were doubtless disappointed, but Brownlie had assembled a good squad of players and most of them would remain for the next campaign.

Amongst all the end of season disappointment a benefit was arranged against Hearts for Jock Kay. On 9th April, a public holiday, a mere 1,000 fans turned out to honour the player who had served United so well for five years. Hearts sent a strong side and United lost 4-3. The Tannadice side also fulfilled a commitment to play St Andrews United as part of the deal that brought keeper Alex Johnstone to the Club. United lost that match 4-3 also, with former player Jimmy Russell scoring a hat-trick for St Andrews. To end the season, United met St Johnstone in Perth for the Wallace Cup and lost 3-1.

As soon as the last ball was kicked, Parker returned to Celtic, having made only three appearances for United. In the first week of May, Johnstone, Fleming, Henderson, McGregor and Ralston were freed. The latter pair both joined Montrose. McHugh, Taylor, Hutchison, Michie and Jacky Kay put pen to paper for United for the next season.

It would be a few weeks before any further signing news was announced, but Tannadice drew the crowds in the summer months for a very different reason.

GREYHOUND RACING IN DUNDEE

Tannadice temporarily goes to the dogs!

Two years earlier the Greyhound Association had been formed, with the first race taking place at Belle Vue Stadium in Manchester on 24th July 1926. In the summer of 1928, greyhound racing came to Dundee, with Tannadice the venue for two meetings each Saturday and one meeting on Wednesday evenings. There were normally seven races at each meeting with five on the flat and two over hurdles. Spectators came out in reasonable numbers but Tannadice was not really suitable for the sport on a long term basis and Dens Park became the regular venue for greyhound meetings in later years.

1928-29

Second Division Champions Again

Over the summer months leading up to the new season, Brownlie negotiated new deals with existing players and by the end of June he had re-signed Walker, Bain and Hart. The only new player at Tannadice initially, was ex-St Johnstone left back Dave McClure, signed from Nelson. Other changes at Tannadice were in the Boardroom, with A. Boyd Carnegie (son of John Carnegie Snr) becoming a Director along with Ernest Robertson.

In early July, several players from the last campaign had yet to re-sign. Dorward and McDonald were still considering their offers and both were soon transfer listed and eventually freed. Campbell refused terms and was transferred to East Stirlingshire. Stalwart Jock Kay also refused terms and he too was transferred, joining Stenhousemuir, but not until November. Dorward went on trial in October to Middlesbrough but was unable to agree terms there.

With only nine signed players and a month to go before the new season was scheduled to begin, Brownlie had to move quickly to find replacements. He became interested in two players who had recently returned from America. One was former international outside right Denis Lawson, who had been with Cardiff City and St Mirren. The other was ex-Dundee, Rangers and Darlington forward, Geordie Henderson. The interest in Lawson petered out, but the Manager was very keen to sign Henderson who, it was assumed, was still a registered Darlington player. United had tried to acquire Henderson a couple of years before but he had moved south to Darlington, costing the English side £1,500. He then played a major role in his new club's winning battle to avoid relegation. When offered re-signing terms there, he had refused and left to join New York Nationals.

United may have balked at the estimated £750 fee for Henderson but on checking the retained list it transpired that Darlington had forgotten to include the player. He was therefore a free agent. After the player himself checked the position with the English FA, Brownlie signed him at the end of July and thus

Geordie Henderson signs for United

acquired a valuable player, for nothing more than a signing on fee. For the next few weeks there were some angry noises from Darlington. They lodged a formal complaint with the English FA, who in turn asked for clarification from the SFA. The incident came to an end after the SFA confirmed that there was nothing to hinder the player's registration and United had acted within the rules.

There was no further signing activity until after the trial match on 7th August. Then, ex-Raith Rovers forward Willie Richmond, and half back David Dorward from North End were signed. Richmond lasted barely a month before being freed.

The season got underway on 11th August with a 4-0 win at Bathgate, but the record of this match and the corresponding 6-1 home win at the end of December were later expunged after Bathgate resigned from the league. Hutchison was immediately back into the scoring groove with a hat-trick in the 4-0 win although that too was obviously wiped from the records! He scored another treble in a 3-1 Dewar Shield win over East Stirlingshire a few days later. His exploits of the previous season had already brought him to the attention of several English sides. Only two games into the new term, Arsenal began showing an interest in the player, and when Wolves joined the list of Hutchison's admirers, United issued a hands-off warning. The Board made it clear that he was not for sale as he was an integral part of a young and talented United side that was aiming for promotion.

Cover was needed for the goalkeeping position and Harry McGregor, a former East Stirlingshire keeper, who had played in the trial match, signed on 22nd August. He was soon to take over from McHugh for the majority of the season's matches. McHugh had played well enough in the 4-1 league win over Bo'ness but after a 3-2 defeat by Aberdeen in the Dewar Shield final, and a 4-1 reversal at Clydebank, McGregor got the jersey. Incidentally, at the time, players still did not wear numbered shirts but the concept was introduced on 25th August 1928, when both Chelsea and Arsenal fielded players wearing numbers. In Scotland, the idea did not take on until after 1945!

Another new signing was made on 31st August when half back William (Patsy) Deuchar signed from Raith Rovers. He went straight into the side that narrowly won 1-0 at home to Dunfermline Athletic. The next game resulted in a

2-2 draw at St Bernard's, with 'Hurricane Hutch' twice levelling for United. Just after that match, Robert Gemmell arrived on trial from Hull City but he failed to impress and left after a month. Wins over East Fife 5-4, Queen of the South 3-2, Armadale 2-0, St Bernard's 3-1 and Morton 3-0 pushed United to the top of the league, a position they then maintained until the end of the campaign. But it was not all plain sailing and there were several hiccups on the road to the championship. Fellow challengers Albion Rovers gave United warning that the passage would not be easy when they won 2-0 on 13th October.

Brownlie lifted the players immediately, and United won the next four games playing some excellent football. The run started with the 5-0 hammering of Alloa Athletic in which all five United forwards scored. King's Park were then beaten 2-0, Leith Athletic 5-3 and Stenhousemuir 8-0. Michie recorded a hat-trick in the latter of these matches but surprisingly perhaps, the prolific Hutchison was not on that score sheet but it was not for the want of trying, as the whole United team tried to set him up to score at various points during the match. A surprise 3-1 defeat from Arthurlie at their Dunterlie Park home gave United another reminder that there was a long way to go, even if they were four points clear at the top.

Arbroath were then beaten 4-3, although the Angus side played much of the second half with only ten men. Hutchison scored another hat-trick in the match but Arbroath almost stole a point with a late fight back from 4-1 down. Against Dumbarton on 1st December, United were without McGregor for a period after half time but still managed a comfortable 3-1 victory. At Forfar Athletic a week later, the home side defended stoutly to keep United to just one goal in the first half and in the second period the Loons took the upper hand to win 2-1. Still, United had a cushion and remained top.

The next match at East Stirlingshire reflected the fighting spirit and resilience that defined United's season. The home side went 2-0 up in the first half and then United were further handicapped when Michie was carried off with a broken leg. The Black and Whites rolled up their sleeves and fought back with three goals to take the points. The loss of Michie seemed to affect United the following week at Bo'ness. A disjointed forward line failed to make any impact and United lost to a single goal. To cover the outside left position normally filled by Michie, Brownlie signed Jim Cameron from Lochee Harp and the outside left played in the 6-1 home win over Bathgate. Unfortunately, his goal, along with Johnny Hart's hat-trick, was wiped out after the West Lothian side resigned from the league following financial problems.

The New Year got off to a flying start with a comfortable 4-0 win over King's Park. Provisional signing John Cunningham, from Vale of Leven Juniors, was called up for that match and made an impressive debut at centre half. Two more players were signed on provisional forms; Eddie Glover of Lochee Harp and George Ross from Dalkeith Thistle. It would be three years before Glover would be called up, but Ross had to wait only a month for his debut.

Three more league points were accumulated with a 2-1 win over Clydebank and a 1-1 draw at Dunfermline Athletic. Scottish Cup business brought a visit by Morton on 19th January and United won 3-1 to advance to the next round with a show of real cup tie spirit. With no match the following week, Chairman Hutchison and Manager Brownlie headed south to London but it was not players they were looking for. The Board at United were so confident of attaining First Division status that plans were drawn up to build a new stand, and Hutchison and Brownlie were in London to find financial backing for the project. Just exactly who they were talking to is not known but they did return with assurances that money would be available if the Club could raise half of the estimated £10,000 cost. An appeal was made to the public and anyone interested in helping fund the project was invited to contact Tannadice. As the months went by there was little response and eventually the plans were shelved.

Two weeks after beating Morton in the Scottish Cup, United survived a difficult cup visit to Stenhousemuir in a 1-1 draw and then made heavy weather of the opening exchanges in the midweek replay. Cameron had one effort disallowed and United missed from the spot before Kay scored. After half time it was all United and Kay made sure with a second. The next round of the cup would bring a local derby at Dens Park but before that United had a tough league match at Dumfries, overcoming Queen of the South by the odd goal in five. When the cup tie came around it took two matches to settle it, with both sides having their chances in the first match that ended 1-1. In the replay at Tannadice, United won through with a single goal scored from the head of Henderson. The next round would take eventual Second Division champions United to Ibrox, to meet eventual First Division champions Rangers. Before that though, United dropped two valuable league points in a 2-0 defeat at Morton before thumping Armadale 5-0 to maintain top spot.

A crowd of 49,000 were at Ibrox for the Scottish Cup tie on 2nd March and they witnessed a fighting display from United who went 3-0 down before scoring a late consolation. They left Ibrox with praise from all corners, but more tangibly a cheque for almost £1,000, as their share of the gate receipts.

With a good run in the cup and steady league form, the players were again attracting attention from clubs in England. Taylor, Cameron and Hutchison were the main interest and valuations of £2,000 and £3,000 had been mentioned in connection with the latter pair respectively. News then emerged that Liverpool had made a bid for Hutchison. Whilst United had no wish to let him go, the player was told of the offer and left to make his own mind up. He opted for Tannadice but this did not stop the Merseyside club who continued to have the player monitored.

Throughout March, United continued their good form, taking eight points from five matches. In the process they scored 20 goals, with eight of those against fellow challengers Albion Rovers in an 8-1 win. In that match Hutchison scored four and Henderson netted a hat-trick. The two points lost to Leith Athletic in 3-2 defeat could have been costly, as it was around that time that Bathgate resigned. All points won by every side against the West Lothian outfit were deducted. This had the effect of tightening the top of the table as United and Morton each lost four points, whereas fellow challengers Arbroath and Albion Rovers were only deducted two. However, by winning 4-1 at Stenhousemuir with the aid of another Hutchison hat-trick, then 4-3 at home to Arthurlie and 2-1 at Arbroath, United were in a strong position. After a 1-1 draw with Dumbarton only one point was required against East Fife to secure promotion and in a close match United won 4-3. The championship was now the objective, but then United unexpectedly lost 3-0 at Alloa Athletic and 1-0 at home to Forfar Athletic. The latter result ended United's 21 game 100% home league record for the season. But it was just a short delay. At home to East Stirlingshire, United secured the top spot in the last game of the league campaign with a 3-1 win. United's scoring rate throughout the league campaign had been excellent and the total goals scored would have been over a century but for the deduction of ten against Bathgate following their resignation from the league. The 99 goals scored were a credit to the side and to Hutchison in particular, who accounted for 34 of these in his 35 appearances.

At the end of season 1928-29 there was also a flurry of cup competitions. United won a Penman Cup tie 2-1 at home to Cowdenbeath and the same score line gave United the Forfarshire Cup, beating Forfar Athletic. United also took up an invitation from Aberdeen to play for the Fleming Charity Shield. After a 2-2 draw, the clubs agreed to toss a coin for the trophy and United won. This last match was notable for one other fact. It was the first time in Scotland a senior side used a substitute; United's Bain replaced the injured McClure in the second half.

At the end of the campaign, every player was re-signed, with the exception of Dave Walker who asked for a free transfer. The Chairman, William Hutchison, had promised the players that they would all be retained if promotion was secured and he kept his word.

1929-30

Hammered Back Down

With fifteen players signed up for the forthcoming First Division campaign there was little signing activity at Tannadice during the summer of 1929. In mid May it was learned that Bill Paterson was leaving Arsenal after failing to settle in London. Although Brownlie might have considered bringing the big keeper back to Tannadice, keepers McGregor and McHugh had been fixed up already.

7th September 1929
Standing: Qusklay (Trainer), Bain, Taylor, McGregor, J. Ross, McHugh,
*   Mr Hutchison, McClure, Deuchar, Gardiner, Cunningham*
Seated: Cameron, Dorward, McNally, Thomson, Hart, Henderson, Jacky Kay, G. Ross

At the end of May, centre half George Gardiner was signed from Clydebank for around £250 and was seen as a direct replacement for Walker. On the same day another half back, George Watson, signed provisionally from Dundee North End. By the end of June yet another half back, Jock Ross, crossed the road from Dens Park. With the emphasis on the half back line, it seems that Brownlie considered that his forward players were strong enough for the challenge of top flight football.

With the plans for the new stand on hold, it was decided to improve the standing areas and some £400 was spent terracing the loose banking around the pitch. Once that was done two trial matches were arranged but no new signings followed.

In front of a crowd of 14,000, Lord Provost Sir William High guided the ropes as Mrs Hutchison unfurled the Second Division championship flag prior to the opening match against Clyde on 10th August. The visitors took the lead after a defensive error before two Hutchison goals put United ahead, but at half time it was 2-2. Clyde went in front again but United battled back, with Kay netting the equaliser for a deserved point. The next match was a Dewar Shield tie against East Stirlingshire which United lost 2-0. There were seven changes in the side, including new signing John McNally from Motherwell Juniors. The team was back on normal lines for the away match at Hamilton Academical and United played well to lead 2-1 at half time, with Kay netting both. But after the break Hamilton were unstoppable and put another four goals past a plucky Tannadice side to win 5-2.

On 24th August, Morton came to Tannadice and despite a nervy second half, United won 3-1 with Hutchison scoring the decisive third goal. Little did any of the 9,000 fans present know, but 'Hurricane Hutch' had just played his last game at Tannadice, at least for the time being. United were approached by Newcastle United for the player early the next week, and although the initial offer was turned down, when the Tynesiders increased the figure to £4,000, it became an offer that United could not refuse. Hutchison was again given the option. This time he decided he had to make the move and try his luck in English football. For his debut at St James' Park on 31st August he was cheered on by a group of employees from James F Low & Co. Ltd from Monifieth. By coincidence the firm's works outing for 300 staff was arranged in Newcastle that very weekend and a number of them went to the game to present Hutch with two good luck horseshoes before the game.

United did not waste any time finding a replacement. George Thomson was bought from Clydebank for £500 and went straight into the centre forward position in the next match, the derby against Dundee at Dens Park. A crowd of 16,000 saw both sides try their best in atrocious weather conditions but the football on view was poor. Dundee won by a single goal and United looked out of their depth at times. A few days after that, a testimonial game for Jackie Baird of Montrose ended in a 4-3 win for United and a week later, Arbroath were easily overcome 4-1 in a Forfarshire Cup tie. In the league however, United won only once in the next six games, a 2-1 victory over Queen's Park. There were problems in a defence that was shipping goals at an alarming rate. Most worrying were 6-1 defeats on consecutive matches at St Mirren and at Ayr United. In early October, United signed Edward Smith, another centre forward, from Carluke Rovers, but neither he nor Thomson seemed able to fill the void left by Hutchison, a loss more keenly felt as the season progressed.

United then surprised even their own fans when they pulled off a deserved 2-2 draw with Celtic at Tannadice on 23rd October. Celtic took a two goal lead against the run of play but Henderson scored twice to earn the point. Two points were collected the following Saturday with a 2-1 win over Cowdenbeath. The Tannadice side then lost to Motherwell, 6-1 for the third away match in a row, but recovered to win 3-2 at home to Partick Thistle and 2-0 at Kilmarnock. This brief run of form lifted United three places up the table. The players were rewarded for their efforts when Chairman, William Hutchison took them on a golf outing. Patsy Deuchar was presented with 100 cigarettes in a mahogany case for his winning round of 83. In the present health conscious society, a prize of this nature would be unthinkable!

Form fell away again and United lost 4-2 when Aberdeen were the visitors to Tannadice and then could only draw 1-1 at home to St Johnstone with Watson making his debut. United also drew the next match, 2-2 with Falkirk, but then injuries to key players hampered the side further and they lost to Hibs, Clyde and Hamilton Academical before the end of the year. In the last of those three matches new signing Andrew Findlay, from St Mirren, made his debut at right back.

The defeats kept coming, with Cowdenbeath, Ayr United and Morton all taking full points against United. The latter was yet another 6-1 thumping. In an effort to recover what was fast becoming a lost cause, Brownlie managed to obtain Andy Haddow from Clyde on loan for the remainder of the season. He also contacted Hearts and signed left half, Bruce Harley. Both made their debuts against Dundee at Tannadice. The result however, was a 1-0 win to the Dark Blues and it sent United to the bottom of the table.

Some respite from the league battle came in the Scottish Cup, with a trip to Stranraer. United won fairly easily with a Deuchar goal and a Michie spot kick conversion early in the first half. That win was followed up with a well earned 4-3 league victory at Airdrieonians, with George Ross netting a hat-trick. Unfortunately it was soon back to the losing trend again. Knocked out of the Scottish Cup, 3-0 by Partick Thistle at home, United then suffered four league defeats in a row, ending with a 7-0 thrashing from Celtic. United had also been forced to sell George Ross just after the Scottish Cup exit. With attendances down, and the bank debt rising, the Board felt they had no option but to accept the offer from Portsmouth. The reported £1,000 fee would go a long way to cover the loss of income through the turnstiles. The Board did however hold on to Bill Taylor, knocking back an offer of over £1,000 from Everton. They had revealed a profit of £1,468 when figures for the year to 30th April 1929 were disclosed in March 1930, but a lot had happened in the interim and the money that had been in the bank had long since been used up to satisfy the debenture holders and meet ongoing running costs.

Early March brought a brief upturn in fortunes with 1-1 draws against Motherwell and Partick Thistle. These results were followed by what was probably the most remarkable outcome of the entire season. Kilmarnock were the visitors to Tannadice on 22nd March and a great team effort saw United win 6-4. The Ayrshire side opened the scoring but Kay levelled from the spot and then he put United ahead. That was all in the first ten minutes. Killie then scored three to lead 4-2 at half time. The second half turned into the Andy Haddow show as he netted four times to earn the two points. If only the team had played like that all season!

Another league point was earned in a hard fought 2-2 draw with Aberdeen at Pittodrie and a week later, Hearts were the visitors to Tannadice as United clung to a slim chance of survival. Haddow put United ahead and they had chances to increase the lead before Hearts equalised. The Edinburgh side then went in front just after half time but United came back again through Haddow. But it was all to no avail as Hearts netted late to win 3-2. Only a miracle could save United from the drop but it was not to be. Fellow relegation contenders St Johnstone inflicted yet another 6-1 defeat, and then Falkirk drove in the final nail with a 5-2 win. The last league game ended in a 2-2 draw with Hibs but there was no consolation in that. United were relegated and a section of the support made their feelings known, citing the loss of Hutchison as the main reason and rather unkindly suggesting that the Club had only themselves to blame for the drop.

The season was wrapped up with a 5-1 Penman Cup defeat at Dens Park where Dundee coasted to a four goal lead by half time. It was soon five and United fans left with heads hung low and only a last minute Hart goal to remember. The defeat however, only served to underline the weakness in a United team that had been hammered into the relegation spot, conceding 109 goals in the league.

The Forfarshire Cup final two days later brought the only consolation of the season with a somewhat fortunate 2-1 win over Montrose. Haddow was again the goal hero and perhaps if he had arrived earlier in the season, the situation might have turned out differently. He was among the top scorers with ten league goals, just behind Henderson on thirteen and Kay on twelve. Henderson and Kay had almost seventy appearances between them whilst Haddow had only fourteen.

After the campaign ended, United retained only eight players; McHugh, Ross, Taylor, Watson, Gardiner, Harley, and Cameron. Haddow returned to Clyde, whilst McGregor, Findlay, McClure, Deuchar, Dorward, Bain, Cunningham,

McNally, Thomson, Smith, Michie, and perhaps more surprisingly Hart and Henderson were all freed. As the Club prepared for a season in the Second Division, they put forward a motion at the Scottish League AGM to raise the guarantee for visiting clubs from £30 to £50. It was estimated that United would be paying around £100 to each side as they left Tannadice, but the return matches would see United obtain not much more than the guarantee. The motion was presented but defeated.

1930-31

Promoted Again

Brownlie was busy again over the summer, adding to the squad for the Second
Division campaign ahead. But he had little, if any, money available to attract
players. The ranks of local junior sides were trawled and in mid May, John
Bateman and Tom Stewart, both of Dundee Violet, were signed up. Of the retained
players, Taylor and Kay were attracting interest from south of the border and
McHugh was the subject of an enquiry from Aberdeen, but the Dons backed off
as the price for the keeper was too high. Any of these three players would most
likely have been sold to ease the debt burden but in the end they all stayed to
begin the new campaign.

Haddow had been offered terms by Clyde but he had refused. United would
almost certainly have taken him back but he was transfer listed at £250 and even
that was too rich for the Tannadice Board. Brownlie therefore had to rely entirely
on free transfers and local juniors and after the trial match on 5th August he
signed both Frank Penson and Colvin Bennett from Fairfield. The latter had
netted four times in the trial. Former Dundee player James Nelson also signed
after showing up well.

The opening encounter of the new season took United to Armadale and after
Bennett gave the visitors the lead, McHugh was the star of the first half pulling off
some good saves to ensure United turned with that one goal advantage. Armadale
equalised just after the break but United then took charge with Cameron scoring
twice and Kay netting the last in a 4-1 win. United then played St Johnstone in
a midweek Dewar Shield tie but lost 2-1 to the Perth side. The league campaign
picked up pace with a point gained against Alloa Athletic in a 1-1 draw, Bennett
grabbing an equaliser. The inexperience of the United players was exposed in that
match and many observers thought that the balance was wrong. In the opinion
of some, the side contained too many young players.

This criticism may have been taken on board by Brownlie, because his next signing was the very experienced William (Tim) Williamson from Montrose. He had been with Hearts, Hamilton Academical and Clyde and made an immediate impact, playing an influential part in a one goal win at Stenhousemuir on 23rd August. The following week he scored his first United goals with a brace at home against former club Montrose. Bennett and Kay got the others in the 4-1 win, with all United's goals coming in a ten minute spell in the first half. Former schoolboy international Eric Mackay then came to United from Dundee on loan for a month, having signed for the Dark Blues only two months earlier, following his return from Canada. He played only once for United scoring both goals in the next match, a 2-2 draw at Forfar Athletic. In the same game United fielded new signing from Dundee Violet, Jimmy Milne who had first appeared on the team sheet as a trialist in the draw at Alloa Athletic two weeks before.

United then suffered a 4-2 midweek Forfarshire Cup defeat at Montrose. That was followed by a 2-1 defeat in a close game with promotion challengers Third Lanark and a 2-0 reversal at St Johnstone. Clydebank were the next visitors to Tannadice and, with Kay scoring a hat-trick, the visitors were as easily beaten as the 5-2 score line suggests. But with a 3-1 defeat at East Stirlingshire and then a 2-1 loss at home to Raith Rovers, United were slipping back in the league race and by mid October, sat nine points adrift of leaders Third Lanark. Brownlie knew he had to strengthen the side and he contacted Geordie Henderson, who was then still unattached. The terms offered were good but Henderson declined, signing instead for Rhyl at the end of the month.

United got back on track with a rather fortunate 4-2 win at Brechin City on 18th October but Brownlie was still in the market for players to improve the squad. He found Denis McCallum at Celtic and the player was acquired on loan, going straight in to the side against Queen of the South at Tannadice. He was joined in the line up on his debut by eighteen year old trialist George (Jock) Bain from Lochgelly Albert. Both players impressed the Tannadice crowd, with Bain scoring one of United's goals in the 5-2 win and he signed for United three days later.

McCallum also proved to be a good capture. In the next match at Dumbarton he was the best player on the field and scored the opening goal for United. Unfortunately Dumbarton were on top form and won 4-1 with four well taken goals. As November progressed United hit form and three home wins in a row consolidated a position amongst the leading group. McCallum and Kay scored two each in the 4-0 win over Arbroath and Williamson netted four as St Bernard's were beaten 5-3. He was also on the mark again in the 2-0 win over King's Park. Midway through this run, keeper McHugh was transferred to Portsmouth. Chairman Hutchison paved the way for McHugh's departure when he revealed that United were losing money every week, due largely to low attendances. The Chairman was not blaming the supporters as he was well aware of the problems caused by high unemployment at the time. He was merely stating a financial fact of football life. With an overdraft in the region of £4,000, the Board had to use whatever means possible to reduce it. The fee for McHugh was not publicised

United v St Bernard's 15th November 1930

at the time but several years later it emerged he had gone for just £400.

Finding a replacement keeper was now the top priority. In the meantime, amateur Willie Felton of local junior side Rioneach Mhor was handed the jersey in the match against King's Park. Felton kept his place at Bo'ness as United won 3-1, and again at Dunfermline Athletic. In that match, United were in the lead three times but had to settle for a point from a 4-4 draw. The rules only allowed Felton to play three times and another trialist (Bennett) stepped in for the 4-0 home win against Armadale.

Scotland junior international goalkeeper, Bill McCallum of YMCA Anchorage was given a trial on 27th December against Alloa Athletic. He had been the target for several other clubs and had recently played against Ireland in a 2-2 draw where he saved two penalties. United played impressively to end Alloa Athletic's nine game unbeaten home record with a 4-1 win. McCallum was then offered terms which he accepted.

January opened with the visit of St Johnstone and the biggest crowd of the season saw Bain equalise an early goal from the Perth side for a deserved point in a 1-1 draw. The visitors also went home with a cheque for £200, probably the largest payment made to any visiting side at any Second Division ground that season. In the next match, United scored all their goals in the first half in a convincing 5-2 win over Stenhousemuir but lost 2-1 the following week to a Montrose side determined to show they did not miss Williamson! Still up with the leading pack, United had a short respite from league pressures as they prepared for the visit of Nithsdale Wanderers in the Scottish Cup.

On 17th January 1931 the team from Sanquhar arrived at Tannadice for the match which would see United register their record win. The headline in the *Dundee Courier* read, "The Goal Diggers" on the following Monday and the match report confirmed that Nithsdale were completely outplayed. Kay, Bain and Harley scored one each and Williamson netted four for a 7-0 half time lead. McCallum and Bain scored two each after the interval and Williamson took his total to five, to add to goals by Kay and Cameron for a final score line of **Dundee United 14 Nithsdale Wanderers 0**. A week later it was reported in the *People's Journal* that Brownlie had instructed his players to ease off! They followed orders and after half time there were numerous chances apparently put deliberately wide or left for the keeper to collect. United could easily have scored a dozen more than they actually did. Disappointingly, a crowd of only around 800 witnessed this historic event, and the full United line up was:-

W McCallum, Taylor and Penson; Milne, Gardiner and Harley; D McCallum, Bain, Williamson, Kay and Cameron.

The next round of the cup drew United against Celtic at Tannadice two weeks later, and a bumper crowd was expected. Before that however, United had a home league match against Forfar Athletic and were fortunate to win. Leading 4-1 at half time, the Loons hit back to make the final score 4-3 but it was a narrow escape for United. Attention then turned to the cup tie scheduled for Saturday 31st January. Unfortunately the weather intervened and it was postponed, despite costly efforts to save the match. It took place four days later on Wednesday afternoon and 13,000 spectators still turned out. United fans were delighted with the team as they led 2-1 at half time with goals from Kay and Bennett, and the Black and Whites were denied a penalty before Celtic equalised. With a quarter of the game still remaining the Glasgow side wrapped it up with a third. United had given a good account of themselves but it was no less disappointing for the fans. The Directors were also disappointed and not just with the result. They had expected a sizeable windfall from a big crowd on the Saturday but that had evaporated and there was barely a profit left for the Club. Gate receipts of only £514 were almost entirely used up making a payment of over £200 to Celtic, players' wages and running costs and then paying for the unproductive work to save the Saturday tie. If the match had gone ahead as scheduled, United would most likely have doubled the gate.

Whilst the exit from the Scottish Cup was hugely disappointing, it made sure everyone at Tannadice was firmly focused on the primary target – promotion. But the next three matches did nothing to improve the chances of going up. A 1-1 draw at Tannadice with East Stirlingshire was fought out on a slush covered pitch on which neither side was able to play decent football. At Third Lanark, United were never in the game as the eventual champions won 4-0 and at Raith Rovers, defences were on top in a 0-0 draw. A formidable display in the 6-0 win at home to Brechin City kept United in the hunt but only a point each was gained from a 0-0 draw at Queen of the South and a 1-1 home draw with Dumbarton, the latter in blizzard conditions.

In an effort to improve promotion prospects, Brownlie again persuaded Clyde to allow Haddow to come on loan for the remainder of the season. He was back at Tannadice in time to face Albion Rovers who were still one of the main challengers for second spot. Haddow scored twice in the 5-0 win over Albion but the victory was inspired by McCallum. Even his sending off with two minutes remaining could not take the shine off the win. A week later Haddow was sent off in the dying minutes as he protested a little too strongly when St Bernard's scored with three minutes left, to win 2-1.

The return of Haddow had a marked impact in the remaining games. He scored twice in the 4-0 win at home to Albion Rovers, once in the 2-1 win at Clydebank and twice away to King's Park in another 2-1 win. United then beat Arbroath 2-1 in the third away match in succession, leaving just one point needed from the last two games to clinch the second promotion spot. The previous four wins had been achieved more through a dogged determination than through good football. It then came as quite a shock to lose 1-0 at home to lowly Bo'ness and that set up a decider between United and Dunfermline Athletic at Tannadice, with United still needing one point.

It was at about that time that a strange rumour began to make the rounds on the west coast. It was alleged that a United official had stated that if second place was achieved, the Club would not accept promotion on the grounds that it would cost too much to run a team in the First Division! It was of course utter nonsense, as Brownlie quickly confirmed. If the Club

Scottish Football Surprise

JIMMY BROWNLIE TO RETIRE

We learned officially last night that Mr James Brownlie is retiring from the managership of Dundee United.

The announcement will be received with surprise in Dundee and elsewhere in view of his club having won promotion to the First Division yesterday.

No one in football has had a greater or more interesting career than the man who guarded Scotland's goal in brilliant fashion on many occasions.

Born in Blantyre, Mr Brownlie joined Third Lanark about thirty years ago. Before that he had played for Celtic, Hearts, and Partick Thistle.

For nineteen years he served Third Lanark unofficially, and was seldom omitted by the Selectors from the Scottish team.

He toured Canada and the States with the first Scottish touring team.

In 1923 he was appointed manager of Dundee United, and had the unique experience of turning out at the last minute for his club against Hearts in a cup-tie. Jimmy still delights in telling how he lost six goals that day!

Sunday Post
26th April 1931

did not want promotion why then, he argued, would they go to all the effort of bringing Haddow back? Chairman Hutchison was also quick to confirm the potential financial benefits, advising that United had lost £3,000 for the season. To have a chance of recouping any of this, First Division football was a must!

In front of a crowd of 7,000, the match against Dunfermline Athletic turned out to be something of an anti-climax as United got their tactics right and Pars got it all wrong. On a heavy pitch, United adopted a route one approach and took the lead through McCallum, but allowed the Pars to level before Haddow got the winner to send United back to the top flight again. The season ended with 93 league goals scored and only Third Lanark could better that. Adding another sixteen from the Scottish Cup gave a total of 109, of which top scorer Kay had 26 and Williamson netted 22. Andy Haddow again had a great strike rate with eight goals in eight appearances.

The celebrations had hardly died down when shock news was announced. Jimmy Brownlie and Dundee United parted company on 25th April 1931! No explanation was given for the sudden resignation of Brownlie, the man who had done so much to lead United out of the wilderness over his eight years at Tannadice. Fans were left to come to their own conclusions and suspicions of a

Willie Reid

Boardroom rift were fuelled by the resignation of William Hutchison two weeks later. He too had been at United for eight years, beginning as a Director then becoming Treasurer and for the last three years, Chairman. It was announced that he had resigned for health reasons but he remained a Director and David Halley took over as Chairman.

The last outing for the team was against Dundee at Dens Park in a Loftus Cup tie. United could manage only a Williamson consolation goal with Dundee already 4-0 up in a game that was largely controlled by the Dark Blues. Immediately after this match Denis McCallum and Haddow returned to their own clubs. Bateman, Stewart and perhaps surprisingly Williamson, were freed. Cameron was placed on the transfer list but he along with Harley and Ross were freed a little later. The retained players were Bill McCallum, Taylor, Penson, Gardiner, Watson, Bennett, Bain and Kay.

United also announced plans to increase the capacity in the stand and improvements to the dressing rooms. The Board advertised the post of Manager/Secretary and received many applications. The applicants were then reduced to a short list of four; former player Johnny Hart, ex-Morton man Jock McIntyre, Hugh Shaw who had been with Hibs, Hearts and East Fife and Willie Reid. The latter was the most experienced candidate having been ten years in management at Albion Rovers. Prior to that, he had played with Morton, Third Lanark, Motherwell, Portsmouth and Rangers. He had also gained international experience in nine appearances for Scotland. His appointment was announced on 1st June and he took over two weeks later.

1931-32

Going Down for the Third Time

There were some interesting revelations concerning the promotion/relegation issue from a Scottish League subcommittee before their AGM on 27th May 1931. The members concluded that automatic promotion had not been a success because it had failed its objective; to improve the standard of teams in the lower league. The subcommittee suggested that there were too many clubs. They put forward a motion to reduce the total number from 38 to 34 with no relegation at the end of 1931-32. They further proposed that the First Division should then detach itself and re-elect 14 teams to form a smaller Second Division! Fortunately for the smaller clubs, the motion was defeated. The only other significant change for the Second Division clubs was the increase in the guarantee from £30 to £50, as United had suggested two years before.

Before United could take their place in the First Division they had to satisfy the League inspection committee that Tannadice met the required standard. Their visit in late May pronounced the ground satisfactory but the pitch had to be widened by a few yards, which meant that a retaining wall had to be repositioned. Improvements were also needed to the changing facilities. The alterations brought additional unwelcome costs at a time when finances were already stretched, but the work had to be carried out and paid for. This left the new Manager with less money available to attract players. Indeed the financial plight was such that United's Directors had to appear in Glasgow before the League Management Committee to discuss the balance sheet. Assurances that measures were being taken to redress the deficit appeased the League.

In late July, George Radcliffe signed from Albion Rovers and William Logie arrived from Portsmouth and they were the only players added before the trial match in August. Once the trial match was over, Reid added Chic McIntosh from Logie and then Andrew Jackson from Dundee North End. But it soon became apparent that a pool of only thirteen players was not enough. Just as the

8th August 1931
Standing: Taylor, Penson, Milne, McCallum, Watson, Gardner, Qusklay (trainer)
Seated: Logie, Bain, Bennett, Kay, Cuthill

season was about to kick off, David Cuthill signed on an amateur form but his registration was cancelled after the first game of the season.

After losing 2-0 at home to Hearts and 3-2 at Celtic in the opening fixtures, keeper McCallum was dropped in favour of McIntosh and United won 2-1 at Queen's Park. Harry Brant was signed from Bury before the next match against Partick Thistle which United won 3-1. Brant had cost Bury £2,000 from Albion Rovers and was listed at £1,250. However, United paid much less, acquiring him for only a nominal fee. Losing 4-2 at both Morton and Airdrieonians sent the Manager back to the transfer market again. He signed Archie Buchanan from Carluke Rovers, but his debut was delayed for two months. United then lost 4-1 at Clyde but drew 0-0 with Cowdenbeath and Kilmarnock at Tannadice, and then 1-1 away to Dundee before picking up only the third win of the season with a 1-0 win at home against St Mirren. Overall, form had been erratic in the opening ten matches with the forwards shouldering much of the blame for failing to turn chances into goals.

Although they lost 2-0 at Ayr United on the last Saturday in September, another two points were picked up in a 3-2 home win against Third Lanark a week later. United adopted a route one approach in that game and goals from Brant, Kay and Jackson in the second half left United with eleven points from thirteen games. That points total was better than at the same time in the previous First Division campaign. However only one point was taken in the next four outings and that was at home to lowly Leith Athletic in a goalless draw. Worse still, in each of the other three games United conceded five goals losing 5-0 at Motherwell, 5-2 at Aberdeen and 5-0 at Rangers, although on each occasion their play did not warrant such heavy punishment.

In an attempt to shore up a leaky defence, half back James Baillie was signed from Fulham prior to the match with Falkirk. United managed a 2-2 draw but the defensive failings were no less evident as the next three games ended in defeat. A 4-2 reversal at Hamilton Academical was followed by yet another 5-0 hammering, at home to Queen's Park. A Brant hat-trick in the next match was not enough as Morton won a close contest 4-3 at Tannadice. A point was salvaged against Clyde in a 1-1 draw but the season hit rock bottom with an 8-0 thrashing at Kilmarnock. It all started with a freak goal scored direct from a corner kick and Killie ran riot, with Aitken netting five.

Changes were considered essential and three new players were signed before the next match against Hearts at Tynecastle. Centre forward Jimmy Dyet was brought from Falkirk and former Scottish international centre half Dave Morris came from Preston North End. He had cost Preston £5,000 and had been listed at £1,500 but arrived at Tannadice for around £500. These two were joined by George McGlynn who signed on an amateur form from St Andrew's University. All three made debuts against Hearts but only McGlynn impressed in yet another 5-0 defeat. The next match produced probably the shock result of the season as United pulled off a one goal win over Celtic on Boxing Day, with a stunning goal from Dyet.

The festive season programme continued with a well earned 1-1 draw at Cowdenbeath on New Year's Day but it was a tired United that lost 3-0 to Dundee at Tannadice the following afternoon. The run of poor league results continued with a 3-0 defeat at Partick Thistle where Eddie Glover made his debut. Signed from Lochee Harp on a provisional form three years earlier, Glover joined United at the same time Radcliffe departed to join Falkirk. United next had to face Second Division Hibs at Easter Road in the Scottish Cup. It was something of a role reversal for the two sides as each was usually found in the opposite league. 14,340 spectators witnessed a first half in which United led 3-1 with one goal from Dyet and two from Brant. Hibs pulled another one back but United went through and left with a share of the second highest gate of the day.

After such a noteworthy win away from home, a Tannadice crowd was stunned a week later as fellow strugglers Airdrieonians thrashed United 7-2 in the league. This result did little to instil any confidence for the impending visit to Dumfries in the next round of the cup. But United recovered and at Palmerston Park, a record crowd of more than 8,000 were treated to a pulsating match that ended 2-2, with McGlynn giving United the lead. Queen of the South levelled from the spot and after half time they went in front but Bennett restored parity. A bumper 12,000 crowd attended the midweek replay with almost half of those taking advantage of reduced price admission for the unemployed. They were not disappointed. Another exciting encounter ended in a 1-1 draw with the sides unable to settle the tie even after extra time. The second replay was scheduled for the following week and United's warm up game at home to Ayr United ended in a 2-1 defeat but the Black and Whites threw it away in the final minutes after leading at half time.

When United and Queen of the South came out for the second replay at Ibrox, they were perhaps surprised to find a crowd of 13,000. United won through and progressed to the next round of the cup, but only with benefit of some good luck on their side. Bennett opened the scoring midway through the first half, but a minute later Queens were level. Dyet grabbed the winner with only six minutes left but either side could have won it.

The next round brought Kilmarnock to Tannadice. Duncan Hutchison was at the game to see his former Club go one up with a Gardiner header from a corner just on half time, but a defensive error cost the equaliser late in the second half. The cup marathon was having an adverse effect on the players and the midweek trip to Rugby Park ended United's interest in the tournament. There were several players carrying injuries and with the home side leading 2-0, United's Gardiner was carried off with a fractured jaw. An already difficult task became impossible and Kilmarnock scored again to win comfortably 3-0. There was of course one major benefit of such a long run in the cup. Over the six cup ties, United shared in total gate money of more than £1,500.

With interest in the cup over, United could now concentrate on the league but the next two games ended in big defeats at Tannadice, with Motherwell winning 6-1 and Aberdeen 4-0. The Club were undoubtedly hampered by a number of injuries and tried, unsuccessfully, to bring players on loan to cover.

A chance of First Division survival was resurrected with a visit to Leith Athletic where United won 5-1. But it was only a temporary relief as they went on to lose the remaining five games against Rangers 5-0, Falkirk 4-0, Third Lanark 4-1, St Mirren 5-1 and Hamilton Academical 5-0, finishing second bottom, fully eight points adrift. Even then a slim flame of redemption flickered when it became known that East Stirlingshire might not be permitted to enter the top flight because of their involvement with greyhound racing at their ground. It came to nothing and, like the drowning man who goes under for the third time, United stayed down for almost thirty years.

The problem all season had been twofold. The defence lost goals too easily and the attack was unable to convert chances. The goals for and against columns confirmed this, with United's record 118 against beaten only by bottom club Leith Athletic. Every other side, including Leith, scored more than United's 40. Top goal scorer for United was Brant, with 14 in league and cup matches. No other player managed to get into double figures. The end of the league campaign also saw the departure of trainer Jack Qusklay. After five seasons at Tannadice, in which he had never missed a game, he left to join Celtic.

The season was rounded off with the local cups. East Fife knocked United out of the Penman Cup with a 2-1 win in Methil. But in the Forfarshire Cup at Dens Park on 27th April, United belied their lowly league position with an excellent display to beat Dundee 3-2. Instead of the usual interest expected for a derby the crowd was a mere 2,000. In the final at Gayfield three days later a tired looking United lost by a single goal to Montrose but in truth it could have been a lot more.

1932-33

Declining Fortunes

There was very little activity at Tannadice during the early summer months of 1932. Charles Whyte was the first new signing, joining United from Arbroath Ardenlea in early June. Most of the squad from the previous season had been released and Reid initially retained only six players from the unsuccessful First Division campaign; McIntosh, Taylor, Penson, Kay, Dyet and Milne. Morris was transfer listed but he too was soon freed.

Following the departure of Qusklay, the job of trainer attracted the most attention and there were hundreds of applicants but very few were seriously considered. In any event, the decision was held over until the Directors made up their minds whether to stay full time or revert to part time. The outcome was perhaps inevitable, as financial constraints decreed that United could only afford to pay part time wages. As if the cut in wages was not bad enough, the players were also informed that there would be no bonuses except in special circumstances, such as a good Scottish Cup run. This latest piece of news brought a transfer request from Kay and United agreed to listen to offers.

Reid then announced a new signing policy. He decided that he would rather have strong young players instead of 'old first leaguers'. He re-signed Watson in early July and by the end of the month he had added Walter Hotson from Falkirk and Joseph Connolly from Leith Athletic. On 22nd July, former Tannadice favourite Johnny Hart was confirmed as the new trainer, a popular choice amongst the support.

Brant and Buchanan re-signed in early August but it took some persuasion from Reid to finally obtain the signature of Kay only two days before the season started. Milne was another who had yet to agree terms and when the season kicked off on 13th August, United only just managed to put a team on the pitch to face Hibs in the opening fixture at Easter Road. It was a sweltering hot day but both sides still produced a good match. Hibs won 2-0, but United took a lot

1932–33
Standing: *Taylor, Penson, McIntosh, Buchanan, Watson, Gardiner*
Seated: *Whyte, Brown, Ouchterlonie, Brant, Kay*

of credit for their display. The Directors were also pleased to leave with a cheque for £170, well above the minimum guarantee of £50 and the largest payment they would receive at any away ground that season. The same eleven then won at Tannadice a week later, more comfortably than the 2-1 score line against Stenhousemuir suggests. Even this early in the campaign the squad was clearly too small. With trialists in for the injured Hotson and Kay in the third match at East Fife, United lost by a single goal. One of the trialists was John Brown of Inverkeithing Juniors and after another outing he was signed up.

Enforced changes were made to the line up before the 4-1 defeat at Raith Rovers and the Manager was glad to finally see Gardiner re-sign in time to face Alloa Athletic in the 1-1 draw a week later. Dundee Osborne's Willie Ouchterlonie played in that match as a trialist. United then lost by a single goal away to Queen of the South but with Ouchterlonie on again, they took two points at home to Arbroath in a 2-1 win and the team was beginning to settle. A week later Dumbarton fell 5-2 at Tannadice, with Dyet getting a hat-trick. The next match, at Armadale, saw Ouchterlonie appear for his third and final trial game. Hotson and Connolly were by now surplus to requirements and had been released. Although United lost 5-3 at Armadale, Ouchterlonie again impressed and was signed just afterwards to become the find of the season, ending it as United's top scorer with fifteen goals. The result against Armadale did not count in the final analysis as the West Lothian side were expelled from the Scottish League at the end of November for failure to pay guarantees. They joined Bo'ness, expelled three weeks earlier for the same reason. The decision to disregard all the matches involved was not made until early April 1933 at which time all the remaining clubs had their points totals adjusted.

During the early part of the season, United were approached more than once by Charlton Athletic for Jimmy Milne on loan for trials but the Directors refused to allow this. Milne was however, transferred in early October to join Preston North End. By then, United had found form and had collected full points with a 1-0 win against St Bernard's, a 4-1 win at Forfar Athletic and a 3-1 victory over Montrose. The improvement had not enticed the fans back to Tannadice though and attendances were well below those of the First Division campaign. The ensuing weeks did not improve the likelihood of bigger crowds as the next thirteen matches produced only seven points. United lost 4-2 at home to Dunfermline Athletic and were then hammered 7-2 at King's Park before managing draws with East Fife 3-3, Arbroath 0-0 and Edinburgh City 1-1. A 2-1 defeat at Leith Athletic followed but United took full points from a 2-0 win against Albion Rovers and a 3-1 win over Brechin City. The next five games however, all ended in defeat.

With his limited resources, the Manager tried to strengthen the squad during December. After playing as trialists, James Lindsay signed from Bowhill Rovers and David Laing from East Craigie. They were joined by former Dundee outside right Peter Gavigan, who had spent a month at Montrose but was by then a free agent. All three eventually made their contribution, but their impact was not as immediate as had been hoped. It was not until the 2-1 result against Raith Rovers on 7th January that they tasted victory.

The following week, United lost 1-0 at Alloa Athletic in the league and then prepared for the Scottish Cup tie at Armadale. It would be the last senior game ever played by the West Lothian side. United had offered a good price to buy the ground rights but Armadale understandably wanted the match on their home ground. United won the tie with ease 2-0, scoring through Brant and Brown in the second half. The Tannadice players warmed up for the next round of the cup with a mid week 3-1 friendly win against a Dundee Junior Select. The cup tie against St Johnstone was next and produced the biggest gate of the season at Tannadice, with a crowd of 19,513. It might have been even bigger had St Johnstone acceded to United's request to open a sixpenny gate for the unemployed, but the Perth club would not agree. Kay put United in front just before half time. St Johnstone drew level with a very harshly given penalty and only after the referee had consulted both linesmen. United were caught cold after the penalty award and by half time it was 3-1 to the Perth side. They got a fourth just after the interval but United rallied and were then denied a clear penalty for hand ball. Dyet scored twice in the last fifteen minutes and the match ended in a 4-3 defeat, with United on the offensive until the final whistle, but unable to get the equaliser they deserved.

After the Scottish Cup exit, there was very little to play for and support dwindled over the remaining few weeks of the season. United were lying more than half way down the league with eight games remaining and that position was not improved with just two points taken from the next four matches. United won well at home to Forfar Athletic 4-1 but suffered league defeats away at St Bernard's 3-2, Montrose 3-0 and Dunfermline Athletic 5-1. They also lost a Forfarshire Cup tie 4-1 at Montrose.

In a local competition for the High Cup, to be played over two legs, United met Dundee at Tannadice on 11th March in the first leg. Despite Ouchterlonie scoring first, Dundee were 4-1 ahead before Brant and Brown got it back to 4-3, but in the end a stronger Dundee scored again to win 5-3. There is incidentally no record of the second leg ever being played. The High Cup match was also the last appearance of Bill Taylor in a United shirt. He had attracted interest from several clubs, with Newcastle United, Celtic and Motherwell all reported to have made offers. When First Division St Johnstone came in with their bid, the Board had little option but to accept and the lack of income through the turnstiles had a significant bearing on the decision. Taylor had been a big favourite with the fans, having racked up 209 competitive matches. In the pre-1945 era, only Duncan Hutchison and Jacky Kay could claim more.

Getting back to league business the following week, United extracted a measure of revenge for the big defeat at King's Park earlier in the campaign. Laing and Ouchterlonie each scored a hat-trick in the 7-3 win at Tannadice but the architect of the victory was Gavigan. Unfortunately there were only around 650 fans present to witness the best display of the season. The following week, only 200 turned out for the 5-0 win over Edinburgh City and at the home match against Leith Athletic a week later, United won 4-3 in front of just 800 spectators.

Two days later United and Dundee met again in yet another local competition, the Robertson Cup. This time it was at Dens Park. There was no real interest in the match with a mere 1,000 turning up to see a 2-2 draw that flattered a full strength Dundee. With no match the following week, United went north on a short highland tour. They lost 2-0 at Elgin City and then travelled to Fraserburgh where the sides played out an entertaining 3-3 draw. Returning home for the last game of the season on 22nd April United ran out 3-1 winners against Brechin City in a league match.

After spending the previous season in the First Division, United had been expected to do a lot better than finish in fourteenth place in the Second Division. The lack of support showed what the fans thought of it, or did it? Times were hard financially with the country in the grip of a recession and unemployment was at record levels. Attendances were rarely in excess of a couple of thousand. The bigger crowds were only likely to turn out to see matches involving local sides

Montrose, Arbroath and Brechin City or against Hibs and of course St Johnstone in the cup. With money so tight, perhaps the fans just had to be very selective, as many could not afford the shilling (5p) for each home game.

After the season ended, United were forced to release a number of players, many of whom under different circumstances might have been kept on. Gardiner, Penson, Buchanan, Watson, Gavigan, Dyet and Whyte were all allowed to leave whilst Brant was transfer listed. As financial considerations were paramount, only six players were retained; McIntosh, Lindsay, Brown, Laing, Kay and Ouchterlonie. Even First Division Dundee had announced that they would not be paying retained players any summer wages, confirming the widespread financial problems in football generally. Alloa Athletic put forward a proposal at the Scottish League to the effect that the guarantee should be scrapped, thus leaving each club to be self supporting financially. The motion was defeated, much to the relief of many of the smaller clubs. But the season ahead would be the most difficult encountered by most of the league clubs and several, including United, would teeter on the brink of collapse.

1933-34

To the Edge of Oblivion

There was some unwelcome news for the players during the summer. The Board decided that bonuses would only be paid if United finished the season in the top three of the league. Once negotiations began with the retained players, Kay and McIntosh were not happy with the terms offered and both were added to the transfer list with a figure of £100 placed against each. Lindsay, Laing, Brown and Ouchterlonie re-signed in July and United also received hundreds of applications from potential new players. Then, in a complete reversal of the previous season's policy, Reid advised that he would be looking to put together a team of experienced First Division men instead of relying on younger players from the juniors!

On 3rd July, Fred Murray from Cowdenbeath was the first new signing and he was quickly followed by Hugh Foy from Bo'ness and keeper Archie Milliken from Kilmarnock. Later that month Reid was successful in bringing back George Ross from Portsmouth. A year earlier, the player had been listed at £750 but had gone to Ireland and played with Bray Unknowns, where he linked up with another former United man, David Dorward. On returning to Portsmouth his fee was reduced to £250 but Reid somehow acquired the player for nothing.

There were further signings after the trial match on 5th August when William Sinclair from Arbroath and William Low from Fraserburgh were added. Low had impressed in the side that had drawn with United at Fraserburgh during the trip north in April. Season tickets for the stand went on sale in late July at 25 shillings (£1.25), but the take up was poor and the crowd for the opening match against East Fife was barely 4,000. United's team was not even fully recruited. Two trialists lined up in the eleven, alongside five players making debuts, plus three from the last campaign along with George Ross. McIntosh was still holding out for improved terms whilst Kay was also unavailable. He had still not agreed terms and was allowed to go to Blackpool on a month's trial. Not surprisingly perhaps, it was a disjointed United that lost 3-1.

A week later, United gained full points from a 2-1 win at Alloa Athletic. In that match Dave Corbett from Ayr United played as a trialist for the second time and was signed a few days later. Charles Campbell from Clyde and Laurie McBain from St Johnstone were added to the side in early September. Milliken and Foy were released whilst James (Chic) Weir was signed on a one month deal after he was freed by Dunfermline Athletic. All this trading in players had only a minimal effect and the next six games brought only three points from a 2-2 draw at home to East Stirlingshire and an easy 2-0 victory at Montrose. Prior to that United had lost four in a row with frequent changes in the line up. First, a sorry display at home to Forfar Athletic resulted in a 3-0 defeat. Then United were unlucky to lose 4-2 at Dumbarton and 2-0 at home to Morton but the 3-0 defeat at St Bernard's could have been much worse if McIntosh, who was by then re-signed, had not been in such good form. New signings Bill Masson from Carluke Rovers and David Willis from Ayr United made their debuts in the East Stirlingshire match as trialists and both were later signed.

United lost another four games in succession beginning with a 3-2 Forfarshire Cup defeat by Dundee. Stenhousemuir then came to Tannadice and won 4-2 with ease and United lost 5-2 at league leaders King's Park. Another 4-2 defeat was inflicted on the visit to Brechin City where ex-United man Osborne did most of the damage. Weir returned to Dunfermline Athletic after his month was up, allowing Ouchterlonie to re-establish himself in the centre forward position. Kay was back out on trial, this time at Crystal Palace whilst Sinclair and Low were both released in early October and Murray in November after failing to meet expectations. Harry Nicolson was transferred from St Johnstone on a one month deal in late October. In his debut, United recorded their first points for a month with a 4-2 win at home to Dunfermline Athletic. United were then unlucky to lose 4-3 at Albion Rovers but were poor against Montrose who won 2-1 at Tannadice. Just after that, United began to string together a few results, starting with a 9-3 win against Edinburgh City in which Ouchterlonie netted five times. Unfortunately only 200 hardy souls witnessed the event, all huddled in the Tannadice stand on a windswept rainy afternoon.

Nicolson left after his one month deal ended to be replaced by Johnnie Herbert from East Fife in time for the game against Alloa Athletic which United won 2-0. After losing the next match 4-1 at home to Raith Rovers, United turned in another good performance in which Ouchterlonie scored four of the goals against Leith Athletic in a 5-1 win. But the most remarkable game was probably the 4-4 draw with Arbroath on 16th December witnessed by United's second biggest crowd of the season, 7,300. Provisional signing Bobby Gardiner scored a debut goal to give United the lead. They held their own until the Red Lichties levelled and then raced into a 4-1 lead. With twenty minutes left, United were reduced to ten men when McBain was carried off with a broken leg. United netted twice through Ross and ex-Dundee forward James (Monty) Munro who

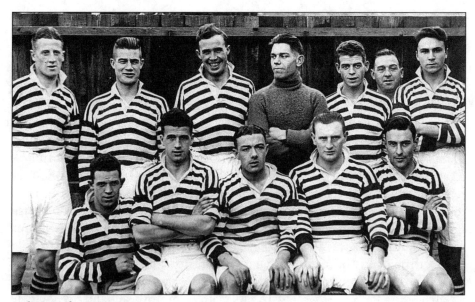

11th November 1933
Back Row: Lindsay, Brown, Corbett, Trialist (Cargill, East Craigie), Campbell, Willis?, Masson
Front Row: Laing, Ross, Ouchterlonie, McBain, Nicolson

had just signed. United almost lost the chance to save the points when the referee stopped play ten minutes too early! He had failed to time the game properly and only restarted after his error was pointed out by United officials and players and confirmed with the linesmen. Gardiner got the equaliser four minutes from the end. United's woes continued however, with a 5-1 defeat at East Fife and a 4-4 draw at home to Dumbarton.

William McIntosh

Off the field, United's troubles appeared even more worrying than on it. The financial statements for the year ended 30th April 1933 were disclosed at the AGM on 19th October. A loss of £3,327 for the year was revealed and the accumulated loss now being carried was £6,189. Wages had accounted for £2,570 but with average attendances reduced by around 4,000 and a poor run in the Scottish Cup, gate receipts were down by £1,350. There were immediate fears that United might soon go the way of Armadale and Bo'ness, especially in view of the continued low attendances. Although it was admitted that drastic action was required, the Directors were still positive. It was not quite time to throw in the towel. All the Directors were present at the AGM and they were joined by several shareholders, including William McIntosh and A B MacBain (both former directors of Dundee) who had acquired shares in Dundee United only weeks before.

In early November there was no sign of any improvement in the Club's financial plight and the assistance of the debenture holders was sought. After a meeting chaired by William Hutchison, they agreed to lend United the sum of £368. This was the balance of the account which held the interest and capital payments that had been made and not yet distributed to the debenture holders. A condition of this loan was that a committee representing the debenture holders and the directors should be formed to establish the way forward. Debenture holders' representatives John Carnegie Jnr, George Greig, W A Clark, James Laird and John Wallace were joined by representatives from the Board for this purpose. Both sides of the table had the best interests of Dundee United to the fore and were eager to find a way to make the Club successful again.

As attendances continued to fall, one Director was quoted by the *Peoples Journal* on 2nd December 1933 saying, "It simply cannot go on. We cannot run a club on the gates we are getting. Unless matters improve, and improve quickly, we will have no choice but to put up the shutters."

Herbert was freed after his month was up. He was replaced by Bobby Gardiner who became a signed player just after the New Year's Day 4-3 defeat at Morton. A few days later, only 500 fans turned up to see Gardiner net twice in a 4-1 win over St Bernard's. The following week in an Angus derby, Brechin City won at Tannadice with a single goal. Much hinged on the outcome of the Scottish Cup when United travelled to Alloa Athletic on 20th January. United had already beaten the Clackmannanshire club twice in league outings and a win was confidently expected. Indeed anything less would be a disaster for United. The 4-2 defeat was therefore more or less the final straw. After United lost the next two league matches 4-2 at Arbroath and 2-1 at Edinburgh City, the Directors decided it was impossible to continue.

As far back as 4th January, Ernest Robertson had expressed doubts as to United's ability to fulfil their fixtures without a successful cup run. A public appeal a week later in the *Dundee Courier* resulted in several prominent businessmen coming forward and a reconstruction proposal was discussed. A Reconstruction Committee was formed and the prospects for the Club looked promising. However, cash was still urgently needed and a further appeal was made on 16th January by the Reconstruction Committee. A subscription list was opened and the committee members were to use their influence to bring in much needed financial help and they pulled no punches, saying, "We want money – that is the long and the short of it".

Little if any cash came in and crisis point was reached around mid February. The Club's liabilities were estimated at £18,000 and an offer to creditors of 5/- (25p) in the pound was made. The largest creditor refused and that action alone prevented any further moves towards reconstruction. That creditor appears to have been the bank, as they insisted that in any reconstruction United would "remain liable for the entire overdraft". This was unacceptable to the parties interested in the reconstruction. There were three home games coming up and that meant payment of guarantees totalling £150. A meeting of shareholders on 16th February agreed that under the prevailing conditions the Club could not go on. Four days later, a letter was sent to the Scottish League advising that Dundee United was withdrawing from the competition, unable to complete the remaining eight fixtures.

At the eleventh hour a scheme to save United was formulated by William McIntosh and Bailie George Greig. They agreed to provide sufficient money to ensure United survived until the end of the season, guaranteeing to cover any losses whilst allowing United to retain any profits. The only stipulation made was that they would take charge of the Club to protect their investment, and at the end of the season the financial position would be reassessed. Although United's letter to the league had been received, it had not yet been tabled, so it was taken off the agenda. On 1st March, United were given the green light to continue. At the same time it was announced that Jimmy Brownlie was to return as Manager. Willie Reid had left at the point United tendered their letter to the Scottish League.

On 3rd March, United were back in business with a home match against King's Park, one of the stronger sides in the league. An unemployed gate was introduced but did little to boost the crowd, numbering only 1,500. They were the lucky ones who saw United hammer eight past the Stirling side and "the Brownlie factor" had a major influence on the outcome. Ross scored two good goals and Laing also hit a beauty, with Ouchterlonie getting the other five. Gardiner though, was the star of the show even without scoring. Leith Athletic were the next to face a United onslaught and the change in fortunes baffled everyone. The Edinburgh side hardly had a chance to play. With two goals in ten minutes and a 4-0 lead by half time, United totally dominated. They eased off but still scored again and won 5-2. Gardiner was again the star and this time he netted two goals for himself.

Meanwhile, more trouble was brewing off the pitch. On 10th March the debenture holders, represented by Charles Stuart had lodged a petition with the Court of Session for the appointment of a Judicial Factor in terms of the security held over Tannadice. During the legal arguments that followed, it emerged that there were in fact two classes of debenture holders. The first group was made up of a large number of subscribers who had paid cash, with their holding covered by a security over Tannadice and they were owed £2,274. The second group were the collateral debenture holders who had received their holding to replace debts due to them by United. Included in this latter group, who were in total owed £7,980, was William Hutchison, the late William Hogg and John Carnegie & Son Ltd. The case would rumble on for a year before a solution was achieved.

The team's return to form did not last and United lost 2-0 to Stenhousemuir, 1-0 to Dunfermline Athletic and 4-1 to Forfar Athletic, all away from home. The next match was again away from home and brought one point in a 1-1 draw on 7th April at East Stirlingshire, another club that had only just survived a financial crisis. A month earlier they had been suspended by the Scottish League for failure to pay a guarantee to a visiting club, but within days they made the payment and were reinstated. The circumstances focused attention on the problems of the smaller clubs. There were those in power who felt that the whole question of a Second Division should be addressed. With the demise of Armadale, Bo'ness, Broxburn United, Bathgate and Clydebank allied to the problems at United, East Stirlingshire and some others, should there indeed be a Second Division and if so should the numbers be reduced? It was even suggested that the bottom two in the current season should be discarded and no clubs re-elected. At Tannadice careful note was taken of these suggestions as United were second bottom at the time.

With a blank league Saturday on 14th April, United faced Dundee at Dens Park in a Penman Cup tie. The Dark Blues won 4-0 with United failing to produce anything in attack. A week later mid-table Raith Rovers were the visitors at Tannadice. Although United won 5-2, the score line was quite flattering but it did set up an intriguing last match. Albion Rovers were the final day visitors to Tannadice and much was at stake. First and foremost, if they were to avoid the need to seek re-election, United had to win to move up one place in the table. Montrose would then fall to second bottom. Arbroath were in second top spot but only a United win would keep them there to gain promotion. Albion Rovers were in third place and had to win to take the championship and go up. With so much at stake, there were supporters from all four clubs in the 8,700 crowd. They witnessed a titanic struggle with some uncompromising play, particularly from the visitors. Two defensive errors gave Albion Rovers the lead and they netted a good third. Tempers ran high and there was an incident on the touchline involving players and spectators. Only the intervention of the police prevented the situation getting out of hand. When calm was restored, United's Lindsay and the visitors' Liddell were ordered to the dressing room. Laing then got two goals back in the final six minutes, both from the spot, but it was not enough and United finished on the second bottom rung.

The following day United announced that only McIntosh, Corbett, Masson, Ross and Gardiner were being retained. Jacky Kay was still on the books but transfer listed. The surprise in the list of freed players was top scorer Ouchterlonie. He had netted 25 of United's 81 goals in the league, a total beaten only by Dunfermline Athletic in second place and Arbroath in third. However in the goals against column, only bottom club Edinburgh City conceded more than United. For the next few weeks it all went quiet at Tannadice, leaving the supporters wondering what the future had in store.

1934-35

The Brownlie Revival

United's continued existence hinged on two events; re-election to the Scottish League and the financial reconstruction. At the Scottish League AGM on 31st May 1934, United were unanimously re-elected along with Edinburgh City. There is little doubt the influence of William McIntosh helped. He had a long association with the governing bodies in Scottish football, having been Honorary Treasurer of the SFA some years before. With that hurdle overcome it was confidently expected that the Club would continue with Greig and McIntosh helping to formulate the financial reconstruction.

Brownlie began to get his team together, but by the end of the first week of August he had re-signed only Gardiner, Corbett, Ross and Masson. McIntosh had asked to be placed on the transfer list and joined Preston North End in mid December. After the trial match on 8th August, at which a crowd of 10,000 attended, only former Ayr United and Aldershot player Bobby Yorke was added. A frantic search for players brought four new faces on the eve of the first league match. They were Alec King and Willie MacRitchie from Clyde, former Hibs centre Jimmy Hart and Jimmy Smith from East Stirlingshire. Jacky Kay re-signed in time to play in the opening match against Forfar Athletic. There was still no replacement goalkeeper and McCormack of Dundee Violet filled in. United had five new men making debuts and won 2-0 with goals from King and Hart.

The following week the Manager added ex-Celtic and Ayr United full back Willie Fleming and keeper Peter Robertson, who had been with Charlton Athletic, to bring the squad up to twelve players. These twelve, plus Arthur Milne who signed in October, made up the squad who would transform United on the park over season 1934-35. Tommy Ross was signed from Osborne in December but his contribution consisted of just a single appearance near the end of the campaign.

11th August 1934
Standing: *Yorke, Corbett, Trialist (McCormack, Violet), Masson, MacRitchie,*
              Kay
Seated: *Ross, Gardiner, Hart, Smith, King*

In the second match of the season it was just like old times at Tannadice. Brownlie had put together a team on a shoestring and the signs were good. 7,000 fans turned out and saw a solid United performance result in a 5-2 win over Dumbarton. But a week later Third Lanark, who would go on to win the Second Division, thumped United 5-0 at Cathkin Park. Dubbed "the mighty atom", Bobby Gardiner was the star of the opening games and against Raith Rovers in the next match he scored twice in United's 4-0 win.

Further developments in the Club's financial situation brought the resignation of Hutchison as trustee for the debenture holders in September and then the Judicial Factor was formally appointed. He took control of Tannadice with the power to sell the ground to meet the debt and when the matter had first been made public six months earlier he did indeed state his intention to put Tannadice up for sale at £2,000! However it made no sense to sell the ground as the debenture holders would not be paid in full.

The early season optimism was waning as United took only five points from the next seven games. First, United lost 3-1 at King's Park on 8th September and then were in the lead three times against Montrose before finally winning 4-3 at Tannadice. A single goal was enough to give St Bernard's the points in the next match and United left it late to win 2-0 against Alloa Athletic. Two up at Morton, United then conceded three goals and were fortunate to level it at 3-3 for a point. The next two games were at home to Third Lanark and Cowdenbeath and on both occasions, the Black and Whites lost 2-0. But when they went to Brechin City on 27th October, United completely overwhelmed the Glebe Park side to establish a record 8-0 away league win. The scorers with two goals each were Yorke, Gardiner, Smith and King. Coincidentally, it was around this time that

United were at loggerheads with Brechin City over the signing of Arthur Milne from junior side, Brechin Victoria. United announced that Milne had signed on 12th October. It therefore came as a surprise when he was listed to play for Brechin City against Dumbarton the following weekend! The case was referred to the SFA and pending the outcome, Milne was unable to play for either side or for his junior team!

United kept the player after the case went before the football authorities but Brechin City were rather severely penalised. The Angus club were fined two guineas (£2.10) and officials Jack Osborne (player/secretary) and Cecil Robertson were both suspended from taking part in football for the rest of the season. The punishment must have been reduced at a later date as ex-United man Osborne, was playing for Brechin City again by December. It later transpired that the Brechin City registration form had been dated in mid August but had not been submitted within the prescribed 14 days. The form received was signed on 15th October with United's on 12th October. It took the League Management Committee until 9th November to confirm United could play Milne and the player himself was exonerated of any wrong doing by the Scottish Junior FA when they completed their own investigation in early December.

After the record win at Brechin City, results were again mixed, with a 3-2 win over Arbroath despite having Fleming injured early and ineffective throughout most of the match. A point was dropped in the 1-1 draw at East Fife after the home side scored in the last minute and against Leith Athletic, United failed to make the best of their superior play and it ended 2-2. A single goal defeat at Cowdenbeath resulted from a poor display by both sides. With Milne now eligible to play, Brownlie decided to give him a debut in the home match against Edinburgh City on 28th November. The outcome in that match produced the highest aggregate number of goals ever scored in a senior match at Tannadice. Fifteen were shared, with United winning 9-6. It may come as surprise to learn that the amateurs from Edinburgh were actually 4-1 up after half an hour with Milne scoring for United, but after that, the show belonged to the debut man. He finished the match with four goals to his credit whilst Ross and King scored two each and Smith scored one.

In the run of six matches that followed, United dropped only one point and that lifted the Club into promotion contention. A 2-1 home win over King's Park was followed by two colossal scores on consecutive Saturdays as United thrashed Edinburgh City 8-2 with the help of a King hat-trick and then thumped Brechin City 9-2 with a Ross hat-trick and four goals from Milne. The excellent run of results continued with a return of five points from three matches over the festive season. The Black and Whites were 3-0 up at Alloa Athletic but then lost three goals themselves including a last minute penalty. They then deservedly won two home matches, 4-1 against Morton and 4-0 against East Fife. After seven games without defeat United came a cropper, losing 5-1 at Dumbarton but the score line flattered the west coast side. Attention was turning towards the Scottish Cup in mid January. As a forerunner to the away tie at Fraserburgh, United had to battle hard for two points in the 5-3 league win over Forfar Athletic.

United travelled to Highland League Fraserburgh on Scottish Cup business and the sides served up a game that was long remembered in the Buchan town. The match was played in winds of up to 60 mph. In the first half a hailstorm lasting twenty minutes caused more problems, but by then United were 4-0 up. Smith and Ross got one each and King scored twice. His second came direct from a corner after the home keeper took a goal kick and the wind blew the ball out for a corner kick. Another freak goal was scored just before half time. Corbett fired in a 30 yard free kick but the referee could not decide if the ball had gone in between the posts or through a hole in the side netting! After consulting both linesmen the goal was given. Against the wind after the break, Gardiner made it 6-0 and only then did the home side come to life with two late goals.

United earned another league point with late goals from Ross and Milne in a 2-2 draw at Arbroath in the run up to the next round of the cup, a home tie with Queen's Park. An unemployed gate costing 7d (3p) helped boost the crowd to more than 21,000, and the match, which ended 6-3 for United, was voted the best game seen in Dundee for years. It was 2-2 at half time with Milne and Smith netting for United. After the break, United had a goal chalked off, then Milne scored three in the space of four minutes and King got the sixth from the spot before the visitors scored their third.

Fellow promotion chasers St Bernard's took a league point at Tannadice a week later in a 3-3 draw, but the cup was still the main focus, with a visit to Hearts awaited. Almost 30,000 witnessed the first encounter at Tynecastle on 23rd February. Milne and King scored with spectacular efforts as United rocked Hearts and led 2-0 at half time. Hearts pulled both goals back and went for a winner but United also had chances and a replay was no less than they deserved. This time there was no unemployed gate as Hearts refused, but still the crowd numbered more than 22,000. Snow, sleet and slippery conditions under foot hampered both teams but they managed to produce an entertaining match. Hearts went in front but United levelled from a Yorke cross that went in off a defender. United then took the lead through Ross with just eight minutes left. A minute later however, Hearts levelled and just into extra time they scored again to make it 3-2. United tired in the latter stages and the Gorgie outfit snatched a fourth. But it had been a good cup run and the money made from the ties was a welcome bonus. Attention then turned back to the league. The prospects of gaining the second promotion spot were realistic but no slip ups could be allowed, and results elsewhere would also be significant.

At the same time the Club's financial situation was again in the headlines. The accounts for the year ended 30th April 1934 disclosed a loss of £1,135 making the accumulated loss carried forward £7,324. Total liabilities were stated at £23,462. Chairman Ernest Robertson along with Directors, Boyd Carnegie, J A Lilburn,

David Wallace, David Halley and newly appointed William McIntosh, confirmed that the reconstruction proposal, would soon be submitted to the shareholders. An extraordinary general meeting was arranged on 25th March at the Mathers Hotel in Dundee where a scheme of financial reconstruction was approved by a majority after a formal motion put forward by William McIntosh and seconded by Pat Reilly. The capital of the company was then 25,000 shares at £1 each of which 3,282 were issued. A petition was submitted to the Court of Session to have the share values reduced to just 2/- (10p) each. At the same time the secured debenture holders were offered 6/8 (33p) in the £ to settle in full.

Another revelation became public during this troubled period. The company formed in 1923 to facilitate the original change of name, Dundee City Athletic Company Ltd. was still in existence and was a shareholder in Dundee United Football Company Ltd.! The only asset was a holding of 1,966 shares in DUFC Ltd and the Directors of Dundee City Athletic Company Ltd (William Hutchison, Pat Reilly, David Wallace and J D Cappon, an accountant) agreed to the reconstruction. Considering the total shareholding of the new company was 3,282, the old company was in effect the majority shareholder!

Back on the field, United won three games in a row to keep up the pressure on the leaders. A good 3-0 win at Raith Rovers was followed by a well deserved 2-1 result at East Stirlingshire. In the next match the *Dundee Courier* headline read "Dazzling Dundee United" as Stenhousemuir took a pounding in another high scoring United home win. It was 8-0, with Milne getting a hat-trick. But the next match put a serious dent in the challenge as Montrose fought back from a goal behind to win 2-1. A week later the prospect of promotion vanished. Even after beating East Stirlingshire 4-0, United were five points behind second placed Arbroath with only two games left. The first goal of the match against East Stirlingshire, scored by Milne, was United's 100th of the league campaign and they went on to end with 105 goals scored. Top scorer was Milne with 23 plus another 5 in the cup. King and Ross both hit a total of 20, with Smith and Gardiner in double figures, on 17 and 14 respectively.

The transformation over twelve months was nothing short of miraculous. From an organisation facing oblivion, Brownlie and the Directors had revived the Club and re-established credibility. Unfortunately, the campaign ended with defeats away at Stenhousemuir 3-2 and Leith Athletic 4-0. In between these two matches United met Montrose, and drew 2-2 in the Forfarshire Cup. Immediately the league season ended, the Black and Whites set off on a whirlwind tour in the north. They played four games in four days using most of the regular first team players and some trialists. Draws at Fraserburgh and Forres were followed by a defeat in Inverness and the trip ended with a commendable 4-1 result against Highland League champions, Elgin City. The last match of 1934-35 was a 3-1 Forfarshire Cup replay win over Montrose on 27th April. It was United's sixth match in eight days.

1935-36

Return of the Hurricane

At the end of the previous campaign, only Fleming, Robertson, Hart and Tom Ross were released whilst Milne, Masson, MacRitchie, Kay, Yorke, Smith, Gardiner and George Ross all re-signed. In June, King successfully applied to the SFA for a free transfer and joined Alloa Athletic. During the tour of the highlands in April, Dave Collington from Scone Thistle had played three times and was signed on 3rd May. Within two weeks Brownlie added the versatile former Montrose and Brechin City forward, Jacky Brown and a month later, Dave Skelligan signed. A former Dundee North End half back, he had played in pre-season trial matches at Tannadice in the past and had spent the previous season at Brechin City.

But the best news, as far as the fans were concerned, was the return of Duncan Hutchison on 18th June. Brownlie had found his name on the Hull City list of players open to transfer and immediately made contact. A deal was struck and Yorke moved in the opposite direction with a nominal cash adjustment. A week later, seventeen year old George Ure from Stobswell, was signed as a reserve utility defender.

There were also new additions to the Board with George Greig, J T Millar and Dr William Donald elected as Directors. It was also announced that yet again, plans for a new stand would remain on the back burner. Brownlie was on duty at Tannadice in the evenings in his role as Secretary, selling season tickets. For a ground ticket, fans would pay 12/6d (62½ p) but a new ticket was introduced for those under fourteen years of age at a cost of 4/- (20p). For the enclosure the price was 17/6d (87½p) and for the stand 25/- (£1.25).

On 20th July, the Court of Session granted the petition to reduce the capital of the company and the Board then settled the secured debenture holders as agreed. At the same time, the collateral debenture holders were issued with second debentures in lieu of their settlement of 5/- (25p) in the pound and they also obtained security over Tannadice for their holding. The Judicial Factor remained in place until January 1936, when he was finally discharged by the Court of Session and the Club then effectively got Tannadice back. During all this, there is no mention of how the ordinary creditors were dealt with but it may be assumed that whilst agreeing to action affecting shareholders and debenture holders, the ordinary creditors were paid in full. Had that not been the case, some other action would have been taken. Once the finances were sorted, Greig and McIntosh provided new money.

There was keen interest in the trial match on 5th August, with a 12,000 crowd eager to see how Hutchison performed after six years away. There was also considerable speculation on how the forwards would line up. Where would Hutchison play? Would he replace Milne at centre? The Brownlie solution was to utilise Hutchison in a supporting role. Over the campaign he occupied all five forward positions at some time. He even filled in at right back when the need arose!

All through the weeks leading up to the start of 1935-36, there was one issue always in the press. United still had to find a goalkeeper, and several names were touted. It was only on 9th August, the day before kick off, that Brownlie acquired the signature of Robert Morrison, formerly with Airdrieonians, Southport and Gateshead. He made his debut in the opening encounter against the previous season's third placed side, St Bernard's. Also making league debuts in the game were Collington, Brown and Skelligan. The latter pair got the goals, as United twice came from behind, to earn a point in a 2-2 draw in front of a crowd of 14,000 at Tannadice. Two days later, only 3,000 fewer saw United earn a creditable 2-2 home draw in a Forfarshire Cup tie against Dundee.

The league campaign continued with a 3-2 win at Alloa Athletic. Milne scored all three goals and United had to come from behind twice to take the points. That was followed by the Forfarshire Cup replay at Dens Park in a match best forgotten as Dundee stormed to a four goal half time lead, and added another four in the second half. Even United's late consolation in the 8-1 defeat came from the boot of a Dundee player! The result also sent Brownlie on another player hunt.

A 1-1 draw at home to King's Park, and a 2-1 defeat at Brechin City were followed by a battling 3-1 home win against undefeated Falkirk, with Hutchison scoring twice to record his first goals since returning. New half back Doug Anderson from Aberdeen made his debut in the match along with inside forward Donovan Reid, signed from Aberdeen East End. In between these matches, the Directors also tried to honour a commitment to a charity match at Fraserburgh, in aid of the RNLI and made the trip north on 4th September. But the match against a Highland League Select had to be cancelled, when the host's Bellslea Park became severely waterlogged. United were hit with injuries to key players over the next two games and despite that handicap they managed a 1-1 draw at Raith Rovers but lost 2-1 at home to St Mirren.

United faced a trip to Dumbarton on 28th September with key players missing again, but signed ex-Dundee defender Robert Hogg on a one month deal. Aberdeen East End trialist, Joe Jamieson also came in to fill the outside left position and netted three in United's 5-3 win. A week later in a 1-1 draw against Morton, both were in the starting line up but failed to impress.

In the next match at Stenhousemuir, United lost 5-0 with the forwards completely out of touch. Reid was injured during the game and then missed the entire league season. In a campaign that was to become one of fluctuating fortunes, a brave 4-2 win over East Fife at Tannadice was followed by a 7-0 thrashing at Cowdenbeath. Granted, Morrison failed to arrive and Collington was forced to deputise in goal, but that alone does not account for such a heavy loss, as the stand in keeper played well in his unaccustomed role.

Following a serious injury to Corbett, Brownlie was forced back into the transfer market. He brought full back Robert Murray from Clyde in time to make his debut in a 4-1 win over Forfar Athletic. The next new signing was John Milne from Benburb but he made little initial impact as United lost 4-2 at Falkirk and 3-1 at Leith Athletic. More proof of the lack of consistency, if it were needed, came in the last two games in November. United comfortably won against Edinburgh City 4-1, but at Montrose they threw away a 2-0 lead, allowing the home side to net three times in the final ten minutes. Just to emphasise the "Jekyll and Hyde United", the side reversed that situation a week later, recovering from two goals down at East Stirlingshire to win 3-2! It would have been two wins in a row for the first time that season, if the next match against Brechin City had finished. The players had braved freezing temperatures and intermittent blizzard conditions. United were leading 5-1 through a Brown hat-trick and two Anderson spot kick conversions, when the referee abandoned the match due to bad light, with less than ten minutes remaining!

Expect the unexpected became the United supporters' watchword, as a week later St Mirren, a team then labelled too good for the Second Division, trounced United 6-2. But United recovered from that to hammer eight past Dumbarton at Tannadice without reply a week later! The Milne clan accounted for six of these with Arthur getting four and John netting two in a score line that was completely justified.

Four fixtures in early January yielded little, with only one point in a 2-2 home draw in the re-arranged game with Brechin City. United lost the other three matches, beginning with a 4-1 defeat at Morton and then 4-3 at East Fife and 3-1 at St Bernard's. Brownlie was particularly unhappy with the centre half Masson and only Ure was immediately available to replace him, but the young defender lacked experience and went to Brechin City on loan. The position was eventually filled by Willie Watson from Ayr United. He had been freed by Hibs during the close season and Brownlie had tried to sign him then but just missed out. Watson was not signed in time for the 4-3 league win over Raith Rovers but made his debut the following week in the Scottish Cup tie at Alloa Athletic. That began a quartet of matches against the Clackmannanshire club.

The cup match on 25th January 1936 at Tannadice ended in a 2-2 draw with Alloa Athletic coming from behind twice to earn a deserved second chance. In the midweek replay at Recreation Park, the home side repeated the feat, coming from a Milne goal behind to draw 1-1. Jerry Kerr was in the opposing line up and played a significant part, marshalling his fellow defenders well. Ex-United man Tim Williamson also played a part, setting up the equaliser. The teams met again on the Saturday at Tannadice on league business and United comfortably won 4-0 with all the goals coming in the first half. The second cup replay followed in midweek at Tynecastle but both the sides looked jaded after three previous meetings. There was little to choose between them as United advanced with a 2-1 win. In the next round they faced Cowdenbeath away and the home side led from the start to finally win 5-3 and knock United out of the competition.

By now there was no prospect of promotion. With key players again absent, United lost the next league match at King's Park 2-1. Montrose then did a double, beating United 4-2 in the Forfarshire Cup and then a week later 3-2 in the league, both times at Tannadice. But no-one could have predicted what would follow. United went on a scoring spree that produced 42 goals in the last six league matches of the season – a record for United and for the UK and a total that would be hard to beat anywhere in senior football.

For the record, Hutchison and Gardiner got two each, and each of the Milnes scored in the 6-3 win at Edinburgh City; Arthur Milne scored a hat-trick and John Milne, Gardiner and Ross one each in the 6-1 home win against Cowdenbeath; another Arthur Milne hat-trick came in the 6-1 home win over Stenhousemuir with Hutchison, Ross and Watson getting the other three; Milne then scored four in the 8-2 demolition of Leith Athletic at Tannadice with Skelligan getting two from spot kicks and Ross and Hutchison one each; Gardiner, Anderson and Ross scored at Forfar Athletic but the run was maintained only because of Skelligan's late goal from the spot for a 4-3 win; the best was saved for last as United annihilated East Stirlingshire in a 12-1 win at Tannadice with Hutchison and Milne each netting a hat-trick, Ross and Kay scored two each and Gardiner and Anderson one each.

In the final table United finished in seventh place scoring a record total of 108 goals with 32 of those coming from Arthur Milne. He scored another three in the cup for a total of 35 with Hutchison, Gardiner and Ross having a combined total of 40. Milne's scoring exploits attracted interest from several clubs with Manchester United, Chelsea and St Johnstone at the head of the queue. Chairman Ernest Robertson made it clear however, that Milne would not leave cheaply and only an offer in the region of £5,000 would tempt United to let him go. Any transfer income would certainly have been welcome as there were signs of financial pressure on the Club again. Towards the end of the season, records show that the Directors were assisting through small short term loans.

Donny Reid made his long awaited return from injury and scored in a 2-0 friendly win over a Dundee Junior Select. United then undertook a short tour in the north again, returning undefeated, with a 3-3 draw at Peterhead, a 4-1 win over Wick Academy, and 1-1 draw at Brora Rangers. In the latter match, trialists James MacFarlane from Fair City Athletic and Robert McIntosh from Blairgowrie played and both later signed.

1936-37

Courting Disaster Again

From the squad of 1935-36, Morrison, MacRitchie, Masson, Smith, Anderson, Murray, Kay and John Milne were released. Most notable in the freed list was Jacky Kay who had been at Tannadice for nine years. He left United after scoring 91 goals in 229 league and 21 Scottish Cup appearances; his total of 250 appearances in major competitions is the Dundee United pre-1945 record. Brechin City moved quickly to sign the player and he would very shortly return to haunt United!

Skelligan and Reid re-signed in late April. Corbett was listed as retained but he never played again and left to join West Ham United in early October. Also listed as retained was Gardiner but after refusing terms he too left and joined English non league side Dartford at the end of July. His move however may have been a loan deal because a year later, when he signed for Bristol Rovers, United received a fee of £250. Gardiner would return to play for United during the Second World War.

In the final week of May, Willie Reid signed from Aberdeen. That was followed by the signings of Partick Thistle outside left Peter Bain and the King's Park keeper Jimmy Milton. Both of these captures were considered quite sensational. The players were transfer listed at £500 and £50 respectively by their clubs but both players had successfully appealed and were granted free transfers. They were unaware of this but Brownlie had been in Glasgow, in the right place at the right time to find out they were available. The Manager and Chairman Ernest Robertson then spent two days tracking the players down to obtain their signatures for United! By the end of May, Collington, Ure, Ross, Brown, Hutchison and Milne had also re-signed.

Next, United announced the signing of full back James Wilkinson, who had spent eight years at Easter Road with Hibs. He was joined by Neil Paterson, an inside left with Leith Athletic. Originally from Buckie, Neil was then a student at Edinburgh University and about to commence a career in journalism. In view of this he signed with United as an amateur to allow him to begin his writing career. He went on to attain fame in America as a writer and won an Oscar for the screenplay of the film *Room At The Top* in 1959. Former Dundee and Brighton defender Tommy McCarthy was added to the squad in mid July.

Many of the players lived out of town and in a then novel approach Brownlie indicated that they would spend two weeks together training at Tannadice prior to the season beginning. The record breaking run at the end of the previous season was still fresh in the memories of supporters and there was an air of confidence around Tannadice. There was even talk of a championship season once again. Looking at the squad for the forthcoming campaign, there were realistic grounds for optimism. The defence comprised some big strong men and the attacking players from the last campaign were all still there, bar Gardiner. After a winning start the rest of the opening results therefore came as a shock.

The first match produced a 4-2 away win over King's Park, with Arthur Milne scoring all four United goals. One criticism levelled at the side was the lack of understanding at times between the players, but this was not completely unexpected. After all, seven of the side were making their United debuts! A week later, United were 3-0 up and coasting after eighteen minutes at home to Brechin City but suffered a second half collapse as the visitors drew level at 3-3. In the end United were lucky to take a point. Former United men Kay, MacRitchie, Robertson and in particular King with two goals, were instrumental in the Brechin City comeback.

15th August 1936
Standing: Collington, McIntosh, Milton, Skelligan, McCarthy, Reid
Seated: Hutchison, Ross, Milne, Paterson, Bain

The next three matches saw United concede four goals on each occasion. Of Airdrieonians' 4-0 win there could be no complaint. But at home to Raith Rovers, United were leading 2-1 before conceding three times in the last fifteen minutes. Paterson had United a goal up at Morton and Milton twice saved penalties to preserve the lead but another collapse occurred and it finished 4-1 to Morton. A point was gained at home to Dumbarton in a poor 1-1 draw and by then there were some furrowed brows at Tannadice. Concerns grew as another four goals were conceded at Ayr United in a 4-1 defeat. The Forfarshire Cup win over Dundee on 23rd September showed what the team could achieve. Changes to the line up for that match saw an improvement in the side and United totally dominated the game for a fully deserved 3-1 win.

The change in fortunes was however, only fleeting. On paper, Brownlie had put together a good side but unfortunately, on the pitch they were underachieving and the search for better quality players went on. Andrew McGillivray from Leith Athletic and John Donnelly from Albion Rovers were signed in early September. Neither lasted long and still there was no improvement. After league defeats of 1-0 at home to Alloa Athletic, 3-0 at St Bernard's and a 4-1 Forfarshire Cup beating from Brechin City at Tannadice, it was announced that one of the existing Directors, George Greig, was to take full control of the Club.

The first indication the fans had of any change was at the home match against Airdrieonians. Much to everyone's surprise, Greig was in the dug-out. It later transpired that Brownlie was watching Dundee Arnot play Arbroath Victoria in a Scottish Junior Cup tie. Spectators also noticed that all the other Directors were absent from their usual places but watched the match from the enclosure instead. United won 2-1, but it was a stumbling victory with Airdrieonians below their best. The players, it appears, knew more than most about what was going on. Greig met with them before the game and left them in no doubt that the Club were in dire financial trouble. Poor results had led to a fall in attendances and a resultant fall in income. United were losing money every week and cut-backs were required. As part of the money saving measures taken, Greig persuaded the players to forego bonuses for the remainder of the season. No-one wanted to see a repeat of 1934!

Three days later a meeting of the shareholders and debenture stock holders took place at Tannadice. The meeting was attended by George Greig, Boyd Carnegie, Ernest Robertson, J T Miller and David Halley (owner of Halley's Bar). Greig, who represented the debenture holders, was unanimously appointed Managing Director until 30th April 1938. He was joined by a new director William McAra, a well known accountant. All the others on the Board agreed, perhaps reluctantly, to resign. None of the resigning directors had enough time available to concentrate on getting United out of their current difficulties. It was then announced that Brownlie had resigned from his post as Manager. Greig had made it clear that there would no new signings and money would be available only to pay the existing players and the trainer. He took control of team matters himself but left all tactics to trainer Johnny Hart. But when it came to the hiring and firing of players, Greig was the sole decision maker. To cut costs he even stopped the players training at Tannadice and left the squad to make their own arrangements close to where each lived. All actions taken were unanimously ratified at another meeting on 16th October and George Greig then had absolute control. United's biggest asset, Arthur Milne immediately attracted interest from several clubs, including Portsmouth, Burnley and Liverpool.

It was not long before Greig began a clear out of players to bring down the wages bill. The team began to pick up points over the remainder of 1936, but the focus of attention was most certainly on the comings and goings, as Greig released several players. McCarthy had left in September, freed by Brownlie. Greig cut the playing staff further, with McGillivray released in October, joined by Watson, Wilkinson and Bain in November. Wilkinson appealed to the SFA but his case was dismissed.

The unhappiest of the players was undoubtedly Arthur Milne. He made a transfer request at the end of October but Greig declared he was not prepared to allow Milne to go and was not in need of the money stating, "I am prepared to spend my own [money] until I put the club in a sound position." Financial records confirm that this is indeed the case with several loans from Greig showing through the cash book. Meanwhile, Willie Reid asked for, and was granted, a free transfer.

In keeping with his tight grip on the purse strings, Greig decided that as far as possible he would sign players from the local junior ranks. He said, "The days of running to the West of Scotland and paying fabulous fees are over. These players have not taken the Club anywhere. I am convinced we have the material at our own door." Several junior trialists did turn out for United over the rest of the season but the only junior signed was Fergus Davidson, in November, from YMCA Anchorage. The only other addition to the playing staff was Alec King who returned to Tannadice in December from Brechin City. At around the same time Brown was freed.

It would appear that most of the players who remained supported Greig, at least publicly. A meeting between Greig and the players took place in late November, with United then ten points behind leaders Ayr United. The players were in confident mood and indicated that they considered ten points was not an insurmountable gap! Indeed the relationship was such that Greig paid for many of the players to attend an international at Dens Park against Wales on 3rd December 1936.

It was inevitable that offers would be made for Milne. Arbroath and Clyde both expressed an interest before Chelsea made an approach at £600. This figure was well below the player's valuation and was of course turned down out of hand. Celtic and Dundee were also keen to land Milne. The Glasgow side reputedly offered £1,000 before the Chelsea bid but it too was declined. Meanwhile, the financial results for the year to 30th April 1936 were made public at the AGM and disclosed a profit of £33. At the same time, Ernest Robertson and Kenneth Lawson were elected to the Board to join Greig and McAra. No matter the opinions at the time, it is evident that Greig was instrumental in turning things round, even if just temporarily. Before he took over, every game resulted in a financial loss but very quickly this turned to profit, even with bare minimum cheques received at away matches. His failing was a lack of knowledge on football matters.

Results on the field over the final three months of 1936 brought five wins, three draws and only four defeats since the radical change of management. That ensured a cushion between United and bottom of the table. In the nine games prior to Greig taking over, United gleaned only four points. Thirteen points were added by the end of the year. United were though, unpredictable and a 5-3 defeat at Cowdenbeath on 17th October was followed by a good performance to win 5-1 at home to Montrose. A 6-4 defeat at home to East Stirlingshire was followed by a hard fought 3-2 win at Raith Rovers and the team was billed as the 'Terriers of Tannadice' for a stunning 5-0 win over Forfar Athletic which included a Paterson hat-trick. The good form continued with a 2-2 home draw with Edinburgh City, a 5-4 win at Dumbarton, a 2-2 draw at Leith Athletic and a goalless draw at home to East Fife before the side lost 2-1 to Ayr United and 2-0 at Alloa Athletic to end the year in a mid table position.

In January, Malcolm Cameron, an amateur, was added to the squad but played just once. Defeats at home to Morton, 4-1 and away to Brechin City, 4-3 were followed by 3-3 draws with both King's Park at Tannadice and away to Forfar Athletic, before United won their first game for almost two months, 3-2 against Stenhousemuir on 23rd January. The main talking point was the Scottish Cup tie at Airdrieonians at the end of the month. United played well against the First Division side and, although beaten 3-1, they were not disgraced and deserved to take something from the encounter.

In February, United played only three games but the fans witnessed plenty of goals starting with a 4-4 draw in the league at East Fife. A 1-1 draw against Cowdenbeath followed and then a Penman Cup tie with Raith Rovers at Tannadice produced another 4-4 draw. Late in the month, there was more off field activity than there was on it. Arthur Milne had lodged an appeal with the SFA claiming that he had not been paid the bonuses of £8.10/- (£8.50) to which he was entitled. To put that in perspective, £8 was around a month's wages for a tradesman. The case was complicated and hinged on the terms of the restructure of the Club's finances in October. Before the SFA could make their decision, there was a considerable amount of correspondence back and forward between the ruling body, the Club and the player. In the end, it seems that the appeal was withdrawn as Milne finally got his wish to move to England when Greig arranged for him to go to Liverpool. It was reported that he had been transferred for a fee of £2,000, but initially, he went to Merseyside on loan. However, it was the end of the player's United career for the time being after accumulating an astonishing 86 goals in 82 competitive league and cup matches.

Milne played his last game for United in a 5-0 defeat at Montrose but the following week, with Hutchison at centre forward, United beat Leith Athletic 4-2 and then won 3-2 at Edinburgh City a week later. The season unfortunately fizzled out after that with a 2-1 league defeat at East Stirlingshire and a 4-1 thumping at Raith Rovers in the second leg of the Penman Cup. St Bernard's then won 3-0 with ease at Tannadice and the final match of the season brought a humiliating 9-2 thrashing at Stenhousemuir. United ended the campaign well ahead of bottom club Edinburgh City, but too close for comfort and only two points in front of second bottom King's Park.

One sad note sounded at the end of the season with the death of Pat Reilly. The man who had been the driving force behind the formation of the Club passed away on 6th April 1937, with barely a mention in the local press. His passing was marked at Tannadice though, and on 10th April the 3,000 fans who attended United's home match against St Bernard's stood with the players in silence for a minute whilst the flag over Tannadice flew at half mast.

As the season wound down, rumours surfaced that United were planning to turn out an all amateur side in the next campaign. These stories were quickly denied by Greig. He did however confirm that there would be no big money buys for 1937-38 and he would be relying on the junior ranks to supply the squad. To emphasise the cost cutting measures, most of the players were freed. Only Hutchison and MacFarlane were retained along with Collington who was in hospital with a fractured pelvis. The big surprise in the list of players allowed to leave was Milton, and he was quickly snapped up by East Fife.

As for Arthur Milne, it was assumed that he was now a Liverpool player. Greig was in touch with the Merseysiders on 7th May, requesting a fee as Milne had completed a loan trial as agreed. Liverpool claimed however that they had not agreed to sign him. The matter was then referred, by United, to the International League Board. Meanwhile in Edinburgh, a sharp-eyed Willie McCartney, Manager of Hibs, noticed that Milne was not on the retained lists of either Liverpool or United. That in effect made the player a free agent. McCartney agreed terms with the player at his Brechin home and he signed for Hibs on 13th May. Greig was understandably angry but there was little he could do until the International Board meeting took place as arranged in September. It is interesting to note that Willie McCartney was caught out by a similar set of circumstances a few years earlier. Then at Hearts, McCartney had allowed Andy Campbell out on loan to Morton and, due to administrative errors, Dundee were able to sign Campbell as a free agent.

1937-38

The Unlikely Saviour

George Greig

The early pre-season news from Tannadice was all about changes in the coaching staff. Greig persuaded Tom Blair, the former Manchester City and Kilmarnock goalkeeper, to take on some of the coaching responsibilities. Shortly after that, trainer Johnny Hart left Tannadice to be replaced by Willie Cameron. Cameron had been with Lochee Harp for fourteen years and had won every honour in the junior ranks. In order to have the pick of the junior crop in the Dundee area, Greig proposed a new concept. Selected players from the junior ranks would receive the benefit of coaching from Blair and Cameron and in return, United would have first call on the players.

The rebuilding of the team began in early July with the signing of Albert Robertson from East Craigie, Tom Clarkson from Kilmarnock and Willie Watson who returned following a short time in England with Lincoln City and then with Dundee. Dan Hutchison, the brother of Duncan, had played in three trial matches in the previous season and he was signed in August from St Joseph's. Nothing much more happened until after the trial match on 9th August which produced a shock 4-1 defeat for United. The opposition comprised mainly of local juniors and some senior old hands. Within a few days, Managing Director/Team Manager, Greig fixed up David Ramsay (a teacher at Colliston who had played with Clydebank, Bo'ness, Forfar Athletic and Brechin City), Bob Black (Forfar Athletic) and John Boland (Forfar Athletic and Brechin City) to complete the squad. An offer for Collington from Chelsea was turned down.

The opening match of the league campaign was a personal disaster for Tom Blair. He was in goal as United were trounced 7-1 at home by St Bernard's. Immediately after the match the keeper hung up his gloves to concentrate on coaching. To replace Blair, Dave Watson (brother of Willie) was signed from Ayr United and his debut match against Raith Rovers was very eventful. In it, Dave Collington played right back, then moved to outside left and finally played in goal when the new keeper went off injured. Raith Rovers took the lead but Clarkston scored twice to put United ahead. The injury to Watson was significant as Raith Rovers went on to score three more to win the match 4-2. Ure made his return to United in this match, after a spell at Brechin City and then Falkirk. A week later, Tommy Adamson was signed from Lochee Harp and Black left Tannadice after only two appearances.

A 2-1 home win against Montrose the following week was slightly overshadowed by the impending AGM on 2nd September, as interest was again briefly focused off the field. The results for the year ended 30th April 1937 disclosed a loss of £1,279, but Greig was at pains to point out that £1,137 of this happened prior to his stewardship and £750 of the loss was caused by a reduction in player valuations. As it was not relevant to the year under discussion, the Arthur Milne situation was not raised at the AGM but had United received the appropriate fee for the player, then the Club would most likely have shown a profit.

28th August 1937
Standing: Collington, Ure, D Watson, Skelligan, W Watson, McFarlane, Cameron
             (Trainer)
Seated: Duncan Hutchison, Boland, Clarkson, Adamson, Dan Hutchison

The case of Arthur Milne came before the International League Board on 25th September 1937. United claimed £1,500 (plus £25 expenses) from Liverpool as the fee payable for the transfer of Milne. Greig was in possession of documents which specified that Milne became a Liverpool player shortly after he went there on loan in March. Liverpool stated that they had never signed Milne and he was only at Anfield on loan. The International League Board invited the two sides to reach a mutual settlement. Although Greig, on behalf of United, was willing to reduce the claim, Liverpool countered with a figure that was considerably lower. This left the Board no option but to adjudicate. There was little debate and the Board found unanimously in favour of United based on the documents provided by Greig. The United chief expressed himself satisfied with the outcome. He felt vindicated by the decision that confirmed the documents he possessed, proved that Milne was a Liverpool player. United received a total of £762.10/- representing half the claim and half of the expenses. Although United were compensated, it was far below the player's true valuation of at least £2,000. And it should not be forgotten that Ernest Robertson had indicated only an offer of £5,000 would tempt the Club to part with the player.

Bobby Yorke returned to United on 8th September after his time with Hull City and at the same time Ramsay was released. A week later former East Craigie, Arbroath and Blackburn Rovers full back Bert Grieve joined the Club, but United's form continued to be erratic, not helped by a series of injuries and illness to players. A 5-1 defeat at Dumbarton was followed by a 5-2 win over Edinburgh City and the already difficult situation was not made any easier when Greig suspended both the Watson brothers, for allegedly 'non-trying' in the next match at Albion Rovers where United lost 4-1. Both later appealed to the SFA and both won their case. United were fined £5 and Dave was allowed to leave on a free transfer but the Club were obliged to keep Willie under contract. Greig was furious with the outcome and vowed that Willie would not play for United again. In the end he had to relent and the player was in the line up for much of the remainder of the season.

A new keeper, George Nicolson, was signed from Kirrie Thistle after a successful trial against Alloa Athletic in a match United drew 2-2. The next match ended 4-4 at King's Park with Duncan Hutchison scoring a hat-trick. Former Falkirk forward Pat Docherty, who was a teacher, made his debut in that match, but bouts of diphtheria and double pneumonia sidelined him for much of the season. Clarkson was the hat-trick hero in the 4-2 win over Dunfermline Athletic on 9th October but a week later, a poor showing at St Bernard's resulted in a 3-0 defeat. A busy October ended with a 1-1 draw at East Stirlingshire and a 2-0 defeat at home to East Fife with Dennis McGurk making his debut. He was a former local junior, who had been with Portadown, but lasted just a few weeks at Tannadice.

After losing the first two games in November, 4-3 at Airdrieonians despite a Robertson hat-trick and 3-1 at Stenhousemuir, United had only nine points from fourteen games. The team then came into some good form with Duncan Hutchison in particular showing some of his old flair. Eleven points were gathered from seven matches starting with the best performance of the season, a 6-1 win over East Stirlingshire on 20th November, unfortunately witnessed by a crowd of just 500. Greig freely admitted that the Club were in danger of winding up as United were losing money again. Support had been dwindling over the season and gate receipts were as low as £50, when at least £120 was needed to break even. It must have been galling to learn that Arthur Milne was then valued at £4,000 by Hibs!

United gradually improved their league position with a 2-0 win over Forfar Athletic, a 3-1 win at Montrose and a tremendous fight back from three goals behind to draw 4-4 with Raith Rovers. Defences were on top as United beat Edinburgh City 2-0 on New Year's Day 1938 but the good run of results ended with defeat by the odd goal in seven at home to Leith Athletic. Willie Wann, a centre forward, made his first appearance for United in that match as a trialist but it was a few more years before he was signed. After that United took only five more league points from the remaining fifteen league games beginning with a 2-0 win against King's Park on 8th January. Willie Rumbles signed from Brechin City on a free transfer and made his debut in a 4-3 defeat at Forfar Athletic, just as McGurk was being released. Then it was all eyes on the Scottish Cup, with Hearts due at Tannadice. That visit produced a match that would prove to be one of the few highlights at Tannadice for some time.

Before kick off, Greig went to the dressing room and delivered a rousing team talk. Hearts were a side filled with players of international standard, including Tommy Walker, but he was well marshalled by the United defence and hardly saw the ball. Adamson put United ahead and Rumbles scored the second just before half time. United went three up when Robertson got the third just after the interval. Hearts scored almost immediately but then Walker missed a penalty and that took the fight out of the Edinburgh side. United continued to dictate play and secured a memorable 3-1 win.

United lost 4-1 to Dumbarton and 3-1 at Cowdenbeath in the league and this did little to help morale in the weeks preceding the next cup match at East Fife. Greig tried his best to encourage a big travelling support. First, he attempted to negotiate a special price of 2/6d (12½p) for the travelling United fans instead of the 3/8d (17p) offered by the railway company. They refused to reduce the price so Greig offered to hire the train himself and then fix his own price, but again the railway company declined.

Grieve was released and John Gilmour was signed in time to play against East Fife. United put up a good fight but in the end they had no luck at all against the Methil side. Collington dislocated a jaw not once, but twice and was eventually carried off unconscious and did not resume. Rumbles broke his wrist and centre half Watson gashed a leg. United held out and were just two goals down but the crocked side wilted in the final fifteen minutes, in which East Fife scored three more to win 5-0. In truth, East Fife were a formidable side and would probably have won even if United had played with a fully fit eleven. The Fife club went on to win the Scottish Cup, beating Kilmarnock in the final.

It was back to league business and United lost to Cowdenbeath 3-2, but managed a 4-2 win at Alloa Athletic a week later. Rumbles played for the last time in that match, scoring the last of his seven goals in seven games. He left United, signing on for a two year voyage to Australia as a ship's carpenter. He was seen as the most promising centre at Tannadice for some time and his departure was a significant factor in the end of season slump.

United lost the next seven league matches in this unremarkable campaign, but the last two games were extraordinary! On 29th April at Methil, United played East Fife, by then Scottish Cup winners, and lost seven goals without reply. However the Fife side won largely because United played much of the game with only nine men. After only a few minutes of the match, Dan Hutchison was stretchered off after he hit his head on a concrete post behind the goal. Duncan, concerned for his brother, also went off. They both returned briefly but Dan was obviously concussed and both again went off. It was no surprise that East Fife scored seven. Had they wanted to they might have scored more.

Surprisingly, on the very next day, Dan was fit and in the side to play Airdrieonians in the last match of the season. Airdrieonians still had a chance of promotion but their hopes were dashed as United matched them all the way. Dan Hutchison completed a hat-trick with a very late equaliser for a final score of 5-5. United also played two Forfarshire Cup ties in April beating Forfar Athletic 5-3 and losing 3-0 away to Dundee. Despite a very poor last quarter to the season, United again finished fourteenth but with a slightly more comfortable six point advantage over second bottom, Edinburgh City. Duncan Hutchison, although never reaching the scoring heights of the late 1920s, still managed to end the season as top scorer with 19 goals.

Greig intimated that he would complete his stewardship as agreed on 30th April 1938, stating that he had achieved all he had set out to do. The Club were in credit and at the AGM a few weeks later, he announced a profit of £303. He definitely lacked experience in football matters and this probably cost United dearly in the case of Milne and there were other less high profile transfer difficulties but none were as costly. Some observers saw George Greig as saint, others as sinner but there is no doubt he had the best interest of United at heart. He and William McIntosh had made sure that Dundee United survived in 1934, and while he was in the Managing Director/Team Manager role for eighteen months, he kept a tight grip on the Club's finances and again ensured survival. But when his period in charge ended the impression gained is that he was glad to leave.

At the end of the season, thirteen players were given free transfers and Duncan Hutchison and Donny Reid were transfer listed. Greig and his fellow directors, including Ernest Robertson, resigned. This left the fans wondering if they would have a team to support in the next campaign.

1938-39

The Third Brownlie Era

Through much of May, no news came from Tannadice, although there was speculation on the appointment of a new Manager. The names of former players Bill Taylor and James Robertson were put forward along with Celtic's Willie McStay. It was also rumoured that William McIntosh would be the new Chairman.

However all speculation ended on 8th June when temporary control of the Club was put in the care of Dr William Donald, Kenneth Lawson and John Carnegie Jnr. The AGM took place a few days later and Dr Donald was formally appointed Chairman. William Hutchison and John Carnegie were the other Directors appointed. The new Board announced that they would co-opt another two directors and two weeks later the news that Jimmy Brownlie was back at Tannadice as a Director, was warmly welcomed by the fans. The Board was completed with the arrival of ex-Dundee and Cardiff City player, Sam Irving, a former Northern Ireland international. Brownlie and Irving were assigned to look after team matters whilst the rest of the Board attended to the business and finance.

Sam Irving

Jimmy Brownlie

The signing of players was an obvious priority and Reid was re-signed almost immediately, along with full back Bob Temple from Aberdeen. Brownlie and Irving then took the unusual step of advertising for players. Once replies were received, the new Joint Managers arranged a trial match. Several experienced players turned out in front of a crowd of 8,000 on 6th August, just one week before the season began. Afterwards there was a crop of signings. The goalkeeping position was filled by Rab Smith of Ayr United. He was joined in defence by former Falkirk and Alloa Athletic full back George Sutherland. The new half back line would be made up of the re-signed Skelligan, Robert Beattie (ex-Motherwell and Alloa Athletic) and Andrew Meikleham from Raith Rovers. Duncan Hutchison, although initially reluctant, also re-signed. He was joined in the forward line by William Benzie (Morton), James Malloy (Cowdenbeath), Pat McCamon (St Mirren) and Bob Howe (St Johnstone).

As the season began, Jimmy Brownlie was quoted saying, "We will carry no passengers. We are out for a class team and if the present players cannot give us the results, immediate steps will be taken to get others."

Nine players made debuts in the opening match of the 1938-39 campaign against Montrose, and in a ding-dong match it was 3-3 at half time. The Gable Endies went 4-3 up with only ten minutes left, but Temple and Malloy scored to win the match 5-4 for United. Defensive frailties and a lack of forward threat resulted in a 4-1 defeat by Cowdenbeath and 1-0 reversal at Airdrieonians and meant that the search for players went on but fees of £750 and £1,000 were being asked and were considered too high. After several rebuffs, United signed centre forward Willie Black on a free transfer from Morton. He went straight into the side against Alloa Athletic and scored the only goal of the game on 3rd September. James Christie, signed from Perth Craigie, also made his debut in that match. On the same day, United opened an OAP gate for the first time.

In the next game, a late goal gave East Fife both points in a 3-2 win, but it was a close contest. Attention then switched to the forthcoming Dundee derby scheduled for 17th September. It was the first time the sides had met in a Second Division match following Dundee's relegation in 1937-38. On the eve of the derby, United won the signature of former Partick Thistle and Blackburn Rovers forward Horace Woolley against stiff competition from Queen of the South, Raith Rovers, St Mirren and Morton. He immediately made his mark with two goals on his debut in a relatively easy 3-0 United win. Woolley arrived with a big reputation and much was expected of him but less than a month later he was released and signed for Morton. George Nicolson was next to re-sign but he was only taken on as the reserve keeper and even then he would turn out for United only once more.

United's form over the next few months was very inconsistent, with defeats from Dumbarton 1-0, St Bernard's 5-3 and Dunfermline Athletic 3-0, whilst a late Temple penalty secured both points in a 2-1 home win against King's Park. A run of four games then netted seven points, with wins against Morton 1-0, Stenhousemuir 2-1 and St Bernard's 5-2, and a 3-3 draw at East Stirlingshire. The latter match should also have brought two points but East Stirlingshire grabbed an equaliser with almost the last kick.

Press reports suggested a happier Tannadice, with players and directors getting on very well and there were regular get-togethers for meals. Forfar West End outside left, Joe Black (brother of Willie), signed in early November after two trial matches. United also beat off competition from Clyde and Arbroath to sign Forthill Athletic's impressive youngster, George Ross. He turned out as a trialist twice in late December before signing in early January.

Although United lost 2-1 to Airdrieonians on 19th November, form improved and they drew 2-2 with Brechin City a week later before collecting full points in a 2-0 win at Leith Athletic and a 4-2 home win over Dumbarton. Forfar Athletic emerged 2-1 winners in a close game at Station Park but the following week, on Christmas Eve, United beat Brechin City by a single goal. Going into the New Year, the Club were well placed in the top half of the league after drawing 2-2 at Cowdenbeath on Hogmanay. The "basement bargain" side, as they had been dubbed, was doing better than had been expected and were steadily picking up points. Interest in United was such, that a supporters' club was formed on 15th December. Jimmy Brownlie carried out the opening ceremony at the clubroom in Murraygate, Dundee. To emphasise the commitment of the Board towards developing a winning side, offers for both Christie and Meikleham were rejected, despite the fact that the transfer fees would have been a welcome boost to the Club.

A wintry January 1939 began with a 5-2 defeat at home to East Fife. Goalkeeper Smith was out through injury and his replacement, Bert Dunbar of Dundee Arnot playing for the second time that season, was unfortunately not up to the task. The following week, United signed Raymond Wallace from Consett Celtic in Durham, on the recommendation of a former colleague of Sam Irving. Wallace was in the side that beat ten-man Dunfermline Athletic with a single goal. But after one more appearance the player was released.

The Scottish Cup came next, with Stenhousemuir at Tannadice in a match that United were expected to win. The visitors lost a player to injury after only thirteen minutes and Ross scored for United almost immediately. United went on to dominate the game but could not find the net again until near the end, when Black got the second. It was not a great cup tie but United deserved the 2-0 win, even if it was against ten men.

Two weeks later in the next round, Motherwell came to Tannadice and produced a highly controversial game. The Lanarkshire side went ahead from a break upfield at a time when United were the stronger looking side. The 'Well keeper then made two great saves to deny United a leveller. Then came the moment of controversy which turned the game. A Motherwell player handled the ball and the incident was apparently spotted by the referee who blew his whistle. Play went on and the ball was punted up the pitch. It was gathered by a Motherwell forward and put into the net with United players static. Everyone in the ground expected the referee to call the play back for the free kick, but astonishingly he

2nd January 1939
Standing: Temple, Sutherland, Trialist (Dunbar, Dundee Arnot), Christie, Beattie,
             Meikleham
Seated: Hutchison, Benzie, Ross, W Black, Howie

placed the ball on the centre circle for United to kick off! Mayhem followed as United protested and there was uproar on the terracing. The decision stood but it all seemed to knock United out of their stride and Motherwell went on to win 5-1. All United had to show was a late Ross consolation.

In between the two cup ties United lost 3-0 at Alloa Athletic and still smarting from the Motherwell result, the Black and Whites also lost 3-1 at home and 3-2 away to the amateurs of Edinburgh City on consecutive Saturdays. United then seemed to find a new impetus and the fans witnessed some excellent performances as the season drew to a close. Six goals were scored in each of the next two games, both at home. The first was a 6-0 win against Forfar Athletic and the second was a 6-1 win over Leith Athletic, the latter achieved without George Ross. After only three months at Tannadice and still only eighteen years old, he was sold to Hibs. The fee was not disclosed but it was said to put United "in a sound financial position" for the rest of the season.

The return derby at Dens on 18th March saw Dundee exact revenge with a 2-0 win. A week later, East Stirlingshire were at Tannadice and came upon a United that just could not help scoring. The luckless visitors conceded ten, with Willie Black netting five of those. In fact, United let their opponents off lightly and that made the following week's 3-2 defeat at King's Park all the harder to take. A 4-3 win at Morton was notable for a Beattie hat-trick but yet again United could not maintain consistency and lost the last two matches. Against Montrose, United were in the lead three times but lost 5-3 to a late double. At Stenhousemuir an experimental line up lost 3-0 in a lacklustre showing to end an average season. However, in the final analysis, the ninth place finish had to be looked on as progress after the previous two campaigns.

The end of season activity also included two Forfarshire Cup ties. A 5-3 win over Forfar Athletic set up a final against Arbroath. The Gayfield side scored twice early in the game against the run of play but over ninety minutes Arbroath were the better side and worth their 2-0 win. One other significant match was the friendly against Hibs. Willie Black stole the show with all four goals in the 4-2 win over the First Division side that included Arthur Milne and George Ross in the line up.

The end of season clear-out resulted in most of the squad receiving free transfers. Only Smith, Temple, Hutchison, Meikleham and the Black brothers were retained. Sutherland was placed on the open to offers list. On 13th May 1939, United advertised for players as they had the year before. At the end of May, Brownlie announced he was resigning from the Board and giving up his managerial role due to the pressure of his own business interests. He left the Club for the third time but was a regular visitor to Tannadice for many years afterwards. New directors were openly invited to join the Board and the year to 30th April 1939 ended with the Club showing a profit of £96.

1939-45

The Second World War Years

Bobby MacKay

In June 1939 the Chairman, Dr William Donald and his fellow directors, John Carnegie Jnr, Sam Irving and William Hutchison were joined by A Arrick Smith, William Robertson and Kenneth Lawson and the first act of the new Board was to advertise for a Manager. Within a week around 50 applications were received but the list came down to a choice of four. Tiny Bradshaw had applied but he was still playing for Third Lanark and a fee would have been involved if he was selected. The others on the short list were ex-Rangers, Liverpool, Sheffield United and East Fife player Archie McPherson, former United player Peter Gavigan who had also been with Dundee and St Johnstone, and the fourth and ultimately successful candidate was Bobby MacKay.

Meanwhile, the job of putting the team together fell to Sam Irving and on 3rd June, he brought in former Bradford City and Gillingham forward, John Ross. Smith re-signed and Jimmy Robertson was acquired from Wellesley Juniors after impressing as a trialist at the end of 1938-39. Irving also re-signed Temple and Meikleham. Ex-Brechin City, Raith Rovers and Montrose outside left Norman Fraser signed at the end of June.

On 5th July United announced the new Manager and it was of course, Bobby MacKay. MacKay owned and operated a billiard saloon in Glasgow at the time, but he was giving that up completely to move to Dundee. Well known in football circles, MacKay had played with Morton, Rangers, Newcastle United, Sunderland, Charlton Athletic, Bristol Rovers (where he had been a team mate of Sam Irving) and Newport County. At international level he had been capped for Scotland against Northern Ireland and Wales.

As soon as he arrived, MacKay arranged two trial matches for early August. Shortly after, he signed inside right William White from Hull City and former Armadale, Rangers, Alloa Athletic and St Bernard's left back Jerry Kerr, the man who would of course lead United to the First Division almost two decades in the future. Centre half Tom Gray (ex-Ayr United, East Fife and Albion Rovers) and inside left John Simpson from St Monance Swifts were also signed soon after the trials.

The league campaign got under way with a match at Edinburgh City and the Black and Whites won. Appropriately it was Black and White who combined well on the day producing two goals for Black in the 3-2 win. A week later United rather fortunately beat Stenhousemuir 4-2 at Tannadice thanks to two goals in the final minute. In the third match of the campaign, a 1-1 draw with East Stirlingshire, Johnny Hutton who had played as a trialist the previous season, made his debut as a signed player. In midweek United were thrashed 6-1 by a strong Dundee side in the Forfarshire Cup.

Archie McPherson, who had applied for the Manager's post, was added to the side but on the day he made his debut, cracks in the defence became evident again as United lost 2-0 to Leith Athletic. However, it all became irrelevant when the Scottish League came to an abrupt halt after Saturday, 2nd September 1939, with the outbreak of World War II on the following day.

The immediate effect of the war was a government order to suspend all football and by 7th September clubs were informed by the SFA that players' contracts were cancelled. A week later friendly games were approved but only on Saturdays and local holidays with small crowds permitted. But in the so called "danger areas" of Edinburgh, Glasgow, Dundee, Dunfermline and Clydebank senior football was still forbidden. Some clubs made the case for regional leagues but the Scottish League, prematurely as it turned out, announced that the league programme would in any case, restart on 23rd September. At the same time, they made cuts in payments to match officials. All payments were more or less halved with First Division referees being paid 21/- (£1.05) but they had the benefit of neutral linesman who were to receive 10/6 (52½ p). In the Second Division each club supplied one of the two linesmen. Dundee United put forward an unsuccessful motion at the Scottish League AGM in June 1939 for neutral linesmen in the lower league also. The payment to Second Division referees was 30/- (£1.50) and was halved to 15/- (75p). As for the players, Second Division wages were limited to £1 per week but it was suggested that clubs making a profit at the end of the season could pay an additional 10/- (50p) per week retrospectively, as a profit sharing bonus. The away team guarantees were also reduced with the First

Division halved to £50 and Second Division to £25.

The Scottish League and SFA then had a consultation with the government on 20th September and it was agreed that regional leagues could take the place of the national leagues. Crowds were to be strictly limited (at Tannadice the limit was 8,000) and the rules on transfers were relaxed. Players would be allowed to turn out for almost any team, provided they had permission from their own club.

The National Service Act was passed on 2nd September 1939 and within a month all men aged between 20 and 22 years of age became liable for conscription. Some players went to war immediately, with Temple, a territorial, one of the first to join up. Bobby MacKay left for Glasgow to find war work as soon as the league had suspended football. Club secretary Arthur Cram took temporary charge of team matters and he contacted every signed player. Within days, Kerr, Meikleham, Robertson, White, Hutton, Ross, Fraser, Black and Simpson all indicated they would be happy to return to United. On 30th September, the new sixteen team Eastern Regional League was set up and United warmed up on 2nd October in a friendly against Dundee. For that match both Dundee and United tried to obtain the services of Bobby Gardiner. Although Dundee made the first request to Bristol Rovers, the player was given the choice of team and had no hesitation in turning out for United. Both teams lacked match fitness and United had to field three juniors to make up the numbers but it was an entertaining match which Dundee won 4-2.

To kick off the new league, United had Smith, Kerr, Meikleham, Robertson, Black, White, Hutton and Fraser. They also obtained permission to play Gardiner and Alex Miller (Bristol City), Arthur Baxter (Barnsley), Alex Glen (Raith Rovers) and soon added Jimmy Littlejohn (Cowdenbeath). Tommy Adamson also returned to United after a short spell at Forfar Athletic.

Irving was still involved in team matters but by November, United had a new Manager with the appointment of Jimmy Allan who had played with Falkirk and Dundee. In the first two matches of the campaign, United beat both Stenhousemuir and King's Park by a single goal. Arthur Milne returned to Tannadice, just hours before the match against Cowdenbeath on 4th November but with two goals conceded in the first minute it was an uphill battle for United who lost 4-2.

The partnership of Milne and Gardiner combined well in the next game and United were 2-0 up with a Gardiner double after only half an hour but St Johnstone levelled the match at 2-2 for a point. On the visit to Tynecastle a week later, United were hammered 9-2 but in the first half United played well and were unlucky to be 3-2 behind. Even after the break the Black and Whites did not play too badly but everything went just right for Hearts. Two players were unfortunate enough to make their debuts that day. Hugh Robertson signed from Forfar Athletic and Peter Monaghan from Bournemouth. Monaghan had actually signed just before the game, using a railway barrow as a table when United arrived at Edinburgh's Waverly Station. He did not settle at Tannadice though, and two weeks later he left to return to his home in the west and later signed for Kilmarnock. On the same day he left, Director William Hutchison resigned due to pressure of work in his own business after all three of his sons had joined the forces. William McCutcheon was co-opted to the Board in his place.

Leading 3-1 at half time against Aberdeen in the next match, United conceded four goals after the interval and it was the superior fitness of the opposition that counted as United tired in the 5-3 defeat. Before the next match, against Dunfermline Athletic, former St Johnstone keeper Charlie Thomson joined United from Exeter City. Milne showed some of his old form and scored a hat-trick in the 5-2 win against the Pars but throughout the rest of December, United picked up only one more point in a 1-1 draw with Raith Rovers at Tannadice. In the other three matches, the Black and Whites lost 6-2 at Hibs, 4-2 at St Bernard's and 2-1 at Alloa Athletic. By then Willie Coull had arrived from Brechin City to join the growing band of players attached to United on temporary transfers.

The New Year's Day match of 1940 brought a local derby with Dundee at Tannadice with the crowd restricted to 8,000 despite a request by United to have the capacity increased to 15,000. As it turned out only 5,685 came to the game. Several dozen fans were turned away by the police as they had forgotten to bring one vital piece of attire – a gas mask! The regulations stated no gas mask – no entry! United won comfortably 2-1 with Alex Glen getting both goals. The following afternoon United were in action again on a visit to East Fife and virtually the same line up made the Methil side look ordinary in a 6-3 win. Missing for United was Milne but his able deputy was Willie Ouchterlonie. Back in United colours for the day he scored two of the goals. Indeed, the entire United forward line that day played exceptionally well and it is worth mentioning that every one of the five had originated from the Dundee junior teams; Glen and Fraser (Forthill), Gardiner (East Craigie), Ouchterlonie (Stobswell) and Adamson (Lochee Harp).

United then beat Arbroath 4-2 but lost to Falkirk by the same score line before the weather intervened to wipe out the majority of football in Scotland for the next four weeks. The backlog of fixtures nationwide was so severe that the league season had to be extended. When United restarted, the versatile former Queen of the South and Notts Forest forward Norman Brand had been added. He too was a former local junior with Stobswell originally and had just returned after some time playing in Ireland. He signed for United as a free agent and went straight into the side to play his part in a 3-1 win on 10th February over St Johnstone.

After next beating Hearts 3-2 to partly avenge the thrashing at Tynecastle earlier in the season, United prepared to face Partick Thistle on 24th February in the newly instigated Emergency War Cup. The first round was a two leg affair and United won the first leg 4-2, completely outplaying the Glasgow side. In fact, had the Tannadice side taken more of the chances created they could have more than doubled their tally. The second leg was watched by a crowd of 9,772 despite a crowd limit of 8,000. Entry to the match was being controlled by the police and not the Club. By comparison to the first leg it was a drab match, but the 1-1 draw ensured that United advanced to the next round. James McLean from Hibs made his first United appearance in the second leg after signing just days before. By then United also had a new Chairman. William McCutcheon was appointed on 14th February in succession to Dr Donald.

On 9th March, Third Lanark were the opposition in the next round of the Emergency War Cup, which was now a straightforward knock out tournament. The match was played in front of another huge crowd (this time there was a recorded 10,463!) and the half time score of 1-0 to United gave little indication of what was to follow. After the break United swamped the more fancied Thirds with six goals including a Milne hat-trick and the 7-1 final score was fully deserved.

Players continued to come and go. Keeper Smith left to assist Celtic in March whilst St Johnstone's Jimmy Tennant came to United. Luton's Tommy Dunsmore was next to transfer in followed by Harry Pinkerton from Falkirk. Additional cover was always required as players were likely to receive calling up papers and others might leave the area on short notice.

A narrow 1-0 win over St Bernard's in the league was not the best preparation for the visit of Kilmarnock in the quarter final of the cup but when the Ayrshire visitors came calling, United made short work of them as they had with Partick and Third Lanark. United set of at a blistering pace and were two goals in front within twenty minutes through Milne and Fraser. Gardiner sealed the 3-0 win near the end in front of 15,629, almost double the crowd limit allowed! United's good spell of form continued with a 5-0 win over a poor Alloa Athletic and that was followed up with a 10-2 thrashing of Stenhousemuir, in which Milne scored four and Gardiner got three. But after five wins and a draw from six home games in a row, United lost 2-1 to Dundee at Dens Park. The same score line resulted at King's Park the week before the cup semi final against Airdrieonians.

Easter Road was the venue for the semi final on 13th April and almost 23,000 supporters packed into the ground to watch a goalless draw, although both sides had chances to score. More remarkable was the 20,000 attendance for the midweek replay. Airdrieonians had obtained the services of England legend, Stanley Matthews for the day but United were not intimidated by the big name player and in fact he had a fairly quiet game. After a goalless first half, United took charge and goals from Glen and Adamson had the Tannadice side two up within five minutes of the restart. Dunsmore added a third from the spot and Airdrieonians scored a late consolation but the 3-1 win took United to the final to face Rangers. Unfortunately the fine cup form was not reflected in league results and prior to the cup final United lost 5-2 at Arbroath, 3-1 at Aberdeen and 3-1 at home to Falkirk.

On 4th May 1940, United and their fans travelled to Hampden to meet Rangers. The official attendance was 75,000 but it is estimated that the permitted capacity was exceeded and several thousand more gained entry. The Black and Whites matched Rangers all the way and should have been in front but were denied a penalty and had a goal disallowed for offside when Woodburn of Rangers made a mess of an attempted clearance and the ball fell to Adamson who scored from close in. There was no protest from Rangers and the crowd were amazed when the goal was chalked off. Later, a Rangers official admitted he thought it was a perfectly good goal. After that incident, the match could have gone either way but the Glasgow side won by a single goal scored by Smith with fifteen minutes remaining.

On their way to Hampden
Littlejohn, Kerr, Thomson, Pinkerton, Miller, Brand, Robertson, Dunsmore, Baxter, Fraser, Milne,
Hutton, Adamson, Glen, Gardiner

United never once put on the brake. See FRASER'S do-or-die expression as he dashes in on Jerry Dawson, with Dougie Gray supervising operations from the background.

Sunday Post
5th May 1940

The players had nothing to show for a gallant effort but they were later presented with medals by United approved by the SFA. The Club did benefit financially of course and received a payment of £1,728 from the gate receipts. Added to the money made throughout the cup run, United ended the season with a profit of £764. Their cup exploits also led to an invitation from Glentoran to visit Belfast but due to the players' weekday work commitments, the trip could not be made.

The cup defeat left United deflated and four days later they were well beaten 5-0 by a Raith Rovers side that included Peter Cabrelli. It was the Kirkcaldy side's last game of the season and Cabrelli actually joined United the following day! United had lost six games in a row in the league and a 3-1 defeat by Hibs and a 2-0 win for Dunfermline Athletic stretched that to eight before the last game of the campaign resulted in a close 3-2 win over East Fife to secure a ninth place finish.

Not surprisingly, the 'mighty midgets' Milne and Gardiner scored most of the goals, sharing 44 (Milne 24, Gardiner 20) over the league and cup campaigns.

With Milne and Millar called for military service the team was already beginning to break up as United took part in a charity match in Coupar Angus. Originally scheduled to play a Black Watch XI, United faced a Perthshire Junior Select instead after the army side were forced to call off on the day before the match. Even on the day of the match there was a problem. Neither side brought a ball! One was eventually found and United went on to win 4-1. The match raised £25 including £5 from the raffle of the ball. As the players returned home they could not know but that was the end of senior football in Dundee for the time being.

An interesting footnote to the season came via the Sheriff Court report in the *Dundee Courier* on 28th May 1940. Tommy Dunsmore was the target of a bribery attempt by John McGinlay and Patrick O'Connor. They were alleged to have offered Adamson £50 to make sure that United lost a match against 'a less publicly favoured club'. More money was promised to other United players if the desired outcome was achieved. Adamson's brother, Willie was also involved and he was apparently offered £20. Evidence was given by Mr Graham of the SFA and also by Arthur Cram and Jimmy Allan to whom Adamson had reported the incident. There were counter allegations but the Sheriff found McGinlay and O'Connor guilty and jailed them for sixty days. Their case was not helped by the fact that O'Connor, who worked for a bookmaker had earlier the same day pled guilty on a charge of football coupon fraud!

Plans for the new season were underway when, on 26th June 1940, the Scottish League Management Committee met and decided to suspend national league football. Clubs were left to arrange local competitions if they wanted to and sixteen west coast based sides quickly formed the Southern League. But in the east matters moved more slowly. During July, many clubs including Dundee and Aberdeen decide to cease operations, with St Johnstone quickly following. United were not prepared to go down without trying to find an alternative and began exploring the prospect of entering a team in the Midlands Junior League. A relaxation of the rules allowed senior players to turn out for junior sides. By 20th July, United had applied for membership of the Scottish Junior FA but also retained membership of the SFA. No difficulties were initially expected.

Meanwhile, moves were afoot to form a Midlands League and a meeting was arranged in Stirling to gauge the opinion of the senior clubs in the area. United and Dundee attended along with Dunfermline Athletic, King's Park, St Bernard's, East Fife, Edinburgh City, Raith Rovers, and Stenhousemuir. East Stirlingshire were in favour but did not attend whilst St Johnstone, Leith Athletic and Alloa

Athletic failed to respond. The proposal for the new league met with a lukewarm reception and only a few clubs appeared interested. The others, including both Dundee sides, decided to discuss the proposal at Boardroom level before reaching a decision. In the end, with little chance of covering even basic costs, United were not in favour and neither were Dundee. At the end of July, both were asked by Dunfermline Athletic, the instigators of the proposal, to reconsider but neither was willing to participate. Without two of the biggest clubs in the area the league had very little prospect of success and with only six teams remaining interested, the league did not go ahead.

United's attempt to get into the junior ranks progressed and in early August the application went before the Emergency Committee of the SJFA. Some members were of the opinion that United should resign their membership of the SFA but others said that request was unfair. Resigning from the SFA meant that United would have to serve a five year probationary period before full SFA membership could be regained. United were elected, by a narrow margin, with dual membership but only for the duration of the war. However, following that decision the SFA then raised their own objection, advising United they could not be a member of both.

It was Arthur Cram who came up with a solution to the problem. A new organisation was formed under the banner of United Juniors with new officials and Ally Gallacher came in from Monifieth Tayside as Manager. Sam Irving and Jimmy Allan were co-opted to the new committee and United Juniors applied for and were accepted into membership of the Midlands Junior League, Forfarshire Junior FA and SJFA. The new club leased Tannadice to play their home games.

As Dundee United, the first match in the Midlands Junior League had already taken place with United winning 8-3 but the match was declared void. Dundee United had also been in the Scottish Junior Cup draw but the tie was declared void also. United Juniors were not allowed into the cup, as they were too late in being formed but they kicked off their league campaign against YMCA Anchorage winning 8-1.

The time taken to get the ball rolling had left the majority of the players from the previous season with no option but to arrange alternative clubs. Gardiner played with Morton for a while and many of the other players were turning out for local junior sides. United Juniors began with just three former Dundee United players in the side; John Ross, Tommy Adamson and Johnny Hutton. Results were mixed but by the turn of the year they held a respectable place in the top half of the league. By the end of November, Arthur Cram was predicting that United Juniors might become a permanent fixture in junior circles.

As a source of revenue, the income from United Juniors was welcome but limited with only small crowds attending. Only twice did more than 1,000 fans turn up and in the total of 22 league and cup matches at Tannadice, on average there were 400 spectators. The Directors however were able to bring in some

Jim Brady

additional money by staging a British Empire Bantamweight championship boxing match. Just over 3,500 boxing fans paying between 3/6 (17½p) and 7/9 (39p) brought in £556, but around a third of this sum had to be paid to the government as entertainment tax. United's share is not known but after paying the boxers and the promoter, the Club might have received around £100. The contest took place on 1st January and Jim Brady of Dundee beat Kid Tanner of British Guiana on points over 15 rounds.

During the season the Board was reduced with the departure of A Arrick Smith who left to take up a new job in London. Everyone connected with the Club was also saddened by the loss of former Chairman, William Hutchison who died suddenly on 16th April 1941.

The diet of junior football alone was not enough for most senior sides in the area and in February 1941 Dundee United's Directors discussed a proposal from the SFA to introduce a new North Eastern League. United were very keen to participate and initially, around a dozen other east coast sides indicated that they wanted to become involved, but in the end only Aberdeen, Dunfermline Athletic, Raith Rover, East Fife, Leith Athletic and St Bernard's took part. The seven North Eastern League sides agreed to play the league in two parts, meeting each other home and away in two series of matches. At the end of the first series they all would participate in a knockout Supplementary Cup competition and after the second series the top four sides would play in a another knockout contest, the Mitchell Trophy.

No set wage structure was put in place with each club left to decide wages at their own discretion. It was also decided that the gate receipts would be split 55% to the home side and 20% to the visitors. The remaining 25% would be pooled and divided equally amongst all the clubs involved in each competition. Dundee were invited to join but chose instead to try for membership of the Southern League as Albion Rovers were planning to drop out of that competition. However, the Coatbridge side had a change of heart and decided to carry on leaving the Dens Park side with nowhere to play.

Meanwhile, United Juniors kept up a run of good form in their league campaign and were also doing well in the Forfarshire Junior Cup. Disposing of the RAF 3-1 in the semi final, United Juniors made history as the first side to reach the final at the first attempt since the inception of the cup. They lost 3-1 to Forfar Celtic in the final but following the match there was a protest from United Juniors. It

United Juniors
Standing: Stevenson, Nolan, Clark, Irvine, Forbes, Lowson
Seated: Anderson, Ross, Arbuthnott, Adamson, Smart

was alleged that three Forfar players had infringed junior status by playing in an unauthorised match against an Army XI. The complaint by United Juniors was however dismissed on a 6-5 vote by the FJFA for lack of proof.

United's AGM held in late June was presided over by Chairman William McCutcheon and the year ended 30th April 1941 resulted in a profit of £682 after payment of £1,000 to the debenture holders. United were in reasonable shape but the Chairman appealed for support for the season ahead. By this time it had been announced that Rangers would enter a team in the Eastern League as well as in the Southern League. The Glasgow side had to confirm that they would not breach Rule 37, which stated that a club must field its strongest side. Rangers advised they had enough reserve strength to field two sides of first team players.

As preparations began for season 1941-42, United still had a small number of retained players, including Jimmy Robertson and John Ross who were both based locally and available. As they had in season 1939-40, players would be allowed to turn out for virtually any side with the permission of their own club. The first player added to the Dundee United playing staff was Cornelius Holland from Grimsby Town and he was soon joined by Polish amateur international goalkeeper Antonia Kellar and another amateur, James Witherspoon.

In late June, Jimmy Allan agreed to carry on as Manager and trainer and he soon had Ian Smart from United Juniors added to the squad. In mid July, Joe Vannet from Arbroath and Eric Sibley from Blackpool were drafted in but the best news for United fans was the acquisition of Jimmy Simpson from Rangers. After playing in a trial match on 2nd August, the ex-United man agreed to return to Tannadice. These nine players were joined by Hanlin and McLean from United Juniors for the opening match of the North Eastern League Series One against East Fife on 9th August. The match ended in a 1-1 draw thanks to a headed second half equaliser from Simpson.

United Juniors would prove to be an invaluable source of players to fill vacancies in the Dundee United line up throughout the season and indeed, in the next match, a friendly against a Scottish Command XI, Forbes and Hadley turned out. However this match was more significant for the debut of a player who would become a scoring sensation for United in the war years. Stationed in the area, Huddersfield Town's reserve centre forward, Albert Juliussen made a scoring debut in the 5-1 defeat and for the next few games played as 'Junior' before signing on 17th September 1941.

Before the next league match, St Johnstone's Willie Clark, ex-Hearts and Dundee half back Bert Adamson and Stan Duncan of Queen's Park were all recruited and made their debuts in a 4-1 win at St Bernard's. A stunning 5-0 win over Aberdeen was followed by a 5-3 defeat at Ibrox, and that set the trend for an up and down season. Leeds United defender Dave Smith moved into the area and joined United but Kellar was just about to play his last game. He was injured in the next match, United's first home defeat of the campaign with Leith Athletic winning 4-1. To replace the keeper, Charlie Brownlee of Brechin City was added and was soon joined by another Brechin City man, right half Lomond Reid. Sid Smith from Norwich City was drafted into the side at the end of September.

After losing 2-1 at Raith Rovers on 13th September, some good league results were achieved by a settled line up over the next few weeks beginning with a 1-1 draw against Dunfermline Athletic and a 2-2 result at East Fife. Juliussen hit the first of many hat-tricks in a 5-2 win at Leith Athletic which was sweet revenge for the defeat at Tannadice. He scored another two goals in a 2-2 home draw with St Bernard's and was fast becoming the star player in the side, scoring in every match since his debut. By mid October he had scored 15 times in just ten appearances. However enforced changes to the side resulted in four big defeats with 25 goals conceded in just four games. A 5-0 defeat at home to Rangers was followed by a 7-2 thrashing at Dunfermline Athletic, a 4-2 defeat at Aberdeen and worst of all, a 9-3 hammering by Raith Rovers at Tannadice.

United had managed to acquire George Watson who had been with Queen's Park Rangers and Willie Cook of Dundee. However, the Manager still had to rely heavily on juniors, trialists or players on temporary transfer almost every week as league football took a short break for the new North Eastern League Supplementary Cup competition in mid November. Another new signing, Willie Fordyce from Arbroath was in the side for the first leg of the tie against St Bernard's and with a dramatic turnaround in fortunes United hammered the Edinburgh side 7-1 with the assistance of six goals from Albert Juliussen, the highest number of goals ever scored by a United player in a single match. A 3-3 draw in the return match a week later was followed by a semi final against East Fife and, with newly signed Patsy Gallacher from Stoke City (not to be confused with the famous Celtic player of the same name) in the side, United carved out a 3-2 win. In the second leg, United introduced former Dundee player, Jimmy

Morgan who had made one appearance for the Club in 1939-40, and Bobby Gardiner also returned for that match. Their influence had a significant bearing on the outcome but not before the Fifers pulled back a goal to make it level on aggregate. The Methil side pressed hard after that but United's defence stood firm and then Juliussen scored to take United into the final.

Aberdeen were the opposition in the two leg final with the first leg at Tannadice on 13th December. There was little to choose between the sides in the first half but United took control after the break and with another Juliussen hat-trick, they chalked up an emphatic 4-1 win. For the second leg a week later, Aberdeen drafted in three new players, including keeper Brown from Clyde to replace Johnstone who had been suspended *sine die*. United were handicapped by the loss of Juliussen as the Scottish Command side had first call on the player and he had to turn out for them instead. His absence alone cannot be blamed for the performance at Pittodrie. United were a goal down in just thirty seconds, four behind at half time and conceded another after the break before making anything of the game. A Watson penalty reduced the deficit with five minutes remaining but Aberdeen scored immediately to restore their two goal aggregate advantage. Gallacher scored in the final minute but it was too late. United's only consolation from the cup run was the cash generated from their share of the gate receipts.

After a comfortable 3-0 win over a Polish Army side in a friendly, the season continued with the North Eastern League Series Two. United were immediately handicapped in the first match, against Dunfermline Athletic, as Juliussen, Cook, Duncan and Dave Smith were all co-opted to a Black Watch side to meet the RAF at Gayfield. Losing players to the services sides was a recurring problem for United throughout the war years but there was little they could do as the forces had first call on them. United lost 5-3 to Dunfermline Athletic on New Year's Day 1942 but a week later managed a 1-1 draw at East Fife. Juliussen was called down to Huddersfield the following week but even without him, United engineered a 2-0 win at home to Aberdeen. The player was back a week later and scored both United goals in the 2-2 draw at Leith Athletic. By this time United had also lost the services of some other players, notably Jimmy Simpson who had been allowed to go to St Mirren and Stan Duncan who had moved south with his unit.

During the next four weeks wintry conditions left United idle but they continued to bring in players. Mansfield Town forward Robert Glassey was signed in late January and he was soon joined by Frank Sargent of Spurs and Bob Smith from Stoke City. Holland was released as he was now based somewhere in Wales. United fans then found out that Sid Smith was not only a good footballer but was also an accomplished boxer, when he won the Midlands District Amateur lightweight title at Brechin on 24th January 1942.

During February, United managed to play just one game, beating Dunfermline

Athletic 2-0 with Sargent and Sid Smith scoring the goals but just days after that match it was announced that both players had left the area. It was three weeks before United played again and there was already a backlog of fixtures. The SFA decreed that the games had to be played on Saturdays and that meant an extension of the season was inevitable. The delay in playing games also held up the draw for the second of the North Eastern League cups, the Mitchell Trophy because only the top four clubs in Series Two were to take part.

After the enforced three week break, David Low from Matrix Rovers joined United and Series Two continued with a 3-1 win at St Bernard's, a 4-2 defeat at Ibrox and a 5-1 home win over Raith Rovers. Ronald Gray joined United from Lincoln City and played his part in the next game, a 2-0 win over St Bernard's. He was also in the side that drew 1-1 at Raith Rovers, with Eric Hampson from Stoke City making his debut. Newcastle's Laurie Nevins was the next player to sign and he made his debut in a memorable match at Tannadice on 18th April. United faced a full strength Rangers side and hammered the Glasgow club 8-1. The score is all the more remarkable as United missed a penalty then gave Rangers the lead before a Juliussen inspired side led 3-1 at half time and simply overwhelmed Rangers in the second half. Amateur player, F B Ellmer of Notts County made the first of three appearances for United in the side that lost 2-0 to East Fife the following week.

United had added Raith Rovers former international half back Alec Low and ex-Rangers and Third Lanark half back Jimmy Melville before meeting Rangers in the Mitchell Trophy semi final. On 2nd May, at Tannadice, United won the first leg 2-1 with Nevins and Glassey scoring. It was a slender lead to take to Ibrox for the second leg. The return match attracted only 5,000 as it was played in direct competition with the Southern League Cup final at Hampden. Charlie McGillivray from Dundee and Robert Rooney from Falkirk were signed in time to play against a strong Rangers side that led 2-1 with only four minutes left. Extra time was looming when Nevins snatched a late goal to level the match and win the tie to set up the second final that season with Aberdeen as the opposition.

Originally, the Mitchell Trophy final was to be played as a one off game but it was then decided to stage the match over two legs to allow both sets of fans the opportunity to see their favourites in action. United won the first leg at Tannadice 4-3. David Low opened the scoring but the Dons levelled before Gardiner gave United a 2-1 half time lead. Glassey made it 3-1 early in the second half but ex-United man Arthur Milne pulled one back immediately and then the Dons were level through Patillo. Glassey scored for United fifteen minutes from the end and United went north a week later with just a one goal advantage. In the second leg Aberdeen scored first and Nevins made it 1-1 at half time. The Dons scored in the second half to take the match into extra time and in the first period, Gourlay scored to win the trophy for Aberdeen. Again United had only the consolation of some good gate receipts. More than the maximum 8,000 allowed had turned up at Tannadice for the matches against both Rangers and Aberdeen and at Pittodrie 12,000 attended. All eight North Eastern League clubs received around £150 each from the pool of money set aside from the Mitchell Trophy and Series Two, to add to £175 received from Series One and the Supplementary Cup.

There were still two league matches to play and the contrasting outcomes of a 5-1 win at Tannadice over Leith Athletic, complete with a Nevins hat-trick, and a 6-1 thrashing at Aberdeen reflected the entire season. A makeshift line up against Aberdeen included newly signed Jack Kirkham, a Bournemouth player who had also been with Wolverhampton Wanderers and Queen's Park Rangers. Kirkham achieved some notoriety during the war. He was captured in North Africa in January 1943 and incarcerated in a prisoner of war camp in Italy but escaped to Switzerland in February 1944.

United had certainly provided entertainment in their forty matches over 1941-42. Spectators had seen an average of five goals per game and player of the season, Juliussen scored 39 goals in his 27 appearances. More than sixty players turned out in the black and white of Dundee United but only Brownlee and Adamson exceeded thirty appearances and Juliussen, Fordyce, Gardiner, Ross, Sibley and Smart made over twenty each. In Series Two, a bonus point was awarded for an aggregate win over each opponent and United finished fourth.

After the North Eastern League was over, the SFA proposed that the eight teams would then join with the sixteen Southern League clubs to take part in the Summer Cup. However the Southern League sides put forward various objections, one of which was that Rangers could enter two teams. They also indicated that due to travelling difficulties and possible interference with work of national importance they could not see their way to take part in the cup but would participate in the competition if it was run on the same lines as last year (i.e. Southern League clubs only!). Travelling difficulties did not however prevent Hearts going to Newcastle for a friendly! Both the Ministry of Transport and Ministry of Labour confirmed they had no objections to the tournament and the SFA advised that the competition would not take place without the North Eastern League sides. In the end a deadlock occurred and to avoid further problems the North Eastern League sides withdrew their 'undoubted claim for inclusion.'

During the summer months new directors Arthur Cram (who was still company secretary), Ernest Robertson and Jimmy Littlejohn joined the Board and Sam Irving resigned. William McCutcheon was re-elected as Chairman and presided over the AGM. United's accounts were made public and showed a loss of £165 for the season but a credit bank balance of £391. This figure did not include money received after 30th April 1942 from cup games and the pool share out. Jimmy Allan remained as Manager and he had Brownlee, Sibley, Fordyce, Melville, Smith, Adamson, Low, Gardiner, Juliussen, and Kirkham all available for 1942-43. Gardiner and Morgan rejoined the squad in early August.

Dundee and St Johnstone considered joining the North Eastern League but ultimately did not apply. Hearts and Hibs, who could both manage to put out two teams, did submit an application and were accepted. That resulted in Leith Athletic and St Bernard's being unceremoniously dumped as their support was far less than the two big guns from Edinburgh.

In addition to those players already committed to United for the new season, the Manager secured several others after the trial match on 1st August 1942 as he wanted as many as possible on standby. Permission was received to play George May from Dulwich Hamlet, George Fairbairn from Fulham and Ted Singleton of Leeds United. From Lochee Harp, Bobby Chalmers joined United initially as a trialist but quickly impressed and was signed. United lost the first match of the new season 2-1 at Rangers but beat Raith Rovers 3-2 at Tannadice a week later and then lost 3-1 at Hearts. That set the trend for Series One of the North Eastern League. United took ten points from five home wins, but lost the other two at home and also lost all seven away matches. Jeffrey Barker from Aston Villa looked to be a good acquisition when he turned out in the 3-1 win over Dunfermline Athletic on 29th August, but a few days later he moved away with his unit. The following week Jimmy Woodburn from Newcastle United made his debut but United lost 3-0 to East Fife and it was the same story for debutant Motherwell left wing pairing Joe Johnstone and Max Turnbull as United lost 4-0 at home to Aberdeen. James Walters of Bolton played the first of his two United games in that match also.

Just after the defeat by Aberdeen, Jimmy Allan announced his resignation as Manager and the *People's Journal* hinted that a 'well known figure, living locally, with experience in both English and Scottish leagues' would be the replacement. A name was never mentioned but before long Jimmy Littlejohn assumed the role of Manager assisted by Willie Arbuckle, the former Dundee trainer. He would remain with United until the Dens Park side started up again in August 1944.

As the new Manager, Littlejohn began with a good 3-1 win over Hibs followed by the same result against Hearts, with Willie Westwater making his first and only war time appearance for United. Although the Black and Whites then lost 4-0 at Raith Rovers on 3rd October, they managed a 3-2 win against Rangers a week later. However, the final four matches of Series One all ended in defeat beginning with a 1-0 home reversal against East Fife. A single goal defeat at Aberdeen was followed by two high scoring games, with United on the wrong end of a 6-4 result at Hibs and a 5-3 at Dunfermline Athletic. The circumstances were of course difficult and it was impossible to field a settled side as players came and went so frequently. In Series One alone United used almost forty players and by the time Series Two ended that figure had risen to around sixty for the second season in succession.

After winning a friendly against an RAF XI, 3-1 at Tannadice with former Portsmouth and Fulham player Jimmy Easson making his first appearance, the team faced Rangers in the North Eastern League Supplementary Cup over two legs. Both matches were good entertainment. Willie Jennet from St Johnstone made his debut at Tannadice on 21st November in a first leg that ended 0-0. A week later at Ibrox, Rangers were leading by a single goal with just minutes remaining when Woodburn scored to take the tie into extra time. Rangers had to battle hard against a resilient United but eventually grabbed a winner early in the second added period.

Out of the cup and with Series Two not scheduled to commence until 1st January 1943, United had all of December free but arranged two friendlies to entertain the fans. On 12th December an ITC XI, complete with Juliussen in the line up, were beaten 5-3 and a week later a Midlands Junior League Select fell 4-2 to a United with a completely changed forward five and Willie Wann netted a hat-trick.

In Series Two teams were again awarded a bonus point for aggregate wins but in the case of United that amounted to just an extra two points as the Club managed only five wins and a draw out of the fourteen games. The first three matches were all at home and should have given United a flying start but because of changes to the line up due to the unavailability of players only three points were gathered. The 1-0 win over Aberdeen was a real shock result, but United then lost 2-1 to East Fife and could only draw 2-2 with Hearts. United also lost the next two matches, away to Raith Rovers 3-1 and Hibs 3-2.

By then, there was a shift in the policy of player recruitment with United looking more to the local juniors for regular players although many experienced players turned out for a game or two. Sandy Elder from United Juniors and George (Piper) MacKay from Elmwood were signed in February 1943 and were joined by Albert Simmons of Dundee Arnot and Alf Burnett from United Juniors in March. Willie Wann had been a trialist as far back as January 1938 and had already turned out for United in several matches during the war before he signed in April 1943. In addition, over a dozen other local juniors played as trialists.

Several senior players were also signed with Peter Martin joining from Raith Rovers in February. Others who turned out on temporary transfers or as guest players were Lyn Thomas (Swansea Town), Sanderson (Preston North End), William Murray, Bernard Nelson and Ernie Scholfield (all Sheffield Wednesday), O'Brien (Watford), Charlie Longdon (Brighton), Fyfe and Urquhart (described only as RAF men), Byrne (Blackpool), Spittal (Derby County), Kelly (Grimsby Town) Graham (Castle Green) and John Brannan (Manchester United). In many cases the players' first names were not given or misquoted and sometimes, no name was listed at all.

After a poor start to Series Two, results remained inconsistent but there were a least a few good wins to celebrate. On 6th February, a depleted United side beat Rangers 2-1 for a well deserved two points and a week later only after an injury to Elder did Aberdeen take command to beat United 3-0. Against Hearts at Tynecastle, the combination of Gardiner and MacKay was crucial in a 4-1 win but injury to Morgan early in the second half a week later at East Fife left United severely weakened and they lost 5-1.

Even short of key players the following week, United still won comfortably 2-0 against Hibs but the sequence of win followed by defeat continued at Ibrox where United lost 3-1. However, it was another United line up affected by call offs and injury. The same problem was evident the next week as United faced Dunfermline Athletic at Tannadice but the makeshift team rose to the challenge and won 4-2. More changes to the eleven were required in the last home league match on 27th March against Raith Rovers and it ended 4-3 in favour of the visitors.

United tried to strengthen the side for the Mitchell Trophy first round tie against Raith Rovers and brought in George Sutherland from Partick Thistle and the old United favourite George A Ross for his third time at United, but lost 5-0 to a very strong Kirkcaldy outfit inspired by the inclusion of the famous Joe 'Ten Goal' Payne of Chelsea (he had notched ten goals for Luton Town on 13th April 1936 as they trounced Bristol Rovers 12-0). A five goal deficit was a lot to turn around and into the side United drafted Joe Harvey of Blackpool and Jock Stein, later to be manager of Celtic and Scotland but then with Albion Rovers. United's chances of reaching the next round were already slim but completely disappeared when Raith Rovers scored twice. United rallied and eventually won 4-3 with Ross getting the winner but it was another cup exit and the season ended with a nothing at stake game at Dunfermline Athletic and United lost 3-1.

At their AGM the North Eastern League witnessed the withdrawal of Hibs and they were replaced by Falkirk. It was also agreed the same two league series system and cup formats would take place but the members agreed to change the points system for Series Two. Home teams would be awarded two points for a win and one for a draw but away wins would result in three points and an away draw would bring two points. To encourage support, prices were reduced from 1/3d (6p) to 1/- (5p) with servicemen and youths paying 7d (3p) and boys under 14 were 3d (1½ p). On the west coast the Southern League clubs decided on an increase in gate prices to 1/6d (7½p).

There had been changes in the Tannadice Boardroom in February with the resignation of Chairman, William McCutcheon. His job as a travelling salesman made it very difficult to attend the weekly meetings and he was replaced by John Carnegie Jnr who was re-elected as Chairman at the AGM in July. At the same meeting, United disclosed a loss of £703 for the year ended 30th April 1943. This was largely attributable to a substantial tax payment made in respect of previous years' profits.

By 24th July 1943, Manager Jimmy Littlejohn was openly inviting players to contact Tannadice if they were interested in turning out for United and a trial match was arranged on 7th August. United had several players available including Brownlee, Martin, Simmons, Elder, Wann, Nevins, Morgan and Juliussen but another big turnover in the playing staff was expected. John Wilson from Chesterfield, Percy Bower from Middlesbrough and Charlie McDermott of Bradford City were all signed up shortly after the trial and after the arrival of George Thomson on loan from Aberdeen, United looked set for the new season.

Hearts were the visitors to Tannadice for the first match of 1943-44 and with debut men McDermott, Thomson, Wilson and Bower all on form and Juliussen at his best with a hat-trick, United won 6-3. Bower in particular looked like a prospect but that was his one and only game for United as his unit left the vicinity the following week. As Bower left, Willie Browning of Queen's Park was added and went straight in to the side to face Rangers at Ibrox. After such a good opening match and with only one change to the line up, the 8-0 defeat at Ibrox came as a big shock.

In the fourteen matches of Series One of the North Eastern League, United used around forty players and the lack of a settled line up brought another run of inconsistent results. Towards the end of August, United brought in George Maxwell from Kilmarnock, Tommy Dougal of Leicester City and Willie Johnston from Queen's Park. The first week of September saw debuts for Robert Perret of Huddersfield Town, and Jimmy Wightman from Blackburn Rovers. Amongst the new signings, United unearthed another gem in Boye Karlsen, a Norwegian international forward who became a firm favourite of the United support over the next couple of years. From the junior ranks, Ronnie McWalter of Lochee Harp played trials in September and signed in October and he was joined by Bobby Moodie from Cowdenbeath, Willie Savage from Queen of the South and, in November, Jack Court from Cardiff City. Jim Brown also joined United around this time.

United won just six matches at home and one away but lost the other seven to finish in fifth place in Series One. After the heavy defeat at Ibrox, United emerged 2-1 winners against Raith Rovers at Tannadice on 28th August but a week later they lost 5-0 at Dunfermline Athletic. A 2-0 home win against Aberdeen was followed by a 3-1 defeat at East Fife and then a 4-1 win at home to Rangers. On 2nd October, United lost 4-2 to Hearts but then recorded a 7-1 win over Falkirk at Tannadice with Juliussen netting four times, but the inconsistency continued with a 3-1 reversal at home to Dunfermline Athletic and a 3-0 defeat at Raith Rovers. United found time to fit in a friendly against an RAF Select and won 7-4 with almost half the United side made up of juniors and trialists, whilst the RAF side contained United regulars Brownlee, Juliussen, Wightman, Johnston, Maxwell and Smith. Series One continued with a 5-1 defeat at Aberdeen but the final two matches brought a feast of goals as United somewhat fortunately won 6-3 at Falkirk and 4-3 at home to East Fife.

It was confidently expected that United would eliminate Hearts in the North Eastern League Supplementary Cup and advance to the next round. But at Tynecastle on 27th November in the first leg, with Hugh Hart on loan from

Dunfermline Athletic, it all went wrong. McGillivray gave United the lead but an unfortunate own goal levelled the match and a young Hearts side ran riot and won 6-2. United however were not aided by a referee who disallowed three goals for offside! The first leg was astonishing but the second, a week later, was beyond belief as far as United fans were concerned. Court scored for United within minutes and with the fans in full voice, United scored three more. Unbelievably, the tie was level on aggregate! But disaster struck just before half time as Brownlee fumbled a cross and the ball fell into the net. That seemed to knock the stuffing out of United and after the interval Hearts scored three more. United passed up several chances before pulling one back but went out on a 10-7 aggregate.

Out of the cup, United were without a game until Series Two began on 1st January 1944 with a trip to Aberdeen and of the eleven who took the field, only Brownlee in goal and Juliussen at centre forward had been in the side that opened Series One. For United, Series Two began well with two points from a 1-1 draw at Pittodrie followed by a 3-1 home win against Raith Rovers, a commendable 2-1 away win at East Fife and then an excellent 6-2 result at home to Rangers. United were top of the league but again, the problems of inconsistency and selection difficulties began to take a toll. A large number of the players from Series One had long since been replaced and in Series Two, more players were added to the season's role call. Ernie Hiles was signed from Fulham and, along with Johnny Osborne of Leicester City, made his debut on 1st January. Several juniors had trials over the next two months but none were signed and the next new addition was John Connor from Queen of the South in March. Ex-Celtic player Bert Duffy came on loan from Hamilton Academical in May along with Bill Shaw, signed from United Juniors.

The team was frequently a makeshift lot, often put together at the last minute and a lack of understanding between the players was evident as they lost 4-1 at Hearts and then suffered a 7-1 drubbing at home to Aberdeen. After gaining nine points from the first four games, only six more were gathered in the remaining ten matches, with home wins against East Fife 3-1, Dunfermline Athletic 2-0 and Falkirk 3-0. Although Series Two was not yet completed a fourth place finish was guaranteed after the Falkirk result and that at least brought entry into the Mitchell Trophy.

By the time the first leg of the Mitchell Trophy was played on 1st April against East Fife at Tannadice, team changes were a little less frequent and United won 2-1 but wasted a number of good chances. All the goals came during a four minute spell around the hour mark with McGillivray and Nevins netting within a minute of each other after East Fife took the lead. As it turned out a one goal lead was not enough and in the second leg United lost 3-0, but the side showed four changes and included three trialists.

To round off 1943-44, United, complete with trialists again, played a friendly against the Norwegian Army XI and won 6-0 with a second half blitz. A week later only four of United's signed players turned out as they lost 4-3 to an ITC XI containing a number of United regulars and the last match of the season was a rescheduled game at Ibrox. With another reshuffled line up United lost 6-1. Despite playing only seventeen times for United Juliussen still managed to score 27 goals and the other regular forwards, McGillivray, by now formally signed from Hibs, and Wann had netted over a dozen times each. They, along with Brownlee were the only players to chalk up more than twenty appearances each. Several players made appearances into double figures but the majority of those turning out in the black and white of United made less than ten.

The season was not quite over and United were invited to participate in the Summer Cup. They drew Falkirk and over two legs lost by an aggregate of 6-0. Yet again United struggled to put a side together and the only positive from the matches were the performances of David Jack signed from Dundee Arnot and Ian Hay from Aberdeen Muggiemoss. John Divers from Airdrieonians had also turned out for United in both games on a short term loan deal.

Team selection was by then such a problem that the Directors indicated they might have to shut down operations all together. There was also newspaper talk of an amalgamation with Dundee, with either Dens Park or Tannadice being sold to a consortium involved in greyhound racing. The latter story had some foundation and there were indeed a number of approaches to both clubs, but suggestions of an amalgamation were completely untrue as neither club wanted to go down that route. Dundee were in fact just about to come out of self imposed exile. They had tried unsuccessfully to join the Southern League more than once but for season 1944-45, they applied for membership of the North Eastern set up. The Forfarshire Cup was also to be revived and it was agreed that United and Dundee would play for the trophy in 1944-45 in a two leg tie.

The proposed return of Dundee to senior football had two other effects at Tannadice. Firstly, trainer Willie Arbuckle went back to Dens Park and was replaced at Tannadice by Willie Cameron. That was followed in early June by the demise of United Juniors.

With two senior teams in the city, Ally Gallacher and his committee decided that there would not be enough support for the juniors. Dundee were admitted to the North Eastern League at the AGM in July at which time Arbroath were also accepted to bring the number of teams up to ten. At the AGM it was also decided that only the top four teams would play for the Supplementary Cup after Series One and the Mitchell Trophy after Series Two,

Charlie McGillivray

although this decision must have been changed later as United finished sixth and still took part in the Mitchell Trophy.

John Carnegie Jnr was re-elected as Chairman, Jimmy Littlejohn remained in charge of team matters and Charlie McGillivray was appointed club captain. By September, McGillivray was acting team Manager with a formal appointment to the position announced in November. It appears that Littlejohn had been suffering ill health and was being assisted by McGillivray but then Littlejohn was forced to step down on medical advice although he remained a Director.

The Club brought in only a few new players prior to the start of season 1944-45. Following the capture of Hay and Jack in June, Ken Gibson was signed from Elmwood. These three joined the retained players McWalter, Shaw, Elder, Wann and MacKay, all from the junior ranks. Others in the squad were Juliussen, Karlsen, Court and Connor.

New keeper Jimmy Adamson, a seventeen year old from Dundee Violet, played as a trialist in the first match of the new campaign, a 2-1 win over East Fife and he was signed immediately after. More signings soon followed with the addition of players on temporary transfer from England including Londoner, Ernie Stygal, Gordon Kennedy from Blackpool and Brighton & Hove Albion goalkeeper Jimmy Revel. Former United Juniors keeper Davie Clark signed in October along with John Sveinsson of Norwegian side Lyn Oslo. George McGeachie from St Johnstone signed in December.

The Series One campaign produced just five wins and three draws out of the eighteen matches. After winning the opening match, United lost 2-1 at Arbroath in a close run match and the derby with Dundee at Tannadice a week later produced the same outcome although it might have gone either way. A then North Eastern League record crowd of 15,500 turned out for the match and the kick off had to be delayed by fifteen minutes to let everyone in. Dundee had gathered together a strong side including Woodburn and Morgan who had been with United and it was no surprise when the Dark Blues took a two goal advantage before half time. United were revitalised in the second half and McGillivray pulled it back to 2-1, but the forwards passed up some good chances that might have brought a deserved point.

United began September with a 2-2 draw at Dunfermline Athletic but lost 2-1 at home to Falkirk before a Juliussen inspired side won 3-0 against Rangers at Tannadice. United lost the next two matches at Hearts 3-0 and at Aberdeen 5-1. Then, a 2-1 first leg Forfarshire Cup defeat away to Dundee on 2nd October was followed by a 5-1 win over Raith Rovers with all five forwards scoring. A Juliussen hat-trick was the highlight of a 5-2 win at East Fife. United lost 4-2 at Falkirk on 21st October but came back from two goals behind to beat Hearts 4-3 with a last minute winner a week later. After that, the side suffered from a run of injuries and there were frequent changes in the line up which meant that United failed to record another win in Series One, picking up just two more points from a 2-2 draw at Dens Park and a 1-1 draw at Raith Rovers. The Black and Whites slipped down the table and finished eighth and there was no place in the Supplementary Cup. Instead United arranged a friendly against a strong Celtic reserve side and won 2-1.

By the end of 1944, the football authorities began to look to the future and plans for the revival of the Scottish Leagues were being informally discussed. United's Directors issued a statement staking a claim to a place in top class football. A total of 75,000 spectators had watched football at Tannadice in the first five months of 1944-45, making an average attendance of almost 9,400. The capacity was easily 25,000 and whilst the dressing rooms, Boardroom and Stand needed upgrading, the work would not take long. The Directors felt that the city of Dundee was easily capable of supporting two top league sides.

As they prepared for Series Two, United brought in Hope of Benburb, Dick Scott from Lochee Harp along with Bobby Ross and Robert Walls both from Crosshill Hearts after they showed up well as trialists. Keeper Pat Kelly arrived from Aberdeen but after just two games he moved south and was replaced by Joe Deans on loan from Dunfermline Athletic. The first five matches of Series Two brought only two wins. The first was a scrambled 1-0 victory at home to Arbroath in the opening match on 1st January and the second a well earned 5-2 win, including a Juliussen hat-trick at home to Raith Rovers, with United kitted out in new red jerseys. In between these two wins United lost away to Dundee, 4-1 and Rangers, 5-1. But those defeats paled in comparison to the 9-1 humiliation at the hands of Aberdeen on 10th February 1945. It was United's biggest ever home defeat and there is no apparent reason other than the fact that most of the team were off form. Alex Hendry from Raith Rovers and Jimmy McIntyre from Queen of the South made their debuts and were the only players to obtain pass marks. Douglas Sneddon was signed in February. Jacky Butchart from YMCA Anchorage signed in April and a month later John Kelly from Morton and John Mooney from Falkirk arrived at Tannadice.

United recovered well from that record defeat and the following week beat Dunfermline Athletic 6-3 with yet another new signing, centre half Syd Nicholson from Aberdeen. A 5-2 defeat at Raith Rovers and a 4-0 reversal at home to Dundee were followed by good wins of 3-0 at Hearts and 3-1 over East Fife and a 1-1 home draw with Rangers. But in the next six matches United could manage only a 2-0 win at Arbroath and a 0-0 draw with Hearts at Tannadice. Four games were lost including a 6-0 defeat at Aberdeen and a 6-1 loss at East Fife. In between these two matches, the second leg of the Forfarshire Cup with Dundee was played and ended in a 2-1 defeat for United at Tannadice. The match was hurriedly arranged as part of the VE Day celebrations following the end of the war in Europe and both sets of fans were in party mood during the game.

Although there was still one fixture to fulfil in the league, the Mitchell Trophy intervened and tied United with Falkirk. United acquired Frank Brennan and

Tommy McCulloch from Airdrieonians on loan for the first leg at Tannadice on 19th May. Alec Shirley was signed from Arbroath and he also made his debut in what was a scrappy match at times, but it was a real cup tie just the same although there was no scoring in the first half. After the break, United came from 2-1 down to level through Shaw and won the game 3-2 with a Scott penalty kick eight minutes from the end. In the return match at Falkirk a week later United were forced into team changes and only five players appeared in both legs. But the reshuffled side took the game to Falkirk and did not deserve to lose 3-1 on the day to go out on aggregate.

Falkirk were the opposition again a week later at Tannadice for the last game of the league season. Although played at Tannadice it was in fact Falkirk's home league match against United and as result the 1-0 win earned United three points. The ever popular Boye Karlsen was captain for the day for what was to be his last game for United before returning to Norway. As he was leaving it emerged that Karlsen, an airman, had taken part in four daring raids over occupied Norway but he had never given any indication that he had been involved. It was also a little known fact at the time that Bobby Moodie had been aboard HMS Ark Royal when she was torpedoed in the Mediterranean.

The last of the war time leagues ended with United in sixth place and Juliussen was yet again the top scorer with 18 goals in his 22 appearances. Seven players turned out twenty times or more but there was still a huge turnover of staff. United had again used over forty signed players and around twenty more as trialists. At the end of the season free transfers were handed to Temple, Moodie, Brand and Hendry but United retained Jimmy Robertson, Norman Fraser, John Simpson, Ian Smart, John Ross, Sid Smith, Bobby Chalmers, Alf Burnett, David Low, Piper MacKay, Sandy Elder, George Maxwell, Ronnie McWalter, Bill Shaw, David Jack, Ian Hay, Tommy Adamson, Willie Jennett, Ernie Stygal, Dave Clark, Dick Scott, Robert Walls, Bob Ross and Alec Shirley. Many of these players were unlikely to play at United again but retaining the registrations might bring in transfer fees once everything returned to normal.

Unlike some other clubs, United survived WW2 and emerged ready to face the future with renewed optimism. Looking back on these early years of Dundee Hibernian/Dundee United it is astonishing that the Club were still in existence at all, having come so close to extinction on at least five occasions. The future, or at least the next several years of it, would not be much better but an unbelievable transformation was going to take place to make the Club a major force in Scottish football and throughout Europe for a time.

The Players

Listed in order of the season that they first played for the Club, the following pages contain career details of all the players known to have signed for Dundee Hibernian/Dundee United from the origins of the Club until August 1945.

To qualify for inclusion, the player must have played at least once in the first team either signed provisionally, professionally, on loan or as a temporary transfer. A player is also included from the point that he made his first appearance as trialist, junior, senior, A N Other, guest or under an assumed name and later signed.

1909–10 Player Profiles

Tom Boland

Tom Boland was the first player to join Dundee Hibernian. Pat Reilly signed him from local junior side St Joseph's on 28th May 1909 just four days after the Club were officially formed. The player was a half back and made his debut in the first Dundee Hibs match, at Tannadice on 18th August 1909 against Edinburgh Hibernian in a friendly match that ended 1-1. He was also in the side that played in Dundee Hibs' first Scottish League match against Leith Athletic on 20th August 1910 and on 15th February 1913 he played against Queen's Park as Dundee Hibs made their debut in the Scottish Cup, scoring the first goal. He stayed with Hibs all through the years of WW1 whilst on active service with the King's Own Scottish Borderers and turned out several times when home on leave. Exactly eight years after he made his debut, he played his last game for Hibs on 18th August 1917 against Dundee in an Eastern League match. He then became the trainer for the team for a short time until the early 1920s.

John Brady was a goalkeeper, signed from Lochgelly United. He made his debut in the first Dundee Hibs match, a friendly against the Edinburgh Hibs on 18th August 1909. In season 1909-10 he shared goalkeeping duties with Tom Timmons and was released in April 1910.

Henry 'Henny' Brown, played at outside right and was signed from Kirkcaldy United. He was one of the eleven to feature in the first ever Dundee Hibernian match against Edinburgh Hibs on 18th August 1909. The player hardly missed a game in the Northern League throughout season 1909-10 but was released at the end of the campaign. He returned to the Club during the latter years of WW1 after some time with St Johnstone and made several more appearances.

James Burns was a centre forward who made a scoring debut in a charity match at Arbroath played in aid of the Elliot Golf Clubhouse Fund on 25th August 1909. James also netted four times in two Northern League matches during a short spell at Dundee Hibs but was displaced by new centre forward Peter Yule in October and then released at the end of the season.

Thomas 'Rocky' Cairns was a former Glossop inside right who made his debut in a Carrie Cup match against Dundee Wanderers on 26th March 1910 but after just two more appearances, both friendly matches, he was released. A year later he left to look for work in the Newcastle area where it was reported that he committed suicide by drowning himself.

James Carroll made his debut on 25th August 1909 in a charity match at Arbroath which was played in aid of the Elliot Golf Clubhouse Fund. An inside right, he was also played on the left side and made several appearances over the season. He re-signed for the next campaign but played only in a few friendlies. He was transfer listed but then released in April 1911.

Tim Dailly was an inside left signed from Dundee reserves. He played in the first ever Dundee Hibs match, a friendly against the Edinburgh Hibs on 18th August 1909. Tim was a regular in the side until February 1910 but was not retained after season 1909-10 and along with many of that squad he was released.

Jamie Docherty was signed from Forfar Athletic and was one of the eleven that turned out in the first match played by Dundee Hibs against Edinburgh Hibs on 18th August 1909. Normally a centre forward, Jamie could fill most forward positions and he was a regular in the line up during that first season. He re-signed for 1910-11, making his Scottish League debut against St Bernard's on 10th September 1910 after which he was selected infrequently. After two seasons at the Club, he was released but appears to have been re-signed in December 1912 after a spell at Partick Thistle. He made only one more appearance before being released again. Jamie has the distinction of scoring Dundee Hibs first goal when he netted the equaliser in the opening friendly and for this achievement he was presented with a commemorative gold medal.

Charlie Donnachie was a former Rangers and Chelsea outside right who had spent some time in the USA and on his return to the UK in March 1910, he signed for Dundee Hibs. He made his first and only appearance for the Club in a Carrie Cup match against Dundee Wanderers on 26th March 1910 at Tannadice and was released shortly after.

Archibald Downie was an outside right signed on 7th October 1909, making his debut two days later in a Northern League match against Dundee 'A'. He became a regular in the line up for the next three months but then fell out of the side and at the conclusion of Dundee Hibs' first season he was released.

Tom Flood signed from Dundee reserves. He could play either outside left or outside right and made his debut in the first Dundee Hibs match, a friendly at Tannadice against the Hibs of Edinburgh on 18th August 1909. Tom played just a small part in the Northern League campaign of 1909-10 and was released at the end of that season but was re-signed in October 1914 and made his Scottish League debut against St Bernard's on 10th October 1914. He remained on the retained list at Tannadice all through WW1 but played just a few times in the latter months of 1914 and was released in May 1919.

Simon Fraser was young player signed in October 1909. He made a scoring debut in a friendly against Morton on 4th October 1909. He played in another friendly that season and was released, but appears to have returned to Dundee Hibs during season 1917-18.

Christopher Gallacher signed from Dundee Wanderers and he was captain of the Dundee Hibs that played Edinburgh Hibs in the friendly at Tannadice on 18th August 1909. The player was used infrequently during the Northern League campaign of 1909-10 in both full back positions but was released at the end of that first season.

E F Gibb was an amateur who made his debut on 25th August 1909 in a charity match at Arbroath in aid of the Elliot Golf Clubhouse Fund. Signed as a reserve, he featured in several positions but in two seasons at Tannadice he played in just a few matches. His debut in major competition came on 31st December 1910 against Cowdenbeath in a Scottish League match. He made just one more appearance before leaving the Club in April 1911.

Jack Hannan was a very experienced player who could fill either full back position. He had started his football career at Lochee United and had also played with Celtic and Everton. Jack was signed from St Johnstone on 2nd June 1909 and made his debut in the friendly match against Edinburgh Hibs on 18th August 1909. He was released at the end of that season but after a short time at Brechin City he was brought back to Tannadice and made his Scottish League debut on 16th December 1911 against Ayr United. He never played in season 1912-13 and was transfer listed in April 1913 but re-signed in August 1913 for another season before leaving Dundee Hibs again in May 1914. On 1st January 1919 he made one last appearance in a friendly against a Canadian XI at Tannadice.

James Loney was a reliable half back signed from Clyde on a loan deal, going straight into the Dundee Hibs side that played in the Qualifying Cup at Brechin City on 4th September 1910. At the end of season 1909-10 he returned to Clyde but was allowed back to Tannadice on loan shortly after. He was in the line up for Dundee Hibs' first Scottish League match on 20th August 1910 against Leith Athletic. At the end of the season, he went back to Clyde again but was brought back to Dundee Hibs for a third time in September 1911. He was allowed to leave at the end of the season, only to re-sign in October 1912. He played just twice that season and was released again in April 1913.

Tom McDermott was a former Dundee inside right signed from Forfar Athletic. He made his Dundee Hibs debut against the Hibs of Edinburgh in the friendly match on 18th August 1909. He stayed just one season at Tannadice, appearing regularly in the line up until November 1909, and was released in April 1910.

Joe 'Dod' McNally was Dundee Hibs' first trainer and he was also a registered player. He turned out just once for the Club when Pat Reilly was short handed for the friendly against Morton on 4th October 1909.

James Mudie was a right back who made his Dundee Hibs debut on 16th October 1909 in a Northern League match against Montrose. In the second half of 1909-10 the player was moved to the forward line and re-signed the following season, but in October 1910 he left to join Cardiff City. In June 1912 he returned to Dundee Hibs and made his first Scottish League appearance at centre forward on 26th October 1912 at Albion Rovers. It was not a happy debut as the home side won 5-1 and James was then dropped and released at the end of the season.

James Ramsay was signed from Brechin City. He was a solid centre half who made his debut in the friendly against Edinburgh Hibs on 18th August 1909. He played a significant part in the 1909-10 season but was released in April 1910 along with many of the players who saw Dundee Hibs through that first campaign. On 21st December 1918 it appears that he made a brief return to play for Hibs in a friendly at Kirkcaldy against Gibson's XI.

James Sheridan was an Irish international inside right who joined Dundee Hibs from Alloa Athletic and made his debut in the Northern League against Dundee 'A' on 26th February 1910. He made just a handful of appearances and was released at the end of the season.

James Snee was previously with Dundee Wanderers. He made his debut for Dundee Hibs in the Club's first Northern League match on 21st August 1909 against his old club and in his short career, played in four different positions before being released at the end of season 1909-10.

James Strachan was formerly with Dundee Violet and St Joseph's. He was regarded as a utility player and whilst he normally played right back he could adapt to any position on the right side of defence or attack. He made his debut in Dundee Hibs' opening match on 18th August 1909 against the Hibs of Edinburgh at Tannadice. His claim to fame was the first goal in Dundee Hibs' first win, 2-1 at Arbroath in a benefit match staged for the Elliot Golf Clubhouse Fund. Although a success in the side, like many others in that first season he was not considered to be up to the rigours of the forthcoming Scottish League campaign and was released.

Tom Timmons was one of the founding committee of Dundee Hibs and held the post of Treasurer. He was also a registered player and an accomplished goalkeeper who shared team duties with John Brady in Dundee Hibs' first season. He made his debut on 9th October 1909 in a Northern League match against Dundee 'A'. During that first season he also played in the forward line on one occasion. In his second season he played as a half back and at full back but again his main role was guarding the net and as reserve to Bill Monteith he made his first Scottish League appearance on 3rd December 1910 against Ayr United. After season 1910-11 it is most likely that he retired.

Peter Yule signed from West End FC and he made his debut against Dundee 'A' in a Northern League match on 9th October 1909. A centre forward, Peter had a good scoring record when he arrived at Tannadice and in a friendly against Arbroath Strollers on 6th November 1909 he became the first Dundee Hibs player to record a hat-trick. He was converted to play centre half in the latter stages of season 1909-10. In his second season at Tannadice he was one of the side that made Dundee Hibs' Scottish League debut against Leith Athletic on 20th August 1910. His appearances were limited to just a few that season and he was released at the end of 1910-11 and soon after signed for Dundee Wanderers. He did return to Dundee Hibs in season 1918-19 and played in several friendlies.

Trialist, Guest, Junior, Newman, A N Other

The following players, listed as one of the above, are those known to have played during the season.

McGlynn at inside right on 3rd January 1910 against Cowdenbeath in a friendly.

McKenzie at outside right on 12th March 1910 against Montrose in Carrie Cup tie.

Simpson at left back on 4th January 1910 against Raith Rovers in a friendly.

1910–11 Player Profiles

Percy Bryson signed from junior side Dundee Harp. He made his debut for Dundee Hibs at centre forward on 7th January 1911 in a Scottish League match against Albion Rovers. Percy made just a handful of appearances during his time with Dundee Hibs and was transfer listed in April 1912, leaving soon after.

John Collins was a former Edinburgh Hibs player signed just prior to the start of Dundee Hibs first season in the Scottish League. He made his debut in the league against Leith Athletic on 20th August 1910. An outside left, John still managed to score both of the goals for his side in that opening match but they lost 3-2. He played in most of the Club's matches over the season but was released in April 1911.

Tom Collins was an outside right signed from Airdrieonians on 1st July 1910. He was in the Dundee Hibs line up that made their Scottish League debut against Leith Athletic on 20th August 1910. His only other outing with the side was at East Stirlingshire. This was a scheduled league match but as the referee failed to arrive it was played as a friendly. Tom was released in April 1911.

Johnny Darroch, a left back signed from Dundee, made his only Hibs appearance on 17th August 1910 against St Johnstone in a friendly. On the books for the entire season, the player never managed to break into the side and was released in April 1911. He later played in Dainty's XI, a fund raising combination during WW1.

P Docherty (first name unknown) made his first appearance for Dundee Hibs in a testimonial for George Guild at Arbroath on 24th August 1910. He played only twice more, once in the Dewar Shield and then in a Northern League match.

John Dunn made his debut at outside left in a Scottish League match against St Bernard's on 24th December 1910. In his next outing a week later, he played on the opposite flank and that was his last game for Dundee Hibs. He was one of several fringe players released in April 1911.

Charlie Dunnian was a former Irish international. He had been with Carlin Shamrock and spent some time on trial with Dundee Hibs in October 1910 but then he went to the Edinburgh Hibs. Four months later he signed for the Tannadice side and he made his debut in a Consolation Cup tie at Cowdenbeath on 25th February 1911. His Scottish League debut was made on 18th March 1911 against Port Glasgow Athletic and, playing at centre forward, Charlie marked the occasion with a memorable hat-trick. Even that was not enough to convince the Manager to retain him and he was transfer listed in May 1911. A year later he was still on the books at Tannadice and appears to have been released in April 1912.

John Dwyer was signed after impressing as a trialist in a Northern League match for Dundee Hibs against Montrose on 15th October 1910. He made his Scottish League debut a week later against Port Glasgow Athletic but in direct competition with the regular outside left John Collins, Dwyer was unable to break into the side and was released in April 1911.

(Timothy) Idwal Evans was a Welsh outside left signed after making his first appearance for Dundee Hibs as a trialist in a Northern League match against Forfar Athletic on 29th April 1911. On 30th September 1911 he made his Scottish League debut against Arthurlie and it turned out also to be his last game. He was released in April 1912.

George Fyfe was an ex-Watford player signed from Edinburgh Hibernian. He could fill any half back or inside forward position and made his first appearance for Dundee Hibs on 17th August 1910 in a friendly against St Johnstone. He was in the side that made a Scottish League debut three days later against Leith Athletic and became an ever present in the league side and missed few of the other games played in national and local competitions. At the end of the season he left to rejoin Hibernian in Edinburgh and from there he appears to have gone to Dumbarton from where Pat Reilly again signed him for Dundee Hibs in December 1911. His second stay at Tannadice was less successful than the first and he was released in April 1912.

Dan Gibson signed from Dundee North End and made his first appearance for Dundee Hibs on 10th April 1911 in a Northern League match against Aberdeen 'A'. His Scottish League debut came five days later at Dumbarton as inside right, but the versatile forward could play anywhere in the attack. In December 1912, Dan was transferred to Glossop for what appears to have been a trial period but by February 1913 he was back at Tannadice only to be released in April 1913. He then spent time with Portsmouth and Merthyr Town but in 1919-20 Dan was back with Hibs again and was one of the squad that did well to win the Eastern League title that season, recording a hat-trick against Brechin City in November 1919. After a spell with Montrose he returned to Dundee Hibs yet again and was one of the squad during the disastrous 1921-22 season that saw Dundee Hibs lose Scottish League status after finishing second from bottom. In January 1922, at his own request Dan was granted a free transfer.

James Govan arrived at Tannadice as a trialist and took part in his first match on 24th December 1910 in a Scottish League match against St Bernard's. It was not until the following season that James made any impact and he became a regular in the side over the next few years. He played mainly at centre half but was also used on both left and right in the half back line as well as getting occasional stints in the attack. Even after the outbreak of WW1 he still turned out for Dundee Hibs on several occasions and netted a hat-trick whilst playing centre forward in an Eastern League match against Broxburn United in March 1916. He played his last game for Dundee Hibs in April 1916.

William Graham was a former Dundee Wanderers inside forward, comfortable on either left or right. He made his debut on 31st August 1910 in a friendly against Arbroath and turned out in his first Scottish League match against Abercorn on 17th September 1910. He missed very few games in the 1910-11 season but in April 1911 he was released.

James Izatt was an Edinburgh based junior and although signed in October 1910 he did not make his debut until 17th December 1910 against Arthurlie in a Scottish League match when regular left half George Fyfe was unavailable. Izatt took over at left back the following week and thereafter he became first choice for that position. In the absence of a goalkeeper he filled in between the posts on four occasions during his Tannadice career and was even utilised at outside left for a short spell in late 1912. By the latter part of season 1912-13 the player had been replaced by George Forbes and was released in April 1913.

Alex Marshall signed from Motherwell and made his debut in a Scottish League match against Cowdenbeath on 1st October 1910. He was with Dundee Hibs for just one season and played mainly at centre forward but also filled in at right half. He was released in April 1911 but in season 1918-19 he appears to have played in a friendly for the Club.

Tommy Miller was a former international left back, and ex-Chelsea player signed from Falkirk just two days before he made his debut on 20th August 1910 against Leith Athletic in Dundee Hibs first Scottish League match. He was well established in the team but was displaced by the arrival of James Izatt in December 1910 and at the end of season 1910-11, Tommy went back to Falkirk.

Bill Monteith was an experienced goalkeeper who had been with Beith and Kilmarnock. He made his first Dundee Hibs appearance in a Qualifying Cup tie against Arbroath on 3rd September 1910 and followed that with his Scottish League debut for Hibs against St Bernard's a week later. He retained his place in the side for half the season but was out for almost three months and replaced by Tom Timmons. The keeper was commuting to Dundee by train but he was not prepared to carry on this way and at the end of the season he left to join Albion Rovers.

James O'Gara was a former Middlesbrough and Airdrieonians player signed from Clapton Orient. When Dundee Hibs made their Scottish League debut against Leith Athletic on 20th August 1910, James was at inside right but he was moved to outside right for the remainder of the season. He hardly missed a match in 1910-11 but was reluctant to remain at Tannadice. However, he re-signed just days into the new campaign but left in November 1911 to join Portsmouth.

John Robertson was a centre half, formerly with Beith and Arthurlie. The player made his debut against Leith Athletic in the first game of the 1910-11 campaign and went on to play in every league and cup match of the season. Although transfer listed, he re-signed for the next season but did not take part in any matches and was transferred to Ayr United on 25th November 1911. During WW1 John returned to Tannadice briefly and turned out several times in Hibs' defence in the Eastern League campaigns and in friendlies.

John James Smith was a centre forward signed from Dundee. He made just one appearance for Dundee Hibs, in a Scottish League match on 3rd December 1910 against Ayr United. He was released in April 1911.

William Swan was a centre forward signed from Arbroath. He made his first appearance in a friendly against a Dundee Junior Select on 16th August 1910. On 10th September 1910 he made a scoring debut in his first Scottish League match for Hibs against St Bernard's and a week later he netted the first Dundee Hibs hat-trick in the Scottish League against Abercorn. He fell out of favour and was used in the side less frequently as the season progressed. The player made his final bow for Dundee Hibs in a Northern League match against Dundee 'A' on 26th April 1911 and was transfer listed shortly after.

J Timmons (first name unknown) played only twice as outside right for Dundee Hibs. His first game was a friendly against a Dundee Junior Select on 16th August 1910 and then he turned out in the testimonial match for Arbroath's George Guild.

Bill Tullis was a goalkeeper, signed from Carnoustie Panmure for the Club's first Scottish League campaign. He made his debut against a Dundee Junior Select in a friendly on 16th August 1910 before playing for Dundee Hibs in their first Scottish League match four days later against Leith Athletic. Unfortunately for Bill, he was replaced by the more experienced Bill Monteith in goal by the time the next league match was scheduled and thereafter Tullis was regarded as the reserve keeper. When Monteith left the Club, Jim Crumley came in as first choice keeper and continued to restrict Tullis to just occasional appearances. Always the understudy and unable to break into the first eleven he was transfer listed in April 1913.

Tom Waterston was an inside left signed from Hearts on 22nd October 1910, initially on a trial basis. He made a scoring debut the same day in a Scottish League match against Port Glasgow Athletic. He scored in each of the next two league matches and appears to have then been taken on for the rest of the season, but a few weeks later he lost his place in the side and was released in April 1911.

William Welsh was signed from Hearts and made his first appearance for Dundee Hibs in a friendly against St Johnstone on 17th August 1910. Three days later he was in the Dundee Hibs side that debuted in the Scottish League against Leith Athletic. A right back, the player was an ever present through the first league campaign but returned to Hearts at the end of the season. In December 1912 he was back at Tannadice again and remained with Dundee Hibs until the outbreak of WWI. He was one of the first from Tannadice to volunteer for military service.

Charles Young made his first appearance for Dundee Hibs against Arbroath in a benefit match for George Guild at Arbroath on 24th August 1910. His Scottish League debut against St Bernard's on 24th December 1910 turned out also to be his last game and he was released in April 1911.

Trialist, Guest, Junior, Newman, A N Other

The following players, listed as one of the above, are those known to have played during the season.

Coventry at left half on 24th August 1910 against Arbroath in a testimonial for George Guild. He was also listed at right back on 31st August against Arbroath in a friendly.

Edwards at inside right on 8th April 1911 against Forfar Athletic in the first of three Northern League matches.

Kermack or McKermack from Pitlochry at outside right on 16th August 1910 against a Dundee Junior Select in a friendly. He also played again a day later, at outside left against St Johnstone in a friendly.

Scrimgeour at left back on 24th August 1910 against Arbroath in a testimonial for George Guild.

Stuart at centre half on 24th August 1910 against Arbroath in a testimonial for George Guild. He also played on 31st August against Arbroath in a friendly.

Sutherland from Brora at right back on 16th August 1910 against a Dundee Junior Select in a friendly. He also played again a day later, at right half against St Johnstone in a friendly.

1911–12 Player Profiles

Johnny Brown was an inside left who made his debut for Dundee Hibs in a Scottish League match against Arthurlie on 30th September 1911 after he signed from Partick Thistle. He was in the side for just three matches and was released in April 1912. It appears that he returned to Tannadice in October 1915 and spent most of that season playing at left half.

John Burns was a centre half and made his debut in a Scottish League match against St Bernard's on 4th November 1911. Although he was a regular in the side for four months, his stay at Tannadice was short and he was released in April 1912.

Bob Craig was an ex-Celtic and Brighton full back. Pat Reilly had tried unsuccessfully to bring the player to Dundee Hibs before but he went instead to Darlington in July 1910, apparently on loan. Just over a year later the Manager succeeded at the second attempt and Bob made his debut in a Scottish League match against East Stirlingshire on 19th August 1911. He was a regular in the side during season 1911-12 but at the start of the following season he was displaced by John McGinness and later by William Welsh. Unable to get back into the side, he accepted a move to Southend United on loan in December 1912. He was released in April 1913 and may have returned to Celtic then.

Jim Crumley was a goalkeeper and made his debut against Albion Rovers on 16th September 1911 in a Scottish League match. He missed just one game throughout season 1911-12 but at the end of the campaign he made the decision to move to Canada. Dundee Hibs however, retained his registration. During WW1 he was back in the UK on military service and made guest appearances

Jim Crumley

for several English sides. He also played twice during the war for Dundee Hibs. In March 1919 he was back in Dundee Hibs' goal on a permanent basis and was the last line of defence during the first half of the successful Eastern League campaign of 1919-20. But lured by the prospect of what was then a substantial £6 weekly wage, he joined Swansea Town in December 1920. He later played for Bristol City, Darlington and Bournemouth & Boscombe Athletic.

William Donaldson was an inside forward who made his debut in a Scottish League match against East Stirlingshire on 6th January 1912. He made one more appearance, in a Consolation Cup tie before being released in April 1912.

William Finlay was a student at St Andrews University. A centre forward, he was signed only as reserve cover and made his debut for Dundee Hibs on 7th October 1911 against Albion Rovers in a Scottish League match. He played just a few more times and was released in April 1912.

William Galloway was signed from Lochee Harp and made his debut on 11 November 1911 against St Johnstone in a Scottish League match. He was an outside left, holding down a first team place for just a short time and was released in April 1912.

Willie Linn

Willie Linn made his debut for Dundee Hibs against St Johnstone on 11th November 1911. Pat Reilly had signed the versatile inside forward from Dundee North End and during his long career, he filled most attacking positions. Over the next four years he was a regular in the Hibs line up and whilst not normally a prolific goal scorer he was top scorer in 1912-13 with 15 goals in major competitions. In April 1915 he signed up for military service but remained a registered Hibs player during WW1, often turning out for Hibs when he was home on leave. By February 1919 he was back in the line up for a short time but left Hibs for a season. He returned in September 1920 and saw the Club through the difficult 1920-21 season in the Central League and the following season in the Scottish League that resulted in Dundee Hibs losing their senior status. The Directors recognised the contribution that Willie had made in his time with the Club and he was the first and only Dundee Hibs player to receive a benefit. Dundee provided the opposition and the match ended in a 1-1 draw with many well known players making guest appearances in the Hibs side. At the end of season 1921-22 he was finally released. His total of 231 appearances is unsurpassed by any other Dundee Hibs player.

George 'Jock' Low was signed from Forfar Athletic and made his first appearance at inside right for Dundee Hibs in a Scottish League match against East Stirlingshire on 19th August 1911 but the arrival of James Robertson saw him switch to outside right, a position that he more or less made his own for the next two years. In April 1913 he moved to Clyde but a year later he was back at Tannadice and he remained with Dundee Hibs, rarely missing a game until he signed up for military service in September 1916. Severely wounded and suffering the effects of a gas attack in August 1917, Jock was unable to play again.

Alex Mitchell joined Dundee Hibs in their second season in the Scottish League. A former Clyde player, Alex was signed from Dundee. He made his debut in a Scottish League match against East Stirlingshire on 19th August 1911 and went on to play in the outside left role for much of the season. He was transfer listed in April 1912 and then released.

Andrew Richardson was signed from Our Boys Blairgowrie for the Consolation Cup tie against Forfar Athletic on 20th January 1912 and he made a scoring debut. His debut in a Scottish League match came on 10th February 1912 against Abercorn but it was in a Forfarshire Cup tie against Dundee on 6th April 1912 that the player became infamous through no fault of his. The match ended in a 2-2 draw but soon afterwards Dundee lodged a protest claiming that Richardson had played in a Perthshire tie and was therefore ineligible. The clubs became embroiled in a public war of words, the outcome of which saw Dundee Hibs scratch from the competition and withdraw from the Forfarshire Association. Andrew was harshly punished with a six month ban and played just twice more, in December 1912.

James Robertson signed from Partick Thistle in August 1911. An inside right, he made his debut for Dundee Hibs against Arthurlie on 30th September 1911 in a Scottish League match but after just ten games the player was transferred to Ayr United.

David Scrimgeour was a centre forward who made his Scottish League debut against St Bernard's on 14th October 1911 and stayed at Tannadice for two seasons. During 1912-13 he hit a seam of form, finding the net frequently and recorded hat-tricks against Forfar Athletic and Johnstone. That brought him to the attention of other clubs and he was transferred to Portsmouth in April 1913. He returned to Tannadice late in season 1918-19 and played in a few friendly matches.

John Sharp signed from Third Lanark and played once for Hibs at right back in a Scottish League match against East Stirlingshire on 19th August 1911. He suffered a serious injury that sidelined him for the rest of the season and he was released in April 1912.

Henry Taylor played at right half during Dundee Hibs' second season in the Scottish League. He signed from East Fife where he had been club captain. His debut for Hibs came on 19th August 1911 against East Stirlingshire in a Scottish League match but over the season, he was limited to just a few appearances. He was released in April 1912.

John Young was an inside left signed from Celtic on loan and he made his debut on 19th August 1911 against East Stirlingshire in a Scottish League match. He made just a few early season appearances and although still with Hibs he took no part in the following season and returned to Celtic in April 1913.

Trialist, Guest, Junior, Newman, A N Other

The following players, listed as one of the above, are those known to have played during the season.

Baptie at right half on 27th April 1912 against Aberdeen 'A' in a Northern League match.

Ferrier in goal on 9th September 1911 against Dundee 'A' in a Northern League match.

1912-13 Player Profiles

Harry Black was an outside left signed from Arbroath. He made his first appearance for Dundee Hibs on 15th August 1912 in a friendly against St Johnstone, scoring one of the goals in a 3-3 draw. Two days later he made his Scottish League debut against East Stirlingshire. For the remainder of season 1912-13 he was used sparingly and was released in April 1913. He made a fleeting return to Tannadice for a friendly in April 1920.

Donald Cameron was a former international goalkeeper, signed from Sheffield United just in time to make his debut in a Qualifying Cup tie at Inverness Caledonian on 2nd November 1912. His Scottish League debut came on 16th November 1912 against Ayr United and he retained the first choice keeper's position for the remainder of the season. On 6th June 1912 he left Dundee Hibs to join Cowdenbeath.

Donald Cameron

James Elrick was a goalkeeper signed from Brechin City to replace Jim Crumley. He made his first appearance for Dundee Hibs on 15th August 1912 in a friendly against St Johnstone. Two days later he made his Scottish League debut against East Stirlingshire but soon after that he was out of the side following an injury. Before he had the chance to recover fully, he was replaced between the posts by Donald Cameron and featured only a couple of times after that. In one of his last appearances for the Club he filled the centre forward position in an emergency against Ayr United on 16th November 1912. He remained at Tannadice during 1912-13 without getting back into the team and was released in April 1913.

George Forbes joined Dundee Hibs from neighbours Dundee and made his first appearance in a Qualifying Cup tie against Forfar Athletic on 21st September 1912. His Scottish League debut came the following week against Arthurlie. He was a left back and once in the side he made the position his own for all but six games over the next three years. He remained with Hibs all through the early years of WW1 but played his last game with the Club in April 1917, signing up for military service in August 1917. He was still a registered player until the end of season 1919-20.

Tom Gallacher was an outside right originally with East Craigie before signing for Dundee. He was acquired from the Dens Park club and made his debut in a Scottish League match against Cowdenbeath on 21st December 1912. Unable to hold a regular place in the side he was transfer listed in April 1913.

David (Chappie) Gowans joined Dundee Hibs just after the start of season 1912-13 from neighbours Dundee. He was an inside right with a good reputation and within three weeks of his debut against Leith Athletic in a Scottish League match on 24th August 1912 he was made Club captain. In March 1913 it was announced that the player planned to live in Canada and on 7th April 1913, after a friendly against Dundee 'A', he was gifted a purse of sovereigns by the directors of his old club. Two days later he left the country by ship for his new home.

Michael Lamb was an outside right from St Bernard's who made his debut for Dundee Hibs in a Qualifying Cup replay against Inverness Caledonian on 9th November 1912. Two weeks later, Michael made his Scottish League debut against Leith Athletic. He was transfer listed in April 1913 and appears to have been released and was later playing with Dundee. During WW1 he turned out again for Dundee Hibs in the Eastern League campaign in 1916-17 and had a positive effect on performance until he left to volunteer for military service in October 1916.

Edward 'Ned' MacDonald was a former Glossop and Arbroath inside right. He made his debut for Dundee Hibs on 28th December 1912 in a friendly against Arbroath Amateurs. His Scottish League debut came on 1st January 1913 against Dumbarton. He had an uninterrupted run at inside right for the remainder of the season and then picked up where he left off after re-signing for season 1913-14, hardly missing a match that term. He successfully moved back to left half in season 1914-15. In April 1915 he joined the Cameron Highlanders but remained on the Dundee Hibs retained list throughout the years of WW1. Ned returned to Dundee Hibs in March 1921 and made a few appearances in the Scottish League campaign of 1921-22.

Alex McDonald began his Hibs career at centre half but the player was also capable of filling any right sided defensive position and even played at outside right when the need arose. He made his first appearance for Dundee Hibs on 15th August 1912 in a friendly against St Johnstone. Two days later he made his Scottish League debut against East Stirlingshire. He was transfer listed in April 1913 but re-signed in June and in his second season at Tannadice he managed only two games, both as a centre forward and was released in April 1914. He appears to have returned to Dundee Hibs for a friendly in April 1920.

John McGinness was a right back signed just in time to make his first appearance for Dundee Hibs on 15th August 1912 in a friendly against St Johnstone. He made his Scottish League debut two days later against East Stirlingshire. John made fourteen appearances in the team before losing his place and was transfer listed in April 1913.

George Parker was a centre forward who made his debut at Tannadice in a Scottish League match against St Bernard's on 2nd January 1913. He played just one more match and was released in April 1913.

John Ross was signed from Arbroath and made his first appearance for Dundee Hibs on 15th August 1912 in a friendly against St Johnstone. Two days later he made his Scottish League debut against East Stirlingshire. That ended his brief career with Dundee Hibs as he was released at the end of the season, although he did return to Tannadice during the years of WW1, playing in several friendlies.

Sam Whyte was a right half signed from either Forfar Athletic or Brechin City. He made his first appearance for Dundee Hibs on 15th August 1912 in a friendly against St Johnstone and two days later he made his Scottish League debut against East Stirlingshire. He remained an integral part of the Dundee Hibs side for two seasons but at the outbreak of WW1 he was one of the first Hibs players to volunteer for military service. He remained a registered player although he never turned out for the Club again and was released in April 1919.

Trialist, Guest, Junior, Newman, A N Other

The following players, listed as one of the above, are those known to have played during the season.

Moreau of Loanhead Mayflower in goal on 7th October 1912 against Dundee 'A' in a friendly.

Lumsden, a junior from Glasgow on 7th October 1912 against Dundee 'A' in a friendly. He scored the only goal of the game.

1913–14 Player Profiles

Gordon Bannerman was an ex-Forfar Athletic and St Johnstone outside right. He made the first of only three appearances for Dundee Hibs in the Northern League against Forfar Athletic on 18th April 1914, scoring on his debut. He was released at the end of season 1913-14.

William Brown (brother of Henry Brown) was an Arbroath junior who played outside right. He made his first appearance for Dundee Hibs in a Qualifying Cup tie against Dunfermline Athletic on 27th September 1913 and three days later started in his first Scottish League match, against Vale of Leven. He was a regular in the side until January 1914 when he lost his place but he re-signed for the following season. However, just after WW1 broke out he volunteered for military service with the Black Watch. In September 1915 he was reported missing in action.

Willie Cavanagh signed from Dundee Violet, one of a group of players who joined towards the end of season 1913-14. He played in several forward positions and at half back, making a scoring debut at outside right in a Scottish League match against Vale of Leven on 4th April 1914. He remained with Dundee Hibs until January 1915, at which time he volunteered for military service. He remained a registered player all through the years of WW1, finally being released in April 1920.

Andrew Crawford was a St Joseph's player. He made his debut on 15th November 1913 against Dunfermline Athletic. During a short career with Dundee Hibs he was used at full back, half back and in the attack but never became established in the side. When WW1 broke out he volunteered for military service and although he remained a registered player he never played after the end of 1913-14 and was released in April 1919.

Pat Currie was a former East Fife outside right who made his debut for Dundee Hibs in a Scottish League match against St Johnstone on 16th August 1913. He was unable to hold down a place in the side during 1913-14, making just a few appearances and although he remained a registered Hibs player throughout the years of WW1, he played just once more, in December 1916 in an Eastern League match. He was released in April 1919.

William Duncan made his debut on St Valentines Day 1914 against Albion Rovers in a Scottish League match. He was an outside right and made little impact in a very short career at Tannadice. After just six consecutive matches he was released in April 1914.

Alex Grieve was one of a group of local juniors signed towards the end of season 1913-14. The keeper made his debut for Dundee Hibs on 4th April 1914 in a Scottish League match against Vale of Leven and had an uninterrupted run in the side until January 1915 when he left Dundee Hibs, perhaps to volunteer for military service. He remained a registered Hibs player throughout the years of WW1 and at the beginning of season 1917-18 he was back between the posts for the Club for a few matches in the Eastern League campaign. He was finally released in April 1919.

Bill Henderson was a former Dundee, Hearts and Bradford City centre half, signed from Grimsby Town. He made his debut for Dundee Hibs in the Scottish League match against St Johnstone on 16th August 1913. On 3rd January 1914 he scored Hibs' 100th league goal in a defeat at home to St Bernard's. He was a regular in the side throughout that season but with the outbreak of WW1 it seems that he either joined the forces or was involved in war work out of the area. Although still a registered Hibs player he did not play again until January 1917 and again in early 1919 in friendly matches.

Joe Hughes was one of a group of local juniors signed at the end of the season 1913-14 with the next campaign in mind. He made his first appearance for Dundee Hibs in a Forfarshire Cup final replay against Arbroath on 28th March 1914 at right half. A week later he moved into his more accustomed centre half role in his Scottish League debut against Vale of Leven and more or less made that position his own. The arrival of Herbert Dainty a year later meant Joe had to move over to the right again. He remained with Hibs through the Eastern League campaigns in the early years of WW1 and in April 1916, it appears that he volunteered for military service. He next featured in the side during a series of friendlies in the final months of 1918-19 and was one of the squad with the Club through the Eastern League championship season of 1919-20. Joe played just a few matches late in the next season and was released in April 1921.

Frank Leckie played his first Dundee Hibs match in the Scottish League against Albion Rovers on 11th October 1913. An inside left, he was an infrequent starter and was released at the end of season 1913-14 but in October 1915 he re-signed to fill the outside left position for a short time when the Club were competing in the Eastern League. He then appears to have volunteered for military service during WW1. He was a registered Dundee Hibs player throughout the war years but played just a few times in friendlies in the spring of 1919 and was released at the end of that season.

David 'Collie' Martin was a former Dundee and Brechin City centre forward. His signing was something of a coup for Pat Reilly, who acquired the player in mid July 1913. He made his debut against St Johnstone on 16th August 1913 in a Scottish League match and went on to star in the Dundee Hibs side that season, playing in every league match, becoming top scorer in Division Two with 22 goals. Despite intense competition from several other sides, Collie was persuaded to remain at Tannadice for 1914-15 and after missing just one league match he was top scorer in the division again with 30 goals including five in one game against Albion Rovers in December 1914. The following season saw the prolific goal scorer on the trail of another record until he volunteered for

David 'Collie' Martin

military service with the Black Watch in November 1915. His record as a Hibs player was truly remarkable including four hat-tricks in local competitions but unfortunately his talent was never to be seen again as he was killed in action in April 1917.

Charlie McPhilips was a former Hearts goalkeeper signed as a direct replacement for Donald Cameron who had left to join Cowdenbeath. Charlie made his debut in a Scottish League match on 16th August 1913 against St Johnstone and remained the first choice keeper until he was displaced by George Sutherland in January 1914. Both keepers were released in April 1914.

William Spence played at right back or right half with Stobswell. He was one of a group of players signed at the end of season 1913-14 and made his debut in a Scottish League match against Vale of Leven on 4th April 1914. He was a regular in the side over the next two years but played less frequently after 1916 making his last appearance in August 1917. He remained a registered player until he was released in April 1919.

Fred Stoessel

Fred Stoessel was an outside left who made his debut on 16th August 1913 against St Johnstone in a Scottish League match. He retained his place in the side for almost the entire season. Fred scored the goals in the Qualifying Cup semi final replay at Tannadice against Inverness Caledonian that took Hibs to the final of that competition for the first and only time. Although he re-signed for season 1914-15, Fred volunteered for military service immediately following the outbreak of WW1. He remained a registered Hibs player all through the war years but it was April 1919 before he was seen playing for the Club again. He was released soon after but returned very briefly towards the end of season 1921-22.

George Sutherland was a former Arbroath keeper. He made his first appearance for Dundee Hibs in a Northern League match on 1st January 1914 against Montrose and on 10th January he made his Scottish League debut against Leith Athletic. He was displaced as first choice keeper following the arrival of Alex Grieve in April 1914 and along with McPhillips he was released in April 1914 and then volunteered for military service in WW1.

Trialist, Guest, Junior, Newman, A N Other

The following players, listed as one of the above, are those known to have played during the season.

Adamson at outside right on 1st January 1914 against Montrose in a Northern League match.

Bertram at left half on 1st January 1914 against Montrose in a Northern League match.

Gordon at centre forward on 1st January 1914 against Montrose in a Northern League match.

1914–19 Player Profiles

John Aitken was a Perth based junior international who signed with Dundee Hibs in the latter stages of season 1915-16. He was a left sided attacking player and made his debut in an Eastern League match against Dunfermline Athletic on 12th February 1916. He was released in April 1916.

Dave Balfour was a former Dundee goalkeeper. He joined Dundee Hibs in the latter years of WW1, making his debut just weeks into the Eastern League season of 1917-18, against East Fife on 22nd September 1917. He missed just one game over the rest of that season and turned out for the Club once more for a friendly in February 1919.

Jimmy Bellamy was a very experienced player who was comfortable in most right sided forward positions or at right half. He had been with a number of English sides including Reading, Woolwich Arsenal, Burnley and Fulham and had also played north of the border with Dundee and Motherwell. The player made his first appearance for Dundee Hibs against Dundee in an Eastern League match on 18th August 1917 and remained with the Club until the conclusion of WW1 at which point he returned south.

Jimmy Bissett was a half back with neighbours Dundee. During February 1919, he played a few times in friendly matches for Dundee Hibs, making his debut on 1st February 1919 against Dainty's XI.

Robert Blackwood was a goalkeeper with Johnstone. He came to Tannadice on loan for a short spell in the second half of season 1915-16, making his debut in the Eastern League against Armadale on 15th January 1916. At the end of the season he returned to his own club.

Jack Brown was a player from the Middlesbrough area. He was stationed locally during WW1, and played for Dundee Hibs, making his first appearance on 9th September 1916 in an Eastern League match against Lochgelly United. Jack was used at centre forward or inside right on a few occasions when he was in the Dundee area.

Charlie Bruce was a goalkeeper with Brechin Hearts and he was signed in February 1915. His first Dundee Hibs appearance was in a Northern League match against Brechin City on 20th February 1915. He retained the keeper's jersey until October 1915 at which time it appears he volunteered for military service. Charlie remained a registered Hibs player throughout WW1 but turned out for the Club just once more and was finally released in April 1919.

Alex Chaplin could play in any full back or half back position. He featured regularly for Dundee Hibs during season 1914-15 after his debut on 15th August 1914 against Dunfermline Athletic in a Scottish League match. It appears that he volunteered for military service in the summer of 1915. Although he remained a registered player all through WW1, Alex never played for Dundee Hibs again and was released in April 1919. He then joined Fulham and had six successful years at the London club.

James Cheyne was signed just as season 1914-15 was under way. He was a centre forward but could fill most attacking roles and made a scoring debut for Dundee Hibs on 29th August 1914 in a Scottish League match against St Johnstone. A year later he volunteered for military service and thereafter played only a few times for the Club in 1916 whilst on leave. He was a registered Hibs player throughout WW1 and was not released until April 1920.

Connolly (first name unknown) was an outside right who played for Dundee Hibs in the latter stages of season 1918-19. He made his first appearance on 22nd March 1919 against Arbroath in a friendly.

William Connolly was a Glasgow based junior goalkeeper. He joined Dundee Hibs in time to make his first appearance in a Loftus Cup tie against Dunfermline Athletic on 30th January 1915. His Scottish League debut came seven days later against East Stirlingshire but he had just one more outing and was released on 15th February 1915.

Herbert Dainty was a former Dundee, Bradford City and Ayr United centre half. He accepted the post of Player/Manager at Dundee Hibs in April 1915 and Ayr United received what was then a Scottish Second Division record fee of £100.

Dundee Hibs had first tried to sign the player late in 1912 and then again in at the end of season 1913-14. Herbert had won a Scottish Cup winner's medal with Dundee in 1910. A very experienced player, his first appearance for Dundee Hibs was in a Northern League match against Forfar Athletic on 24th April 1915. During WW1, whilst with Dundee Hibs, he became involved in fund raising for the war effort with his own team, 'Dainty's XI'. As a result, he stopped playing for Dundee Hibs in December 1917 at which point he was elevated to the Board of Directors at the Club. Pat Reilly then returned to take over as Manager. By the start of season 1919-20, Herbert was the Chairman of Dundee Hibs. He was replaced as Chairman in June 1922 and a few months later, with several new Directors appointed to the Board, he resigned due to his other business commitments.

Herbert Dainty

Charlie Dinnie was a former Dundee player. He moved to Huddersfield Town in 1911 and remained on their books for ten years. During WW1 the player was with Dundee Hibs for the Eastern League campaign of 1916-17. He made his debut against Lochgelly United on 19th August 1916 and went on to take part in most of the matches that season.

Tom Dorward was a versatile forward signed from Dundee. Pat Reilly unsuccessfully tried to sign the player for season 1910-11 but he did eventually join Dundee Hibs and made his debut in an Eastern League match against Bathgate on 9th October 1915. Throughout his one season at Hibs, 1915-16 he played in various attacking positions.

Dunn (first name unknown) was a goalkeeper who turned out for Dundee Hibs during season 1918-19. It may have been Stephen Dunn who was in the army during WW1 and later played for Arsenal. He made his debut on 30th November 1918 in a friendly against Keith & Blackmans, a works team from Arbroath.

David Ferguson was a former Dundee Wanderers and Forfar Athletic player. He was the first of Herbert Dainty's signings and made his debut in an Eastern League match on 21st August 1915 against East Stirlingshire. David could play in either full back position and turned out regularly until December 1915. After that he more than likely volunteered for military service. David remained a registered Dundee Hibs player throughout the years of WW1 and was finally released in April 1920.

'Ref' Ferrier (first name was either Frank or Robert) had played for Dundee in the late 1890s. He was a full back or half back and made his debut for Dundee Hibs in an Eastern League match on 19th August 1916 against Lochgelly United. He stayed with the Club through the latter years of WW1 and probably went back to Dundee once the Scottish League started up again.

Johnny Fitzpatrick could play at either right or left half. Also known as 'Fitchie', he was one of a family of five brothers, all well known in football circles in the area. He joined Dundee Hibs from junior side St Joseph's and made his first appearance on 25th August 1917 against East Fife in an Eastern League match and went on to serve the Club for two seasons.

David Gillies was a former Hearts inside right signed for Dundee Hibs from Arbroath in August 1915. He made a scoring debut in the Eastern League on 21st August 1915 against East Stirlingshire but made just two more appearances for the Club and it is presumed he then joined the armed forces.

Sam Gilligan was one of a number of Dundee players to join Dundee Hibs in the latter years of WW1. He made a scoring debut against Dundee on 10th November 1917 in a Loftus Cup tie. Sam made just one more appearance for Hibs, two weeks later in the Loftus Cup replay against Dundee at Tannadice and he scored again.

James Herron was a former Dundee outside right. He moved to Arbroath but turned out for Dundee Hibs on 11th December 1915 in a friendly against the 2/7 Argyll & Sutherland Highlanders side. In April 1916 he made three more appearances for Hibs and signed again in season 1919-20 when he played a big part in Hibs' Eastern League championship campaign in which he was an ever present. He was also in the Dundee Hibs side that competed in the Central League in the following season but left the Club in May 1921.

Tom Houston was an inside forward and turned out for Hibs in several friendlies in the latter part of season 1918-19 making a debut on 9th April 1919 against St Joseph's. He signed for the Club two years later from junior side Roselea and made his Scottish League debut against Alloa Athletic on 10th December 1921. He then made several appearances before he was released at the end of that campaign.

Bob Husson was formerly a left back with Dundee, and joined Dundee Hibs for the 1916-17 season making his first appearance in an Eastern League match on 26th August 1916 against East Stirlingshire. He returned to his former club in August 1917.

Joe Johnston was a half back with Dundee and spent some time with Dundee Hibs during season 1918-19, making his debut on 21st September 1918 against the Highland Light Infantry side in a friendly match.

Kennedy (first name unknown) was a goalkeeper with North End. The player was with Dundee Hibs through most of season 1916-17, making his debut in an Eastern League match on 19th August 1916 against Lochgelly United.

Gordon Kerr was a goalkeeper who played twice for Dundee Hibs in 1916. His debut was on 15th April 1916 against Dunfermline Athletic in an Eastern League match.

John Knowles was a local junior who made his debut at right half in a Scottish League match against Cowdenbeath on 12th September 1914. He played in just a handful of games for Dundee Hibs and was released in April 1915.

Val Lawrence made a scoring debut for Dundee Hibs on 18th September 1915 against Kirkcaldy United in an Eastern League match. An inside right, he had been with Newcastle United, Forfar Athletic, Manchester City, Oldham Athletic and Leeds City. He played just four times for Hibs whilst in this area and was back briefly in March 1919 before returning south to resume his career in England.

Ernie Levett was from the Newcastle area and had played with non league West Kirk and Silksworth. Whilst serving in the forces he assisted Dundee Hibs on several occasions, making a scoring debut in an Eastern League match against Dunfermline Athletic on 8th December 1917. He returned south when WW1 ended and later joined Brentford.

Adam Lindsay was able to play at either outside or inside left and turned out in Dundee Hibs colours for the first time in a friendly against St Johnstone on 29th March 1919. He was in the line up again in friendlies during April 1921 and then signed for the Club in the latter stages of the Scottish Alliance season of 1922-23 after a successful trial against Ayr United 'A' on 17th February 1923.

McCabe (first name unknown) was formerly in the ranks of Dundee reserves and made his debut for Dundee Hibs on 21st October 1916 in an Eastern League match against Dunfermline Athletic. Available for most forward positions, he remained at Dundee Hibs through the remaining years of WW1. It appears that he may have returned to Hibs in the early 1920's as assistant trainer.

Tom McCulloch was an inside right. A well known player with Dundee, he joined Dundee Hibs during WW1, making his debut against Armadale on 8th September 1917 in an Eastern League match. He remained with the Club for two seasons and then returned to Dundee for the resumption of Scottish League football in August 1919.

George McGregor was an outside left with Partick Thistle. He joined Dundee Hibs for a short period in 1916, making his debut in a Forfarshire Cup semi final second replay against Arbroath at Dens Park on 11th March 1916. He left again at the end of that season but appears to have played for Hibs on one more occasion, a friendly against the Hibs of Edinburgh in April 1919.

James McGuire was signed from St Johnstone and made his debut for Dundee Hibs in an Eastern League match against Kirkcaldy United on 18th September 1915. He was a versatile forward who played in almost all attacking positions. The player remained with Hibs throughout WW1 taking part in all three Eastern League seasons between 1915 and 1918. In season 1918-19 he played in some of the friendly matches that were organised and twice recorded hat-tricks against a Labour Garrison XI in October 1918.

McKee (first name unknown) was an inside left who turned out for Hibs towards the end of season 1918-19. He scored a goal in his first appearance which was against Dainty's XI on 1st February 1919.

Charlie McKenzie was a junior international inside right who assisted Dundee Hibs just twice during WW1. He made his first appearance on 11th November 1916 against Broxburn United in an Eastern League match.

McKerracher (first name unknown) was a goalkeeper from the Falkirk area who played a few times for Dundee Hibs during the Eastern League campaign of 1915-16. He made his debut on 23rd October 1915 against Broxburn United.

McKirdy (first name unknown) was an outside left who turned out for Hibs towards the end of season 1918-19. He made a scoring debut for Dundee Hibs against Dainty's XI on 1st February 1919.

McNeil (first name unknown) was a defender who made his debut for Dundee Hibs in the match against Keith & Blackmans works team on 30th November 1918. During season 1918-19 he was a frequent member of the side.

David Millar made his debut in an Eastern Cup match on 3rd March 1917 against Dunfermline Athletic. He made a few appearances the following season in friendlies. In 1919-20 he re-signed and over the season he played in several positions both in attack and at half back before he left the Club in April 1920.

Milne (first name unknown) was in the Dundee Hibs side briefly during the latter stages of 1918-19. A defender, he made his debut in a friendly against junior side Glenisla on 30th April 1919.

John Mulholland made his first appearance for Dundee Hibs against Forfar Athletic in a friendly on 12th April 1919. He scored a debut goal from an unaccustomed centre forward position. In the Eastern League championship season he was the first choice left back. John remained with the Club during the 1920-21 Central League season and signed again for the unsuccessful Scottish League season a year later, making his first appearance in that competition on 20th August 1921 against Bo'ness. After three years at Hibs he was released in April 1922.

John Mulholland

Tom Murray was a local junior who made his Dundee Hibs debut in an Eastern League match against East Fife on 13th November 1915. He played for Hibs in most forward positions until February 1916 when he appears to have volunteered for military service. In October 1918 he was back at Tannadice and marked his return with four goals in a friendly against an Army Select. In the Eastern League championship season of 1919-20, Tom was a frequent starter in the side but he was released at the end of that campaign.

Albert 'Bert' Neal made his Hibs debut in the Eastern League on 21st August 1915 against East Stirlingshire. The former Northampton Town, Dundee and St Johnstone player could play in a number of positions but was generally used at right back. He was with Dundee Hibs for just one season and then he volunteered for military service in WW1.

George Nicolson was an outside left, signed from Arbroath. He made his debut in an Eastern League match for Dundee Hibs on 9th October 1915 against Bathgate but played just once more for the Club.

Vic Outerson played his first game for Dundee Hibs against East Stirlingshire on 26th August 1916 in an Eastern League match. He could play at either outside left or right and featured in many of the matches during season 1916-17. He left Hibs in August 1917.

William Reid played a few times for Dundee Hibs during season 1918-19. He made his first appearance for the Club on 21st December 1918 against Gibson's XI (a select made up from players of Hearts and Raith Rovers).

Charles Rennie was a full back who joined Dundee Hibs at the beginning of season 1917-18. He made his first appearance against Dundee in an Eastern League match on 18th August 1917 but three months later he left the Club.

James Ritchie was an outside left signed from Arbroath. He made a scoring debut in the Eastern League on 21st August 1915 against East Stirlingshire. In October 1915 he appears to have left Dundee Hibs and volunteered for military service.

Willie Robb was a goalkeeper who had played with Birmingham City. He turned out for Dundee Hibs in season 1918-19, making his debut on 21st September 1918 against a Highland Light Infantry side in a friendly. He later played with Armadale, Rangers and Aldershot.

Rutherford (first name unknown) was listed twice for Dundee Hibs making his debut on 19th August 1916 against Lochgelly United in an Eastern League match.

Jimmy Sharp was with Dundee Hibs during WW1. He had started his career with Dundee before moving south to join Fulham. He then spent time with Woolwich Arsenal and Rangers before returning to Fulham and then moving to Chelsea. He turned out for Hibs for the first time on 18th September 1915 against Kirkcaldy United in an Eastern League match and was a regular in the side until he volunteered for military service with the Black Watch in April 1916. He returned to Tannadice briefly in February 1919 and then went back south to sign for Fulham for a third time.

William Stalker was a former Everton player who made his first appearance for Dundee Hibs in an Eastern League match against Dunfermline Athletic on 8th December 1917. He then became a regular at right back for the remainder of that season. He returned to Tannadice for the 1919-20 season and played a major role in the Eastern League championship winning side. He featured for

Hibs in the early part of the next season but fell out of favour in the latter half and was released in April 1921.

Henry Steel was formerly a goalkeeper with Dundee Wanderers and was signed following the departure of Alex Grieve in January 1915. Henry made his debut on 16th January 1915 in a Scottish League match against Abercorn. He had just one more outing before he was released on 1st February 1915 but appears to have returned in December to play in a friendly.

Archie Taylor was a former Dundee centre forward who made his debut for Dundee Hibs on 15th April 1916 against Dunfermline Athletic in an Eastern League match at half back. He reverted to his favoured position in season 1915-16 and became Hibs top scorer netting twelve times in his seventeen appearances. Included in his tally were hat-tricks against Lochgelly United and Bathgate. In the following season Archie played exclusively at left back and as a result he scored no more goals. In his last season at Tannadice, 1918-19 he played in several friendlies. Following the appointment of Jimmy Brownlie as Manager in 1923, Archie was brought

Archie Taylor

back to Tannadice as the team's trainer. He had built up a solid reputation on the coaching side in the preceding years as assistant trainer with Dundee. The 1924-25 promotion winning side were coached by Archie and much of the credit for that successful campaign was attributed to him. In September 1926 he left the Club, to take up the post of trainer at Huddersfield Town. It is not known how long he remained with the English side but in the two seasons following his move there, they finished second top of the English League.

David 'Napper' Thomson was better known as a player with neighbours Dundee. He was with Dundee Hibs for two seasons, making his debut in an Eastern League match against Dunfermline Athletic on 1st September 1917. Generally considered a centre half he was capable of filling virtually any defensive role. Although rumoured to be staying with Hibs, at the beginning of 1919-20, with the resumption of the Scottish League, he returned to Dens Park.

'Napper' Thomson

George Wilkie

George Wilkie played his first game for Dundee Hibs in a friendly against the Highland Light Infantry on 21st September 1918. Initially a forward, he played throughout that season and signed on with Hibs again for the Eastern League championship season of 1919-20. Mid way through that campaign he was converted to half back and although he filled a forward berth from time to time, the rest of his career was played in the mid line. He made his first appearance in a Scottish League match on 20th August 1921 against Bo'ness but played just a few of the games during the unsuccessful campaign of 1921-22 and was released at the end of that season.

Whitson (first name unknown) (sometimes listed as Winston) was a member of the Dundee Hibs squad during the latter stages of season 1918-19. He made his debut on 22nd March 1919 against Arbroath in a friendly. He was a defender and may have been Tony Whitson who had played with Newcastle United.

Matthew Wilson was a centre forward signed in September 1913. He was probably released in the summer of 1914 without ever making it into the side. In season 1918-19, it appears that he played in many of Hibs' friendlies making a scoring debut on 6th April 1918 against East Fife. He was a prolific goal scorer, netting five in one game against an RAF XI and he scored four against a Royal Garrison Artillery side.

Trialist, Guest, Junior, Newman, A N Other

The following players, listed as one of the above, are those known to have played during the war years.

Alexander (ex-Dundee) at right back on 5th October 1914 against Dundee 'A' in a Northern League match.

Allan at outside left on 3rd March 1917 against Dunfermline Athletic in an Eastern Cup tie.

Baird in goal on 4th November 1916 against East Fife in an Eastern League match.

Bebbington at left half on 19th August 1916 against Lochgelly United in an Eastern League match.

Bennett at outside left on 17th April 1915 against St Johnstone in a Loftus Cup tie.

Besser at right back on 2nd December 1916 against St Bernard's in an Eastern League match.

Bruce at inside right on 9th April 1919 against St Joseph's in a friendly, scoring two goals.

Burge at centre forward in four consecutive Eastern League matches beginning on 26th January 1918 against Dundee. In his four games he scored two goals.

Andrew Cabrelli at inside left on 9th November 1918 against the Army Pay Corps in a friendly.

Luigi Cabrelli at right back on 9th November 1918 against the Army Pay Corps in a friendly.

Cabrelli in goal on 23rd November 1918 against the Highland Light Infantry in a friendly.

Campbell at left back on 2nd December 1916 against St Bernard's in an Eastern League match.

Chalmers at right half on 22nd February 1919 against a Dundee Shipyard Select in a friendly.

Charlesworth at inside right on 28th October 1916 against East Fife in a Loftus Cup tie.

Clark at left half on 21st December 1918 against Gibson's XI in a friendly.

Connolly at inside left on 24th April 1915 against Forfar Athletic in a Northern League match.

Cook at centre forward on 15th March 1919 against Dundee in a friendly.

Coyle or McCoyle at outside left on 1st January 1917 against East Stirlingshire in a Loftus Cup tie. He also played at outside right on 3rd March 1917 against Dunfermline Athletic in an Eastern Cup tie.

Davidson at centre half on 19th October 1918 against an Army Select in a friendly.

Dow at inside right on 23rd November 1918 against a Highland Light Infantry side in a friendly.

Edwards at right back on 28th October 1916 against East Fife in a Loftus Cup tie. He played again on 4th November 1916 against East Fife in an Eastern League match.

Elder at centre half on 25th August 1917 against East Fife in an Eastern League match.

Galt at centre forward on 23rd February 1918 against Dundee in an Eastern League match, scoring a goal.

Gordon at right back on 3rd March 1917 against Dunfermline Athletic in an Eastern Cup tie.

Gordon at inside left on 21st April 1917 against the Royal Garrison Artillery in a friendly, scoring twice.

Hopkins of Maryhill at centre forward on 9th March 1918 against Raith Rovers in an Eastern League match.

Johnstone of Brechin City at left back on 3rd April 1915 against Forfar Athletic in a Northern League match.

Laing at outside left on 2nd January 1918 against Armadale in an Eastern League match.

Lithgow at outside left on 28th October 1916 against East Fife in a Loftus Cup tie.

MacKay at right half on 5th October 1918 against a Labour Centre Garrison XI in a friendly (also billed as a Loftus Cup match).

McClure in goal on 1st March 1919 against Hibernian in a friendly.

McLachlan at outside right on 7th October 1916 against Bathgate in an Eastern League match.

McLeod in goal on 22nd February 1919 against a Dundee Shipyard Select in a friendly.

Martin at right half on 23rd November 1918 against the Highland Light Infantry in the first of three friendly matches.

Mullen at outside right on 30th November 1918 against Keith & Blackmans works team. He also played at centre forward on 21st December 1918 against Gibson's XI in a friendly.

Nairn at centre forward on 24th November 1917 against Dundee in a Loftus Cup tie.

O'Fee at right half on 15th March 1919 against Dundee in a friendly.

Patterson at outside left on 7th October 1916 against Bathgate in an Eastern League match. He also played at inside left on 28th October 1916 against East Fife in a Loftus Cup tie.

Peckwith, a Royal Navy man, on 1st January 1917 against East Stirlingshire in a Loftus Cup tie.

Preston at inside left on 8th April 1916 against Leith Athletic in an Eastern Cup tie.

Ramsay at centre forward on 30th December 1916 against Cowdenbeath in an Eastern League match.

Reid at centre forward on 28th October 1916 against East Fife in a Loftus Cup tie.

Reid at inside right on 25th August 1917 against East Fife in an Eastern League match, scoring a goal.

Robertson at outside left on 9th November 1918 against the Army Pay Corps in a friendly, scoring a goal.

H Robertson at centre half on 9th November 1918 against the Army Pay Corps in a friendly.

Rourke or O'Rourke of St Joseph's in goal on 20th November 1915 against East Stirlingshire in the first of two Eastern League matches.

Shaw at inside right on 22nd March 1919 against Arbroath in a friendly.

Simpson at outside left on 6th October 1917 against Armadale in an Eastern League match.

Simpson at right back on 21st December 1918 against Gibson's XI in the first of two friendly matches.

Smith at inside left on 30th January 1915 against Dunfermline Athletic in a Loftus Cup tie.

Sutherland at inside left on 30th November 1918 against Keith & Blackmans works team in a friendly.

Thomson at outside right on 30th December 1916 against Cowdenbeath in an Eastern League match.

Thomson at centre forward on 22nd September 1917 against East Fife, in the first of three Eastern League matches.

Timmons at inside right on 21st October 1916 against Dunfermline Athletic in an Eastern League match.

Wood of Glossop at inside right on 5th October 1918 against a Labour Centre Garrison XI in a friendly.

1919–20 Player Profiles

George Aimer was a full back who made his first appearance for Dundee Hibs as a trialist on 27th December 1919 against Lochgelly United in an Eastern League match. He was signed for season 1920-21 in the Central League and hardly missed a game over that campaign but left to join neighbours Dundee in May 1921. He later joined Fulham and also spent some time in America with Providence Clamdiggers, Fall River FC and New York Giants.

George Aimer

Jimmy Bradley

Jimmy Bradley began his career at Luton Town and then signed for Dundee before joining Dundee Hibs. He made a scoring debut on 23rd August 1919 in an Eastern League match against Montrose. Jimmy could play in either inside forward position and was an important part of the Eastern League championship side of 1919-20. He was released in May 1920 and returned to England. He then had a short spell back at Luton Town and also with Clapton Orient.

David Cargill was an outside right signed from Dundee. He made his Dundee Hibs debut on 23rd August 1919 against Montrose in an Eastern League match. He was an important part of the side that won the championship that season but left the Club in May 1920.

Mick Cosgrove was an attacking player from Dundee North End. His first appearance for Dundee Hibs was in a Northern League match against Arbroath on 24th January 1920. He turned out for Hibs infrequently over 1920-21 but in June 1921 he joined Tottenham Hotspur. He later played for Celtic before moving to America, returning in 1924 to play with Barnsley, Aberdeen and Bristol City.

Mick Cosgrove

Bob Crumley was an experienced goalkeeper with Newcastle United, Dundee and Arbroath. He made just one appearance for Dundee Hibs when he stepped in to cover the unavailability of both regular keepers on 12th April 1920 in a Loftus Cup tie against Raith Rovers 'A'. In August 1926, then with Lochee United as trainer, he took the same post at Dundee United after Archie Taylor left to join Huddersfield Town.

Peter Fisher from Forthill Athletic played his first game for Dundee Hibs at centre forward in a Northern League match against Arbroath on 14th February 1920. He was not signed until the beginning of the 1922-23 season when Hibs were in the Scottish Alliance and he filled the outside right berth. Although released in November 1922 it appears he returned a month later to play as an emergency right back.

David Gibb was a centre forward who joined Dundee Hibs from Montrose and made his debut in an Eastern Cup match against St Johnstone on 5th April 1920, listed as 'Anderson' on the team sheet. Using a pseudonym in minor competitions was a fairly common occurrence at the time. However when the name 'Anderson' was used again in the Forfarshire Cup final against Dundee on 24th May, it resulted in a protest by the Dens Park club and a replay was ordered. Just as in the first match Hibs won the replay 1-0. He signed up with the Club for the Central League campaign of 1920-21 and featured regularly in the line up but was released in May 1921.

Andy Henderson

Andy Henderson was a very experienced goalkeeper with Falkirk. He joined Dundee Hibs at the end of season 1919-20, making his first appearance for the Club on 7th April 1920 in a friendly against a Forfarshire Junior XI. He then signed up for the following season in the Central League. When Hibs were re-admitted to the Scottish League in season 1921-22, Andy was still the first choice keeper and made his Scottish League debut for Hibs on 20th August 1921 against Bo'ness. He was one of just three players to remain with the Club when they lost Scottish League status at the end of that season, beginning his third year with Hibs in the Scottish Alliance. He left in January 1923, half way through the campaign.

William Miller was a goalkeeper signed from Stobswell. He made his first appearance for Dundee Hibs against Lochgelly United on 27th December 1919 in an Eastern League match and hardly missed a game over the rest of the season. He re-signed for the Central League campaign of 1920-21 but took very little part in it and was released in November 1920.

James Morrison was a former St Patrick's defender. His first appearance for Dundee Hibs was on 7th April 1920 against a Forfarshire Junior XI. He then signed for the 1920-21 season in the Central League. James made a significant contribution at full back or half back during the campaign but he was released in May 1921.

Frank Murray was a former Dundee player. He was the crucial signing of the 1919-20 Eastern League season and was vital to winning the championship. He made his debut in a Qualifying Cup tie against Cowdenbeath on 20th September 1919 and hardly missed a game after that. He was top scorer for the season with 10 goals including a hat-trick against Lochgelly United but at the end of the campaign, he left the Club.

Frank Murray

John Smith was a half back who signed in August 1919, making his debut in the first Eastern League match of the championship season 1919-20 against Montrose on 23rd August. Used sparingly in the campaign he was released in April 1920.

John Stirling was a former Dundee half back who made his first appearance for Dundee Hibs in the Eastern League championship winning season on 30th August 1919 against Arbroath. He played a major part in the campaign and stayed with the Club through the following season in the Central League and was released in May 1921.

James Webster had been with Blackburn Rovers and joined Dundee Hibs in time to make his debut in a Forfarshire Cup tie against Montrose on 3rd April 1920. He signed for the Central League season in 1920-21, regularly turning out at right half but left the Club in May 1921.

Joe Wilson joined Dundee Hibs from Blackburn Rovers during the Eastern League championship winning season of 1919-20. He made his debut at centre forward against St Johnstone on 13th December 1919. Joe remained with Hibs during the following season whilst the Club were in the Central League but was released in April 1921

Trialist, Guest, Junior, Newman, A N Other

The following players, listed as one of the above, are those known to have played during the season.

Anderson of Forfar North End at inside right on 14th February 1920 against Arbroath in a Northern League match.

Duncan at outside right on 23rd August 1919 against Montrose in an Eastern League match.

Henderson at outside left on 29th November 1919 against Brechin City in an Eastern League match, scoring a goal. He also turned out on 10th January 1920 against Aberdeen 'A' in a Northern League match.

G or J Miller at right half on 23rd August 1919 against Montrose in the first of two Eastern League matches.

Newton at inside left on 7th April 1920 against a Forfarshire Junior XI in a friendly.

Sime at inside left on 27th December 1919 against Lochgelly United in an Eastern League match.

George 'Doddy' Steven at inside left on 5th May 1920 against St Johnstone in a testimonial for their trainer J McVean.

1920-21 Player Profiles

George Adams

George Adams was a full back with Montrose when he made his first appearance for Dundee Hibs as a trialist against East Stirlingshire in the last Central League match of 1920-21 on 30th April. He then signed up for the Scottish League season and made his debut in that competition on 20th August 1921 against Bo'ness. He played regularly in the first half of the season but in the latter stages he featured just once in the side for an Eastern League match. George was released in May 1922.

Joseph Allison was an inside right who arrived at Tannadice from Banknock Juniors initially for a one month trial. He made his first appearance on 30th October 1920 in a Central League match against King's Park. He was then signed but played only a few times before being released in January 1921.

Lowingham Braidford was an inside forward who made his debut for Dundee Hibs as a trialist in a Central League match against Broxburn United on 12th February 1921. With Dundee Hibs restored to the Scottish League, he re-signed for the following season, and made his first Scottish League appearance against Bo'ness on 20th August 1921. The player missed just one game in the disastrous 1921-22 season and was released in May 1922. He then signed for Hartlepool United before spending a short time in America and then returning to play for Northampton Town.

Lowingham Braidford

Adam Brown signed for Dundee Hibs from Forthill Athletic and made his first appearance on 16th August 1920 against Dunfermline Athletic in a Loftus Cup tie. He remained with the Club throughout season 1920-21 in the Central League, frequently filling the left half position and occasionally outside left. He was released at the end of the season.

Dave Brown was with Morton before joining Dundee. He came to Dundee Hibs on a short term loan deal, making his first appearance on 21st August 1920 against Armadale in a Central League match. He returned to his own club within ten days of arriving at Tannadice. Dave later moved to Peebles Rovers before going south of the border where he played for Stoke City and Notts County. He then returned for a short spell at Kilmarnock but was soon down south again with Darlington, Crewe Alexandra and finally Barrow.

Tom Dick was a centre forward with Bonnybridge Thistle and came to Dundee Hibs on trial initially, making his first appearance against East Fife in a Central League match on 11th December 1920. He signed in January 1921 and became a regular in the side throughout the season but left when the campaign ended.

Frank Gray was a former Dundee Osborne outside left who had also been with Brechin City. He signed for Hibs and made his first appearance on 18th December 1920 against Hearts 'A' in a Central League match. He made a successful move to centre forward in the latter stages of the season but left the Club at the end of the campaign.

Willie Kay was a centre forward who joined Dundee Hibs from Plymouth Argyle in July 1920, making his debut for the Club on 16th August 1920 in a Loftus Cup tie against Dunfermline Athletic. In November 1920 he was offered and accepted a free transfer and a cash settlement of £12.

Joe Kinsella was a goalkeeper who joined Dundee Hibs from St Joseph's and made his debut in a Central League match on 1st January 1921 against Broxburn United. He was second choice behind Andy Henderson for the keeper's jersey in the Scottish League season of 1921-22 playing his first Scottish League game on 24th September 1921 against Bathgate. He was released in July 1922.

George Lamb was a former Dundee outside right. He made his Dundee Hibs debut in a Loftus Cup tie against Dunfermline Athletic on 16th August 1920. He was with the Club for just four months and was released in December 1920.

John McMahon was formerly with Hamilton Academical and made his Dundee Hibs debut in a Loftus Cup tie against Dunfermline Athletic on 16th August 1920. An inside forward, he made just a few appearances during his three months at the Club and left to join Clackmannan in December 1920.

James M Ritchie

James M Ritchie arrived at Dundee Hibs on loan from Aberdeen and made his first appearance in the final Central League match of season 1920-21 against East Stirlingshire on 30th April 1921. He signed for the Scottish League campaign of 1921-22 making his debut in that competition on 20th August 1921 against Bo'ness. He was a regular in the side in the early part of the campaign but in the latter stages he featured less and was released in May 1922.

Norman Thain was an outside right with Forthill Athletic. He joined Dundee Hibs towards the end of season 1920-21 for trials and made his first appearance for the Club in a Northern League match against Forfar Athletic on 16th April 1921. He was signed three months into the Scottish League season that followed, making his debut in that competition on 5th November 1921 against East Fife. At the end of the season he was released.

John Waugh could play at inside forward or half back and had a short spell at Sunderland before he moved north to join Dunfermline Athletic. Dundee Hibs acquired him for a fee of £15 and he made his debut on 18th September 1920 in the Qualifying Cup second replay at neutral Station Park, Forfar, against Arbroath. He was with Hibs for just three months and was then sold to Gillingham and later joined Darlington.

Trialist, Guest, Junior, Newman, A N Other

The following players, listed as one of the above, are those known to have played during the season.

Clark at left half on 5th January 1921 against Montrose in a friendly.

Duff at outside right on 9th April 1921 against Alloa Athletic in a Central League match.

Fox of Osborne at centre half on 30th April 1921 against East Stirlingshire in a Central League match. He played again the following season at left half on 29th October 1921 against King's Park in a Scottish League match.

Hill in goal on 3rd January 1921 against Dunfermline Athletic in a Loftus Cup tie and on 5th March 1921 against Bo'ness in a Central League match.

Jackson at centre forward on 25th December 1920 against Cowdenbeath in a Central League match.

James at centre half on 5th January 1921 against Montrose in a friendly.

MacFarlane at outside left on 1st January 1921 against Broxburn United in the first of three matches in the Central League.

Simpson at outside left on 27th November 1920 against Falkirk 'A' in a Central League match.

Smith in goal on 5th January 1921 against Montrose in a friendly.

Swinney of Grange Rovers at centre forward on 19th March 1921 against Armadale in the first of three Central League matches.

John Waugh

1921–22 Player Profiles

Tom Bannister

Tom Bannister was a former Dundee centre half. He made his debut for Dundee Hibs on 15th August 1921 against St Johnstone in a friendly. Five days later he made his Scottish League debut for the Club in the opening match of the 1921-22 campaign against Bo'ness. He missed just two league matches over the season and was one of just three players who stayed with the Club into the Scottish Alliance season of 1922-23 after Scottish League status was lost. In April 1923 he was released.

Joe Bibby played with Blackburn Rovers and Wigan Borough before he signed for Dundee Hibs. He made his debut on 8th April 1922 in a Scottish League match against Dunfermline Athletic but was released shortly after, with just a handful of appearances to his credit.

David Duncan was a centre half, signed for Dundee Hibs from Hearts, probably on loan. He made his debut in the Scottish League on 18th February 1922 against Cowdenbeath. David played in all of the remaining league matches in that season but then he left the Club.

James Headrick was signed from Stirling Emmet and made his debut against Forfar Athletic in a Scottish League match on 15th October 1921. An accomplished right back, the player never missed a league match over the remainder of the season and was twice used as an emergency centre forward. When the campaign ended and Hibs lost their Scottish League status, he was initially retained but left the Club soon after without playing another game. He later signed for Alloa Athletic but was tragically killed in a motor cycle accident in June 1925.

James Headrick

Willie Hogg was an experienced outside right who had started his career at Sunderland. After nine years there he moved north and had spells at Rangers, Dundee and Raith Rovers. He then joined Montrose before signing with Dundee Hibs for season 1921-22. He made his first appearance in a friendly against St Johnstone on 15th August 1921 and five days later made his Scottish League debut for the Club against Bo'ness. Willie made a good start and played in ten consecutive games but was dropped in October and then released in November 1921.

Willie Hogg

Peter Kelly was a right sided attacker who made his debut on 31st December 1921 in a Scottish League match against Vale of Leven. During the latter part of season 1921-22 he was a regular in the side but was released at the end of the campaign.

Pat Maxwell was signed from Hibernian in Edinburgh and joined Dundee Hibs in the latter stages of season 1921-22, possibly on loan. An attacking player, he made his debut in a Scottish League match against Forfar Athletic on 25th February 1922 and in two months at the Club he made just a handful of appearances, before leaving at the end of the season.

Alex McCulloch was an inside left. He was a much travelled player who began his career with Leith Athletic and then had experience with numerous English sides before signing for Raith Rovers and then Lincoln City. Just before joining Dundee Hibs he played in Wales for Merthyr Town and Llanelli. Alex made his debut for Hibs in a Scottish League match against St Bernard's on 4th March 1922 and played in all the remaining league matches of that campaign. At the end of the season it appears that he retired.

William McDonagh was a left back signed from Croy Celtic. He made his Dundee Hibs debut on 14th January 1922 against Bo'ness in a Scottish League match. He made just a few appearances for the Club and in May 1922 he was transfer listed at £25 but was possibly released shortly afterwards.

Dan McInnes

Dan McInnes was previously with St Johnstone and then joined Raith Rovers. A full back, he could play on either flank. Dan came to Dundee Hibs on loan for season 1921-22, making his first appearance on 15th August 1921 in a friendly against St Johnstone. He made his Scottish League debut for the Club against Armadale on 17th September 1921 but was used only occasionally in the side and returned to his own club at the end of the campaign.

James McKimmie signed for Dundee Hibs from junior side St Joseph's as a reserve for the half back line. He made his debut in a Scottish League match on 1st October 1921 against Clackmannan and made several more appearances over the season but was released at the end of the campaign.

Willie Oswald

Willie Oswald made his first appearance for Dundee Hibs as a trialist on 29th April 1922, scoring twice in a 4-1 win against Armadale in the Scottish League. He was not signed at the time and instead went to Gillingham and later to St Johnstone. He came to Tannadice as a signed player just after the beginning of season 1924-25 by which time the Club had become Dundee United. Willie became a regular, playing at inside right in the side that won the Second Division championship that season. He made a significant contribution to the Club's first season in the top flight of Scottish football and was perhaps surprisingly released at the end of the campaign. He then joined Brighton & Hove Albion before moving to the United States where he played with Providence Gold Bugs, Fall River FC and New York Yankees.

John Rae was a centre half signed from Albion Rovers and made his first appearance for Dundee Hibs in a friendly against Dundee on 11th January 1922. He then signed in time to play in the Scottish Cup tie against Broxburn United on 28th January 1922. The player retained his place in the remaining matches of the Scottish League campaign that season and was signed again just into the next season in the Scottish Alliance League. He featured frequently that season but was released in April 1923.

Barney Smith was an experienced half back with Hibernian of Edinburgh. He came to Dundee Hibs on a one month loan deal and made his debut in a Scottish League match against St Johnstone on 10th September 1921 but after just one more game, he was released.

George Stuart was an ex-Dundee half back signed from Leeds United. He made his debut against East Stirlingshire in a Scottish League match on 3rd September 1921 in his usual position but at the end the campaign he was tried at centre forward during a crisis. In May 1922 he was released after Hibs lost Scottish League status.

Horace Williams was a centre forward who began his career at St Johnstone then moved to Edinburgh Hibernian. He came to Dundee Hibs for a fee of £30 and made a scoring debut in a friendly against St Johnstone on 15th August 1921. He then scored twice in a Scottish League match for the Tannadice side, five days later against Bo'ness. His scoring record included a hat-trick against Lochgelly United and he finished season 1921-22 as top scorer with 13 goals. He was transfer listed at £200 in December 1921 and moved to Gillingham. Horace later played for Wrexham, New Brighton and Blackpool and also a number of English non league sides.

Horace Williams

Trialist, Guest, Junior, Newman, A N Other

The following players, listed as one of the above, are those known to have played during the season.

Farquharson at outside left on 1st April 1922 against East Stirlingshire in the first of two Scottish League matches. He also played on 12th April 1922 against Dundee in the testimonial for Willie Linn.

Ferrier at right back on 12th April 1922 against Dundee in the testimonial for Willie Linn.

Gilligan at outside left on 25th March 1922 against Broxburn United in a Scottish League match.

Gray at centre half on 15th February 1922 against Bathgate in a Scottish League match.

Irvine of YMCA Anchorage at outside right on 22nd October 1921 against Broxburn United in the first of two Scottish League matches.

Low of Dundee Violet at centre forward on 4th March 1922 against St Bernard's in the first of two Scottish League matches. He also played on 12th April 1922 against Dundee in the testimonial for Willie Linn. He scored three goals in total from his three games.

McGuire at centre half on 11th January 1922 against Dundee in a friendly.

Page at centre forward on 22nd April 1922 against Clackmannan in a Scottish League match.

Paton at left half on 31st December 1921 against Vale of Leven in a Scottish League match.

Smith of North End at inside left on 12th April 1922 against Dundee in the testimonial for Willie Linn.

Weldon at outside left on 15th February 1922 against Bathgate in a Scottish League match.

Wilson at inside right on 15th February 1922 against Bathgate in a Scottish League match.

1922–23 Player Profiles

Joe Baillie was the goalkeeper signed after Andy Henderson left. Joe came from the Edinburgh Hibernian and made his debut for Dundee Hibs on 6th January 1923 in a Scottish Alliance match against Dundee 'A'. The following week he made his first appearance in a major competition for the Club when he played in a Scottish Cup tie on 13th January 1923 against Beith. He retained the keeper's jersey for an uninterrupted run until the end of the season but was then released.

James Balloch was a former Clackmannan and Hearts centre half who signed for Dundee Hibs at the beginning of season 1922-23. He made his debut for the Club against Partick Thistle 'A' in a Scottish Alliance match on 19th August 1922 and his first appearance in major competition came when he lined up in the side that met Beith in a Scottish Cup tie on 13th January 1923. James had a long run in the side and was often used as an emergency forward. Towards the end of the campaign he found it harder to get into the line up and was released in May 1923.

Bowman (first name unknown) was a reserve goalkeeper with Dundee. He joined Dundee Hibs on loan as cover for regular keeper Andy Henderson. Bowman made his debut in a Scottish Alliance match against Hearts 'A' on 9th September 1922 but only played once more before returning to his own club.

John Chester was an outside right who made his debut for Dundee Hibs in an Eastern League match against Montrose on 16th December 1922. He made his first appearance in a major competition for Hibs when he was in the line up for a Scottish Cup tie against Beith on 13th January 1923. A few days later, the post of trainer at the Club became vacant and it was offered to him jointly with James Terris but both turned it down. He lost his place in the team just afterwards and was released in February 1923.

John Clark was signed from Carlisle United on a one month loan deal and registered just in time to make his debut for Dundee Hibs in a Scottish Cup tie against Beith on 13th January 1923. He made a scoring debut and after appearing as an ever present in a short Hibs career he returned to his own club.

Fred Howard was a centre forward signed from Clyde on a short term deal. He made his debut in a Forfarshire Cup tie against Forfar Athletic on 18th April 1923, but left the Club after playing just twice more.

George 'Dod' Hutchison was signed from St Monance Swifts and made his debut for Dundee Hibs in a Scottish Alliance match against St Mirren 'A' on 2nd September 1922. He was released in November 1922 after playing just a few games for the Club.

Walter Mackintosh was a junior player from Blairgowrie. He made his debut for Dundee Hibs in a Scottish Alliance match against Albion Rovers 'A' on 10th February 1923. He could play on either side of the half back line and retained his place in the side until the end of the season. When new Manager Jimmy Brownlie arrived at Tannadice, Walter was still on the books but was released soon after.

Willie McAndrew

Willie McAndrew was the first signing made by new Manager, Peter O'Rourke. The player, who had been with Queen's Park and Clyde, joined Dundee Hibs from Third Lanark. He made his debut on 9th December 1922 in a Scottish Alliance match against Kilmarnock 'A'. Willie made his first appearance for Hibs in a major competition when he turned out against Beith in a Scottish Cup tie on 13th January 1923 and over the rest of the season found himself filling all three half back positions. When O'Rourke resigned as Manager in early March 1923, McAndrew took charge of the team until the end of the season at which time he left the Club.

Robert McDonald made his debut for Dundee Hibs on 26th August 1922 in a Scottish Alliance match against St Mirren 'A'. His first appearance in a major competition for Hibs was on 13th January 1923 against Beith in a Scottish Cup tie. He was a regular in the Hibs line up at either right back or left back until he was released in April 1923.

Robert McDonald

Joseph Murray was a right sided attacking player who also turned out at centre forward and right half. He made his debut for Dundee Hibs in a Scottish Alliance match on 23rd September 1922 against Queen's Park Strollers. He was with the Club for just two months and was released at the end of December 1922.

Michael O'Rourke was a son of newly appointed Manager, Peter O'Rourke and made his debut for Dundee Hibs in a Scottish Alliance match against Dundee 'A' on 23rd December 1922. He played in a few positions but latterly was the regular outside right. Following the resignation of his father, he stayed on but left at the end of the season.

Peter O'Rourke was an inside forward. A son of the Dundee Hibs Manager of the same name, he joined the Club shortly after his father was appointed. He made his debut in a Scottish Alliance match against Kilmarnock 'A' on 9th December 1922. Several clubs kept close tabs on the player whilst he was at Tannadice and at the end of the season he opted to go south and signed for Bradford Park Avenue. He was later on the books at Northampton Town and Norwich City.

Jamie Scullion was an inside forward who also played in defence. He signed from Hamilton Academical and made his Dundee Hibs debut in a Scottish Alliance match against Aberdeen 'A' on 2nd October 1922. His first match in a major competition for Hibs was a Scottish Cup tie against Beith on 13th January 1923. Jamie remained with Hibs until the end of the season when he moved to Bury. He later joined King's Park but was soon back south of the border where he enjoyed success with Fulham, Stockport County, Crewe Alexandra, Wigan Borough and then with numerous non league sides.

Jamie Scullion

Harry Smillie was a left sided attacker who also played at centre forward. Signed from St Johnstone, he made his debut in a Scottish Cup tie against Nithsdale Wanderers on 24th January 1923. Harry played in most of the remaining matches that season but was released in April 1923.

William Stewart signed from Arbroath and played at inside right for Dundee Hibs during the Scottish Alliance season of 1922-23, making a scoring debut on 19th August 1922 against Partick Thistle 'A'. He also scored a goal in his first appearance in a major competition, a Scottish Cup tie against Beith on 13th January 1923. At the end of that season he was released.

George Stoddart

George Stoddart was a former Raith Rovers player. He was signed from Hull City and made his debut for Dundee Hibs in a Scottish Alliance match against Partick Thistle 'A' on 19th August 1922. He was an inside left and played just a few games for the Club before being released in November 1922. He later played for Stenhousemuir.

Russell Sutherland was a former half back with Dundee who had spent a season with Barrow before signing with Dundee Hibs. He made his first appearance on 19th August 1922 against Partick Thistle 'A'. Russell was released in November 1922 after his short term contract expired.

James Terris was a former Cowdenbeath and Hearts half back who joined Dundee Hibs from Millwall Athletic and made his debut on 19th August 1922 in a Scottish Alliance match against Partick Thistle 'A'. The player made his first appearance in a major competition for Hibs in a Scottish Cup tie against Beith on 13th January 1923. He was a regular in the side throughout season 1922-23 and was offered but declined the position of joint trainer along with John Chester in February 1923. When Hibs returned to the Scottish League the following season, new Manager Jimmy Brownlie wanted to retain the player but was not prepared to pay the transfer fee of £250 requested. James then joined Falkirk and was later on the books at Liverpool before his career took him across the Atlantic to the USA to play.

James Terris

W Thomson was a centre forward stationed nearby in either the army or RAF. He made a scoring debut in Hibs' Scottish Alliance season against Partick Thistle 'A' on 19th August 1922. After a few more games he was released.

Willie Wilson was signed from Raith Rovers and made his debut for Dundee Hibs on 19th August 1922 against Partick Thistle 'A' in a Scottish Alliance fixture. He was an outside left and was a regular in the side, making his first appearance in a major competition for Hibs in a Scottish Cup tie against Beith on 13th January 1923. In late February 1923 he was allowed to go to St Johnstone to help the Perth side's promotion bid from the Scottish Second Division, unsuccessful as it transpired.

John Young was a full back signed for Dundee Hibs from Morton and made his debut in a Scottish Alliance match against Partick Thistle 'A' on 19th August 1922. He managed just three games in total before he was released.

Trialist, Guest, Junior, Newman, A N Other

The following players, listed as one of the above, are those known to have played during the season.

Anderson of Lochee United at right back on 19th August 1922 against Partick Thistle 'A' in a Scottish Alliance match.

Ballantyne of Partick Thistle at centre forward on 12th May 1923 against Aberdeen in a charity match.

Bryce at left back on 1st January 1923 against St Johnstone in a Wallace Cup tie.

Cargill at outside right on 2nd December 1922 against Raith Rovers 'A' in a Scottish Alliance match.

Crighton at right back on 18th April 1923 against Forfar Athletic in a Forfarshire Cup tie.

Dickie of Dundee at outside left on 24th February 1923 against Third Lanark 'A' in a Scottish Alliance match.

Dow at inside right on 26th August 1922 against St Mirren 'A' in a Scottish Alliance match.

Elder or Edwards at right back on 24th March 1923 against Third Lanark 'A' in a Scottish Alliance match.

Finney at centre forward on 3rd March 1923 against Hearts 'A' in a Scottish Alliance match.

Heggie at centre forward on 23rd December 1922 against Dundee 'A' in a Scottish Alliance match, scoring a goal.

Kilpatrick of Ayr United at outside right on 12th May 1923 against Aberdeen in a charity match.

MacKay of Petershill at centre forward on 6th January 1923 against Dundee 'A' in the first of two Scottish Alliance matches.

McArthur at outside right on 25th November 1922 against Kilmarnock 'A' in a Scottish Alliance match.

McAvoy at outside right on 2nd October 1922 against Aberdeen 'A' in a Scottish Alliance match.

McCloy at right back on 12th May 1923 against Aberdeen in a charity match.

McCormick of Third Lanark at left back on 12th May 1923 against Aberdeen in a charity match.

McGhee of Brechin City at inside right on 28th October 1922 against Airdrieonians 'A' in a Scottish Alliance match.

Malcolm at centre half on 9th April 1923 against Aberdeen 'A' in an Eastern League match.

Mannion of Dumbarton at inside right on 20th January 1923 against Clackmannan in a Scottish Alliance match.

Mathie at centre forward on 2nd September 1922 against St Mirren 'A' in a Scottish Alliance match.

Muir of Kelty Rangers at inside left on 6th January 1923 against Dundee 'A' in a Scottish Alliance match.

O'Neil a Dunfermline junior at centre forward on 30th September 1922 against Rangers 'A' for the first of three Scottish Alliance matches.

Patterson at right back on 24th February 1923 against Third Lanark 'A' in a Scottish Alliance match.

Robb of Lochee Harp at centre forward on 2nd December 1922 against Raith Rovers 'A' in the first of two Scottish Alliance matches.

Salisbury of Partick Thistle at outside left on 12th May 1923 against Aberdeen in a charity match.

Sharp at left half on 1st January 1923 against St Johnstone in a Wallace Cup tie.

Simpson of Osborne at centre forward on 18th November 1922 against Leith Athletic in an Eastern League match, scoring a goal. This may have been Tommy Simpson who later signed.

Slade of Ayr United at inside right on 12th May 1923 against Aberdeen in a charity match.

Smith from Perth at inside left on 24th March 1923 against Third Lanark 'A', in the first of three Scottish Alliance matches, scoring once. He also played on 9th April 1923 against Aberdeen 'A' in an Eastern League match.

Thomson at centre forward on 25th November 1922 against Kilmarnock 'A' in a Scottish Alliance match.

1923–24 Player Profiles

Jimmy Brownlie was a goalkeeper with international experience who had been with Third Lanark for several years. He joined Dundee Hibs as a Player/Manager, making his first appearance in a charity match against Aberdeen on 12th May 1923. A few days later, he was interviewed but his appointment was not announced until 11th June 1923. He made his debut in a major competition for Hibs on 18th August 1923 in a Scottish League match against Cowdenbeath. Jimmy chose himself for the keeper's position until he relinquished that role in April 1924 to Frank Bridgeford. The old keeper was however, forced to return in one or two emergency situations, most notably, his last appearance as a player against Hearts in a 6-0 defeat on 1st February 1926 in the second replay of a Scottish Cup tie. His first spell as Manager continued until April 1931 and during that period, he took the Club (by then Dundee United) to promotion three times, twice as Second Division champions. His bond with the Club never diminished and he returned to manage the side again from March 1934 until October 1936. Jimmy was appointed a Director of Dundee United and took on the role of Manager for a third time, jointly with Sam Irving, in August 1938 until the outbreak of WW2. He was a regular in the Tannadice stand for many years afterwards and saw the Club gain promotion again in April 1960.

Tom Cottingham

Tom Cottingham was an inside right with Hamilton Academical before spending a short time with Luton Town. He left the English side to join Dundee Hibs, making his first appearance in a Penman Cup tie against St Johnstone on 15th August 1923. Three days later he made his Scottish League debut against Cowdenbeath. After the Club changed its name, Tom played in the first match as Dundee United against Dumbarton on 27th October 1923 but it turned out to be his last appearance and he was released shortly after. He then joined Carlisle United and later played with Bo'ness.

Eddie Gilfeather

Eddie Gilfeather spent two seasons at Tannadice on loan from Celtic. A left half, he made his debut for Dundee Hibs on 29th September 1923 against Vale of Leven in a Scottish League match. He was in the line up on the first occasion that the Club played as Dundee United and became a regular in the side over the rest of the season. He returned to his own club in April 1923, but Jimmy Brownlie successfully negotiated for his return for a second season. Eddie had a major influence in the side that won the Second Division championship in season 1924-25. There was speculation that the player would sign for United but he returned to Celtic and shortly afterwards, went to Hibernian.

Sandy Gilmour was an inside left signed from Hearts. He made his first appearance for Dundee Hibs in a Penman Cup tie against St Johnstone on 15th August 1923 and three days later, made his Scottish League debut against Cowdenbeath. He was in the side that played the first game under the new name of Dundee United and continued to turn out regularly over the season, playing in the half back line or in the attack. He re-signed the following term and was an important part of the side that won the Second Division championship, spending almost the entire campaign at outside left. He did not stay on for the First Division challenge and left to join St Bernard's.

Sandy Gilmour

George Hannah

George Hannah was a former Broxburn United outside left signed from Hamilton Academical. He made his first appearance for Dundee Hibs on 15th August 1923 in a Penman Cup tie against St Johnstone and then on 18th August he made his Scottish League debut against Cowdenbeath. The player had an uninterrupted run of twelve games for the Club but was then sidelined because of a serious health problem. He was advised to give up the game as a result, and was released in April 1923.

Jock Kay was a versatile full back who had been with Armadale before he joined Third Lanark and then Dundee Hibs. He made his first appearance for the Tannadice side on 15th August 1923 against St Johnstone in a Penman Cup tie and three days later turned out for his Scottish League debut against Cowdenbeath. After the name change he played in the first match as Dundee United on 27th October 1923 against Dumbarton and remained with the Club for over five years. He was in the Second Division championship squad of 1924-25 and was one of just a handful of players retained for the challenge of top flight football. He became a regular in the side during two seasons in Division One of the Scottish League but encountered relegation back to Division Two at the end of 1926-27. Although tempted with a move to the USA he remained with United for another full season and was rewarded with a benefit match on 9th April 1928. However, he did not re-sign and joined Stenhousemuir in November 1928.

Jock Kay

Bobby Knox

Bobby Knox was a former Airdrieonians and Third Lanark half back who made his Dundee Hibs debut on 15th August 1923 against St Johnstone in a Penman Cup tie. Three days later, he made his Scottish League debut for the Club against Cowdenbeath. His Hibs career was hampered by injury and he was in the side only occasionally, finally being allowed to leave in April 1924.

James Mackie was a former Aberdeen and Ayr United centre forward. He signed from Bo'ness and made a scoring debut for Hibs in a Wallace Cup tie against St Johnstone on 12th September 1923. He also made a scoring debut for the Club in the Scottish League against Johnstone three days later. He was one of the players who lined up against Dumbarton on 27th October 1923 for the first match under the new name of Dundee United but James did not come up to the Manager's expectation and he was released in December 1923. He then signed for King's Park.

Bobby McEwan was an outside right signed from Dumbarton and made his debut on 15th August 1923 in a Penman Cup tie against St Johnstone. On 18th August he made his first Scottish League appearance for the Club against Cowdenbeath. Over the next two months he missed just one game. On the day that the Club played under the new name of Dundee United for the first time, Bobby was in his usual place but it turned out to be his last appearance and he was released shortly afterwards.

Joe O'Kane could play in any inside forward position and at centre forward. He was one of Jimmy Brownlie's first acquisitions for Dundee Hibs when he signed from Celtic and had been on loan with Clydebank, Stockport County, Stevenston United and Stalybridge Celtic. He made his debut in a Penman Cup tie against St Johnstone on 15th August 1923 and then made his first appearance in a major competition for the Club three days later in a Scottish League match against Cowdenbeath. With just nine goals scored he was top scorer in 1923-24. He left after requesting a free transfer in February 1925 and signed for Arthurlie.

Bobby McEwan *Joe O'Kane* *James Porter*

James Porter was signed from Hearts and made his first appearance for Dundee Hibs on 15th August 1923 in a Penman Cup tie against St Johnstone at left back, although he later played in the half back line. He made his Scottish League debut three days later against Cowdenbeath. James was with the Club through the 1923-24 season and re-signed for the next campaign although his appearances seem to have been severely restricted because of injury. He left to join Bathgate in December 1924.

Dave Richards was a right back or centre half who joined Dundee Hibs after a short spell at Port Vale. He made his debut on 15th August 1923 in a Penman Cup tie against St Johnstone and then three days later turned out for the Club in a Scottish League match against Cowdenbeath. He was in the first line up to play under the new name of Dundee United three months later and also one of the squad which won the Second Division championship in season 1924-25. The player would have been re-signed for the following term in the First Division but was snapped up by Luton Town. He was later transferred to Watford.

Ed Stirling was a left half signed from the ranks of Dundee reserves. He made his first appearance for Dundee Hibs on 15th August 1923 against St Johnstone in a Penman Cup match and three days later made his Scottish League debut for the Club against Cowdenbeath. After the name change, Ed was in the first Dundee United side when they met Dumbarton on 27th October 1923. He missed just a few games during the season but was released in May 1924 and then joined Rochdale.

John Swan was a right half signed from Clydebank. He made his debut in a Scottish League match against Arbroath on 22nd September 1923. John was the last player to sign for Dundee Hibs before the change of name to Dundee United. He was in the side that met Dumbarton on 27th October 1923 as Dundee United and went on to turn out frequently over the remainder of the season but was released in April 1924.

Dave Richards

Ed Stirling

Bobby Bauld

DUNDEE UNITED

1923-24 Player Profiles

Bobby Bauld was an inside forward who had a trial with Spurs before signing for Raith Rovers where he then spent three years. He was acquired from the Kirkcaldy side for a fee of £100 and was the first player signed after the Club became Dundee United. Bobby made a scoring debut against St Bernard's in a Scottish League match on 3rd November 1923. A regular in the side for two seasons, he was one of the promotion winning squad of 1924-25 and one of only four players retained at the end of that campaign to face the challenge of First Division football. He was in the line up when Dundee United made their debut in the top flight of Scottish football on 25th August 1925 against Raith Rovers. United lasted just two seasons in Division One and Bobby, by then playing at left half, was rarely out of the side. However, he did not relish the prospect of playing in the lower league again when the Club were relegated in April 1927. Initially offered a deal in the United States where he would have gone for no fee, he was eventually sold to Bradford City for £350. He remained there for seven years and then moved to Chesterfield.

Frank Bridgeford

Frank Bridgeford was the goalkeeper signed from Forfar Celtic to fill the vacancy left when Jimmy Brownlie decided to end his playing days. He made his first appearance for United as a trialist against Bo'ness in the Scottish League on 15th March 1924 and signed shortly afterwards. During season 1924-25 he was the first choice keeper in the side that won promotion to the First Division, missing just one league match. However, it appears that he was not considered up to the challenge of top flight football and was released in April 1925.

Jimmy Russell was a centre forward, signed from Rosslyn Juniors. He made his first appearance for United scoring twice as a trialist against Armadale on 12th January 1924 in a Scottish League match. Apparently the answer to the Club's centre forward problem, he was then signed but did not achieve what was expected. He was retained for the next league campaign but could not hold down a first team place and was allowed on loan to Third Lanark in November for a short spell. He returned to Tannadice a few weeks later but was released in April 1925. He then spent some time with Raith Rovers and then returned to the junior ranks with St Andrews United.

Tommy Simpson was an outside right who joined United from local junior side, Osborne. He made his debut against Johnstone on 22nd December 1923 in a Scottish League match and missed just one game during his first two seasons at Tannadice. He played an important part in the promotion winning side of 1924-25 and was one of just four players retained to play in the First Division campaign that followed. When the side was chosen to make Dundee United's debut in the top flight against Raith Rovers on 15th August 1925, Tommy was in his usual berth and was rarely out of the line up for the next nine months. He was

Tommy Simpson

less frequently in the side during the relegation season of 1926-27 and left to join Brighton & Hove Albion at the end of that campaign. He spent just one season with the English side and then returned north to join Montrose.

Jimmy Walker joined United on loan from Dundee when regular outside left George Hannah became ill. The former Arniston Rangers player was initially reluctant to cross the road but was eventually persuaded and made his first appearance for the Tannadice side against St Bernard's in a Scottish League match on 3rd November 1923, scoring one of the goals. He remained with United for the season and returned to his own club at the end of 1923-24.

Trialist, Guest, Junior, Newman, A N Other

The following players, listed as one of the above, are those known to have played during the season.

Forbes at left half on 26th April 1924 against Forfar Athletic in a Scottish League match.

Freebairn, a Perth junior at inside right on 16th April 1924 against Stenhousemuir in a Scottish League match.

McDonald in goal on 22nd September 1923 against Arbroath in a Scottish League match.

Bobby Main of Shawfield Juniors at outside right on 15th December 1923 against Bo'ness in a Scottish League match.

1924–25 Player Profiles

Jimmy Cameron was an outside left with Lochee Harp when he made a scoring debut for United as trialist against Johnstone in a Scottish League match on 3rd April 1925. He played once more that season as emergency cover but did not sign for United until three years later. Jimmy became an integral part of the side that won promotion in season 1928-29, whilst attracting a lot of interest from other clubs. He was in the side again for much of the unsuccessful season in the First Division and after relegation in April 1930, he signed again for the Second Division campaign. Surprisingly, he was transfer listed at the end of 1930-

Jimmy Cameron

31 and then released. He joined Chester City after he left United and later crossed the Irish Sea and played with Shelbourne. In 1932 he signed for Celtic before moving to Forfar Athletic and then Arbroath. Tragically, at the age of just 29 he died from pneumonia in December 1935.

Andy Cant was one of a number of players released by Dunfermline Athletic just as season 1924-25 got under way. With a good reputation as a goal scoring centre forward, he was quickly snapped up by United and made his debut on 13th September 1924 in a Scottish League match against King's Park. After a few weeks at centre, he had not lived up to expectation and lost his place, making one more appearance before being released at the end of the season.

Hugh Collins came from Partick Thistle on loan in March 1925 as United tried to maintain their push for promotion. He made his debut on 7th March 1925 in a Scottish League match against Alloa Athletic and went on to make just a handful of appearances before returning to his own club. Interestingly, although United won the Second Division title, they did it with little help from Hugh, as he never played in a winning United side.

James Harvey had been with Kilmarnock and St Johnstone. A right half, he joined United, making his debut against Bo'ness in a Scottish League match on 16th August 1924 and then made the right half position his own for most of the campaign. Despite being one of the squad that won the Second Division championship that season, he was released in April 1925.

Johnny McRoberts

Johnny McRoberts joined United from St Johnstone for a nominal fee and made his debut against Bo'ness on 16th August 1924 in a Scottish League match. He was made team captain and his performances at centre half, where he was a regular, were an important factor in the Second Division championship win of 1924-25. Initially, he was not one of the players retained for the First Division challenge but after reconsideration, he was re-signed. However, he managed only two outings at the higher level and left United in December 1925 to join East Stirlingshire.

William Mackie was a centre forward who was signed from Albion Rovers and made his debut for United in a Scottish League match against Dunfermline Athletic on 15th November 1924. He was a frequent starter in the side, but despite being a part of the Second Division championship winning squad, he was one of many players released at the end of the season.

Jacky Osborne was a left back signed from Lochee Central. He made his debut for United as a trialist on 20th September 1924 in a Scottish League match against East Fife. He was signed shortly after and went on to play a major role in the side that won the Second Division championship in season 1924-25. He was one of the four players retained for the First Division campaign the following season but was then unable to win a first team place. He left to join Forfar Athletic in January 1926 and later went to Brechin City.

Jacky Osborne

Robert Rintoul began his career at Bo'ness and then moved to Lochgelly United before joining Dundee United on a one month trial. He was brought in for the injured Gilmour and made his first appearance as a trialist against Arthurlie in a Scottish League match on 17th January 1925 at outside left. It was a scoring debut but he made just four more appearances and was released when his one month deal ran out.

James 'Snyder' Smith was a centre forward who joined United from Clyde and made his debut on 16th August 1924 against Bo'ness in a Scottish League match, scoring twice. He scored again in the next match, against his former club but after just one more appearance he was released.

Trialist, Guest, Junior, Newman, A N Other

James 'Snyder' Smith

The following players, listed as one of the above, are those known to have played during the season.

Hill of Forfar West End at left back on 13th September 1924 against King's Park in a Scottish League match.

Soutar of Clydemore in goal on 29th April 1925 against St Johnstone in a friendly.

1925–26 Player Profiles

Malcolm Campbell

Malcolm 'Micky' Campbell was the first signing made in anticipation of the challenge of First Division football in season 1925-26. He was a right sided defender who had started his career at Stenhousemuir and then moved to Falkirk. Micky made his debut as the Club stepped on to the First Division stage for the first time on 15th August 1925 against Raith Rovers. Converted to an attacking player he played in most forward positions for United over two seasons in the top flight and was top scorer for the Club in 1925-26, with eleven league and cup goals. He remained with United for the season following relegation at the end of 1926-27. Initially retained for season 1928-29 the player refused the terms offered and left to join East Stirlingshire in July 1928. He later played with Ballymena in Ireland.

Andrew Finlay was an inside left who had played with Port Vale, Airdrieonians and Crewe Alexandra. He joined United from Third Lanark and made his debut on 17th October 1925 against Queen's Park in a Scottish League match. He kept his place in the side for eight weeks but following injury, was unable to regain a regular first team slot. In April 1926 he was released and joined Hibernian.

Andrew Finlay

Tom Gilroy was a nineteen year old full back signed from Fauldhouse Juniors. He made his debut against Rangers in a Scottish League match on 19th December 1925 and then made the left back position his own for much of the remaining season and the next, in the top flight. After United were relegated he was one of several players sold due to the Club's troubled financial situation, joining Falkirk for a fee of around £550. He later played for Albion Rovers.

Jimmy Howieson had started his senior career at Airdrieonians before moving to St Johnstone. He became available for transfer in May 1925 and was signed by United, going into the side to face Raith Rovers as the Club made their debut in the First Division. Jimmy scored both United goals in the match but United still lost 4-2. An inside left, Jimmy was one of the star performers in the side but was surprisingly sold to St Mirren for a fee of £1,000 in October 1925 after just three months at Tannadice. Hull City had also been interested in signing him and he joined them the following season. He then had a spell in the USA with New Bedford Whalers before returning to Hull City in 1929. Jimmy later played with Shelbourne, Clyde, Alloa Athletic, Glenavon and Belfast Celtic.

Jimmy Howieson

Hugh McBride signed from Hamilton Academical and made his first appearance as United made their debut in the First Division against Raith Rovers on 15th August 1925. He was the regular left back during the first half of the season but then found it more difficult to get into the starting eleven. In April 1926 he was released and later joined East Fife.

Jock (Smiler) McDonald was an outside left who had started his career with Linfield before joining Blackburn Rovers in 1919. After two years with the English side he moved north and signed for Dundee but in the summer of 1925, unable to agree terms at Dens Park, he crossed the road to join United. He was in the United side that debuted in the First Division against Raith Rovers on 15th August 1925 and missed just two games over that season. He repeated that feat in season 1926-27 and after the Club were relegated he re-signed for the Second Division campaign. Again, he hardly missed a match but when season 1927-28 ended he was unable to agree terms and after being initially listed for transfer, he was released.

Jock McDonald

William MacDonald was an outside right signed from junior side Law Scotia and he made his debut for United in a Scottish League match against Motherwell on 5th September 1925. After just three games for the Club, the player was released.

Bob McFarlane was formerly with Partick Thistle and signed for United from Arbroath on a short term loan deal to cover for the absence of Willie Welsh through illness. He made his debut for United in a Scottish Cup tie against Hearts on 23rd January 1926 and was released just three weeks later when his contract expired.

Bob McFarlane

Mickey McGregor

Mitchell 'Mickey' McGregor was an outside right, signed from local junior side Stobswell. He made his debut for United against Raith Rovers in a Scottish League match on 6th March 1926, one of only two appearances he made that season. In the next campaign, he became a regular in the side and although United were relegated, Mickey remained with the Club for the following season in the Second Division and was a regular again. He was released in April 1928, joined Montrose and later played with Arbroath and Falkirk.

Peter McMillan was a centre forward who had been with Portsmouth and Southend United. He made a scoring debut for United against St Johnstone on 12th September 1925 in a Scottish League match. One of several players who were unsuccessful in the centre forward position around that time, he played just twice more and was released at the end of the season.

Dave Nicoll joined United on a short term loan deal from Forfar Athletic to cover for Dave Walker who was suspended. Formerly with neighbours Dundee, Dave made his debut for United in a Scottish Cup tie against Hearts on 23rd January 1926. He played just a handful of games for the Club and was released at the end of the agreed period.

Peter McMillan

Dave Nicoll

Bill Paterson was a very experienced goalkeeper who had started his career at Dunfermline Athletic before moving to the United States to play with Boston Wonder Workers. He then returned to Dunfermline Athletic but was offered by them to United in May 1925. The big keeper was signed up very quickly and made his debut for United on 15th August 1925 when the Club played Raith Rovers in their first top flight match in the Scottish League. He missed just one game in his first season but it was a costly one as United lost 6-0 to Hearts in a Scottish Cup tie with Jimmy Brownlie in goal. Just over half way through 1926-27 Bill was injured and was out for much of the remainder of the season. He re-signed for United after the Club were relegated at the end of that campaign but after just a handful of games he was injured again and out for several weeks. Soon after he returned to the side, his performances brought him to the attention of Arsenal and he signed for the English side in January 1928. He did not settle in London and in the summer of 1929 he was back in Scotland and joined Airdrieonians.

Bill Paterson

Joe Shandley was signed from Queen of the South and played his first game for United at right half in a Penman Cup tie against Dundee on 26th August 1925. His next game saw him move to centre forward as he made a scoring debut in the Scottish League against Queen's Park on 9th September 1925. He was released after just one more game, a Forfarshire Cup tie.

Jimmy Simpson was one of the best signings made during the first Jimmy Brownlie era. At seventeen years old he was a schoolboy international and signed for United as a centre forward from Newburgh West End but could play in just about any forward or half back position. He made his debut as United stepped onto the First Division stage for the first time on 15th August 1925 against Raith Rovers. Although just two seasons at Tannadice, Jimmy was a big favourite with the fans and they were disappointed when he left at the end of season 1926-27, still just eighteen years old, to join Rangers. At the time, United were experiencing severe financial difficulties so were forced to sell the player for a fee said to be in the region of £2,500 (although some reports quoted the figure at much less). Jimmy went on to enjoy considerable success with Rangers in a centre half role. He also played for Scotland fourteen times and was the team captain for all bar one of his international appearances. In 1941 Jimmy returned to United for a short spell before moving on to join St Mirren. His son was Ronnie Simpson the popular Celtic and Scotland goalkeeper. When Jimmy ended his playing career, he went into management with Buckie Thistle and then with Alloa Athletic.

Jimmy Simpson   *Dave Walker*   *Jimmy Walker*

Dave Walker joined United from St Johnstone in July 1925 and made his first appearance for the Tannadice side when they made their debut in the First Division against Raith Rovers on 15th August 1925. Normally a centre half, Dave was capable in any defensive role and was a regular in the team during the two seasons in the top flight. Following relegation at the end of 1926-27, Dave signed up for the Second Division campaign that followed and was again one of the first choices on any team sheet. The following season, in which United won promotion again, the player was less frequently chosen and at the end of that campaign he was granted a free transfer at his own request.

Jimmy Walker joined United from Third Lanark in the summer of 1925 and was in the United side that played for the first time in a First Division match on 15th August 1925 against Raith Rovers. He filled the right half berth for United for most of season but at the end of the campaign he gave up football to pursue his career in teaching. He took a position as head teacher in Bishopbriggs and occasionally wrote as a guest reporter in the Sunday Post.

Willie Welsh was a twenty one year old centre forward who joined United on loan from Hearts, where he had been for three years. He made a scoring debut against Hamilton Academical in the Scottish League on 10th October 1925. He quickly settled into the side and netted a hat-trick against Kilmarnock in just his third game and it appeared that United had found the solution to their goal scoring problems. However, it was almost four months before he found the net again. After the season ended the player returned to Hearts but was immediately released and United moved in to sign him for the forthcoming campaign. Willie missed just a handful of games during that season and netted another

Willie Welsh

hat-trick, against Dunfermline Athletic in February 1927. He always seemed to save his best performances for the matches against his old club and twice he was instrumental in United wins over Hearts. With finances tight at Tannadice the player moved to Charlton Athletic for around £1,000 at the end of the season. He later played with Wigan Borough, Southport, Newport County, Wrexham, Gateshead, Hartlepool United and Jarrow.

1926–27 Player Profiles

Eddie Carroll

Eddie Carroll was an Irish international who had been with Glenavon. He was brought in from Aberdeen on loan and made a scoring debut at centre forward against Kilmarnock in a Scottish League match on 4th September 1926. During his short spell with United he had a good scoring record including a memorable hat-trick against Hearts in December 1926. At the end of the season he returned to his own club but was almost immediately released and returned to Ireland to join Dundalk.

Frank Carroll was the brother of Eddie Carroll. He began his career at Belfast Celtic before spending three seasons at Manchester City. He then became player manager at Newry Town until the end of season 1925-26. Frank made his debut for United on 2nd October 1926 at centre half against Queen's Park in a Scottish League match. After just three appearances for United he was dropped and then released in April 1927.

James Dempster was an experienced goalkeeper who had been with Sunderland, Airdrieonians and St Johnstone before he signed for United, initially on loan for a month as cover for the injured Bill Paterson. He made his debut against Vale of Leven in a Scottish Cup tie on 5th February 1927 and with Paterson's injury keeping him on the sidelines, James was signed for the remainder of the season. After the Club were relegated in April 1927, the keeper left to join newly promoted Bo'ness and he later played for Bathgate.

James Dempster

Tom Fleming was a versatile full back who joined United from neighbours Dundee, making his debut in a Scottish Cup tie against Montrose on 23rd February 1927. After United were relegated at the end of season 1926-27, Tom re-signed and was with the Club through the Second Division campaign that followed but was released in May 1928.

Johnny Hart had been with Albion Rovers and Motherwell and signed for United from St Johnstone. As a centre forward he made his debut in a Scottish League match against Rangers on 14th August 1926 just as the Club entered a second season in Division One. He was also played frequently as a half back with United and from that position he scored a hat-trick against Arbroath Athletic in a 7-0 Scottish Cup win in January 1927. After United were relegated in April 1927, Johnny remained with the Club all through the next two seasons and he was an influential attacking player in the side that won promotion again in season

Johnny Hart

1928-29. During that campaign he netted another hat-trick but it was expunged from the official records after the opposition, Bathgate resigned from the Scottish League. The First Division campaign of 1929-30 ended in relegation again and surprisingly, Johnny was one of the players released when the season ended. He went to Ross County as player/coach but never lost his affection for United and applied, unsuccessfully, for the vacant Manager's job in May 1931. United fans did not have long to wait for Johnny's return to Tannadice and he was appointed team trainer in July 1932. He left that job five years later but was back again in 1946 in the same role. After another seven years with the Club he gave up his coaching position but carried on as a scout for several more years.

Alex Henderson signed from local junior side North End in August 1926, mainly as a reserve and made his debut at right half in a Scottish League match against St Johnstone on 6th November 1926. He featured in the side in several different positions over his two seasons with United but his appearances were infrequent. He was released in April 1928.

James Meagher arrived at United on loan from neighbours Dundee at a time when United were short of players due to injuries. A former Newtongrange Star player, James made his debut for United at inside left in a Scottish League match against Hamilton Academical on 2nd March 1927. He remained with the Club until the end of the season when he returned to his own side.

James Meagher

Andy Miller was an inside right signed from Wishaw Juniors. He made his debut for United against Kilmarnock in a Scottish League match on 4th September 1926. Andy was a promising young player but when United were relegated at the end of season 1926-27, the Club were experiencing severe financial problems and he was one of a number of players sold, joining Hearts for a fee of £1,000.

John Moore was a half back who had been with Aberdeen, Crystal Palace, Hamilton Academical and also spent some time in the USA with Brooklyn Wanderers. He made just one appearance for United in a Scottish League match against Kilmarnock on 4th September 1926. After leaving United, he joined Arthurlie.

Andy Ramage

Andy Ramage was a bustling centre forward with Dundee and during a period of injuries to several players at Tannadice he arrived on loan for one match, against Partick Thistle in a Scottish Cup tie on 5th March 1927. Two months after he played for United, he was in a Dundee side that thumped United 7-2 in a Forfarshire Cup tie. Andy scored four of the goals for the Dens Park side.

1927-28 Player Profiles

John Bain arrived at United from Dunfermline Athletic during the summer of 1927. He made his debut at left half in the opening match of season 1927-28 against Bathgate in the Scottish League on 13th August 1927 and over the next two years he never missed a competitive match. John has the unique distinction of being the first United player ever to take the field as a substitute when he came on to replace Dave McClure in the second half of a match against Aberdeen in the Fleming Charity Shield. After helping the Club to promotion in 1928-29 he featured less frequently in the First Division campaign of 1929-30 and was allowed to leave in May 1930 to join St Johnstone.

John Bain

John Dorward

John Dorward was a left back signed from local junior side, Logie. He made his debut on 13th August 1927 against Bathgate in a Scottish League match and was the first choice left back for almost the entire season. At the start of the next campaign, he could not agree terms and was transfer listed. He had a trial at Middlesbrough but returned after a few weeks and was released in May 1929 without making any further appearances for United.

Duncan Hutchison

Duncan Hutchison is undoubtedly one of the best signings ever made during the Jimmy Brownlie era. At twenty one years old, he was released by Dunfermline Athletic and joined United, making a scoring debut against Bathgate in a Scottish League match on 13th August 1927. A centre forward with a good eye for a goal scoring opportunity, he completed his first season as top scorer with 32 league and cup goals including hat-tricks against Arthurlie and Third Lanark. The following season he netted another 35 goals with hat-tricks against Arbroath and Stenhousemuir and four goals in one match against Albion Rovers. A hat-trick against Bathgate was expunged after the opposition resigned from the Scottish League. During that campaign there was a lot of interest being shown by other clubs and a Liverpool offer for the player was only rejected as 'Hurricane Hutch' wanted to stay at Tannadice. As United began season 1929-30 in Division One, the player was in top form but when an offer of around £4,000 was received from Newcastle United, he decided it was time to try his luck at a higher level. He had two years with the Tyneside club and then moved to Derby County and finally to Hull City. In June 1935 he was transfer listed by Hull City and the ever alert Brownlie quickly brought him back to United in a swap deal involving Bobby Yorke. With Arthur Milne as the established centre by then, Duncan took on the role of a supporting forward but he had lost little of his attacking prowess and notched 49 goals as a regular in the side over the next three seasons, netting hat-tricks against East Stirlingshire and King's Park. 1938-39 was his last full season as a player for United and after turning out once in the next campaign he left immediately after the outbreak of WW2. He was invited to join the Board at Dundee United in 1953 and took temporary charge of team matters between the resignation of Andy McCall and the appointment of Reggie Smith as Manager. In 1963 Duncan became Chairman of Dundee United. He was in that position for just a brief spell but remained a Director until his death in 1973.

Alex Johnstone was a goalkeeper with St Andrews United and played in a trial match at Tannadice in August 1927. After Bill Paterson was injured in October, Alex was quickly added to the squad and the keeper made his debut for United against St Bernard's on 8th October 1927 in a Scottish League match. As Paterson was out for extended periods, Alex played regularly throughout the campaign but he soon faced competition with the arrival of Jock McHugh. Alex was released at the end of the season.

Alex Johnstone

Jacky Kay was signed from Motherwell Juniors and made his debut at inside left against Bathgate in a Scottish League match on 13th August 1927. He made the inside left position his own for the next two years whilst United were in Division Two and helped the Club to promotion at the end of season 1928-29. He was more or less an ever present in the side as United yo-yoed between the two Scottish Leagues over the next three years. Jacky was top scorer in the promotion winning season of 1930-31 with 26 goals including a hat-trick against Clydebank. At the

Jacky Kay

beginning of season 1933-34, the player was unhappy with the terms offered by United who were by then in a difficult financial position. He was transfer listed and allowed out on loan at Blackpool, Chester City and Crystal Palace. However, his differences with the Club were resolved and he continued to play regularly until May 1936, when, after nine years at United, he was released. Jacky then joined Brechin City and later became trainer with Dundee. He holds the Dundee United record for appearances for a pre WW2 player.

George Mason was a utility forward signed from Falkirk on a short term deal. He made his debut on 3rd January 1928 against King's Park in a Scottish League match but after just one more game, he was released.

Jock McHugh

John 'Jock' McHugh was a goalkeeper signed from Burnbank Athletic following the departure of Bill Paterson to Arsenal. Jock made his debut in the highly charged atmosphere of a Scottish Cup replay against Dundee at Dens Park on 8th February 1928. He shared the keeper's position with Alex Johnstone for the rest of season 1927-28. In the following campaign he was understudy to Harry McGregor and spent some time on loan at Montrose. United were promoted to the First Division for season 1929-30 and Jock broke into the side in mid November to become first choice for much of the remainder of the season. Following relegation, he re-signed for 1930-31 in the Second Division but was attracting attention from other clubs and in November 1930 he was transferred to Portsmouth for a fee of around £400. He did not stay long at Portsmouth and was soon transferred to Watford and whilst there he went on loan to Southend United.

Harry Michie

Henry 'Harry' Michie was a promising outside left signed from Alva Albion Rangers. He made his debut on 10th December 1927 against Ayr United in a Scottish League match. In that game he played as centre forward but reverted to his natural position soon after. For a winger, he had a good scoring record including a hat-trick against Stenhousemuir in November 1927. He lost his place in the side through serious injury shortly afterwards and it was almost a year before he was back in the side again. Unfortunately he managed just a few more appearances before he was released in April 1930.

Tom Parker was a former Bathgate player who had signed for Celtic and came to United on loan. He made his debut at inside right against Third Lanark in a Scottish League match on 17th March 1928 and made just two further appearances before he returned to his own club at the end of the season.

Archie Ralston was an inside right signed from Law Scotia. He made a scoring debut with two goals against Bathgate on 13th August 1927 in a Scottish League match. Archie faced stiff competition for the inside right berth from Johnny Hart and as a result he never commanded a regular first team place and he was released in May 1928.

Bill Taylor joined United from Longriggend Rob Roy and made his debut as a trialist on 26th November 1927 against Dumbarton in a Scottish League match. He quickly established himself as the first choice at right back and retained that position for two years. In his second season with United, 1928-29 he played an important part in the promotion winning side. In the First Division campaign that followed he was again a regular in the side and for three seasons after that. He was considered one of the stars of the side and was

Bill Taylor

frequently the subject of transfer speculation. Several clubs were interested in taking the player from United and offers were turned down until Bill left to join First Division St Johnstone in March 1933.

Trialist, Guest, Junior, Newman, A N Other

The following players, listed as one of the above, are those known to have played during the season.

Blyth of Motherwell Juniors at right back on 5th November 1927 against East Stirlingshire in a Scottish League match.

Duffy of Lochgelly Celtic at centre forward on 9th April 1928 against Hearts in a testimonial for Jock Kay. He scored a hat-trick in the match.

Jack at outside right on 14th April 1928 against Ayr United in a Scottish League match.

Stewart Ross of St Andrews United at outside left on 27th August 1927 against Queen of the South in a Scottish League match.

1928–29 Player Profiles

John Cunningham was a centre half with Vale of Leven Juniors before he signed for United, initially on a provisional form. He made his debut on 2nd January 1929 against King's Park in a Scottish League match and two weeks later signed professionally. He was taken on as reserve cover and made just a few appearances over his two seasons with United and was released in April 1930.

William (Patsy) Deuchar was a right half but was comfortable in most defensive positions. He joined United from Raith Rovers and made his debut against Dunfermline Athletic on 1st September 1928 in a Scottish League match. He remained with United for two seasons and was a regular in the side that won the Second Division title in 1928-29. Less frequently used in the following season, he was released in April 1930 after United were relegated again.

Patsy Deuchar

David Dorward

David Dorward signed from local junior side North End. A right half, he played for the first time for United against Bathgate on 11th August 1928 but that match was later expunged from the records and his official debut is therefore a Dewar Shield match four days later against East Stirlingshire. His official debut in a major competition was on 18th August 1928 in the Scottish League against Bo'ness. David played a significant part in the promotion winning side of 1928-

29 and was with United through the unsuccessful First Division campaign the following season. He was released in April 1930 to sign for Charlton Athletic, and later played in Ireland with Bray Unknowns.

George 'Geordie' Henderson arrived at Tannadice as something of a signing coup by Jimmy Brownlie. Geordie was a former Forfar Athletic, Dundee and Rangers player and Brownlie had tried to sign him in 1926 before he went to Darlington for £1,500. He helped the English side avoid relegation and then spent some time in the USA with New York Nationals but had returned to England after a year. Due to an administrative error, Darlington failed to register the player and as a result he was able to sign for United as a free agent. He made his debut

Geordie Henderson

against Bathgate on 11th August 1928 but that match was later expunged from the records and his official debut is therefore a Dewar Shield match four days later against East Stirlingshire. His official debut in a major competition came on 18th August 1928 in the Scottish League against Bo'ness. Geordie starred for United at outside right, notching a respectable goal tally including a hat-trick against Albion Rovers in March 1929. He was an important part of the side that won promotion and in the First Division campaign that followed he turned out in most forward positions. After relegation at the end of 1929-30 he was initially freed but was then offered terms. Unfortunately for United he decided to move south and became player/coach at Rhyl.

Dave McClure

Dave McClure was a former St Johnstone player who joined United from Nelson FC in the summer of 1928. He made his debut against Bathgate on 11th August 1928 but that match was later expunged from the records. His official debut is therefore a Dewar Shield match four days later against East Stirlingshire and his official debut in major competitions was on 18th August 1928 in the Scottish League against Bo'ness. A hard tackling right back, Dave missed just one league match in season 1928-29 and played a major role in the successful drive for promotion. When United met Aberdeen in the Fleming Charity Shield match on 4th May 1929, Dave became the first United player to be substituted when he went off injured. In the First Division the following season, he was no longer an automatic first choice and played just a handful of games. United were relegated again and Dave was released in April 1930.

Harry McGregor

Harry McGregor was a goalkeeper signed from East Stirlingshire after showing up well in the public trial in August 1928. He made his debut on 1st September 1928 in a Scottish League match against Dunfermline Athletic, displacing Jock McHugh between the posts. He became the first choice keeper for the rest of the season and helped the side to promotion. During the First Division campaign that followed Harry became the understudy to McHugh until the end of the season and was in the side for just two short runs. In April 1930 he was released and joined Alloa Athletic.

Willie Richmond was an inside right signed from Raith Rovers. He made his first appearance for United against Bathgate on 11th August 1928 but that match was later expunged from the records and his official debut is therefore a Dewar Shield match four days later against East Stirlingshire. His first official game in major competition was on 18th August 1928 in the Scottish League against Bo'ness. He was with United for just over a month and was released at the end of September 1928.

George A Ross was an inside right from Dalkeith Thistle and made his United debut in a Scottish Cup replay against Stenhousemuir on 6th February 1929. He established himself as a regular in the side during the following season and he was developing into a good player. Although not renowned as a goal scorer, he netted a hat-trick against Airdrieonians in January 1930. Still just twenty years old, his talent was soon to be lost to United fans as financial difficulties forced the Club to accept an offer of £1,000 from Portsmouth soon afterwards. More than three years later however, he was back at Tannadice after an unsuccessful time

George A Ross

in the south and he had also spent time in Ireland with Bray Unknowns. He became a regular in the United line up, playing in most forward positions and had a creditable scoring record over the next five years, netting another hat-trick, against Brechin City in December 1934. George was released in April 1937 and then joined Leith Athletic but during the years of WW2, he made a return to play for the Club twice in 1943.

Trialist, Guest, Junior, Newman, A N Other

The following players, listed as one of the above, are those known to have played during the season.

Aitken of Vale of Leven at left half on 27th February 1929 against Armadale in a Scottish League match.

Daly from Paisley at centre half on 20th October 1928 against Alloa Athletic in a Scottish League match.

Dickson at right back on 8th April 1929 against East Fife in the first of two Scottish League matches.

Logie of Vale of Leven at left back on 27th February 1929 against Armadale in a Scottish League match.

M McNeil of Kilsyth Emmet at centre half on 6th October 1928 against Morton in a Scottish League match.

1929–30 Player Profiles

Andrew Findlay was an experienced right back who joined United from St Mirren and made his debut against Hamilton Academical on 28th December 1929 in a Scottish League match. He remained with United until the end of the season but after the Club was relegated he was released along with a number of other players.

Andrew Findlay

George Gardiner

George Gardiner was a centre half signed from Clydebank in the summer of 1929 in preparation for the return to First Division football. He made his debut in the opening match of the campaign against Clyde on 10th August 1929 and was rarely out of the side that season. He remained with United after they were relegated again and was in the line up for most of the campaign that followed in Division Two in 1929-30. George helped the side regain a First Division place a year later. Unfortunately season 1931-32 was a poor one for United and they were relegated yet again. George was a regular in that unsuccessful campaign and stayed with United in the lower league for another year before he was released in April 1933. He then joined Leith Athletic.

Andy Haddow was a centre forward who had been with Morton, Burnley, New York Nationals and then Clyde. United acquired him on loan and he made his debut in a Scottish League match against Dundee on 11th January 1930. Andy had a significant impact in the side, scoring regularly, including four goals in one match against Kilmarnock in March 1930. But it was too late to save United from relegation and at the end of the season he returned to his own club. United tried to sign the player for the next season but could not afford the £250 price tag then placed on him, but he did return to Tannadice in March 1931 on another loan deal from Clyde. This time his late contribution helped United back into the top flight, but when the campaign ended Andy went back to Clyde. Shortly afterwards he was released by them and joined Ballymena in Ireland.

Andy Haddow

Bruce Harley

Bruce Harley was a left half signed from Hearts and he made his debut for United on 11th January 1930 against Dundee in a Scottish League match. He played regularly in the side until the end of the season. United were then struggling in the lower reaches of the First Division and were eventually relegated and Bruce was one of the few players retained for the Second Division campaign that followed. He was in the line up for many of the early games in season 1930-31 but in the latter stages he could not get a starting place and was released in April 1931.

John McNally was signed from Motherwell Juniors as reserve cover for the outside right position. He made his first appearance for United in a Dewar Shield match against East Stirlingshire on 14th August 1929. His debut in a major competition followed on 7th September 1929 against Airdrieonians in a Scottish League match. He was used in the side only occasionally and was one of a large number of players released following relegation in April 1930.

John 'Jock' Ross was a half back signed from Dundee and he made his debut for United at right back on 10th August 1929 against Clyde as United made their return to the top flight in Scottish football. He was with United for just one season during which he was a regular in the side. After the Club was relegated in April 1930, Jock was released and joined Welsh side Connah's Quay.

Jock Ross

Eddie Smith

Eddie Smith was signed from Carluke Rovers and made his debut for United in a Scottish League match against St Mirren on 5th October 1929. He was another centre forward signed by United to fill the gap left by Duncan Hutchison but he was also one of a number who did not come up to expectation. Eddie managed just a few games and was released in April 1930 after United were relegated.

George Thomson was the centre forward brought in from Clydebank for £500 to fill the gap left immediately after the departure of Duncan Hutchison. He had a hard act to follow and made his debut in a difficult derby against Dundee in the Scottish League on 31 August 1929. George never quite found his shooting boots at United and was released at the end of season 1929-30 following relegation from the First Division.

George Watson was a versatile half back signed from local junior side North End in the summer of 1929 as reserve cover. He did not have long to wait for his debut which came against St Johnstone on 30th November 1929 in a Scottish League match, making just a few more appearances that season. United were relegated at the end of it but George was retained for the Second Division campaign that followed. He became the first choice left half in February 1931 helping the Club to regain a First Division spot and retained his position for the first half of season 1931-32 in the top flight. His appearances became less frequent thereafter but when the Club were relegated, he was kept on for another season. George managed just a few more outings before being released in April 1933.

1930–31 Player Profiles

George 'Jock' Bain was signed from Lochgelly Albert. As an eighteen year old, he made a scoring debut for United as a trialist during a Scottish League match against Queen of the South on 25th October 1930. He played in both inside forward positions during the promotion winning season of 1930-31 scoring frequently. Included in his goal tally was a Scottish Cup hat-trick against Nithsdale Wanderers as United ran up a record 14-0 win. In the unsuccessful First Division campaign of 1931-32, George made just a few appearances and was released in April 1932 to join Brechin City.

Jock Bain	*John Bateman*	*Colvin Bennett*

John Bateman was signed from Dundee Violet just after the end of season 1929-30. An inside right, he made his debut in the first match of the following season on 9th August 1930 against Armadale in the Scottish League. He made little impact over the campaign with only a handful of appearances and was released in April 1931.

Colvin Bennett was a centre forward signed from local junior side Fairfield after playing well in a public trial match. He made a scoring debut in the opening match of season 1930-31 against Armadale in the Scottish League. He scored in each of his first five matches and went on to find the net regularly over the early part of the campaign until the arrival of Tim Williamson. The two players then shared the centre forward role and both played their part as United won promotion to the First Division. In April 1931 Colvin was re-signed for the challenge of the top flight and started the campaign as the first choice centre forward. The arrival of Jimmy Dyet pushed Colvin into an outside right role which he filled frequently. It was an unsuccessful return to the First Division for the Club and Colvin was released at the end of the season along with many of the squad.

Eric MacKay was a former schoolboy international who had gone to Canada but had not settled, returning to sign for Dundee in early 1930. He arrived at United on loan for a month and made a scoring debut, netting twice against Forfar Athletic on 6th September 1930 in a Scottish League match. That was his first and only appearance for United.

Eric MacKay *Denis McCallum* *Bill McCallum*

Denis McCallum came from Celtic on loan and made his debut at outside right on 25th October 1930 against Queen of the South in a Scottish League match. He kept his place in the side for most of the remainder of the season and helped the Club to win promotion but returned to Celtic when the loan deal expired in April 1931.

Bill McCallum was a goalkeeper signed from local junior side YMCA Anchorage. He made his debut as a trialist in a Scottish League match against Alloa Athletic on 27th December 1930 and signed just days later. A junior international, Bill was the mainstay in goal for the rest of the season and played a big part as United won promotion to the First Division. However, despite playing the first two matches of the new season, the arrival of Chic McIntosh effectively ended his career at Tannadice and although still in the squad he made just one more appearance before he was released in April 1932.

Jimmy Milne made his debut at centre half for United as a trialist against Alloa Athletic in a Scottish League match on 16th August 1930. A junior with Dundee Violet, he signed shortly afterwards and went on to feature regularly at right half and played his part in the promotion winning side that season. He was rarely out of the line up during season 1931-32 in the First Division campaign. Financial constraints forced the Club to transfer list the player following relegation in April 1932 and after initial interest from Charlton Athletic he went to Preston North End. He was with the Lancashire club for seven years and later played for Wigan Athletic and Morecambe. In 1961 he became the manager at Preston North End and remained in that post for seven years.

Jimmy Milne

James Nelson was an outside right signed from Dundee. He made his debut for United on 9th August 1930 against Armadale in a Scottish League match. After just three games he was released.

Frank Penson signed for United from local junior side Fairfield after showing up well in a public trial match. A left back, he made his debut against Armadale in a Scottish League match on 9th August 1930 and he retained the left back slot for the entire season. He made a vital contribution to the promotion winning side and was retained for the ultimately unsuccessful assault on the First Division in 1931-32, missing just two games over that campaign. Back in Division Two again, Frank kept his place for most of 1932-33 but was released at the end of that season.

Tom Stewart

Tom Stewart was a left half signed from Dundee Violet just after the end of season 1929-30. He made his debut in the first match of the following season on 9th August 1930 against Armadale in a Scottish League match. He began his United career well and featured regularly in the side but in the latter stages of 1930-31 he dropped out of contention and was released in April 1931.

William (Tim) Williamson was a much travelled inside right signed from Montrose. He had played on both sides of the border with around a dozen clubs before joining United. He made his debut against Stenhousemuir on 23rd August 1930 in a Scottish League match. Tim was often used at centre forward and from that position he netted several goals including four in one game against St Bernard's in November 1930 and five against Nithsdale Wanderers in Dundee United's record 14-0 win in the Scottish Cup. Despite playing a big part in winning promotion with the Club, he was released at the end of season 1930-31. He then joined Accrington Stanley before moving on to play with Southport and Rochdale. He returned to Scotland with Alloa Athletic and Leith Athletic and had a spell with Distillery in Ireland before ending his career at Montrose.

Tim Williamson

Trialist, Guest, Junior, Newman, A N Other

The following players, listed as one of the above, are those known to have played during the season.

Attilio Becci of Arbroath Roselea at outside right on 27th September 1930 against Clydebank in a Scottish League match.

Bennett of Cumbernauld Thistle in goal on 20th December 1930 against Armadale in a Scottish League match.

Willie Felton of Rioneach Mhor in goal on 29th November 1930 against King's Park in the first of three Scottish League matches.

Lumsden of Dundee Violet at outside right on 20th September 1930 against St Johnstone in a Scottish League match.

Reid of Stobswell at outside right on 30th August 1930 against Montrose in a Scottish League match.

Ross of Dundee North End at outside right on 23rd August 1930 against Stenhousemuir in a Scottish League match.

1931–32 Player Profiles

Jim Baillie was a right half, formerly with Cardiff City, Derry City and Fulham before he joined United. He made his first appearance on 7th November 1931 against Falkirk in a Scottish League match. After just a handful of games he was released. Jim later played for French club Lille.

Jim Baillie

Harry Brant

Henry 'Harry' Brant joined Bury from Albion Rovers for a fee of £2,000 in the summer of 1929 but for personal reasons he was keen to return to Scotland. Listed by Bury at £1,250, he came to United for a fee of much less than that and made his debut at inside left on 22nd August 1931 against Partick Thistle in a Scottish League match. He went on to play in both inside forward positions over the season, finding the net regularly and netting a hat-trick against Morton. United were relegated at the end of that season and Harry was one of the few players to sign up for the campaign that followed in the Second Division. With the Club in dire financial circumstances at the end of season 1932-33 Harry was transfer listed but with no interest being shown from any other club he was eventually released.

Archie Buchanan

Archie Buchanan joined United from junior side Carluke Rovers and made his debut at right back on 28th November 1931 against Morton in a Scottish League match. He made several more appearances in the side that season in the right half berth. Following relegation to the Second Division, he was re-signed and became a regular in the line up during 1932-33 but was released at the end of that campaign.

David Cuthill was an outside left with Grove FP. He signed for United on an amateur form and made his debut against Hearts on 8th August 1931 in a Scottish League match. That was his only appearance as his registration was cancelled four days later.

Jimmy Dyet was a bustling centre forward who began his career at King's Park scoring eight goals on his debut in January 1930. Six months later he moved to Falkirk from where he was acquired by United. He made his debut on 19th December 1931 against Hearts in a Scottish League match and went on to retain the centre forward position for much of the remainder of season 1931-32 in which United were relegated from Division One. He was re-signed for the Second Division challenge in the following season and continued a good run of form including a hat-trick against Dumbarton in September 1932. He was released in May 1933 and returned to King's Park.

Jimmy Dyet

Edmund 'Eddie' Glover was an outside right with Lochee Harp when he provisionally signed for United in January 1929. He had to wait three years to make his debut against Partick Thistle on 9th January 1932 in a Scottish League match and his stay at the Club lasted only until the end of that season with just occasional appearances. He was studying to become a teacher and appears to have pursued that career instead of football.

Andrew Jackson

Andrew Jackson was an inside right signed from local junior side North End. He made a good impression during a public trial and was signed shortly afterwards. His first appearance came in a Scottish League match against Celtic on 15th August 1931 and he went on to play regularly during that season in the First Division. United were unsuccessful in the campaign of 1931-32 and were relegated at the end of it. Andrew was one of several players released then.

William Logie was a former Dundee Violet player who joined United from Portsmouth after a successful outing in a public trial match. An outside right, he made his debut in a Scottish League match against Hearts on 8th August 1931 as United began a season in the First Division after winning promotion. William began as a regular in the line up but in the latter stages of the campaign he appeared infrequently. After the Club was relegated at the end of season 1931-32, he was released along with a number of other players.

George McGlynn was an amateur outside left who played with United whilst studying at St Andrews University. He made his debut on 19th December 1931 against Hearts in a Scottish League match and kept his place in the side for much of the remainder of an ultimately unsuccessful season in the First Division. He left the Club in May 1932.

William Logie   *George McGlynn*   *Chic McIntosh*

Chic McIntosh was signed from local junior side Logie after an impressive performance in a public trial match. He replaced Bill McCallum in goal against Queen's Park on 18th August 1931 and went on to retain the keeper's jersey for all bar one match in the rest of season 1931-32. He was one of the few players retained following relegation in April 1932 and in the following season in Division Two he missed jut one league match due to injury. At the beginning of 1933-34 Chic was unhappy with the terms he was offered and was transfer listed. A new keeper, Archie Milliken was brought in and began the campaign but Chic took over again after four matches. He was the first choice keeper from that point in the season until March 1934 at which time he again refused the terms offered to re-sign and was dropped. At his own request, he was transfer listed at £150. In November 1934 he went for trials at Preston North End and signed for them a month later.

Dave Morris

Dave Morris began his professional career at Raith Rovers and moved to Preston North End in 1925 for a fee of £5,000. He was transfer listed and spent some time on loan at Chester City before moving north to join United for £500. A centre half, Dave made his debut for United against Hearts on 19th December 1931 in a Scottish League match and went on to play regularly over the rest of the season. At the end of the campaign United were relegated and Dave was initially transfer listed but was soon released and he joined Leith Athletic.

George Radcliffe joined United from Albion Rovers for the return to First Division football. He made his debut against Celtic in a Scottish League match on 15th August 1931 at outside left. George was used frequently throughout the first half of the season on either flank but in January 1932, he left to join Falkirk.

1932–33 Player Profiles

John Brown joined United from Inverkeithing Juniors after two successful trial matches beginning with a Scottish League encounter against East Fife on 24th August 1932. An inside right, he missed very few games over the next two years and was a regular goal scorer for the Club. Due to financial difficulties the player was one of many released at the end of season 1933-34 and he then joined Cowdenbeath.

John Brown

Joe Connolly

Peter Gavigan

Joe Connolly was an outside right signed from Leith Athletic. He made his debut for United on 13th August 1932 against Hibs in a Scottish League match. Joe did not stay long at Tannadice and was released two months into season 1932-33.

Peter Gavigan was a much travelled outside right. He had spent four years with Fulham and two seasons at Clapton Orient before returning to Scotland to join St Johnstone and then Dundee. He was with Montrose for a short period before he signed for United. Peter made his debut on 10th December 1932 against Brechin City in a Scottish League match and then played regularly until the end of season 1933-34 when he was released. In 1939, Peter applied unsuccessfully for the vacant Manager's job at United.

Walter Hotson was a former Armadale right back who signed for United from Falkirk on a short term deal. He made his debut on 13th August 1932 against Hibs in a Scottish League match but within a few weeks, he was released.

David Laing was an outside left with local junior side East Craigie. He made his debut for United as a trialist in a Scottish League match against Albion Rovers on 3rd December 1932. After two more trial games he was signed and became a regular in the side. Even from his wide attacking position he had a knack for finding the net and managed to record a hat-trick against King's Park in March 1933. He re-signed for the following season and was again a regular but with finances at Tannadice strained, he was one of several players released in April 1934.

James Lindsay was a left half with Bowhill Rovers and made his first appearance for United as a trialist on 26th November 1932 against Leith Athletic in a Scottish League match. After one more trial game he was signed and was a regular in the line up for two seasons. Along with several other players he was released at the end of season 1933-34 with the Club experiencing financial problems. He then signed for Welsh side Rhyl and later played for Brechin City.

David Laing   *James Lindsay*   *Willie Ouchterlonie*

Willie Ouchterlonie was a centre forward with local junior side Osborne. He played his first game for United as a trialist on 3rd September 1932 against Alloa Athletic in a Scottish League match. After a second trial two weeks later he was signed and then became a regular feature of the side at centre or outside right. He was on the score sheet more often than not including a hat-trick against King's Park in March 1933 and ended his first season as top goal scorer. He re-signed for season 1933-34 and was again the top marksman in the side. His tally that season included five goals against both Edinburgh City and King's Park and four against Leith Athletic. It came as something of a surprise when he was released in April 1934. He then joined Raith Rovers and later played for Barrow and Wrexham. In January 1940 he made a fleeting return to United for one more game and scored a brace.

Charles Whyte was signed from junior side Arbroath Ardenlea in the summer of 1932. An outside left, he made his debut against Hibs on 13th August 1932 as United returned to the Second Division following relegation. In the latter stages of the campaign he played in either outside position but when the season was over he was released.

Charles Whyte

Trialist, Guest, Junior, Newman, A N Other

The following players, listed as one of the above, are those known to have played during the season.

Alec Farmer of Osborne at inside left on 8th October 1932 against Forfar Athletic in a Scottish League match. He later moved to Stobswell and turned out for United again on 30th December 1933 against Dumbarton in a Scottish League match.

Gardiner of Inverkeithing Juniors at left back on 1st October 1932 against St Bernard's in the first of two Scottish League matches.

Johnston at left back on 17th December 1932 against Albion Rovers in a Scottish League match.

Bert Lamb of East Craigie in goal on 15th March 1933 against Dundee in a High Cup tie. He later moved to Dundee Violet and near the end of season 1933-34 he made three Scottish League appearances for United.

Gordon McDonald of Alyth United at right back on 5th November 1932 against East Fife in a Scottish League match.

McAvan of Dundee Celtic at inside left on 15th October 1932 against Montrose in a Scottish League match.

Sullivan of Newburgh West End at outside left on 12th November 1932 against Arbroath in a Scottish League match.

Whitelaw of Inverkeithing Juniors at centre half on 24th August 1932 against East Fife in a Scottish League match.

1933–34 Player Profiles

Charles Campbell was a left back signed from Clyde. He made his debut for United on 2nd September 1933 against Dumbarton in a Scottish League match. The player retained his place in the side for almost the entire season but at the end of the campaign, he was released, largely because the Club was experiencing severe financial difficulties.

Dave Corbett

Dave Corbett had been with Hearts and signed for United from Ayr United. He was a right half and made his first appearance as a trialist in a Scottish League match against East Fife on 12th August 1933. During a difficult period in the Club's history, Dave was a stalwart of the side and was one of only five players retained at the end of 1933-34. He re-signed for the next two campaigns and was rarely out of the line up until he was sidelined by injury in November 1935. Two months later he was back in the team and a regular starter until the end of the season. Although re-signed for season 1935-36 he left the Club in October 1936 to join West Ham United and was later with Southport before returning to Scotland to play with Dumbarton and St Mirren. He returned to United for one outing in October 1945.

Hugh Foy was a right back signed from Bo'ness. He made his debut for United against East Fife on 12th August 1933 but a few weeks later, after just four games he was released.

Bobby Gardiner was the find of the season in 1933-34. Playing as a trialist on 16th December 1933 he scored twice against Arbroath in a Scottish League match. He was with Broughty Ex-Service Club at the time and was quickly signed by

United after an impressive debut and was one of the few successes in the side over season 1933-34. Nicknamed 'the mighty atom' by the fans, he was one of just five players retained at the end of the season during a time when the Club was in financial difficulties. In season 1934-35 he was joined in the attack by Arthur Milne at centre forward and this pairing became known as 'the mighty midgets'. They were an effective partnership for the best part of two seasons and lifted United from the doldrums of second bottom of the Second Division to a challenging position near the top. In the summer of 1936 Bobby refused the terms offered and left United to join non league Dartford. A year later, and still registered with United, he joined Bristol Rovers, earning United a fee of around £250. Just after the outbreak of WW2 Bobby returned to Tannadice for season 1939-40 in the North Eastern League and played for the Club in the Emergency War Cup final in 1940. After a spell in junior football the following season, he was back with United and appeared regularly until April 1943. Shortly afterwards he returned to Bristol Rovers, with whom he was still registered but after the war he came north and ended his career with Arbroath.

Bobby Gardiner

Johnnie Herbert

Johnnie Herbert was an East Fife inside left who had been on trial with Raith Rovers. He then joined United for a one month trial and made his debut against Alloa Athletic in a Scottish League match on 25th November 1933. At the end of the agreed period he was released.

William Low was first spotted on a brief tour of the Highlands when he played for Fraserburgh against United in April 1933. An outside right, he made his debut in the opening match of season 1933-34 against East Fife on 12th August but a few weeks later he was released.

Bill Masson made his first appearance for United at left back as a trialist against East Stirlingshire in a Scottish League match on 23rd September 1933. He played at centre half in two more trial matches and then signed in early November from Carluke Rovers. He went on to play in the centre half position for the rest of the season and was one of just five players retained at the end of 1933-34 as United encountered financial problems. He was an ever present in the side in 1934-35 but featured less frequently in the season that followed and he was released in April 1936.

Bill Masson

James (Monty) Munro

Laurie McBain

Lawrence 'Laurie' McBain was a half back who began his career at Queen's Park. He joined United from St Johnstone and made his debut on 9th September 1933 in a Scottish League match against Morton. Laurie was settling in well to the side and beginning to have a major influence when he suffered a broken leg that ended his career in December 1933.

Archie Milliken was a goalkeeper signed from Kilmarnock. He made his debut for United in the first league match of Season 1933-34 against East Fife on 12th August 1933. After just four outings for the Club he was replaced by Chic McIntosh and then released in September 1933.

James (Monty) Munro was signed by United from Dundee initially on a one month deal which was later extended. An outside left, he made a scoring debut against Arbroath on 16th December 1933 in a Scottish League match. After a short run in the team in early 1934, he was released at a point which coincided with the crisis in United's financial position, February 1934. Monty died just two years later, still aged just 23 years.

Fred Murray signed from Cowdenbeath. A centre forward, he made his debut for United on 12th August 1933 against East Fife in a Scottish League match. He was released in November 1933 after just a few appearances.

Fred Murray

Henry 'Harry' Nicolson was an outside left signed from St Johnstone on a one month deal. He made a scoring debut against Dunfermline Athletic in a Scottish League match on 28th October 1933 but when his loan agreement expired, he was released.

William Sinclair was a centre half signed from Arbroath after he showed up well in a public trial match in August 1933. He made his debut for United in a Scottish League match against East Fife on 12th August 1933. William was soon replaced in the side and surplus to requirements, he was released in October 1933.

Harry Nicholson   *William Sinclair*   *James (Chic) Weir*

James (Chic) Weir had started his career with Kilmarnock and had also been with Hamilton Academical and Queen of the South before moving south to join Norwich City in 1930. After a year there, he returned north and played with Armadale and Bo'ness before going to Dunfermline Athletic. From there he was released and signed for United on a one month deal just as season 1933-34 was under way. A centre forward, he scored twice on his debut against Dumbarton on 2nd September 1933 in a Scottish League match. He played well during his month with United and found the net regularly but at the end of the loan agreement, Dunfermline Athletic took him back, having witnessed the upturn in his form.

David Willis was a right back signed from Ayr United. He made his debut as a trialist against East Stirlingshire on 23rd September 1933 in a Scottish League match. Signed shortly afterwards, he went on to retain the right back position for most of season 1933-34. Along with the majority of the playing staff, he was released in April 1934.

Trialist, Guest, Junior, Newman, A N Other

The following players, listed as one of the above, are those known to have played during the season.

Cargill of East Craigie in goal on 11th November 1933 against Montrose in a Scottish League match.

Lawrence of Lochee Harp in goal on 18th November 1933 against Edinburgh City in a Scottish League match.

Willie McConnachie of Dundee Celtic in goal on 21st April 1934 against Raith Rovers in a Scottish League match.

Orchison of Forfar Celtic in goal on 14th April 1934 against Dundee in a Penman Cup tie.

Bertie Paterson of Logie at centre forward on 31st March 1934 against Forfar Athletic in a Scottish League match, scoring a goal.

A Peden in goal on 28th April 1934 against Albion Rovers in a Scottish League match.

Wallace of Perth YMCA at left half on 30th December 1933 against Dumbarton in a Scottish League match.

Whyte, a Forfar junior at centre half on 16th September 1933 against St Bernard's in a Scottish League match.

1934–35 Player Profiles

Dave Collington was a right back from Scone Thistle. His first match for United was as a trialist against Forres Mechanics on 23rd April 1935 in a friendly during United's short Highland tour. He signed soon after and then made his debut in major competition against St Bernard's in the opening Scottish League match of 1935-36. He did not feature much in the side until the latter stages of that campaign but then became a regular in the side for the next two years. The player had an unfortunate time with injuries, suffering a broken pelvis and broken jaw at different times in his United career but surprisingly, these injuries did not keep him out of the side for long. He was however released in April 1938.

Willie Fleming was a right back who had been with Celtic and Ayr United. He made his debut for United in a Scottish League match against Third Lanark on 25th August 1934. Willie went on to play a major part in the 1934-35 league campaign but despite a good record with the Club he was released in April 1935.

Jimmy Hart was a centre forward who had been with Portadown and Hibernian. He made a scoring debut for United on 11th August 1934 against Forfar Athletic in a Scottish League match. He lost his place in the side shortly after the arrival of Arthur Milne and was released in April 1935. He then joined Cowdenbeath.

Alec King joined United on 11th August 1934 from Clyde and made a scoring debut on the same day against Forfar Athletic in the opening Scottish League match of 1934-35. He was an outside left and over the season he missed just one game, racking up a respectable goal tally including a hat-trick against Edinburgh City in December 1934. Alec applied to the SFA for a free transfer in June 1935 and it was granted, allowing him to join Alloa Athletic. He later went to Brechin City and in December 1936 he returned to United but was released again in April 1937.

Alec King

Willie MacRitchie signed from Clyde just in time to make his debut for United in the opening Scottish League match of 1934-35 against Forfar Athletic. A left back, he went on to become a regular in the side and missed just two matches that season. Re-signed for 1935-36 he began the campaign in his left back role again but towards the end of the season he lost his place and was released in April 1936.

Arthur Milne

Arthur Milne was one of the best signings made by Jimmy Brownlie. Signed from Brechin Victoria, Arthur made a sensational debut on 28th November 1934 scoring four goals in a Scottish League match against Edinburgh City and that set the trend for the high scoring centre. He netted another four in a match against Brechin City not long after to bring his opening tally to eleven in just four games. He struck up an immediate understanding with Bobby Gardiner and the pair soon became known as 'the mighty midgets'. Arthur netted another four goals in one match against Queen's Park and a hat-trick against Stenhousemuir to end the season as top scorer with 28 goals from 22 league and cup appearances. He re-signed for the next campaign and again he was the star forward. Hat-tricks against Alloa Athletic, Cowdenbeath, Stenhousemuir and East Stirlingshire were outdone by four goals against Dumbarton and Leith Athletic for a season's total of 35 goals in 31 games. His exploits brought him to the attention of other clubs but United were determined to hold on to their biggest asset and offers from other clubs were turned down. There were radical changes at the Club in October 1934 including cancellation of the player's bonus scheme. Arthur was the only player to challenge that decision and eventually it led to his departure from Tannadice. He lodged an appeal with the SFA for his bonus money but before it could be heard he was allowed to go to Liverpool on loan in March. He was still top scorer for the third season in a row by the end of 1936-37. Following an administrative error the player became a free agent and was signed by Hibs. United claimed that Liverpool had signed the player and after a hearing at the International Board, Liverpool were ordered to pay United £750 plus expenses. That was well below the valuation on the player but more importantly the player was a big loss to the team. In November 1939 he returned to United and featured regularly in the side during season 1939-40 and he was in the line up as United faced Rangers in the Emergency War Cup final in May 1940. His record in 1939-40 merely confirmed him as one of the most prolific goal scorers ever to don a United jersey.

Peter Robertson was a goalkeeper who started his senior career at Dundee before moving south to join Charlton Athletic and then Crystal Palace. He joined United just after the beginning of season 1934-35, making his debut against Dumbarton in a Scottish League match on 18th August 1934. He was in the side for the rest of the campaign but was released in April 1935.

Peter Robertson

Tommy Ross was signed from local junior side Osborne in December 1934. He made a scoring debut at outside right against East Stirlingshire in a Scottish League match on 30th March 1935. Tommy then took part in the tour of the Highlands in April 1935 but did not impress sufficiently and was released shortly afterwards.

Jimmy Smith signed for United from East Stirlingshire and made his debut on 11th August 1934 against Forfar Athletic in a Scottish League match. Normally an inside left, Jimmy could fill most forward positions and made a significant contribution during season 1934-35. He re-signed for the following season and was again featured regularly in the side but was released in April 1936.

Bobby Yorke

Bobby Yorke was a former Ayr United and Dunfermline Athletic player who signed for United from Aldershot after he played well in a public trial match. He made his debut at right half on 11th August 1934 in the opening Scottish League match of the new season against Forfar Athletic. Bobby was capable of filling either half back position and also lined up at centre forward with some success early in season 1934-35. In June 1935 he moved to Hull City as part of the deal that brought Duncan Hutchison back to Tannadice but Bobby too would return for a second stint with the Club. It appears he left Hull City and joined Ayr United again for a time but Bobby returned to United in September 1937 and was at the Club for another two seasons. He was released in April 1938 and then joined Montrose.

Trialist, Guest, Junior, Newman, A N Other

The following players, listed as one of the above, are those known to have played during the season.

Bremner of Rothes in goal on 25th April 1935 against Elgin City in a friendly.

Falconer of Dundee Violet at left back on 22nd September 1934 against St Bernard's in a Scottish League match.

A McCormack of Dundee Violet in goal on 11th August 1934 against Forfar Athletic in a Scottish League match.

McGrory of Dundee North End at left half on 23rd April 1935 against Forres Mechanics in the first of two friendlies, scoring twice in the second match.

Millar at outside left on 23rd April 1935 against Forres Mechanics in a friendly.

Parle of Elgin City in goal on 24th April 1935 against Inverness Thistle in a friendly.

1935–36 Player Profiles

Doug Anderson was a half back signed from Aberdeen. He made his debut for United in a Scottish League match against Falkirk on 7th September 1935. Doug became a regular in the side at left half until he was released in April 1937 after just one season. He then joined Hibs.

John 'Jacky' Brown was a former Montrose and Brechin City outside left. He made a scoring debut for United against St Bernard's in the opening Scottish League match of season 1935-36. Jacky was tried in several positions including centre forward from where he netted a hat-trick against Brechin City. Unfortunately the match was abandoned and the record of his feat expunged along with the 5-1 score in favour of United. He was re-signed for the next season but never established himself in the side again and was finally released in December 1936. He then signed for Forfar Athletic.

Robert Hogg was a former Dundee and Partick Thistle defender who came to United on a one month trial. He made his debut as a trialist against Dumbarton on 28th September 1935 but after just one more appearance he was released.

James MacFarlane signed from Perth junior side Fair City Athletic in May 1936 after a successful trial against Brora Rangers on 29th April 1936 during United's short Highland tour. He made his next appearance in a Forfarshire Cup tie against Dundee on 23rd September and his debut in major competition three days later against Alloa Athletic in a Scottish League match. Usually a left half, James lined up in several defensive positions and was even pressed into service in the forward line on two occasions. He was a regular in the side during 1936-37 but was fielded less frequently in his second season. In April 1938 he was released along with most of the squad that term.

James MacFarlane

Robert McIntosh was a left back who signed from junior side Blairgowrie after making a good impression as a trialist with United on a brief tour of the Highlands in April 1936. He played his first game for United against Brora Rangers on 29th April 1936. Robert made his debut in major competition on 8th August 1936 against King's Park in a Scottish League match. He went on to make the position his own for the entire season bar one game in which he played at outside left but was one of a large group of players released in April 1937.

John Milne was an outside left who joined United from Benburb after he had been seen playing for the junior side just once. He made his debut on 16th November 1935 in a Scottish League match against Leith Athletic and went on to complete the season with the Club missing just a few games. Despite a good scoring record, he was released in May 1936.

Bob Morrison was a former Airdrieonians goalkeeper who had moved to England to join Southport. He then spent some time with Gateshead before joining United. Bob made his debut for the Club on 10th August 1935 against St Bernard's in a Scottish League match and was the first choice keeper for the rest of the season, missing just one match. He was released in May 1936 and joined Albion Rovers but later returned south to play for Workington before returning to Scotland to join Forfar Athletic.

Robert Murray was a versatile full back with Hearts and then Clyde. He joined United, making his debut in a Scottish League match on 2nd November 1935 against Forfar Athletic. The player was in the side for most of the remaining games that season but was released at the end of the campaign. He was then reinstated to the junior ranks.

Donovan 'Donny' Reid was an inside forward signed from Aberdeen East End. He made his debut on 7th September 1935 against Falkirk in a Scottish League match but went on to appear just a few times in his first season after an injury in October sidelined him until the latter stages. Donny featured more regularly in 1936-37 but was released at the end of that campaign. He was back with United in September 1937 but could not get into the side and was transfer listed in April 1938. However, he re-signed again for the next campaign but still unable to command a regular place, he was released in April 1939.

Dave Skelligan was a defender who had appeared in public trial matches in 1930 and 1931 but he was not signed until June 1935 from Brechin City. He could play in almost any defensive role and made a scoring debut at left half in a Scottish League match against St Bernard's on 10th August 1935. Dave was a stalwart in the defence for four seasons at United but was released in April 1939. He then joined Forfar Athletic.

George Ure was just seventeen years old when he signed from Stobswell as a reserve utility defender. He made his debut at right back against Cowdenbeath on 26th October 1935 in a Scottish League match. George made only three appearances during season 1935-36 and spent some time on loan at both Brechin City and Falkirk before returning to United for season 1937-38. He was then in and out of the side covering almost every defensive position at some point but at the end of the campaign he was released.

George Ure

Willie Watson was a centre half signed from Ayr United, making his debut for Dundee United in a Scottish Cup tie against Alloa Athletic on 25th January 1936. He was a regular in the line up for the remainder of the season and re-signed for season 1936-37, but after three months he was released and went south to join Lincoln City. He then appears to have moved back to Scotland and joined Dundee briefly but at the beginning of season 1937-38 he was back with United. After a match in which United were beaten 4-1 by Albion Rovers, Willie and his brother, goalkeeper Dave Watson were both suspended by then Manager/Managing Director, George Greig for 'not trying'. Both appealed to the SFA and in the case of Willie, United were obliged to honour his contract. Greig vowed he would never play for United again but soon relented and Willie was back in the side for much of the remainder of season. He was however, released in April 1938.

Trialist, Guest, Junior, Newman, A N Other

The following players, listed as one of the above, are those known to have played during the season.

David Dair of Alyth United at left back on 1st February 1936 against Alloa Athletic in a Scottish League match.

Joe Jamieson of Aberdeen East End at outside left on 28th September 1935 against Dumbarton, scoring a hat-trick in the first of two Scottish League matches.

Robert Mennie, an Aberdeen junior at outside right on 25th April 1936 against Peterhead, scoring a goal in the first of two friendly matches.

Sutherland of Dundee Arnot at right half on 1st February 1936 against Alloa Athletic in a Scottish League match.

1936–37 Player Profiles

Peter Bain

Peter Bain joined United from Partick Thistle. He was an outside left and made his debut on 8th August 1936 against King's Park in a Scottish League match. Peter had been on the Partick Thistle transfer list at £500 but had successfully appealed to the SFA who ruled he should be given a free transfer and was therefore acquired for nothing. He appeared to be doing well for the Club but a change of Manager occurred in October 1936 and Peter was released. He then joined Raith Rovers.

Malcolm Cameron was an amateur who played just one game for United. He was at inside right against King's Park in a Scottish League match on 9th January 1937.

Fergus Davidson was an amateur signed from YMCA Anchorage just after control of the Club was given to Managing Director/Team Manager George Greig. Fergus made his debut at centre half against Raith Rovers in a Scottish League match on 7th November 1936. He retained his place for much of the remaining campaign, even playing as a forward twice. As an amateur he was automatically released at the end of the season and was not re-signed.

Fergus Davidson

John Donnelly was a right half who signed for United from Albion Rovers and made his debut against Morton in a Scottish League match on 5th September 1936. After just one month at the Club he was released.

Dan Hutchison was the younger brother of Duncan Hutchison and played his first game for United as a trialist against Alloa Athletic in a Boxing Day Scottish League match in 1936. He was still with local junior side St Joseph's when he played as a trialist for the second time at the end of season 1936-37 and then signed. An outside left, Dan featured in the side infrequently but recorded a hat-trick in a 5-5 draw with Airdrieonians in his last game for the Club on the final day of season 1937-38. The hat-trick was remarkable insofar as Dan had been carried from the field unconscious in the previous game, just a day earlier! He was one of thirteen players released in May 1938.

Tom McCarthy had been with Dundee and on loan at Montrose before moving south to join Brighton & Hove Albion. A centre half, he was signed in May 1936 and made his debut against King's Park in a Scottish League match on 8th August 1936 but left the Club after just four outings. He went to London to find work.

Andrew McGillivray was a left half who signed for United from Leith Athletic and made his debut against Dumbarton in a Scottish League match on 12th September 1936. His time at Tannadice was short and within weeks of arriving he had been released.

Jimmy Milton was a goalkeeper with King's Park. He was transfer listed at £50 but appealed to the SFA and was granted a free transfer. Jimmy then joined United and made his debut in the opening Scottish League match of the new season on 8th August 1936 against his former club. After a fairly successful season with United as an ever present in the line up, he was surprisingly released at the end of the campaign and joined East Fife. In the following year, he helped his new club lift the Scottish Cup.

Jimmy Milton

Neil Paterson

J E Neil Paterson was a student at Edinburgh University and an amateur player with Leith Athletic. He was an inside left and made his debut for United on 8th August 1936 against King's Park in a Scottish League match. Neil came to Dundee to begin his career in journalism and remained with United for a season during which he proved his worth with a creditable haul of goals including a hat-trick in November against Forfar Athletic. As an amateur he was automatically released at the end of the season and did not re-sign although he did turn out for United once more in an emergency. Neil eventually moved to the USA where he achieved some notoriety as an author and screenwriter. He won the Atlantic Award for Literature in 1946 and later became a governor in the British Film Institute. His screenplay for the 1959 film *Room At The Top*, based on his own novel *Man On A Tightrope*, won him an Oscar.

Willie Reid

Willie Reid was a left half signed from Aberdeen and he made his debut in the first match of season 1936-37 against King's Park on 8th August 1936. After just a few weeks with United, Willie requested and was granted a free transfer. He later played for Forfar Athletic and then Hibernian.

James Wilkinson was a right back with Hibernian for eight seasons before he signed for United, making his debut on 8th August 1936 against King's Park in a Scottish League match. He was released in November 1936 when a change of management at United took place. James appealed to the SFA against his free transfer but they upheld the Club's decision.

Trialist, Guest, Junior, Newman, A N Other

The following players, listed as one of the above, are those known to have played during the season.

Barclay of St Johnstone YMCA at outside left on 6th March 1937 against Montrose in a Scottish League match.

Breen of Dundee Arnot at inside right on 1st January 1937 against Morton in the first of two Scottish League matches. He also played on 2nd October 1939 against Dundee in a friendly.

Pat Casciani of Osborne at right half on 19th December 1936 against Ayr United in a Scottish League match. He also played at outside left on 5th April 1937 against Raith Rovers in a Penman Cup tie.

Hill of Clepington at inside right on 10th April 1937 against St Bernard's in a Scottish League match.

McKenzie at left back on 5th April 1937 against Raith Rovers in a Penman Cup tie.

Napier of Brechin Victoria at inside right on 2nd January 1937 against Brechin City in a Scottish League match.

Smith of Forfar East End at left half on 23rd January 1937 against Stenhousemuir in a Scottish League match.

Soutar of Clepington at outside left on 24th October 1936 against Montrose in a Scottish League match.

Dougie Sword of Fairfield at right half on 26th December 1936 against Alloa Athletic in a Scottish League match.

Ronnie Sword of Fairfield at centre half on 9th January 1937 against King's Park in the first of two Scottish League matches.

1937–38 Player Profiles

Tommy Adamson signed for United from local junior side, Lochee Harp. He made his debut against Montrose on 28th August 1937 in a Scottish League match at inside left. Throughout the season he was a regular in the side, usually at inside left but sometimes at outside left or occasionally at left half. At the end of the season the Club released most of the playing staff including Tommy and he joined Forfar Athletic. After the outbreak of WW2, Tommy returned to United for season 1939-40 and was a regular on the left again. He was part of the side that went all the way to the final of the Emergency War Cup. Tommy scored for United in the final but his 'goal' was controversially disallowed and opponents Rangers went on to lift the trophy. After that he was on active service but turned out for United again at the end of season 1944-45.

Robert Black was a former Forfar Athletic inside right who signed for United just before the start of season 1937-38. He made his debut for United on 14th August 1937 against St Bernard's in a Scottish League match but after just two games he was released.

Tom Blair was a very experienced goalkeeper who had been with Kilmarnock, Manchester City and several clubs in Canada and the United States. He had also been with Ayr United and Linfield before he joined Dundee United as player/coach in May 1937. He was part of the George Greig plan to develop local junior talent for United and on the coaching side he was relatively successful. However, his playing career at United started and ended on his debut against St Bernard's in a Scottish League match. United were hammered 7-1 and Tom decided to hang up his boots immediately after.

John Boland had been with Forfar Athletic and Brechin City before signing for United at the beginning of season 1937-38. He made his debut against St Bernard's in a Scottish League match at inside left on 14th August 1937 but he was comfortable in most forward roles, most of which he played in over the season. John was a regular in the team but at the end of the campaign, he was one of thirteen players released.

Tom Clarkson was a centre forward who joined United from Kilmarnock, making a scoring debut on 14th August 1937 against St Bernard's in a Scottish League match. He was one of several players used to cover the troublesome centre forward role in season 1937-38. Tom was no worse than any other player in the role, and indeed had a fairly good scoring rate including a hat-trick against Dunfermline Athletic. At the end of the campaign he was released along with most of the squad.

Pat Docherty was a local school teacher who had played for Falkirk and Leith Athletic. He made his debut for United at inside right against King's Park in a Scottish League match on 2nd October 1937 but shortly afterwards he was hospitalised through illness. His recovery took over six months and he did not return to the side until the last few games of the season. Along with many other players, he was released in May 1938.

John 'Jock' Gilmour was a former Dundee left back who made his first appearance for United in a Scottish Cup tie against East Fife on 12th February 1938 following the sudden departure of Robert Grieve. Jock was a regular in the side until the end of the season and was then released.

Jock Gilmour

Robert Grieve

Robert Grieve had been with Arbroath and Blackburn Rovers before he signed for United. He made his debut as a trialist at left back against Albion Rovers on 18th September 1937 in a Scottish League match. Robert signed soon after that match and kept his place for most of the next four months but was suddenly released in early February 1938.

Dennis McGurk was a former YMCA Anchorage and Dundee Violet player who had suffered a career threatening injury as a young player. He recovered and returned to football with Portadown in Ireland. From there he signed for United and made his debut as an inside right on 30th October 1937 against East Fife in a Scottish League match. He was just a few weeks at the Club before he was released.

George Nicolson was a goalkeeper signed from junior side Kirrie Thistle, making his debut as a trialist on 25th September 1937 against Alloa Athletic in a Scottish League match. He was quickly signed after the match as a replacement for the suspended Dave Watson. George retained the keeper's jersey for the rest of the season but along with a dozen others, he was released at the end of the campaign. The player signed again for the club just after season 1938-39 was under way but he was taken on then purely as a reserve and made just one further appearance.

George Nicolson

David Ramsay was a teacher at Colliston and had played with Clydebank, Bo'ness, Forfar Athletic and Brechin City before joining United just before the beginning of season 1937-38. He made his debut on 14th August 1937 at left back against St Bernard's in a Scottish League match but after just one more appearance, three weeks later, he was released.

Albert Robertson signed for United from local junior side East Craigie in July 1937. Unfortunately, the player had also signed for Stobswell on the same day and as a result he was suspended by the SFA for a month from the start of the season which delayed his debut. He was an inside forward and eventually made his first appearance on 18th September 1937 against Albion Rovers in a Scottish League match. His time at Tannadice was relatively successful and he found the net frequently, including a hat-trick against Airdrieonians in November 1937. At the end of the season he was one of thirteen players released.

Willie Rumbles was a free agent when he offered his services to United in October 1937. Initially the Club were not interested and the player then signed for Brechin City. Then, after just three months there, he was released and came to United, making a scoring debut against Forfar Athletic on 15th January 1938 in

Willie Rumbles

a Scottish League match. At the time United had a problem finding a scoring centre forward and Willie seemed to have been the solution scoring seven times in seven outings. However, without warning, he left the Club at the end of February 1938 and signed on for a two year voyage to the southern hemisphere as a ship's carpenter.

Willie Wann was a centre forward but could fill most attacking positions. He made his first appearance for United as a trialist on 3rd January 1938 against Leith Athletic in a Scottish League match after spending time with Brechin City and Forfar Athletic. He then returned to junior football with St Johnstone YMCA and later played with United Juniors. Willie was one of several players who turned out for Dundee United from the junior side but unlike most, he was eventually signed. During 1942 he played several times and found the net regularly including a hat-trick against a Midlands Junior Select in December 1942. He was signed in April 1943. Willie was in the side on a regular basis until October 1944 when he was on loan at Raith Rovers, returning to United for the last few games of season 1944-45. Although he was retained for the following season he never took part and was probably reinstated to the junior ranks.

Dave Watson was signed from Ayr United and replaced the retired Tom Blair in goal for a short period. He made his debut on 21st August 1937 against Raith Rovers in a Scottish League match. Following a match against Albion Rovers that United lost 4-1, Dave along with his brother Willie, was suspended by the Club for allegedly 'not trying'. They both appealed the decision to the SFA and the Club were instructed to give Dave a free transfer.

Trialist, Guest, Junior, Newman, A N Other

The following players, listed as one of the above, are those known to have played during the season.

Gold of Stobswell at outside right on 29th April 1938 against East Fife in a Scottish League match.

Hughes of Stobswell at inside left on 29th April 1938 against East Fife in a Scottish League match.

Lannan, a Perth junior at outside left on 21st August 1937 against Raith Rovers in a Scottish League match.

Linton, a Brechin junior at left back on 11th September 1937 against Edinburgh City in a Scottish League match.

Nicholl of Kirrie Thistle at centre forward on 12th March 1938 against Brechin City in a Scottish League match, scoring once.

Davie Reid of YMCA Anchorage at inside left on 12th March 1938 against Brechin City in a Scottish League match, scoring a goal.

Jimmy Reid of YMCA Anchorage at inside right on 5th March 1938 against Brechin City in a Scottish League match.

Robertson of YMCA Anchorage at right half on 19th March 1938 against Stenhousemuir in the first of two Scottish League matches.

Tom Sturrock of Dundee North End at right half on 13th November 1937 against Stenhousemuir in a Scottish League match.

J Thomson of YMCA Anchorage at right half on 26th March 1938 against Leith Athletic in a Scottish League match.

Alec Watson of Brechin City at inside right on 27th April 1938 against Dundee in a Forfarshire Cup tie.

1938–39 Player Profiles

Robert Beattie had been with Ayr United and Motherwell and was signed for United after a good performance in a public trial match. He made his debut on 13th August 1938 against Montrose in a Scottish League match, one of nine players making debuts that day. Something of a utility player, he was used at both right half and left half and occasionally, inside left and it was whilst in that position he scored a hat-trick against Morton in April 1939. Despite an apparently good season with United, he was released in May 1939.

William Benzie was an inside right, signed from Morton after he showed up well in a public trial match. He made his debut for United in a Scottish League match on 13th August 1938 against Montrose, retaining the position throughout most of the season. He found the net frequently but when the campaign was over, along with most of the squad, he was released.

Robert Beattie

William Benzie

Joe Black

John 'Joe' Black (brother of Willie Black) was an outside right with Forfar East End. He made his debut for United as a trialist against Morton on 22nd October 1938 in a Scottish League match. Joe shared the outside left position with Bob Howe over the rest of the season and was one of many players released at the end of the campaign.

Willie Black

Willie Black (brother of Joe Black) was a postal van driver in Forfar but he played with Morton. United tried several times to persuade the player to come to Tannadice before he finally signed. A centre forward, he made a scoring debut against Alloa Athletic in a Scottish League match on 3rd September 1938. He was a regular starter in the side and a frequent goal scorer, netting a hat-trick against St Bernard's in October and scoring five goals in one match against East Stirlingshire in March 1939. His undoubted skill in front of goal meant he was one of just a few players retained for the following season. Willie featured less frequently in the side during 1939-40 and as the Club did not participate in senior football the next season, he was released.

James Christie joined United from junior side Perth Craigie. He made his debut at centre half as a trialist against Alloa Athletic in a Scottish League match on 3rd September 1938. James was in the line up throughout most of season 1938-39 but was released when the campaign was over.

Bob Howe was signed after playing well in a public trial match. He was a former St Johnstone outside left and made a scoring debut for United against Montrose on 13th August 1938 in a Scottish League match. Bob made his main contribution to the Club in the first half of season 1938-39 and was released in April 1939 along with most of the players from that campaign.

Bob Howe

Johnny Hutton was an inside right with local side Broughty Ex-Service Club. He made his debut for United as a trialist in a Scottish League match, scoring twice against Leith Athletic on 11th March 1939. He was re-signed for season 1939-40 and in the early part of the season he was often in the side. Johnny was called up for active service in December 1939 and remained a registered player, but was only able to turn out once during the war. After he was demobbed in 1945, he returned to United but in February 1946 he was transferred to Millwall at his own request as he wished to settle in London.

James Malloy was a former Cowdenbeath centre forward who signed for United after playing well in the annual public trial. One of nine players making debuts on 13th August 1938 against Montrose in the Scottish League, he scored in the match. Over the season James was in and out of the team and never became an established first choice and failed to find the net again. He was released at the end of season 1938-39.

Pat McCamon was signed from St Mirren and was one of nine players making a United debut on 13th August 1938 in a Scottish League match against Montrose. An inside right, he had signed after playing in the annual public trial match but he never established himself in the side and was released in December 1938 after just a few outings.

Andrew Meikleham was considered a utility player when he signed from Raith Rovers after a successful appearance in a public trial match in August 1938. He made his debut for United at left half against Montrose in a Scottish League match on 13th August 1938 and went on to fill that role in every game in season 1938-39 apart from one outing at inside left and one match he missed. He was one of a handful of players re-signed for the next campaign. Just a few weeks into the campaign, WW2 broke out and although Andrew turned out for United briefly, it appears he left the Club to join the armed forces around October 1939.

Jimmy Robertson

Jimmy Robertson was a half back signed from Wellesley Juniors and he made his first appearance for United as a trialist against Hibernian in a friendly on 10th April 1939. He then signed and made his debut in major competition in a Scottish League match against Stenhousemuir on 29th April 1939. Jimmy re-signed for season 1939-40 and following the outbreak of WW2 turned out regularly for the Club, filling several different positions. He was in the line up against Rangers in the Emergency War Cup final in 1940. Jimmy appears to have signed up for military service but remained on United's retained list and turned out on a few occasion during the war. In season 1945-46 he was still with the Club but was released at the end of that season.

George S Ross signed for United from local junior side Forthill Athletic. He was a centre forward and made his debut for the Club as a trialist against Cowdenbeath in a Scottish League match on 31st December 1938. After one more trial match he was signed and in his first few games he was very impressive. After just three months with United and still just eighteen years old he was sold to Hibernian for a fee which was undisclosed but left the Club financially secure for the remainder of the season.

Rab Smith

Rab Smith was a goalkeeper signed from Ayr United after a public trial match in August 1938. He made his debut on 13th August 1938 against Montrose in a Scottish League match, becoming a regular in the side. Rab went on to retain the keeper's jersey for all but four games that season. He was one of the few players re-signed for the next season but shortly after the outbreak of WW2, he moved to the west coast to work and was signed by Celtic.

George D Sutherland was a full back who had been with Falkirk and Alloa Athletic. He made his debut for United on 13th August 1938 against Montrose in a Scottish League match at right back and went on to play in the same position for most of that campaign. He lost his place in the side in March 1939 and at the end of the season, he was placed on the transfer list. With the outbreak of WW2 all players' contracts were cancelled in September and he became a free agent.

Bob Temple was one of nine players who made their debuts for United on 13th August 1938 in a Scottish League match against Montrose. He was a former King's Park player who had moved to Aberdeen at the start of season 1935-36. From Aberdeen, he joined United. He was made Club captain and playing at left back he scored on his debut and became a big favourite with the fans. Bob was an ever present in his first season and was readily re-signed for the next, but with the outbreak of WW2, he was soon in the army. As a territorial, he was one of the first to be called up for active service. He remained on United's retained list throughout the war and was released in May 1945.

Bob Temple

Raymond Wallace was signed on a one month deal from Consett Celtic in County Durham on the recommendation of a friend of Director, Sam Irving who was temporarily in charge of team matters at the time. An outside right, he made his debut on 14th January 1938 against Dunfermline Athletic in a Scottish League match but after just one more outing he was released.

Horace Woolley had been with Partick Thistle before moving south to join Blackburn Rovers. Released by the English club, he was in great demand in September 1938, receiving offers from Queen of the South, Raith Rovers,

Dunfermline Athletic, St Mirren and Morton before he joined United on a short term deal. He made a scoring debut at centre forward, netting twice against Dundee on 17th September 1938 in a Scottish League match. His initial promise quickly evaporated and he was released after just two more games. He then joined Morton.

Horace Woolley

Trialist, Guest, Junior, Newman, A N Other

The following players, listed as one of the above, are those known to have played during the season.

Clark of Greyfriars at outside left on 11th February 1939 against Edinburgh City in a Scottish League match.

Davidson of Lochee Central at inside left on 1st April 1939 against King's Park in a Scottish League match.

Bert Dunbar of Dundee Arnot in goal on 1st October 1938 against King's Park in the first of two Scottish League matches. He also played on 3rd October 1942 against Raith Rovers in a North Eastern League match.

Ferguson of Perth Celtic at outside right on 3rd September 1938 against Alloa Athletic in the first of two Scottish League matches, scoring a goal in his second outing.

Lawson of St Andrews at outside left on 8th April 1939 against Morton in the first of three Scottish League matches.

Vernon Mullaney (ex-Dundee Osborne and Leicester City) at inside right on 11th February 1939 against Edinburgh City in a Scottish League match.

Robertson of Forthill Athletic at right back on 8th April 1939 against Morton in a Scottish League match.

Vic Scott of Downfield at right back on 25th March 1939 against East Stirlingshire in a Scottish League match.

George Smith of Dundee Arnot at centre half on 24th December 1938 against Brechin City in a Scottish League match. He also later played in two friendlies.

Webster of East Craigie at outside right on 10th April 1939 against Hibernian in a friendly.

Wilson of Dundee Arnot at inside left on 27th August 1938 against Airdrieonians in a Scottish League match.

1939–40 Player Profiles

Arthur Baxter

Arthur Baxter was a forward with Barnsley and had been with Dundee North End, Portsmouth, Falkirk and Dundee. At the outbreak of WW2 he was based locally and United obtained permission from his club to play him. He made a scoring debut against Stenhousemuir in an Eastern Regional League match on 21st October 1939. Arthur was a regular in the side throughout 1939-40, playing at right half for most of the season. He was an important part of the side that went all the way to the Emergency War Cup final against Rangers. For the following season there was no senior football in the area and Arthur played at junior level. He was later on active service and was reported as killed in action in September 1944.

Norman Brand had played with Queen of the South, Nottingham Forest, Larne, Ballymena and Glenavon before the outbreak of WW2. A versatile player, he made his debut for United at left half on 10th February 1940 against St Johnstone in an Eastern Regional League match and then turned out for the Club in various positions over the rest of the war years until he was released in May 1945.

Peter Cabrelli was an inside forward who had played with Forfar Athletic, Falkirk, King's Park and Raith Rovers. He had also spent some time playing in Italy. He joined United from Raith Rovers at the end of season 1939-40, making his debut on 11th May 1940 against Hibernian in an Eastern Regional League match. After three more matches that season, he left. He was called up for national service in 1941 and during the war years he turned out for several English and Scottish clubs including two appearances

Peter Cabrelli

for United. He signed for United again and made his second debut against Airdrieonians in a Southern League B match on 29th September 1945. He was released at the end of the season and then joined Montrose.

Willie Coull was a left half who joined United from Brechin City. He made only two appearances including his debut on 16th December 1939 in an Eastern Regional League match against St Bernard's.

Tommy Dunsmore was a left back and began his career with Hibernian before moving south to join Luton Town. He joined United during WW2, making his debut on 30th March 1940 against Alloa Athletic in an Eastern Regional League match. He scored the crucial third goal from a penalty against Airdrieonians in the semi-final replay of the Emergency War Cup in 1940 and went on to play in the final against Rangers. When senior football was suspended in June 1940 he left United but returned for one more game in October 1945 against Arbroath in a Southern League B Division match and then went back to Luton Town.

Norman Fraser was a left winger with Brechin City, Raith Rovers and Montrose before he joined United. His first appearance came in a Scottish League match against Edinburgh City on 12th August 1939 but following the outbreak of WW2 the league was abandoned and the record of the match expunged. Norman remained with United throughout season 1939-40 and was in the side that faced Rangers in the Emergency War Cup final of 1940. The Club abandoned senior football in June 1940 but amongst others, Norman was kept on the retained list. He joined the armed forces, playing only once more for United but was not released until May 1946.

Norman Fraser

Alex Glen

Alex Glen was a former Forthill Athletic right winger who was with Raith Rovers at the outbreak of WW2. As he was based in the local area, United obtained permission from his club to play him and he made his debut in a friendly against Dundee on 2nd October 1939. He was in the right wing position for all but one of United's matches for the rest of the season, including all the matches in the Emergency War Cup. In the following season, United did not operate a side in senior football and Alex enlisted for military service.

Tom Gray was a centre half who had been with Ayr United, East Fife and Albion Rovers before he signed for United. He made his debut in a Scottish League match against Edinburgh City on 12th August 1939 but following the outbreak of WW2, the league was abandoned and the record of the match expunged. All player contracts were suspended with the outbreak of the war and at that point Tom left United.

John 'Jerry' Kerr was a former Armadale, Rangers, Alloa Athletic and St Bernard's left back. He joined United in season 1939-40 and made his debut against Edinburgh City in a Scottish League match on 12th August 1939 but following the outbreak of WW2 the league was abandoned and the record of the match expunged. The Eastern Regional League was then formed and Jerry remained with United throughout the season missing just a handful of games. He was in the side that turned out for the Emergency War Cup final against Rangers in 1940. The end of that season marked a temporary end to senior football and all the players went elsewhere. Jerry is of course, much better known for making his mark at United as Manager. He took the job in July 1959 and within a year he had led the Club from the depths of the Second Division to promotion into the top flight. He remained in charge for twelve years during which time he transformed United into an established First Division side competing at the top level and in Europe. He relinquished the post of Manager to Jim McLean in December 1971, taking the role of General Manager until 1973. Thirty years later the Club recognised the huge contribution Jerry had made throughout his time in charge when they renamed the south stand the Jerry Kerr Stand. During its construction in the early 1960's Jerry had in fact been the clerk of works for the project.

Jimmy Littlejohn was a centre half who had been with Cowdenbeath until the outbreak of WW2. United received permission to play him and he made his debut on 28th October 1939 against King's Park in an Eastern Regional League match. He went on to complete the season, missing just a few games and helped the side reach the final of the Emergency War Cup against Rangers. Senior football was then suspended for a season but Jimmy retained a close link with United and in July 1942 he was elected to the Board of Directors. He was also joint team Manager with Jimmy Allan until the latter stepped down three months later. He then took sole charge of team matters until Charlie McGillivray was appointed in November 1944 after a short spell working together. In February 1957, after fifteen years on the Board, Jimmy resigned for health reasons but he was re-appointed in February 1960 and remained on the Board until his death in 1989.

James McLean was an inside left from Hibs who made his debut for United on 2nd March 1940 against Partick Thistle in the first round of the Emergency War Cup. That was his only game for United in season 1939-40 and when senior football was suspended the following season he appears to have played for United Juniors. In season 1941-42 he turned out for United again but just occasionally.

Archie McPherson was with Rangers and Bathgate before he moved south to join Liverpool in 1929. He was then transferred to Sheffield United before he returned to Scotland with Falkirk and then East Fife. He had unsuccessfully applied for the post of Manager at United in 1939. He was signed for season 1939-40 and made his only appearance for United at inside left on 2nd September 1939 against Leith Athletic in a Scottish League match. However, the record of this game was expunged when the leagues were abandoned following the outbreak of WW2.

Archie McPherson

Alex Miller

Alex Miller was a full back who had started his senior career at East Fife before moving south to joined Bristol Rovers and then Bristol City. At the outbreak of WW2, United obtained permission to play him and he made his debut in an Eastern Regional League match against Stenhousemuir on 21st October 1939. He was an important member of the side throughout season 1939-40 and played his part in taking United to the Emergency War Cup final against Rangers. He was called up for military service in May 1940.

Peter Monaghan joined United from Bournemouth & Boscombe Athletic and made his debut on 18th November 1939 against Hearts in an Eastern Regional League match. After just one more game, he left United as he wanted to be closer to his home on the west coast. He then joined Kilmarnock.

Peter Monaghan

Jimmy Morgan was a former Dundee half back who made his debut for United in a friendly against a Perthshire Junior Select on 30th May 1940. He did not turn out again until December 1941 and was a regular for the rest of that season. Jimmy was re-signed for season 1942-43 and played at centre half until he dropped out of the side in February 1943. At the beginning of the next season he was in his usual place until he was called up and joined the navy towards the end of 1943.

Harry Pinkerton was a left half who had been with Hull City, Port Vale and Burnley before joining Falkirk. United received permission to play him and he made his debut against Stenhousemuir on 3rd April 1940 in an Eastern Regional League match. He made just three more appearances before the end of the season and then left United. Harry was a reserve in the travelling party for the Emergency War Cup final against Rangers but took no part in the game.

Jimmy Morgan   *Harry Pinkerton*   *John Ross*

Hugh Robertson was a right back from Forfar Athletic who was unfortunate enough to make his debut on 18th November 1939 in an Eastern Regional League match which United lost 9-2 to Hearts. After two more games he left the Club.

John Ross was a right winger with Gateshead and Gillingham before he signed for United. He made his first appearance and scored a goal in a Scottish League match against Edinburgh City on 12th August 1939, but following the outbreak of WW2 the league was abandoned and the record of the match expunged. John left the Club on a free transfer in November 1939 but returned two years later, playing often during 1941 and 1942 whilst serving in the armed forces. In season 1945-46 he signed for United again scoring a hat-trick in his first game back, against Airdrieonians in a Southern League match. After playing frequently in the first eleven in that campaign, he re-signed for 1946-47 but made just a few appearances over the season. He was released in April 1947.

John Simpson was an inside left signed from St Monance Swifts. His first appearance came in a Scottish League match against Edinburgh City on 12th August 1939 but following the outbreak of WW2 the league was abandoned and the record of the match expunged. Players' contracts were suspended when the war broke out and John left United then.

Jimmy Tennant was a left winger who was temporarily transferred from St Johnstone as cover for Norman Fraser. He made just one appearance for United on 8th April 1940 against King's Park in an Eastern Regional League match.

Charlie Thomson was an experienced goalkeeper who had been with Alloa Athletic and Falkirk before he went south to join Brighton & Hove Albion in 1934. He moved to Exeter City in 1939 and following the outbreak of WW2 he was based in the local area and joined United, making his debut on 2nd December 1939 against Dunfermline Athletic in an Eastern Regional League match. Charlie retained the keeper's jersey for the rest of the season and was in the side that went all the way to the Emergency War Cup final against Rangers. There was no senior football in Dundee during the following season and Charlie left United. He rejoined Exeter City after the war ended.

Willie White had been with Lochgelly United before moving south of the border. He played with eleven English sides and signed for United from Hull City. His first appearance came in a Scottish League match against Edinburgh City on 12th August 1939 but following the outbreak of WW2 the league was abandoned and the record of the match expunged. Willie stayed just briefly with United and appears to have joined the armed services early in the conflict.

Trialist, Guest, Junior, Newman, A N Other

The following players, listed as one of the above, are those known to have played during the season.

Bert Hood of Brechin City in goal on 2nd October 1939 against Dundee in a friendly. Bert was signed for United reserves in August 1949 and then played three times in Scottish League C Division (North East).

Mudie of Dundee Celtic at outside right on 11th May 1940 against Hibs in an Eastern Regional League match, scoring a goal.

1940-41

No players signed as Dundee United did not compete.

1941–42 Player Profiles

Robert 'Bert' Adamson was a left half who had played with Hearts, Dundee and Wrexham. He was with Carlisle United at the outbreak of WW2 and was then based locally, which allowed him to join United. Bert made his debut on 16th August 1941 against St Bernard's in a North Eastern League match and played regularly for United during 1941-42. However, just a few games into the following season he appears to have left the area.

Charlie Brownlee was a goalkeeper with Brechin City before he joined United, making his debut in a North Eastern League match against Raith Rovers on 13th September 1941. He was the Club's first choice keeper for the next three years, hardly missing a game until he was transferred to Arbroath at the end of season 1943-44. When United were in dire need of a reserve keeper in February 1952 Charlie returned to Tannadice to fill the vacancy but was released again three months later. However, he signed for United a third time, in October 1952, again answering an urgent call for a keeper at Tannadice. He was released again in May 1953.

Bert Adamson

Charlie Brownlee

Willie Clark was a full back with St Johnstone and he joined United briefly during WW2. He made his debut on 16th August 1941 against St Bernard's in a North Eastern League match but after just two months he left the Club.

Willie Cook

Willie Cook was a left winger who joined Dundee in 1925 from Forfar Athletic. In 1928 he was transferred to Bolton Wanderers and later played with Blackpool and Reading before returning to Dundee just before the outbreak of WW2. After his own club decided not to compete in senior football, permission was given for him to play for United and he made his debut on 8th November 1941 against Raith Rovers in a North Eastern League match. Willie played just a few games for United while he was stationed locally with the RAF.

Stan Duncan joined United from Queen's Park during WW2 and made his debut on 16th August 1941 against St Bernard's in a North Eastern League match. An inside forward he turned out frequently until his unit was moved south in January 1942.

F B Ellmer was an amateur half back who had been with Notts County. He made his debut for United against East Fife on 25th April 1942 in a North Eastern League match and played twice more before leaving the area.

Willie Fordyce was a left back with Arbroath who joined United during WW2. He made his debut against St Bernard's in a North Eastern League Supplementary Cup match on 15th November 1941 and went on to keep his place in the side for the rest of the season. In season 1942-43, he was again a regular feature in the United line up but he left to join East Fife in July 1943.

Willie Fordyce

Patsy Gallacher

Patsy Gallacher was an Irish international inside forward who joined Sunderland in 1929. After ten years there he moved to Stoke City just before WW2 began and was then stationed in the Dundee area which allowed him to turn out for United. He made his debut in a North Eastern League Supplementary Cup match against East Fife on 29th November 1941. After just three more games he left the area again.

Bob Glassey was an inside forward who had played with Liverpool, Stoke City and Mansfield Town prior to the outbreak of WW2. Before joining United he had been with Third Lanark. Bob made his United debut on 21st February 1942 against Dunfermline Athletic in a North Eastern League match. He was an inside forward with an eye for goal but unfortunately, like so many other players during this era, he was not with United for long, leaving to join Raith Rovers in the early months of 1943.

Bob Glassey

Ronald Gray was a right half who had been with Sheffield United before moving to Lincoln City. He signed for United during WW2 with permission from his club and made his debut on 4th April 1942 in a North Eastern League match against St Bernard's. After just three games it appears he left the area.

Eric Hampson was a right winger from Stoke City reserves. He was briefly stationed locally with the RAF and turned out for United twice, making his first appearance on 11th April 1942 against Raith Rovers in a North Eastern League match. Permission was received to field the player in season 1942-43 but it appears he then left the area.

Cornelius Holland was an inside right who had been with Folkestone and Grimsby Town before the outbreak of WW2. He joined United for season 1941-42 making his debut against East Fife in a North Eastern League match on 9th August 1941. Like so many of the war signings he was not in the area long and left the Club when his army unit moved back to England. He was released in February 1942 by which time he was somewhere in Wales.

Cornelius Holland

Albert Juliussen

Albert Juliussen was a reserve player with Huddersfield Town and during WW2 he was based in Perth as an instructor with the army. He joined United and made a scoring debut at centre forward on 13th August 1941 against a Scottish Command XI. The player turned out for United again three days later as a trialist against St Bernard's in a North Eastern League match. He scored twice in that match and found the net at least once in each of his next eight games, including a hat-trick against Leith Athletic. His scoring record in season 1941-42 was extraordinary and in one match, against St Bernard's he set the record for a United player with six goals in one game. 'Juli' had another hat-trick against Aberdeen and by the end of the campaign, he had netted 38 goals in 26 appearances. In the following season he appeared much less frequently but in 1943-44 he was back on the scoring trail with 25 goals in sixteen games, including hat-tricks against Hearts and Rangers and four goals in one game against Falkirk. He began the next season with Jeanfield Swifts but was soon back with United and he netted 17 times from 21 appearances with hat-tricks against East Fife and Raith Rovers. On 11th August 1945 United fans were stunned when the player signed for Dundee, with Huddersfield picking up a £2,000 fee in the process. He joined Portsmouth in March 1948 and later moved to Everton and spent two years on loan at Berwick Rangers. 'Juli' was re-signed by United and had a short stay with the Club in 1953 and then he moved to Brechin City.

Antonia Kellar

Antonia Kellar was a Polish amateur international goalkeeper who had taken part in the Olympics for his country. He joined United whilst he was stationed in the local area during WW2 and made his debut against East Fife in a North Eastern League match on 9th August 1941. He was injured a few weeks later and was replaced by Charlie Brownlee. Antonia then appears to have left the area again.

Jack Kirkham was an inside forward with Bournemouth & Boscombe Athletic and he had also played for Wolverhampton Wanderers and Queen's Park Rangers. In 1942 he was in the local area, training with his army unit and United were granted permission to play him. He made his debut in the last game of the season on 6th June 1942 against Aberdeen in a North Eastern League match. Jack was permitted to play for United in the next season but was only available occasionally until he left the area in October 1942. In January 1943 he was reported missing in action but was soon confirmed as a prisoner of war. In February 1944, he escaped from a POW camp in Italy and reached Switzerland.

Alec Low was a Scottish international who had been with Raith Rovers. He was a half back and made his debut for United in a Mitchell Trophy match against Rangers on 2nd May 1942. At the end of the season, a few weeks later, he left United.

David S Low was a player with local club Matrix. He was a right winger and made a scoring debut for United on 28th March 1942 against Raith Rovers in a North Eastern League match and turned out regularly until the end of the season. He was re-signed for the next campaign but after just a few games he left United.

Charlie McGillivray was a former Ayr United, Celtic, Manchester United, Motherwell and Dundee inside forward. During WW2 he was with Hibs but was given permission to play for United and made his debut on 9th May 1942 against Rangers in a Mitchell Trophy tie. He did not turn out again until October 1943, playing a few more times before formally joining United in January 1944. In the following season, he became team captain and was a regular in the side, also assisting Manager Jimmy Littlejohn with team matters. Charlie took over the Manager's job officially in November 1944 at which time he stopped playing. However, in September 1945, with the team on a poor run of results he put himself back in the side, scoring three times in two games. In July 1945, Arthur Cram stepped down as Secretary at United and the Directors offered Charlie the post of Manager/Secretary but he declined. The position was then advertised and Charlie was given a free transfer but he stayed on as Manager until Willie MacFadyen was appointed at the end of October 1945.

Jimmy Melville was a former Rangers and Third Lanark half back who joined United during WW2, making his debut against his old club, Rangers on 2nd May 1942 in a Mitchell Trophy tie. He turned out for the Club until the end of the season and was re-signed for 1942-43 but was fielded only occasionally and he appears to have left United in January 1943.

Jimmy Melville

Laurie Nevins

Laurie Nevins signed for Newcastle United in September 1940 but was based locally with the Royal Navy during WW2 and joined Dundee United with permission from his club. He made a scoring debut on 18th April 1942 against Rangers in a famous 8-1 win for United in the North Eastern League. Laurie was a left winger with a good goal scoring record including a hat-trick against

Leith Athletic in May 1942. The player was able to turn out for the Club regularly over the next two seasons and was again with United at the beginning of 1944-45. In November 1944 he appears to have left the area again and after the war ended he went back to Newcastle and later played with Hartlepool United and Brighton & Hove Albion.

Lomond Reid was a right half with Brechin Victoria and signed for United during WW2. He made his debut against Dunfermline Athletic in a North Eastern League match on 20th September 1941. Lomond was with United for just a few months and left the area in January 1942. He was still on United's list of retained players until he was released in April 1946.

Robert Rooney was a centre forward with Falkirk and had also been with Clyde and Dunfermline Athletic. He joined United for one game only and scored against Rangers in a second leg tie in the Mitchell Trophy on 9th May 1942.

Fred Sargent

Fred Sargent was a left winger with Spurs at the outbreak of WW2. He was transferred to United temporarily, whilst he was based locally, and he made a scoring debut on 21st February 1942 against Dunfermline Athletic in a North Eastern League match. It was thought that Fred would be in the area for a while but his unit was moved south after he had played just once for United but he returned in November and played once more.

Eric Sibley was a right back who joined United from Blackpool during WW2. He had started his career at Spurs in 1934 and had also spent some time with Bournemouth & Boscombe Athletic. Eric made his United debut against East Fife on 9th August 1941 in a North Eastern League match and played for the Club frequently over the next two seasons as he was in the RAF and stationed near Dundee. He left the area in January 1943 and at the end of the war, he returned to Blackpool and later played for Grimsby Town and Chester City.

Ian Smart was a left winger who had been with United Juniors and then Monifieth Tayside before he signed for United at the beginning of season 1941-42. He made his debut on 9th August 1941 against East Fife in a North Eastern League match and went on to become a regular that season operating on either flank or at centre. In the following season Ian remained on United's retained list

Ian Smart

but moved to local junior side Violet and turned out for United just once more before WW2 ended. In August 1946, he was back with the Club again and remained a United player, latterly as a full back, until he was released in May 1952. Something of an unsung hero during his time at United, Ian played 144 times in major competition and also turned out more than 50 times for Dundee United 'A' in Scottish League C Division matches. Whilst with the Club, Ian continued in his career as an art teacher.

Dave Smith was a defender with Leeds United although he was more than likely in the reserves there. He joined Dundee United during WW2 whilst stationed in the vicinity, initially as a guest but he was released by his own club and signed for the Tannadice side in January 1942. He made his debut in a North Eastern League match against Leith Athletic on 6th September 1941 and was an infrequent starter for United over the remaining war years until he was released in May 1945.

Bob Smith was a Stoke City reserve half back who joined United during WW2, making his debut on 21st February 1942 against Dunfermline Athletic in a North Eastern League match. He was in the area for only a short time and after three matches he left United.

Sid Smith was a left winger with Norwich City. He joined United on a temporary transfer and made his debut against East Fife on 27th September 1941. He was released by Norwich City in December 1941 and then became a signed United player, although he was with the Club for a very short time. He was also an accomplished amateur boxer and won the Midlands and District Lightweight Amateur title in Brechin on 24th January 1942. A month later he left the area, although United retained his registration until he was released in April 1946.

Joe Vannet was a right half who played for United after permission was received from his club, Arbroath, at the beginning of season 1941-42. He made his debut against East Fife on 9th August 1941 in a North Eastern League match. Like so many other players during WW2, he was with United only temporarily and left in November 1941.

George Watson was an inside left with Queen's Park who spent some time with United during WW2. He made his debut on 1st November 1941 against Aberdeen in a North Eastern League match. George played in a few more games that season but then appears to have left the Club. He remained on the United retained list, turning out again in October 1944 in a Forfarshire Cup tie.

James Witherspoon

James Witherspoon was an amateur right winger signed by United during WW2. He made his debut against East Fife in a North Eastern League match on 9th August 1941 but a few weeks later he appears to have left the area.

Trialist, Guest, Junior, Newman, A N Other

The following players, listed as one of the above, are those known to have played during the season.

Donaldson of Scone Thistle at right half on 28th March 1942 against Raith Rovers in a North Eastern League match.

Tommy Findlay of Aberdeen Parkvale at right back on 1st November 1941 against Aberdeen in a North Eastern League match.

William Forbes of United Juniors at centre half on 13th August 1941 against a Scottish Command XI in the first of two friendlies. He also played on 27th March 1943 against Raith Rovers in a North Eastern League match.

Joseph Hadley of United Juniors at left back on 13th August 1941 against a Scottish Command XI in a friendly.

Haig, a Black Watch soldier at left back on 1st November 1941 against Aberdeen in the first of two North Eastern League matches.

Andrew Hanlin of United Juniors at left back on 9th August 1941 against East Fife in the first of three North Eastern League matches.

D Lewis at left back on 1st November 1941 against Aberdeen in a North Eastern League match.

Lorimer of Elmwood at inside left on 10th January 1942 against Aberdeen in a North Eastern League match.

McQueen of East Craigie at centre forward on 30th May 1942 against Leith Athletic in a North Eastern League match.

Moore at inside left on 27th September 1941 against East Fife in a North Eastern League match.

Rhodes at left wing on 1st November 1941 against Aberdeen in a North Eastern League match.

Stevenson at right wing on 18th October 1941 against Rangers in a North Eastern League match.

Wilde, a Black Watch soldier at inside left on 20th September 1941 against Dunfermline Athletic in a North Eastern League match.

1942–43 Player Profiles

Jeffrey Barker was a half back with Aston Villa. United secured permission to play him and he made his debut on 29th August 1942 against Dunfermline Athletic in a North Eastern League match. It was his only appearance for United as he left the area the following day.

John Brannan was a half back on the books of Manchester United. He joined Dundee United briefly during WW2, making his debut on 20th February 1943 against Hearts in a North Eastern League match. John played only three times before leaving the area again.

Alf Burnett

Alf Burnett was a centre forward from United Juniors who made his first Dundee United appearance as a trialist on 29th August 1942 against Dunfermline Athletic in a North Eastern League match. Soon afterwards he went on military service. Alf played for United again in March 1943 by which time he was a signed player. After he was demobbed, he starred for Dundee United 'A' in Scottish League C Division, netting 15 goals in just 11 appearances. That earned him a first team place on 9th November 1946 against Alloa Athletic but that was his last outing with United. He then went on loan to Barrow and spent some time with Lancaster City before moving to Barrow permanently in July 1947. In 1949 he joined Lincoln City.

Bobby Chalmers was a junior footballer who had been with Petershill and Lochee Harp before he joined United. He was a left winger and made his debut as a trialist against Rangers on 8th August 1942 in a North Eastern League

Bobby Chalmers

match. After two more games he was signed by the Club and made several appearances in the side that season, before leaving the area with his unit. He remained on the list of retained players and made two appearances in season 1945-46 but was released at the end of that campaign.

Jimmy Easson was a local junior half back with Carnoustie Panmure. He had spent several years at Portsmouth and a short time at Fulham. Jimmy turned out for United twice during WW2 making a scoring debut in a friendly against an RAF XI on 14th November 1942.

Sandy Elder had previously been with United Juniors, Jeanfield Swifts and St Johnstone. He was a half back but made his first appearance for United on the right wing against a Midlands Junior Select on 19th December 1942. He played again under the alias of 'Scott' before finally signing with Dundee United in February 1943. Sandy featured frequently in the line up over the next eighteen months and then appears to have left the area. He was reported playing for Spurs in November 1944 and later joined Hartlepool United before moving north again to join Forfar Athletic.

Sandy Elder

Fyfe

George Fairbairn

George Fairbairn was a registered Fulham right half who made his debut for United against Raith Rovers on 15th August 1942 in a North Eastern League match. He was with United for just three months and then went on active service to North Africa where he was reported killed in action in February 1943.

Fyfe (first name unknown) was based locally with the RAF and was not attached to any other club when he joined United. He made his debut on 1st January 1943 at left half against Aberdeen in a North Eastern League match and featured in the line up often over the next three months but then dropped out of the side. In January 1944 he was back again for two more outings.

Joe Harvey, who had been with Wolverhampton Wanderers and Bournemouth & Boscombe Athletic joined United on a temporary transfer from Bradford City and made his debut in a Mitchell Trophy tie against Raith Rovers on 10th April 1943. After one more game he returned to his own club. He joined Newcastle United after the war and later became their manager.

Willie Jennett

Willie Jennett was a left half who joined United during WW2 from St Johnstone. He made his debut on 21st November 1942 against Rangers in a North Eastern League Supplementary Cup tie and made a few more appearances with the permission of his club before signing for United permanently in August 1944. He featured in the line up more often than not that season and was retained for 1945-46 although he never played and was transfer listed in June.

Joe Johnstone was a left winger from Motherwell who joined United briefly during WW2. He made his debut in a North Eastern League match against Raith Rovers on 3rd October 1942 but left the area a few weeks later.

Charlie Longdon was a Brighton & Hove Albion player. United obtained permission to play him and he made his debut in a North Eastern League Supplementary Cup tie against Rangers on 28th November 1942. He also played in a friendly two weeks later before he left the area again.

George (Piper) MacKay, so called because he could indeed play the bagpipes, was from local junior side Elmwood and made his debut for United on 16th January 1943 against Hearts in a North Eastern League match. He also played under the alias of 'Thomson' twice before eventually signing. He was a very talented left winger who could also play on the right if required and was a regular in the United line up during the latter years of WW2. 'Piper' was re-signed after the war ended and was a big favourite with the fans for the next two seasons. His skills did not go unnoticed by other clubs and he almost left United in

Piper MacKay

January 1947 to join Blackpool in exchange for George Eastham but that deal fell through. However, on Christmas Day 1947 it was announced that he was moving to First Division Dundee and the deal went through the following day after Jimmy Dickson agreed to move in the opposite direction, joining United.

Peter Martin was a Raith Rovers full back who made his debut for United playing under the alias of 'Stewart' on 6th February 1943 against Rangers in a North Eastern League match. He played under the same alias for a month before officially joining United in March 1943. Peter stayed until the end of season 1943-44 and was in the squad at the start of the next season but left after just one more appearance.

George May had been with West Bromwich Albion and Notts County but at the outbreak of WW2 he was playing with Dulwich Hamlet. Permission was received from his club and he made his debut for United against Rangers at inside left on 8th August 1942 in a North Eastern League match. His stay in the area was short and after three more games he left.

Bernard Nelson was a Sheffield Wednesday inside forward who had permission to play for United briefly during WW2. He made his debut in a friendly against a Midlands Junior Select on 19th December 1942 and remained with United for three months before leaving the area.

Kinnaird Ouchterlonie was an inside forward, formerly with Dundee. He made his first appearance for United as a trialist against Rangers in a North Eastern League match on 13th March 1943. More than five years later, he became a signed player and made his debut in major competition against St Johnstone on 11th September 1948 in a League Cup tie. He was the first choice inside right until the arrival of new players in December 1948 pushed him out of the side and into the reserves where he finished his United career. He was released in May 1949.

Kinnaird Ouchterlonie

Ernie Scholfield was a registered player with Sheffield Wednesday and he joined United on a temporary transfer during WW2. He made a scoring debut on 12th December 1942 against an ITC XI in a friendly but after just two more appearances, he left the area.

Albert Simmons was an inside right with local junior side Arnot. He made his United debut as a trialist on 6th March 1943 in a North Eastern League match against Hibs and then signed. After five appearances, he went on military service but was retained as a registered United player although he never played again other than in a friendly in September 1949 against Newburgh Juniors.

Ted Singleton was a centre forward with Southend United and possibly Leeds United. He joined Dundee United in the midst of WW2 whilst he was temporarily based locally and made a scoring debut against Raith Rovers on 15th August 1942 in a North Eastern League match. By mid October he had left the area and was soon on active service in North Africa.

Ted Singleton

Jock Stein

Jock Stein was a centre half with Albion Rovers. He made his only appearance for United on a temporary transfer for a Mitchell Trophy tie against Raith Rovers on 10th April 1943. Jock of course went on to achieve fame as manager of Celtic and later Scotland.

George Sutherland was a centre half signed from Partick Thistle. He made his debut against Raith Rovers in a Mitchell Trophy tie on 3rd April 1943 but made just one more appearance before leaving United.

Lyn Thomas was a centre forward with Swansea Town and during WW2, he appears to have turned out with United twice, making his debut in a North Eastern League match against Aberdeen on 24th October 1942.

Max Turnbull was an inside forward with Motherwell before he joined United during WW2. He made his debut in a North Eastern League match on 3rd October 1942 against Raith Rovers and remained with United for two months.

Urquhart (first name unknown) was based locally with the RAF but not attached to any other club. He joined United, making his debut on the right wing against Aberdeen on 1st January 1943 in a North Eastern League match. He featured in the side again on three occasions over the next few weeks but then appears to have left the area.

James Walters was a registered Bolton Wanderers player. He turned out twice for United in WW2 at centre forward making his first appearance on 12th September 1942 against Aberdeen in a North Eastern League match.

Willie Westwater was a former Dundee left back who made his first appearance for United as a trialist in a North Eastern League match against Hearts on 22nd August 1942. He signed for United more than ten years later and made his competitive debut on 8th August 1953 against Morton in a League Cup tie. He was not with United long and was released in January 1954 and then went to Canada.

Willie Westwater

Jimmy Woodburn

Jimmy Woodburn was a left half with Newcastle United. He was based locally during WW2 when United obtained permission to play him. His debut came on 5th September 1942 against East Fife in a North Eastern League match. Jimmy made just a few appearances before leaving the area. He returned in 1944 but he played with Dundee during his stay that time.

Trialist, Guest, Junior, Newman, A N Other

The following players, listed as one of the above, are those known to have played during the season.

Byrne of Blackpool at inside right on 16th January 1943 against Hearts in the first of two North Eastern League matches.

Carse of Dundee North End at left half on 19th December 1942 against a Midlands Junior League Select in a friendly.

Clark at left half on 20th March 1943 against Dunfermline Athletic in a North Eastern League match.

Dalgleish of Aberdeen Parkvale at inside left on 30th January 1943 against Hibernian in a North Eastern League match.

Dickson of Dundee North End at left back on 31st October 1942 against Hibernian in a North Eastern League match.

Glackin of Carnoustie Panmure at outside right on 19th September 1942 against Hibernian in a North Eastern League match.

Norman Ireland of Dundee North End at outside right on 24th October 1942 against Aberdeen in the first of two North Eastern League matches.

William Murray of Sheffield Wednesday at left back on 14th November 1942 against an RAF XI in a friendly.

O'Brien of Watford at right half on 14th November 1942 against an RAF XI in a friendly.

Robertson at right back on 13th March 1943 against Rangers in the first of two North Eastern League matches.

Sanderson of Preston North End at outside right on 14th November 1942 against an RAF XI in a friendly.

Spittal of Derby County at right back on 23rd January 1943 against Raith Rovers in a North Eastern League match.

Martin Walker of St Andrews United at centre half on 13th March 1943 against Rangers in a North Eastern League match.

1943-44 Player Profiles

Percy Bower joined United briefly from Middlesbrough, making a scoring debut against Hearts in a North Eastern League match on 14th August 1943. He left the area almost immediately after.

Jim Brown appears to have been a utility player who made his debut for United on 23rd October 1943 against Raith Rovers in a North Eastern League match. He then crops up in various positions over the next year but nothing else is known about his playing career.

Willie Browning

Willie Browning joined United from Queen's Park and made his debut at inside left against Rangers in a North Eastern League match on 21st August 1943. He was with United until November 1943 at which time he appears to have left the area.

Johnny Connor was a centre forward with Queen of the South. Whilst stationed in the vicinity during WW2 he was temporarily transferred to United, making his debut on 11th March 1944 against Dunfermline Athletic in a North Eastern League match. A few weeks later his time with United ended when he left the area.

Jack Court was an inside forward with Cardiff City and during WW2 he joined the Royal Marines. Whilst he was stationed locally, he joined United, making his debut in a North Eastern League match against Aberdeen on 6th November 1943. Jack made several appearances over the remainder of that season but for the following campaign, he joined Arbroath. He rejoined United for season 1948-49 and made his debut

Jack Court

in major competition against Dumbarton in a Scottish League match on 14th August 1948. However, a few weeks later he requested a transfer and soon left to join neighbours, Dundee. Later, he went south again and joined Swindon Town.

John Divers was a winger with Airdrieonians. He arrived at United on loan for both legs of the Summer Cup tie against Falkirk, making his debut on 3rd June 1944. After the second leg he returned to his own club.

Tommy Dougal was a registered player with Leicester City. A right winger, he made his debut for United on 28th August 1943 in a North Eastern League match against Raith Rovers but he played just twice more before leaving the area.

Bert Duffy was a former Celtic half back, playing with Hamilton Academical. He arrived at United on loan for the closing stages of season 1943-44, making his debut against Rangers on 27th May 1944 in a North Eastern League match. He also took part in United's two leg Summer Cup tie against Falkirk before returning to his own club.

Tommy Dougal

Ken Gibson signed from local junior side Elmwood. He made his debut at left half against East Fife in a North Eastern League match on 19th February 1944. After another outing before the end of the season, he was re-signed for 1944-45 making several appearances before leaving the Club in April 1945.

Hugh Hart was a centre half with Dunfermline Athletic. He joined United on a temporary transfer for a two leg North Eastern League Supplementary Cup tie against Hearts, making his debut on 27th November 1943.

Ian Hay was a centre forward signed from junior side Aberdeen Mugiemoss. He made his debut in the last game of season 1943-44 against Falkirk in the second leg of a Summer Cup tie on 10th June 1944. Ian could also play in either inside forward position and over season 1944-45 he featured regularly. He was signed for the next season but played just once before going to Brechin City on loan in September. He was released in May 1946.

Ian Hay

Ernie Hiles was a centre half and captain of Fulham. He joined United whilst he was stationed in the vicinity, making his debut on 1st January 1944 against Aberdeen in a North Eastern League match. Ernie was a regular in the side for the rest of the season but moved away soon after.

David Jack was signed from local junior side Arnot. A right back, he made his debut in the first leg of a Summer Cup tie against Falkirk on 3rd June 1944. David spent the next two seasons with United and featured regularly in the line up until he was released in April 1946.

Ernie Hiles   *David Jack*   *Willie Johnston*   *Boye Karlsen*

Willie Johnston was a left back with Queen's Park. He joined United whilst he was stationed in the vicinity and made his debut on 28th August 1943 against Raith Rovers in a North Eastern League match. During season 1943-44 he was in and out of the area and played for United when he could. After February 1944 he was no longer available.

Boye Karlsen was a Norwegian international inside forward who joined United whilst stationed in the area during WW2. He made his debut against Rangers on 25th September 1943 and became a big favourite with the fans. Boye turned out for United regularly over the next eighteen months until he was posted south in January 1945. He played again in March, and in June that year he was back at Tannadice to play in his final game before returning home to Norway. A few months later it was reported that he was back in the UK playing with Exeter City.

George (Bud) Maxwell was a full back with Kilmarnock who signed for United during WW2. He made his debut against Raith Rovers on 28th August 1943 in a North Eastern League match and then appeared regularly in the side until his army unit was posted out of the district in December. 'Bud' remained on United's list of players until he was released in April 1946.

George Maxwell

Charlie McDermott was a left back with Bradford City. He turned out in a pre-season trial match for 1943-44 and joined United immediately afterwards, making his debut on 14th August 1943 against Hearts in a North Eastern League match. Throughout the season he was available only occasionally and left United when the season was over.

Ronnie McWalter was a right back with local junior side Lochee Harp. He made his debut for United as a trialist on 11th September 1943 in a North Eastern League match against Aberdeen and then featured frequently in the side for the rest of the season. Ronnie was re-signed for 1944-45 and was in the side during the first half of the season but only featured once in the latter stages. In 1945-46 he was in the squad but played just once and at the end of the season he was released and joined Arbroath.

Charlie McDermott

Bobby Moodie

Bobby Moodie joined United from Cowdenbeath. He was an inside right and made his debut as a trialist on 16th October 1943 against Dunfermline Athletic in a North Eastern League match. Bobby became a regular in the side until he was posted out of the area in April 1944, at which point he joined Falkirk. He returned in November 1944 for a few more games with United but was released at the end of the season.

Johnny Osborne was a centre half with Leicester City. He joined United and made his debut on 1st January 1944 against Aberdeen in a North Eastern League match but left the area again just a few days later.

Robert Perret had been with Bournemouth & Boscombe Athletic, Huddersfield Town and Southampton. He joined United whilst he was stationed in the locality during WW2. He made his debut on 4th September 1943 against Dunfermline Athletic in a North Eastern league match but played just once more before his unit left the area..

Willie Savage was a right back with Queen of the South. Whilst stationed near Dundee he joined United on a temporary transfer, making his debut on 23rd October 1943 against Raith Rovers in a North Eastern League match. After just one more appearance, in a friendly against an RAF Select, he appears to have left the area.

Bill Shaw was a centre half with United Juniors. He signed for Dundee United at the end of season 1943-44, making his debut against Rangers on 27th May 1944 in a North Eastern League match. Bill made a significant contribution in the league campaign in the following season and was retained for 1945-46 but in September 1945, he was allowed to leave and joined Brechin City.

George Thomson was a half back signed on loan from Aberdeen in time to make his debut for United against Hearts in a North Eastern League match on 14th August 1943. He made a good start to the campaign but was recalled by Aberdeen in November, returning to play for United just once more, in May 1945.

| Willie Savage | George Thomson | Jock Wightman |

John 'Jock' Wightman was a very experienced half back who had played with York City, Huddersfield Town and Bradford Park Avenue before joining Blackburn Rovers. He came to United on a temporary transfer whilst stationed locally and made his debut on 25th September 1943 against Rangers in a North Eastern League match. Jock played as often as he could in season 1943-44 and was re-signed for the following season but after just one more game, he left the area.

John Wilson joined United from Chesterfield at the beginning of season 1943-44 and made his debut on 14th August 1943 against Hearts in a North Eastern League match. He turned out just three times at the start of the season and twice later in the campaign. By February 1944 he appears to have left the area.

Trialist, Guest, Junior, Newman, A N Other

The following players, listed as one of the above, are those known to have played during the season.

Allen at left back on 29th January 1944 against Aberdeen in a North Eastern League match.

Anderson at left half on 30th October 1943 against an RAF Select in a friendly.

Duncan of Lochee Harp at right back on 28th August 1943 against Raith Rovers in the first of three North Eastern League matches.

Fraser of YMCA Anchorage at right back on 26th February 1944 against Hearts in the first of two North Eastern League matches.

Eggo of Forfar Celtic at right back on 22nd January 1944 against Hearts in a North Eastern League match.

Gillies of St Johnstone YMCA at inside right on 30th October 1943 against an RAF Select in a friendly.

Grain at right back on 4th September 1943 against Dunfermline Athletic in a North Eastern League match.

Graham of Castle Green at centre forward on 28th August 1943 against Raith Rovers in a North Eastern League match.

Horne of Dundee Violet at right back on 12th February 1944 against Falkirk in a North Eastern League match.

Neil at left wing on 8th April 1944 against East Fife in a Mitchell Trophy tie.

T V Nicholls at left half on 22nd January 1944 against Hearts in the first of two North Eastern League matches.

H Temple at right back on 29th January 1944 against Aberdeen in a North Eastern League match.

Thomson at left wing on 3rd June 1944 against Falkirk in a Summer Cup tie.

Webb of United Juniors at left back on 30th October 1943 against an RAF Select in a friendly.

Gorrie Wilson of YMCA Anchorage at left back on 15th January 1944 against Rangers in a North Eastern League match.

1944–45 Player Profiles

Jimmy Adamson was a seventeen year old Harris Academy pupil who was a goalkeeper with local junior side Violet. He impressed in a pre-season trial and signed with United, making his debut against East Fife in a North Eastern League match on 12th August 1944. After playing in the opening nine matches of the season he was replaced by the more experienced Dave Clark. Jimmy made just one more appearance that season and although he was re-signed for 1945-46 he was farmed out on loan to Brechin City. Later called up for military service, Jimmy was eventually released in April 1947.

Frank Brennan was a centre half with Airdrieonians. He played for United in a Mitchell Trophy first leg tie against Falkirk on 19th May 1945 along with his team mate Tom McCulloch. They were on loan at United who were at the time, very short of players.

Jimmy Adamson

Jacky Butchart

Jacky Butchart was a right winger signed from local junior side YMCA Anchorage. He made his debut as a trialist on 28th April 1945 against Hearts in a North Eastern League match but after just one more game his United career was over.

Dave Clark

Dave Clark was a goalkeeper who had been with United Juniors. He made his Dundee United debut on 7th October 1944 against Raith Rovers in a North Eastern League match. Dave was the first choice keeper for three seasons, missing very few games but was released in April 1947. He then signed for East Fife.

Joe Deans was a goalkeeper with Dunfermline Athletic. He came to United on a short term loan deal, making his debut against Rangers in a North Eastern League match on 6th January 1945. After two more outings with United he returned to his own club.

Alex Hendry was signed from Raith Rovers but made just one appearance, at right half on 10th February 1945 against Aberdeen in a North Eastern League match. He was released in May 1945.

Hope (first name unknown but may have been Tommy) joined United from Benburb. He was a right winger who made his debut on 1st January 1945 in a North Eastern League match against Arbroath but made just a few more appearances over the remainder of that season.

John Kelly played for United in a Forfarshire Cup tie against Dundee on 9th May 1945. He was a Morton player and turned out for United that day as a last minute replacement on the right wing.

Pat Kelly was a South African goalkeeper playing for Aberdeen. He made his debut for United on 1st January 1945 against Arbroath in a North Eastern League match but after just one more game, he left the area with his army unit.

Gordon Kennedy was a full back with Blackpool. He joined United during the final year of WW2, making his debut on 25th November 1944 against Raith Rovers in a North Eastern League match. During the remainder of the season he made several appearances at left back, right back and on the right wing. He was re-signed for the following season and again made several appearances and also played for Brechin City before returning to Blackpool late in the season.

Tom McCulloch was a right winger with Airdrieonians. He played for United in a Mitchell Trophy first leg tie against Falkirk on 19th May 1945 along with his team mate Frank Brennan. They were on loan at United who were very short of players at the time.

George McGeachie joined United from St Johnstone and made his debut in a friendly against a Celtic XI on 23rd December 1944. He remained with United for the remainder of the season playing in his usual position of right half.

Jimmy McIntyre signed for United from Queen of the South. He was an inside left and made his debut on 10th February 1945 against Aberdeen in a North Eastern League match and remained with United until the end of the season.

Tom McCulloch	*George McGeachie*	*Jimmy McIntyre*	*Syd Nicholson*

John Mooney was a St Mirren player who turned out for United on 12th May 1945 in a North Eastern League match against East Fife. He filled the centre half position as United were short of players.

Syd Nicholson had been with Bournemouth & Boscombe Athletic and Barnsley before joining Aberdeen. He came to United on loan and made his debut against Dunfermline Athletic in a North Eastern League match on 17th February 1945. Syd played just a few times before returning to his own club.

Jimmy Revel was a goalkeeper with Brighton & Hove Albion. He played for United just once, in a North Eastern League match against Rangers on 16th December 1944.

Bobby Ross signed for United from Crosshill Hearts. He was a centre half, making his first appearance for United as a trialist against Rangers on 6th January 1945 and was signed immediately after the match. Bobby was a regular in the side for most of the remaining games that season and was re-signed for 1945-46. For the next seven

Bobby Ross

seasons, Bobby was one of the Club's most consistent performers, making his debut in major competition in the Scottish League on 10th August 1946 against Dunfermline Athletic. In August 1952 he requested a transfer to a London club as he wanted to start a business there. He was a taxi driver in Cowdenbeath at the time and felt that he could make a success of a similar venture in London. As a result he was transferred to Millwall but he did not settle in the area and was soon back north playing with Cowdenbeath.

Dick Scott joined United from Lochee Harp. He was an inside right but made his debut at centre forward on 1st January 1945 against Arbroath in a North Eastern League match. Dick featured regularly for the rest of the season and was re-signed for season 1945-46 but played just one more time before being released in April 1946.

Dick Scott   *Alec Shirley*

Alec Shirley was a centre forward signed for United from Arbroath. He made his debut in a Mitchell Trophy first round first leg tie against Falkirk on 19th May 1945. Alec was re-signed by United for the following season, making a number of appearances early in the campaign. In November 1945, shortly after he became married, he moved south to join Halifax Town.

Douglas Sneddon joined United from St Johnstone for just one game, at inside right against Raith Rovers on 24th February 1945 in a North Eastern League match when United were desperately short of players.

Ernie Stygal was an unattached player who came from London. He made his debut for United at right half against Dundee in a Forfarshire Cup tie on 2nd October 1944 and featured frequently in the side over the next three months. He never played for the Club again but remained a United player after he was transferred south with his army unit. He was eventually released in May 1946.

Svein (John) Sveinsson was a Norwegian international inside forward with Lyn Oslo. He made a scoring debut for United as a trialist against Raith Rovers in a North Eastern League match on 7th October 1944. He was with United for just a month before leaving the district. However his affection for United came in useful more than twenty years later, by which time he was an official at Lyn Oslo. He accompanied Finn Seemann as a guest of United at Easter Road in October 1965 just before Finn signed for the Club.

John Sveinsson

Robert Walls

Robert Walls joined United from Crosshill Hearts and made his first appearance at right back as a trialist against Arbroath on 1st January 1945. He was then signed and turned out for United frequently over the rest of the season. Robert was retained for the following season but never played again.

Trialist, Guest, Junior, Newman, A N Other

The following players, listed as one of the above, are those known to have played during the season.

Crowe of Stobswell at inside left on 18th November 1944 against Arbroath in the first of two North Eastern League matches.

Gardiner of Dundee Arnot at left half on 18th November 1944 against Arbroath in a North Eastern League match.

Kinder of Carnoustie Panmure at inside left on 17th February 1945 against Dunfermline Athletic in a North Eastern League match.

Norman Hay of Dundee Arnot at centre forward on 2nd December 1944 against Dunfermline Athletic in a North Eastern League match.

McCann of Dundee North End at right half on 16th December 1944 against Rangers in a North Eastern League match.

Bobby McGregor of Hall & Co. at left back on 7th April 1945 against Arbroath in a North Eastern League match.

The Statistics

The following chart lists the appearances and goals scored by Dundee United players signed from August 1909 – June 1945.

The total appearances in Scottish League, Scottish Cup, League Cup, European matches and in the Forfarshire Cup are self evident.

Matches grouped as 'Other Competitions' include all major national competitions other than the above.

Matches grouped under Misc Matches include all minor and local competitions, friendlies, testimonials, benefits, charity matches, tour games, abandoned and expunged matches.

Debut	Name	Scottish League		Scottish Cup		League Cup		Other Comp		Forfarshire Cup		Misc Matches	
		App	Gls	App	Gls	App	Gls	App	Gls	App	Gls	App	Gls
30-Apr-21	Adams G	12						8		1		3	
12-Aug-44	Adamson J											1	
16-Aug-41	Adamson R							37					
28-Aug-37	Adamson T	30	2	2	1			33	7	2		2	2
27-Dec-19	Aimer G							3		5	1	43	1
12-Feb-16	Aitken J									2		2	
30-Oct-20	Allison J											7	
07-Sep-35	Anderson D	27	6									5	2
07-Nov-31	Baillie James	5										14	
06-Jan-23	Baillie Joe			2						4			
25-Oct-30	Bain Jock	21	4	1	3								
13-Aug-27	Bain John	85	7	10						4		11	1
08-Aug-36	Bain P	10	3										
22-Sep-17	Balfour D											24	4
19-Aug-22	Balloch J			2								21	1
18-Apr-14	Bannerman G											3	1
15-Aug-21	Bannister T	36	4	3						3		24	1
29-Aug-42	Barker J							1		1		1	
09-Aug-30	Bateman J	4	1							3		7	
03-Nov-23	Bauld R	134	28	9	2			32	3			1	
21-Oct-39	Baxter A											1	
13-Aug-38	Beattie R	21	6	2						2	1	27	2
18-Aug-17	Bellamy J											3	1
09-Aug-30	Bennett C	50	19	6	4					1	1	3	
13-Aug-38	Benzie W	29	15	2						2		1	
08-Apr-22	Bibby J	3										2	
01-Feb-19	Bissett J											4	
15-Aug-12	Black H	5								2		2	1
22-Oct-38	Black J	13	2								1	1	
14-Aug-37	Black R	2											
03-Sep-38	Black W	29	23	2	1			9	1	3	1	6	7
15-Jan-16	Blackwood R									4		5	
14-Aug-37	Blair T	1											
14-Aug-37	Boland J	26	7							1			

Debut	Name	Scottish League		Scottish Cup		League Cup		Other Comp		Forfarshire Cup		Misc Matches	
		App	Gls	App	Gls	App	Gls	App	Gls	App	Gls	App	Gls
18-Aug-09	Boland T	73	1	2	1			27	1	8		60	1
14-Aug-43	Bower P							1	1				
09-Sep-22	Bowman											2	
23-Aug-19	Bradley J							2	1	4	3	24	7
18-Aug-09	Brady J							1		1		22	
12-Feb-21	Braidford L	35	6	1						2		17	3
10-Feb-40	Brand N							11	5			2	
20-Feb-43	Brannan J							3					
22-Aug-31	Brant H	57	20	7	3					2	1	7	2
19-May-45	Brennan F							1					
15-Mar-24	Bridgeford F	44		2						2		4	
16-Aug-20	Brown A							3				20	
21-Aug-20	Brown D											3	3
18-Aug-09	Brown H							2		1		42	9
09-Sep-16	Brown Jack											9	3
10-Aug-35	Brown Jacky	15	2							3		5	5
23-Oct-43	Brown Jim							11					
24-Aug-32	Brown John	63	19	3	2					2	1	7	3
30-Sep-11	Brown John	2						9	2	4		15	
27-Sep-13	Brown W	5						9	2			2	
21-Aug-43	Browning W	1						95					
13-Sep-41	Brownlee C			2								6	
12-May-23	Brownlie J	30		2						2		3	
20-Feb-15	Bruce C									2		20	
07-Jan-11	Bryson P	4						5	2			3	
28-Nov-31	Buchanan A	44	2	2				2		3		6	
29-Aug-42	Burnett A	1						1					
25-Aug-09	Burns James							4				6	5
04-Nov-11	Burns John	12										1	
28-Apr-45	Butchart J							2					
11-May-40	Cabrelli P							24	2			1	1
26-Mar-10	Cairns T											3	
02-Nov-12	Cameron D	19		1				2				4	
03-Apr-25	Cameron J S	70	19	8	1					4	1	5	2

Debut	Name	Scottish League		Scottish Cup		League Cup		Other Comp		Forfarshire Cup		Misc Matches	
		App	Gls	App	Gls	App	Gls	App	Gls	App	Gls	App	Gls
09-Jan-37	Cameron M	1											
02-Sep-33	Campbell C	29		1								1	
15-Aug-25	Campbell M	68	17	6	1					1		2	
13-Sep-24	Cant A	8	2							1		1	
23-Aug-19	Cargill D							2	1	4		22	4
04-Sep-26	Carroll E	21	11	4	2					1	1		
02-Oct-26	Carroll F	3											
25-Aug-09	Carroll J									1		13	1
04-Apr-14	Cavanagh W	20	2										
08-Aug-42	Chalmers R											5	2
15-Aug-14	Chaplin A	23						10	1	2		8	
16-Dec-22	Chester J			2	1			1				9	
29-Aug-14	Cheyne J	20	6							5	4	12	3
03-Sep-38	Christie J	27								2			
07-Oct-44	Clark D	21		1		6		58		5		1	
13-Jan-23	Clark J			2	1							4	1
16-Aug-41	Clark W							9					
14-Aug-37	Clarkson T	25	11	2						2	3		
23-Apr-35	Collington D	62	1	3						2		9	
07-Mar-25	Collins H	4	1									1	
20-Aug-10	Collins J	15	3					5	1	2	1	7	
20-Aug-10	Collins T	1										1	
22-Mar-19	Connolly											7	2
13-Aug-32	Connolly J	8	1										
30-Jan-15	Connolly W	2						3				1	
11-Mar-44	Connor J											1	1
08-Nov-41	Cook W							6					
12-Aug-33	Corbett D	84	6	9	2			1		5		1	
24-Jan-20	Cosgrove M	10	1									5	1
15-Aug-23	Cottingham T									1		2	
16-Dec-39	Coull W							2					
06-Nov-43	Court J	6	1			5	1	11	3				
19-Aug-11	Craig R	19	4					5		2		9	
15-Nov-13	Crawford A	7	1							1		4	

Debut	Name	Scottish League App	Gls	Scottish Cup App	Gls	League Cup App	Gls	Other Comp App	Gls	Forfarshire Cup App	Gls	Misc Matches App	Gls
16-Sep-11	Crumley J	19						6		2		38	
12-Apr-20	Crumley R											1	
02-Jan-29	Cunningham J	9								1		4	
16-Aug-13	Currie P	7						1	1			1	
08-Aug-31	Cuthill D	1											
18-Aug-09	Dailly T							1		4		12	4
24-Apr-15	Dainty H											29	
17-Aug-10	Darroch J											1	
07-Nov-36	Davidson F	18		1								2	
06-Jan-45	Deans J							3					
05-Feb-27	Dempster J	13		4						2		3	
01-Sep-28	Deuchar W	52		8	1					2		15	3
11-Dec-20	Dick T											17	
19-Aug-16	Dinnie C												
03-Jun-44	Divers J							2					
18-Aug-09	Docherty J	4						2		1		31	7
24-Aug-10	Docherty P											3	
02-Oct-37	Docherty Pat	4								1	1		
06-Jan-12	Donaldson W	1						1				1	
26-Mar-10	Donnachie C												
05-Sep-36	Donnelly J	3								1			
11-Aug-28	Dorward D	44	1	6						2		8	
13-Aug-27	Dorward J	36		4						1		3	
09-Oct-15	Dorward T							3		3		14	2
28-Aug-43	Dougal T							3					
09-Oct-09	Downie A							1				12	3
27-May-44	Duffy A							3					
18-Feb-22	Duncan D	11										1	
16-Aug-41	Duncan S							13	1				
14-Feb-14	Duncan W	4								2			
30-Nov-18	Dunn											6	
24-Dec-10	Dunn J	2											
25-Feb-11	Dunnian C	3	4					1		2	1	4	
30-Mar-40	Dunsmore T							10	2				

Debut	Name	Scottish League		Scottish Cup		League Cup		Other Comp		Forfarshire Cup		Misc Matches	
		App	Gls	App	Gls	App	Gls	App	Gls	App	Gls	App	Gls
15-Oct-10	Dwyer J	4										1	4
19-Dec-31	Dyet J	35	14	5	4					3	1	4	1
14-Nov-42	Easson J											1	
19-Dec-42	Elder A							1	2			2	
25-Apr-42	Ellmer F B							31					
15-Aug-12	Elrick J	6						3				2	
29-Apr-11	Evans I	1						2				1	
15-Aug-42	Fairbairn G											11	
21-Aug-15	Ferguson D							11	1			49	
19-Aug-16	Ferrier 'Ref'												3
28-Dec-29	Findlay A	9		2									
17-Oct-25	Finlay A	13	1	1								1	
07-Oct-11	Finlay W	5	1										
14-Feb-20	Fisher P											10	
25-Aug-17	Fitzpatrick J											37	
23-Feb-27	Fleming T	21		1						1			
25-Aug-34	Fleming W	30		4						2			
18-Aug-09	Flood T	8										8	1
21-Sep-12	Forbes G	67		2				15		5		47	1
15-Nov-41	Fordyce W							50				3	
12-Aug-33	Foy H	4											
12-Aug-39	Fraser N							30	8	1		5	2
04-Oct-09	Fraser S											14	4
01-Jan-43	Fyfe							10	1				
17-Aug-10	Fyfe G	27	1					5	1	2		13	
18-Aug-09	Gallacher C							1	1	1		9	
29-Nov-41	Gallacher P							4				1	1
21-Dec-12	Gallacher T	9	2										
11-Nov-11	Galloway W	6	1									2	1
10-Aug-29	Gardiner G	129	6	12	1					6		8	
16-Dec-33	Gardiner R	77	35	7	2			82	29	5	2	13	
10-Dec-32	Gavigan P	13		2						1		2	4
05-Apr-20	Gibb D							2		5		28	7
25-Aug-09	Gibb E	2										7	

Debut	Name	Scottish League		Scottish Cup		League Cup		Other Comp		Forfarshire Cup		Misc Matches	
		App	Gls	App	Gls	App	Gls	App	Gls	App	Gls	App	Gls
10-Apr-11	Gibson D	26	13					10	3	5	2	29	6
19-Feb-44	Gibson K							11		1		1	
29-Sep-23	Gilfeather E	58	3	2						2		4	1
21-Aug-15	Gillies D											3	
10-Nov-17	Gilligan S											2	2
15-Aug-23	Gilmour A	68	10	1						4		7	
12-Feb-38	Gilmour J	8		1						1		1	
19-Dec-25	Gilroy T	46		5						1		1	1
21-Feb-42	Glassey R							20	13			2	
02-Oct-39	Glen A							35	5	2	1	1	
09-Jan-32	Glover E	5		3				5	1	5		35	7
24-Dec-10	Govan J	50	2	2				5				3	
24-Aug-12	Gowans D	11		1						2	2	11	
31-Aug-10	Graham W	18						5		4		16	5
18-Dec-20	Gray F							3					
04-Apr-42	Gray R	25								1		4	
12-Aug-39	Gray T							1				10	
04-Apr-14	Grieve A	16		1									
18-Sep-37	Grieve R	22	18										
11-Jan-30	Haddow A			2				2		1	2	2	
11-Apr-42	Hampson E	9								1		2	
15-Aug-23	Hannah G	10								1		33	1
18-Aug-09	Hannan J	25						10					
11-Jan-30	Harley B			4	1			2					
27-Nov-43	Hart H							2					
11-Aug-34	Hart Jimmy	10	6							1	1	10	5
14-Aug-26	Hart John	117	24	14	4					3		3	
16-Aug-24	Harvey James	33	2	2				2	1	2		2	
10-Apr-43	Harvey Joe							17	3				
10-Jun-44	Hay I									1		3	
15-Oct-21	Headrick J	30	2	1	1								
06-Nov-26	Henderson Alex	7	1	1						1			
07-Apr-20	Henderson Andy	29		1				3		7		60	
11-Aug-28	Henderson G	69	23	8	2					3		8	2

Debut	Name	Scottish League		Scottish Cup		League Cup		Other Comp		Forfarshire Cup		Misc Matches	
		App	Gls	App	Gls	App	Gls	App	Gls	App	Gls	App	Gls
16-Aug-13	Henderson W	19	1	1				10		3		7	1
10-Feb-45	Hendry A							1					
25-Nov-33	Herbert J	4											
11-Dec-15	Herron J							5	1	9	2	57	9
01-Jan-44	Hiles E							14					
28-Sep-35	Hogg R	2											
15-Aug-21	Hogg W	9	2										
09-Aug-41	Holland C							7	5			1	
01-Jan-45	Hope							6	1			1	
13-Aug-32	Hotson W	3										1	1
09-Apr-19	Houston T	9		1								8	1
18-Apr-23	Howard F									2		1	1
13-Aug-38	Howe R	18	2	2									
15-Aug-25	Howieson J	10	5							1		1	
28-Mar-14	Hughes J	27						3		8		84	5
26-Aug-16	Husson R											12	1
26-Dec-36	Hutchison Dan	17	5							2			
13-Aug-27	Hutchison Dunc	197	116	18	6					10	4	19	16
02-Sep-22	Hutchison G											7	
11-Mar-39	Hutton J	1	2					12	4	1		4	2
17-Dec-10	Izatt J	40						9		4		16	
03-Jun-44	Jack D							51		3		1	
15-Aug-31	Jackson A	26	5							2		1	
21-Nov-42	Jennett W							28	2			1	1
28-Aug-43	Johnston W							16					
21-Sep-18	Johnston J											18	
08-Oct-27	Johnstone A	18		3								1	
03-Oct-42	Johnstone J							4					
13-Aug-41	Juliussen A					3	2	73	87	2	1	3	4
25-Sep-43	Karlsen B							38	7	1		2	
15-Aug-23	Kay J C (Jock)	177	3	14						5		11	
13-Aug-27	Kay J S (Jacky)	228	80	21	11					8	3	23	4
16-Aug-20	Kay W							3				10	4
09-Aug-41	Kellar A							5				1	

Debut	Name	Scottish League		Scottish Cup		League Cup		Other Comp		Forfarshire Cup		Misc Matches	
		App	Gls	App	Gls	App	Gls	App	Gls	App	Gls	App	Gls
09-May-45	Kelly J									1			
01-Jan-45	Kelly Pat							2				2	2
31-Dec-21	Kelly Peter	15		1								20	
19-Aug-16	Kennedy									2		1	
25-Nov-44	Kennedy G							26				2	
15-Apr-16	Kerr G									1		5	
12-Aug-39	Kerr J	47	21					28	7	2	1	5	2
11-Aug-34	King A	9		5	4							6	
01-Jan-21	Kinsella J												
06-Jun-42	Kirkham J	4						4					
12-Sep-14	Knowles J	13										1	
15-Aug-23	Knox R	40	15							2		1	
03-Dec-32	Laing D									2		5	
16-Aug-20	Lamb G	4						2	1			7	2
09-Nov-12	Lamb M							1				5	2
18-Sep-15	Lawrence V	7										6	4
11-Oct-13	Leckie F											19	1
08-Dec-17	Levett E											8	1
29-Mar-19	Lindsay A	39	1	3						3		10	1
26-Nov-32	Lindsay J	105	27	2						2		3	
11-Nov-11	Linn W							22	6	13	3	88	15
28-Oct-39	Littlejohn J							31					
08-Aug-31	Logie W	20	1	1									
04-Sep-09	Loney J	38	1					11		5	1	41	
28-Nov-42	Longdon C							1				1	
02-May-42	Low A							6					
28-Mar-42	Low D							13	6				
19-Aug-11	Low G	70	9					10		8		57	9
12-Aug-33	Low W	5											
28-Dec-12	MacDonald E	60	6	2				11		5	2	21	
05-Sep-25	MacDonald W	3											
29-Apr-36	MacFarlane J	39	1	1						1		3	1
06-Sep-30	MacKay E	1	2										
16-Jan-43	Mackay G	24	5	1		10		93	12	6		4	1

Debut	Name	Scottish League		Scottish Cup		League Cup		Other Comp		Forfarshire Cup		Misc Matches	
		App	Gls	App	Gls	App	Gls	App	Gls	App	Gls	App	Gls
12-Sep-23	Mackie J	11	5							1	1	1	1
15-Nov-24	Mackie W	16	7							1			
10-Feb-23	Mackintosh W									4		10	1
11-Aug-34	MacRitchie W	55		8						5		5	
13-Aug-38	Malloy J	12	1										
01-Oct-10	Marshall A	8	2									2	
16-Aug-13	Martin D	47	48	1				11	5	5	6	28	21
06-Feb-43	Martin P							13	2				
03-Jan-28	Mason G	2	1										
23-Sep-33	Masson W	74	1	5				12		4		9	
28-Aug-43	Maxwell G							12					
25-Feb-22	Maxwell P	5											
08-Aug-42	May G							4					
09-Dec-22	McAndrew W			2						3		12	
09-Sep-33	McBain L	15	3							1			
15-Aug-25	McBride H	20								1		1	
21-Oct-16	McCabe											58	13
25-Oct-30	McCallum D	24	8	2									
27-Dec-30	McCallum W	21		2	2							1	
13-Aug-38	McCamon P	3											
08-Aug-36	McCarthy T	4											
11-Aug-28	McClure D	44	1	6						1		7	
04-Mar-22	McCulloch A	9	1									1	
08-Sep-17	McCulloch Thomas											33	
19-May-45	McCulloch Thomas							1					
14-Aug-43	McDermott C							12					
18-Aug-09	McDermott T							1				8	
14-Jan-22	McDonagh W	5		1									
15-Aug-12	McDonald A	17		1				2				6	1
15-Aug-25	McDonald J	103	11	12						3		3	
26-Aug-22	McDonald R	2		2						2		28	
15-Aug-23	McEwan R	10								1		2	
23-Jan-26	McFarlane R	2		3									
23-Dec-44	McGeachie G							15				1	

Debut	Name	Scottish League		Scottish Cup		League Cup		Other Comp		Forfarshire Cup		Misc Matches	
		App	Gls	App	Gls	App	Gls	App	Gls	App	Gls	App	Gls
12-Sep-36	McGillivray A	2										3	5
09-May-42	McGillivray C							38	19	1		2	
15-Aug-12	McGinness J	7						5					
19-Dec-31	McGlynn G	12		6	1								
11-Mar-16	McGregor G	43		6						2		5	
01-Sep-28	McGregor H									2	1	3	
06-Mar-26	McGregor M	55	6	8	3					1		3	1
18-Sep-15	McGuire J									4	1	75	22
30-Oct-37	McGurk D	5	1										
08-Feb-28	McHugh J	52		3						2		9	
15-Aug-21	McInnes Dan	8										1	
18-Aug-31	McIntosh C	91		9						4		6	
29-Apr-36	McIntosh R	34		1						2		2	
10-Feb-45	McIntyre J							11	2	1			
01-Feb-19	McKee											4	2
11-Nov-16	McKenzie C											2	
23-Oct-15	McKerracher	9										6	
01-Oct-21	McKimmie J											1	1
01-Feb-19	McKirdy											5	
02-Mar-40	McLean J							5					
16-Aug-20	McMahon J							1				3	
12-Sep-25	McMillan P	3	1										
04-Oct-09	McNally Joe											1	
14-Aug-29	McNally John	10										2	
30-Nov-18	McNeil											19	
02-Sep-39	McPherson A											1	
16-Aug-13	McPhilips C	11						10				2	
16-Aug-24	McRoberts J	38		1						2		1	
11-Sep-43	McWalter R	9						29		1		1	
02-Mar-27	Meagher J	9	3	1				1		1	1		
13-Aug-38	Meikleham A	33	1	2						3	1	5	
02-May-42	Melville J							15					
10-Dec-27	Michie H	32	13	1	1					2		6	
03-Mar-17	Millar D			1	1			2	1			12	1

Debut	Name	Scottish League		Scottish Cup		League Cup		Other Comp		Forfarshire Cup		Misc Matches	
		App	Gls	App	Gls	App	Gls	App	Gls	App	Gls	App	Gls
21-Oct-39	Miller Alex	18	1					31					
04-Sep-26	Miller Andy	15	1	3						1		3	
20-Aug-10	Miller T							1					
27-Dec-19	Miller W									4		15	
12-Aug-33	Milliken A	4											
30-Apr-19	Milne											4	
28-Nov-34	Milne A	73	77	9	8			29	24	6	3	7	4
16-Aug-30	Milne Jimmy	74	7	8						2		2	
16-Nov-35	Milne John	15	7	1									
08-Aug-36	Milton J	34		1						2		2	
19-Aug-11	Mitchell A	16						4		2		7	
18-Nov-39	Monaghan P							2					
03-Sep-10	Monteith W	17						1				1	
16-Oct-43	Moodie R							27	10			2	2
12-May-45	Mooney J							1					
04-Sep-26	Moore John	1											
30-May-40	Morgan J							42	3			5	
19-Dec-31	Morris D	12		6									
07-Apr-20	Morrison J									2		30	1
10-Aug-35	Morrison R	33		4						3		5	
16-Oct-09	Mudie J	1						2		1	1	20	5
12-Apr-19	Mulholland J	23						5		10		69	4
16-Dec-33	Munro J	8	2	1									
20-Sep-19	Murray Frank							1		5	1	26	10
12-Aug-33	Murray Fred	5								1	1		
23-Sep-22	Murray J											13	3
02-Nov-35	Murray R	21	1	4						1		2	
13-Nov-15	Murray T									2		26	8
21-Aug-15	Neal A									4		28	1
19-Dec-42	Nelson B							9	4			1	
09-Aug-30	Nelson J	2										1	
18-Apr-42	Nevins L							50	23	1		5	4
17-Feb-45	Nicholson S							7	3				
23-Jan-26	Nicoll D	2		3									

337

Debut	Name	Scottish League		Scottish Cup		League Cup		Other Comp		Forfarshire Cup		Misc Matches	
		App	Gls	App	Gls	App	Gls	App	Gls	App	Gls	App	Gls
25-Sep-37	Nicolson George	29		2						2			
09-Oct-15	Nicolson George											2	
28-Oct-33	Nicolson H	4	1										
20-Aug-10	O'Gara J	23	5					5		1		10	
15-Aug-23	O'Kane J	44	14	3	3					3		3	2
23-Dec-22	O'Rourke M									4		13	1
09-Dec-22	O'Rourke P									4	2	16	2
20-Sep-24	Osborne Jacky	30		2								3	
01-Jan-44	Osborne Johnny							1					
29-Apr-22	Oswald W	50	17	3	2					2		5	
13-Mar-43	Ouchterlonie K	9	2			5	1	2		1		1	
03-Sep-32	Ouchterlonie W	51	40	2				1	2	1	1	7	5
26-Aug-16	Outerson V											16	1
02-Jan-13	Parker G	2											
17-Mar-28	Parker T	3	1										
08-Aug-36	Paterson J N	26	9	1	1					1	2	1	1
15-Aug-25	Paterson W	77		3						3		3	
09-Aug-30	Penson F	98		10						4		8	
04-Sep-43	Perret R							2					
03-Apr-40	Pinkerton H							4					
15-Aug-23	Porter J	39	3	1						2	1	5	
15-Aug-31	Radcliffe G	14	1	1									
11-Jan-22	Rae J	13	1	1						1		19	
13-Aug-27	Ralston A	7	4	1						1		3	
05-Mar-27	Ramage A			1									
14-Aug-37	Ramsay D	2											
18-Aug-09	Ramsay J							1				18	1
07-Sep-35	Reid D	32	5							3	1	5	2
20-Sep-41	Reid L							13				1	
21-Dec-18	Reid William											4	1
08-Aug-36	Reid Willie	6											
18-Aug-17	Rennie C											11	
16-Dec-44	Revel J							1					
15-Aug-23	Richards D	49	3	2	1					4		7	1

Debut	Name	Scottish League		Scottish Cup		League Cup		Other Comp		Forfarshire Cup		Misc Matches	
		App	Gls	App	Gls	App	Gls	App	Gls	App	Gls	App	Gls
20-Jan-12	Richardson A	4	1					3	1	1		1	
11-Aug-28	Richmond W	2										3	
17-Jan-25	Rintoul R	3	1	2									
21-Aug-15	Ritchie J											8	3
30-Apr-21	Ritchie J M	22	2									6	
21-Sep-18	Robb W											8	
18-Sep-37	Robertson A	21	9	2	1					2			
18-Nov-39	Robertson H	9						3					
30-Sep-11	Robertson James											1	
10-Apr-39	Robertson Jimmy	1						40		1		6	
20-Aug-10	Robertson John	22						5		2		17	
18-Aug-34	Robertson P	33		4						2		2	
09-May-42	Rooney R							1	1				
06-Feb-29	Ross G A	143	60	13	3			3	2	9	1	9	3
31-Dec-38	Ross G S	7	5	2	2								
10-Aug-29	Ross Jock	35		2						2		3	
15-Aug-12	Ross John	1										15	
12-Aug-39	Ross John	7	1					41	13	3		7	1
06-Jan-45	Ross R	146	1	13		26	1	34		15		14	1
30-Mar-35	Ross T	1	1									3	
15-Jan-38	Rumbles W	5	6	2	1								
12-Jan-24	Russell J	17	6	1						2	2	3	
19-Aug-16	Rutherford											2	
21-Feb-42	Sargent F							2	2				
23-Oct-43	Savage W							1				1	
12-Dec-42	Scholfield E							1				2	1
01-Jan-45	Scott R							17	10				
14-Oct-11	Scrimgeour D	28	8	1	1			5	4	1		10	5
02-Oct-22	Scullion J			2						4		21	2
26-Aug-25	Shandley J	1	1							1		1	
18-Sep-15	Sharp James									4		23	1
19-Aug-11	Sharp John	1											
27-May-44	Shaw W							30	1	2		1	
26-Feb-10	Sheridan J											5	2

Debut	Name	Scottish League		Scottish Cup		League Cup		Other Comp		Forfarshire Cup		Misc Matches	
		App	Gls	App	Gls	App	Gls	App	Gls	App	Gls	App	Gls
19-May-45	Shirley A							12	2				
09-Aug-41	Sibley E							36				2	
06-Mar-43	Simmons A							6				1	
15-Aug-25	Simpson Jimmy	53	7	7				18	1	2		2	
12-Aug-39	Simpson John	99	13	6	2					1		3	1
22-Dec-23	Simpson T									5		7	
12-Aug-33	Sinclair W	6								1			
15-Aug-42	Singleton E							5	3				
10-Aug-35	Skelligan D	120	16	9	1					8	1	7	1
09-Aug-41	Smart I	91	9	5		21	2	27	6	12		12	1
24-Jan-23	Smillie H			1						4	2	10	4
10-Sep-21	Smith B	2											
21-Feb-42	Smith Bob							3					
06-Sep-41	Smith Dave							22	2			3	
05-Oct-29	Smith E	8	2										
11-Aug-34	Smith J A	51	19	8	3					5	1	4	1
03-Dec-10	Smith J J	1	3										
16-Aug-24	Smith James	3											
23-Aug-19	Smith John							1				9	
13-Aug-38	Smith Rab	30		2				6		3		5	1
27-Sep-41	Smith S							6	1			1	
24-Feb-45	Sneddon D							1					
21-Aug-09	Snee J							1				5	1
04-Apr-14	Spence W	24								2		35	1
08-Dec-17	Stalker W							2		7		53	
16-Jan-15	Steel H	2										1	
10-Apr-43	Stein J							1					
09-Aug-30	Stewart T	15								1		1	
19-Aug-22	Stewart W			1	1					1		26	4
15-Aug-23	Stirling E	31								1		3	
30-Aug-19	Stirling J							5		11		65	3
19-Aug-22	Stoddart G											7	2
16-Aug-13	Stoessel F	22	6	1				11	3	3	3	15	
18-Aug-09	Strachan J							2	1	1		30	4

Debut	Name	Scottish League		Scottish Cup		League Cup		Other Comp		Forfarshire Cup		Misc Matches	
		App	Gls	App	Gls	App	Gls	App	Gls	App	Gls	App	Gls
03-Sep-21	Stuart G	25	6	1						1		3	
02-Oct-44	Stygal E									3		1	
01-Jan-14	Sutherland G	8		1								1	
13-Aug-38	Sutherland G D	28		2				6					
03-Apr-43	Sutherland George							2					
19-Aug-22	Sutherland R											10	
07-Oct-44	Sveinsson J							5	2				
22-Sep-23	Swan J	20		1				1		1		1	
16-Aug-10	Swan W	8	6					1	1			8	1
15-Apr-16	Taylor A											60	12
19-Aug-11	Taylor H	3						1				1	
26-Nov-27	Taylor W	187	1	22						6		15	
13-Aug-38	Temple R	34	9	2						3	1	4	1
08-Apr-40	Tennant J							1					
19-Aug-22	Terris J			2						3		27	1
16-Apr-21	Thain N	14	1	1								4	
24-Oct-42	Thomas L							2	1				
02-Dec-39	Thomson C							30				1	
01-Sep-17	Thomson D											38	5
31-Aug-29	Thomson George	15	2	1				11	3	1		1	
14-Aug-43	Thomson George										2		
19-Aug-22	Thomson W											5	2
16-Aug-10	Timmons J											2	1
09-Oct-09	Timmons T	4						5		2		17	
16-Aug-10	Tullis W	3						1				10	
03-Oct-42	Turnbull M	13						8				1	
26-Oct-35	Ure G							4					
01-Jan-43	Urquhart							9	1				
09-Aug-41	Vannet J											1	
15-Aug-25	Walker D	111	18	9	2					3			
15-Aug-25	Walker James	33	3	1								3	
03-Nov-23	Walker Jimmy	22	2	1						1		1	
14-Jan-39	Wallace R	2										2	
01-Jan-45	Walls R							11		1			

Debut	Name	Scottish League		Scottish Cup		League Cup		Other Comp		Forfarshire Cup		Misc Matches	
		App	Gls	App	Gls	App	Gls	App	Gls	App	Gls	App	Gls
12-Sep-42	Walters J							2	2				
03-Jan-38	Wann W	2	1					46	19	1		5	7
22-Oct-10	Waterston T	9	3							1		1	
21-Aug-37	Watson D	5											
30-Nov-29	Watson George	63		1				9	7	1		7	
01-Nov-41	Watson George									1			
25-Jan-36	Watson W	43	2	6				1		5			
18-Sep-20	Waugh J											11	3
03-Apr-20	Webster J									8		26	
02-Sep-33	Weir J	6	5										
17-Aug-10	Welsh William	50	3	2				7	1	5		16	
10-Oct-25	Welsh Willie	57	19	4	2					1		2	3
22-Aug-42	Westwater W	3				6		1				1	
12-Aug-39	White W							4				3	
22-Mar-19	Whitson											11	
13-Aug-32	Whyte C	21	3	1				15	1			5	1
15-Aug-12	Whyte S	39		1				11	1	2		10	
25-Sep-43	Wightman J												
21-Sep-18	Wilkie G	8						5	1	9	1	72	10
08-Aug-36	Wilkinson J	8								2			
15-Aug-21	Williams H	24	13	1						1		2	1
23-Aug-30	Williamson T	36	17	2	5					1		1	1
23-Sep-33	Willis D	24	1	1								1	
13-Dec-19	Wilson Joe							1		9	1	39	11
14-Aug-43	Wilson John							5	2			19	
06-Apr-18	Wilson M											25	20
19-Aug-22	Wilson W			2						1		1	1
09-Aug-41	Witherspoon J							5					
05-Sep-42	Woodburn J							6	1				
17-Sep-38	Woolley H	3	2										
11-Aug-34	Yorke R	64	10	6						3	2	4	
24-Aug-10	Young C	1										2	
19-Aug-11	Young John	3						1				1	
19-Aug-22	Young John											3	
09-Oct-09	Yule P	8	1					1		1		32	7

Bibliography

My main information sources were periodicals produced by D C Thomson & Co Ltd.

The Dundee Courier & Advertiser
The Dundee Advertiser
The Dundee Courier & Argos
The Evening Telegraph & Post
The Saturday Evening Post
The Sporting Post
The Sunday Post
The People's Journal

Amongst countless internet sites the following were most useful and worth a visit by anyone looking for historical football data:-
www.since1888.com
www.londonhearts.com
http://geocities.com/br1anmccoll/
www.scottishfa.co.uk
www.soccerbase.com
www.wikipedia.com

Other websites of interest to Dundee United fans include:-
www.dundeeunitedfc.co.uk
www.youthatunited.com
www.feddusc.com
www.a90arabs.net
www.weejimsta.co.uk
www.glenrothesarabs.co.uk
www.eastangusarabs.co.uk
www.ediarabs.co.uk

www.glsarabs.co.uk
www.southlondontangerines.co.uk
www.arabtrust.org.uk

Other sources of information.
Dundee United Who's Who by Pat Kelly, John Donald Publishers Ltd.
Rags To Riches by Mike Watson, David Winter & Son Ltd.
They Wore the Dark Blue by Norrie Price.